The Opportunity Gap

Achievement and Inequality
in Education

The Opportunity Gap

Achievement and Inequality
in Education

EDITED BY

CAROL DESHANO DA SILVA

JAMES PHILIP HUGULEY

ZENUB KAKLI

RADHIKA RAO

AFTERWORD BY

RONALD F. FERGUSON

HARVARD EDUCATIONAL REVIEW
REPRINT SERIES NO. 43

Library of Congress Control Number 2006939812

ISBN 978-0-916690-47-2

Published by the Harvard Educational Review,
an imprint of the Harvard Education Publishing Group

Harvard Educational Review
8 Story Street
Cambridge, MA 02138

Cover Design: Josh Silverman, Schwadesign, Inc.

The typefaces used in this book are ITC New Baskerville for the text
and Univers Condensed for display.

Printed in Canada

We dedicate this book
to our families for guiding us to where we are now;
to all students facing limited opportunities;
and to the educators and visionaries working tirelessly
to expand those opportunities

Contents

Part Three:
Expanding Opportunities, Fostering Achievement   229

Afterword

Introduction

The extension of the Elementary and Secondary Education Act through the 2002 No Child Left Behind Act (NCLB) has been of great interest to educators, education researchers, and the American public. The title of the reauthorization itself, perhaps by political design, waves the flag of equity and has galvanized people across the political spectrum. Yet only four years later there are many questions about the potential impact of NCLB and whether it will in fact be able to create educational equity through testing and accountability. This collection of articles from the pages of the *Harvard Educational Review* suggests that, as with previous sweeping solutions to entrenched educational disparities, the promised outcome is unlikely. Developing a common national barometer for student and school progress, particularly across socially significant groupings, has certainly been an asset for educators and policymakers, but accountability alone will not yield equity. We must recognize that the gaps in educational achievement that we are so fond of discussing are produced by even more unwieldy gaps in opportunity. Ironically, educational institutions are not expected to reflect these opportunity gaps; they are in fact often asked to correct them. Any proposed remedies for achievement gaps must include a broader discussion that addresses these larger gaps in opportunity, and with this volume we aim to open that discussion.

The history of public education in the United States tells us that issues of equity and have always been tied closely to educational attainment. President John Adams once said, "Laws for the liberal education of youth, especially for the lower classes of people, are so extremely wise and useful that to a humane and generous mind, no expense for this purpose would be thought extravagant" (Institute for American Liberty, 1998). And today, under a law initiated by President George W. Bush, it is federal policy that no child should be left behind. These voices from the oval office across more than two centuries of national history show just how committed our nation, at least in principle, has been to the equal education of all its citizenry.

Unfortunately, achieving educational equity has been far more elusive in reality than in principle. From a broad perspective, there is certainly reason to celebrate the development of our national education infrastructure. One fundamental principle of mid-nineteenth century's common schools was to alleviate the burgeoning social-class tensions of the time. Horace Mann, the father of these schools, advocated for his vision of an education system that was "common in the highest sense, as the air and light were common; because it was not

1

only the cheapest but the best, not only accessible to all, but as a general rule, enjoyed by all" (Reese, 2005, p. 11).

The establishment of common schools resulted in substantial increases of enrollment rates for previously uneducated populations, which led to the relatively high level of access in the U.S. today. When the common school era ended around the turn of the twentieth century, an unprecedented 51 percent of Americans between the ages of five and nineteen were attending grade school (Snyder, 1993). One hundred years later, America's public schools are serving over 48 million students (National Council of Educational Statistics [NCES], 2006). It seems then that the dream of access held by Horace Mann and others has in many ways been realized. But what of the class divisions he was concerned about? And what about race and gender differences? Has the vastly increased access to school provided the equal opportunity for all that American leaders, from John Adams to President Bush, have worked for? Sadly, the answer is no; in fact, inequality in education remains one of the most pervasive issues in our field today. The 1999 National Assessment of Educational Progress, for example, shows that White seventeen year olds scored on average over 30 points higher than their African American counterparts (NCES, 2006).[1] Similar gaps in achievement also exist across socio-economic and regional groupings. Ultimately, it is clear that equal access is not synonymous with equal achievement or equal opportunity.

Today, what is still true is that young people from groups with fewer resources, such as lower socio-economic status, limited social capital, or non-dominant cultural position, are often far less likely to have access to first-rate educational opportunities (Diamond, 2006). Socioeconomic differences are associated with inequities in educational resources, teacher qualifications, and class size. Disparities in social capital relate to differences in the knowledge of social systems as well as social connections that mediate students' educational attainment. And non-dominant cultural positioning often correlates with lower expectations and systematic exclusions, to the detriment of the students in subordinate cultural positions (Carter, 2005). Moreover, even in seemingly equitable educational settings — students in the same suburban school with comparable levels of effort, for example (Ferguson, 2002) — social forces still contribute to unequal achievement within schools. Thus, it seems that groups of students with socially significant differences such as wealth, maternal education level, race, and community climate, will have disparate levels of academic achievement. We are left then, searching for ways to remedy a complex set of educational problems, so that the vision of educational equity that generations of American leaders have held can become a reality.

Successive reform movements over the last century have sought panaceas to resolve the complex problems of achieving equity in educational attainment, and all have had limited success in leveling the educational landscape. The progressive education movement of the early twentieth century, which was largely influenced by Dewey's ideas of the dualism of education and democracy, has been criticized for lacking the social conscience to adequately challenge the racism and sexism of the time (Berube, 1995). The *Mendez v. Westminster School District* (1946) and *Brown v. Board of Education* (1954) Supreme Court decisions, along with subsequent education and school desegregation efforts, aimed to address educational disparities by challenging the "separate but equal" concept that, by legitimizing the de facto segregation in schools, was clearly having a negative impact on the achievement of Black and Latino populations (Carter, Flores, & Reddick, 2004). Unfortunately, the political will of mainstream America to embrace race and class diversity may have been overestimated. Today, more fifty years after *Brown*, many U.S. schools are rapidly resegregating (Orfield & Lee, 2004). Thus, the promise of educational equity through desegregation seems to have been undone by prejudice and racism in the greater society.

In the 1980s, in response to the infamous report on American educational woes, *A Nation at Risk* (National Commission on Excellence in Education, 1983), a powerful player joined the education reform movement: the business sector. Startled by the suggested connections between the U.S. economic struggles of the 1970s and declining educational achievement nationally, businesspeople descended upon public education in a variety of roles, including philanthropy, policymaking, and school leadership (Berube, 1995). The thought was that achievement could be improved if business models of efficiency and the business community's substantial financial resources could be tapped. Berube notes, however, that the assumed generosity of the business sector was overstated, and the transferability of business organizational models to educational institutions was unsuccessful. Critics such as former labor secretary Robert Reich noted that corporate giving to primary and secondary education was actually relatively low, compared to the overall investment in higher education. He noted further that the giving that did exist was motivated considerably by taxbreaks, which paradoxically, undermined the ultimate goal of the collaboration by weakening the revenue base that schools draw on in the first place (in Berube, 1995). In the end, high hopes for improving opportunities for disadvantaged students with the help of the business community were undermined by the economic interests of those of higher socioeconomic classes.

Today, the latest panacea for resolving inequity in U.S. Education is that of accountability. In the forward to the NCLB Act of 2002, President George W. Bush notes that NCLB's reforms "express my deep belief in our public schools and their mission to build the mind and character of every child, from every background, in every part of America" (p. 1). And while the policy outlines several areas needing school reform, including prioritizing effective programming, reducing bureaucracy, and empowering parents, the accountability component is generally the primary force of policy. Unfortunately, the impact that NCLB will ultimately have is debatable. Many states and school districts are not able to keep up with the NCLB proficiency requirements and, consequently, are reporting increasing numbers of failing schools. Another primary criticism of NCLB is that federal money is not available to support the mandated testing, which drains the educational resources of states and districts and forces them to cut other areas of programming. Connecticut has gone so far as to sue the federal government for mandating the legislation, without providing the resources to support it (Blumenthal, 2006; Sternberg, 2006).

Still other scholars point to the hopelessness of accountability alone as a way to rectify educational inequity in the face of the vast social, economic, and power disparities that exist across groups in the United States. Kantor and Lowe (2006) suggest that NCLB actually represents a gradual decline in federal involvement with social issues, in that it centralizes efforts to achieve social equity around education in a true, although not explicitly acknowledged, panacean approach. In the end, after more than a century of reform efforts our schoolchildren still do not have equal opportunities. Perhaps, then, what is missing from these popular reform efforts is the recognition that educational achievement does not exist in a vacuum; it parallels social structures that can enable or inhibit it. Thus, the story does not begin with an achievement gap, but with a more fundamental gap in opportunity that precludes achievement of educational equity in many ways. The recognition of, implications of, and potential solutions to such opportunity gaps are the subject of this volume.

By no means is the acknowledgment of these broader obstacles inhibiting educational inequity novel. Education scholars for many years have been discussing the impact that social inequities have on the promise of opportunity through education, both in the United States and abroad. And in our seventy-six years of history, the *Harvard Educational Review* has fully participated in these discussions by providing a venue for practitioners, theorists, and researchers to present important work that advances our understanding of opportunity gaps. In this volume, we revisit several of these important works, with the hope of troubling the tradition of narrow solutions to complex educational problems. History has shown us that differences in educational achievement among groups cannot be addressed by one-dimensional approaches such as pedagogical shifts, desegregation, or accountability. We must first acknowledge not only that there is a gap in educational achievement, both in the United States and abroad, but also that a larger gap in opportunity precedes its manifestation in the educational realm.

Thus, we produced this volume to revisit influential contributions to the pages of *HER*, largely over the last twenty years, that chronicle the societal parallels to disparities in educational achievement. These works both document how these parallels are manifested in our educational settings and present informed approaches that have found success through bold and imaginative actions. Part One, Social Structures, Institutions, and Education, explores broader social inequalities, both domestic and international, and their relationship with educational achievement is discussed in realistic terms. These authors are not despairing; rather they suggest areas where educational initiatives may have a positive impact within the context of more systemic inequities. Part Two, The Interactions among Schools, Students, and Communities, narrows the lens of these inquiries, and focuses on the manifestations of disparities in opportunity, such as race and class-based power dynamics, in the school context. Issues of tracking, preferential treatment, and school culture are connected to these larger social inequities, which ultimately have adverse affects on the most vulnerable students. Finally, Part Three, Expanding Opportunities, Fostering Achievement, presents remedies that are truly promising because they employ strategies that acknowledge the greater systemic issues and do not profess to be panacean solutions. Here, the class and racial power dynamics of the larger society are exposed and countered. Additionally, once these skewed lenses, are removed we see the true potential of collaboration across communities, classes, and professions. In all, Part Three shows that well-informed initiatives with humble perspectives can make a difference, creating real opportunities for students in need.

As John Adams suggested long ago, creating equity in education is an investment, one that requires more than economically shrewd and politically lukewarm solutions. It requires a clear vision of the true landscape of opportunity, an understanding of our schools as one of many stages where these opportunity gaps play out, and finally imaginative solutions that are modest yet effective. It is our hope that these pages tell just that story, a story that, in the world of educational reform, may replace our naïve overconfidence with informed and hopeful prudence.

Note

1. On average, Whites scored 294.6, while African Americans on average scored 263.9. The total population mean for seventeen-year-olds was 287.8.

References

Berube, M. (1995). *American school reform: Progressive, equity, and excellence movements, 1883-1993.* Westport, CT: Praeger.

Blumenthal, R. (in press). Why Connecticut sued the federal government over No Child Left Behind. *Harvard Educational Review, 76*(4).

Bush, G. W. (2002). Foreword. In *No child left behind.* Retrieved October 23, 2006, from http://www.whitehouse.gov/news/reports/no-child-left-behind.html

Carter, D., Flores, S., & Reddick, R. (Eds.). (2004). *Legacies of* Brown: *Multiracial equity in American education.* Cambridge, MA: Harvard Educational Review.

Carter, P. (2005). *Keepin' it real: School success beyond black and white.* New York: Oxford University Press.

Diamond, J. B. (2006). Still separate and unequal: Examining race, opportunity, and school achievement integrated suburbs. *Journal of Negro Education, 75*(3).

Ferguson, R. (2002). *What doesn't meet the eye: Understanding and addressing racial achievement gaps in high achieving suburban schools.* Retrieved October 23, 2006, from North Central Regional Educational Laboratory website, available online at http://www.ncrel.org/gap/ferg/

Institute for American Liberty. (1998). *John Adams "Thoughts on government."* Retrieved October 23, 2006, from http://www.liberty1.org/thoughts.htm

Kantor, H., & Lowe, R. (in press). From new deal to no deal: No child left behind and the devolution of responsibility for equal opportunity. *Harvard Educational Review, 76*(4).

National Commission on Excellence in Education. (1983, April). *A nation at risk: The imperative for educational reform.* Retrieved October 23, 2006, from http://www.ed.gov/pubs/NatAtRisk/index.html

National Council of Education Statistics (NCES). (2006). *The condition of education.* Retrieved October 23, 2006, from http://nces.ed.gov/programs/coe/2006/section1/indicator03.asp#info

Orfield, G., & Lee, C. (2004). *Brown at 50: King's dream or Plessey's nightmare?* Retrieved October 23, 2006, from The Civil Rights Project at Harvard University website, available online at http://www.civilrightsproject.harvard.edu/research/reseg04/resegregation04.php

Reese, W. (2005). America's public schools: From the common school to "No Child Left Behind." Baltimore: Johns Hopkins University Press.

Snyder, T. D. (1993). *120 years of American education: A statistical portrait.* Washington, DC: National Center for Education Statistics.

Sternberg, B. (in press). Real improvement for real students: Test smarter, serve better. *Harvard Educational Review, 76*(4).

Part One

Social Structures, Institutions, and Education

Part One

Introduction

Educators and the general public have long considered education to be the silver bullet for achieving social equality. Current reform discourse promotes education —carefully monitored by "standards" and "accountability" — as the tool for safeguarding the U.S. position in the global market. But this way of thinking obscures the interrelated nature of the economy, public health, and racial, ethnic, and gender relations with the institution of education in the United States and around the world. Considering these institutional and structural factors is essential to constructing an education system that will serve the higher goals not only of providing life opportunities to individuals or fostering national economic growth, but also of promoting social justice.

Authors in Part One are intended to examine the ways educational institutions have failed to respond adequately to the different social backgrounds of their students in order to reduce inequalities in attainment; present a straightforward assessment of the limitations of education to cure existing institutional and structural inequalities; and, finally, to illuminate the potential role of education in guaranteeing the opportunity for academic and life achievement for all.

In "Poverty and Education," Raewyn Connell begins by attempting to answer one of the most important questions educators consider: How can schools as institutions offer equal educational opportunity to children living in poverty? The author takes a cross-national approach to this question, examining the schooling of children in poverty in Australia, Britain, Canada, and the United States. Connell examines the definition of poverty, shows how these definitions differ according to context, and explains how historical factors contributed to the rise of compensatory programs to aid impoverished students. Connell critiques compensatory education as a policy solution to raising poor children's educational performance, based on the fact those programs are born out of a misunderstanding of both the population and the solution. To remedy that misunderstanding, Connell encourages educators to rethink the role of power relations and the accountability and standards policies that encourage competition rather than inclusion in today's schools, as well as the curriculum and pedagogy that poor students and their teachers experience and conduct. Finally, Connell calls for academics and policymakers to partner with teachers and poor students and their families to carry out a broad-based institutional change, not only to increase educational opportunity but also to achieve social justice.

In "Cognitive Skill and Economic Inequality: Findings from the National Adult Literacy Survey," Stephen W. Raudenbush and Rafa M. Kasim also tackle the issue of social justice, focusing on the link between educational opportunity for women and racial minorities and economic inequality. Conducting a quantitative analysis of a large-scale dataset of American adults who were in the labor force in 1992 — the National Adult Literacy Survey, which includes a measure of adult literacy skill as a proxy for cognitive ability — the authors test these hypotheses, finding that the relationship between cognitive ability and earnings differs when considering race and gender. Both the earnings gap between racial minorities and non minorities and the unemployment experienced by racial minorities are, in part, explained by differences in literacy skill — suggesting that schools may not adequately prepare students of color for the cognitive skills necessary to achieve in the workforce. Although this was not found to be true for women, the authors did find that the existing gender gaps occurred within occupations, indicating that gaps did not exist because women chose lower-paying careers. The authors' findings support the hypothesis that cognitive ability measured by performance on a literacy test partially explained economic inequality and refuted the hypothesis of career preferences, but the most striking finding was that large proportions of these racial and gender gaps were left unexplained by literacy measures. Raudenbush and Kasim propose that labor market discrimination and social competition and segregation might explain why gender and racial gaps remain, indicating the important role the institution of education has to play in improving educational and life opportunities for students of color and women, through policies like affirmative action.

In "Improve the Women": Mass Schooling, Female Literacy, and World-Wide Social Change," Robert LeVine, Sarah LeVine, and Beatrice Schnell investigate the potential relationship between the education of women and their children's health. The authors begin by reviewing the research on this topic, focusing largely on developing countries, and positing a theory of how investing in women's education might foster social change. LeVine et al. argue that participating in schooling influences women's aspirations, identity formation, communications skills, and models of learning and teaching as adaptive strategies, which in turn leads them to desire more for themselves and their children and to act on those desires in ways that result in improved health outcomes. The authors' argument is supported by their quantitative analysis of the relationship between women's literacy skills and their ability to gain access to health information in Nepal and Venezuela. The findings make a strong claim for the power of the institution of schooling to improve life opportunities: The cognitive skills women learned were related to their access to and comprehension of health information. This conclusion reinforces the importance of equal educational opportunity as being beneficial not only to women as individuals, but to society as a whole.

The authors in this section present a broad look at the intersection of education and social inequality, economic inequality, and public health. They span the literature on educational opportunity and achievement in terms of the populations and contexts studied — children and adults, the industrialized and developing world — and explore the important issues of race, gender, and poverty. All suggest that educators and policymakers must better understand how greater social inequality in the forms of inadequate health care, residential segregation, or poverty, for example, might influence education policy and how education policy may impact such inequalities.

Poverty and Education

RAEWYN CONNELL*

H ow schools address poverty is an important test of an education system. Children from poor families are, generally speaking, the least successful by conventional measures and the hardest to teach by traditional methods. They are the least powerful of the schools' clients, the least able to enforce their claims or insist their needs be met, yet the most dependent on schools for their educational resources.

Since modern school systems persistently do fail children in poverty, a sense of outrage runs through much educational writing about disadvantage. Several authors have recently added a note of urgency to this discussion. Natriello, McDill, and Pallas (1990) give their survey of U.S. practice the subtitle, "Racing against Catastrophe." Kozol's (1991) book, Savage Inequalities, presents an even bleaker portrait of willful neglect and deepening tragedy. Korbin (1992) speaks of the "devastation" of children in the United States. This note has also been heard outside education in discussions of the urban "underclass" and is given strength by the 1992 violence in Los Angeles and the rise of neo-fascism in Europe.

In its first year, the Clinton administration signalled no sharp break from the educational policies of the 1980s. But Clinton's election has created a political space in the United States for reconsidering compensatory programs, which were already gaining renewed support after a period of skepticism and narrowed horizons.[1] The secretary of education speaks, for instance, of a "revolutionary" plan for "reinventing" Chapter I, the major U.S. compensatory program (Riley, 1994). Rhetoric aside, there is certainly a need to rethink the underlying logic of compensatory programs, which have not changed in their basic design and political justification, either in the United States or in other countries, since the 1960s. Meanwhile, child poverty has grown dramatically, and the difficulties faced by some parts of the school system have reached crisis proportions.

Such rethinking can draw on two assets that were not available in the 1960s. The first is the accumulated practical experience of teachers and parents with compensatory programs. A great fund of such experience is found outside the United States, which Weinberg (1981) has documented in a vast "world bibliog-

*This article was originally published under the name R. W. Connell.

Harvard Educational Review   Vol. 64   No. 2   Summer 1994, 125–149

raphy." A more international perspective can help one to see both the deeper roots of the problems and a broader range of responses; however, participants in the debate in the United States rarely consider it.

The second asset is a much more sophisticated sociology of education. In discussion of how inequalities are produced, the focus has gradually shifted from the characteristics of the disadvantaged to the institutional character of school systems and the cultural processes that occur in them. Compensatory programs cannot be reinvented in isolation; the rethinking leads us inevitably to larger questions about education.

Education used to be represented in political rhetoric as a panacea for poverty. This is now rare, but education for the poor is still an arena for confident pronouncements by many economists and businesspeople, welfare specialists, and political and cultural entrepreneurs of various persuasions — some of whom are startlingly naive about the educational effects of what they propose. I hope to show that teachers' experience and educational reasoning are central to a strategy for reconstruction.

The purposes of this article are to question the social and educational assumptions behind the general design of compensatory programs; to propose an alternative way of thinking about the education of children in poverty, drawn from current practice and social research; and to explore some broad questions about the strategy of reform this rethinking implies. My focus is on the educational systems of industrialized, predominantly English-speaking, liberal-capitalist states (Australia, Britain, Canada, and the United States), though in broad outline the argument should also apply to other countries with comparable economic and political systems.

Poverties and Programs

"Poverty" is not a single thing, nor a simple concept. On a world scale, distinctly different situations are embraced in the term. MacPherson (1987) speaks of five hundred million children living in poverty in developing countries, most in rural settings. The quality of the schooling that reaches them is debated; Avalos (1992), for example, argues that the formal pedagogy conventional in their schools is profoundly inappropriate. Poverty in agricultural villages is different from poverty in the explosively growing cities, from Mexico City to Port Moresby, that now dominate the politics of the developing world. It was in the context of migration into such urban settings that Lewis (1968) formulated the idea of a "culture of poverty," which has had a profound effect on compensatory education in wealthy countries.

In industrial capitalist countries with high average incomes, poverty is the effect of unequal distribution, rather than the effect of absolute level of resources. Even in these countries, welfare researchers have pointed to the diversity of situations. As early as 1962, in *The Other America*, Harrington distinguished the aged, minorities, agricultural workers, and industrial rejects as belonging to different "subcultures of poverty." Such complexity is reemphasized in more recent and more systematic welfare research (for example, Devine & Wright, 1993).

There is complexity in two senses, first in the very definition of poverty. Low incomes are part of everyone's concept of poverty, but incomes vary in character as well as amount: some are regular and others are intermittent; some are paid all in money and some are partly "in kind"; some are shared in a household (or a wider group) and some are individual. Further, people's economic situations depend on what they own, as well as on their current incomes. The distribution of wealth is known to be markedly more unequal than the distribution of income, so a simple income measure of poverty is likely to underestimate the severity or extent of deprivation. Further, there are other types of resources beyond income and wealth that cannot be cashed out on an individual basis, but where inequality is materially significant: for example, access to public institutions such as libraries, colleges, and hospitals; to public utilities; and to safety and community health.

Official statisticians generally throw up their hands at this complexity, and settle for a single index that allows a "poverty line" to be drawn. The most widely used is an austere income-based poverty line adopted in the United States in 1964 (based on earlier government calculations about emergency food needs for families), and subsequently applied in other countries. The great virtue of a poverty-line approach is that it allows a straightforward calculation of the number of people living in poverty. For example, in 1991 the United States counted fourteen million children in poverty (U.S. Bureau of the Census, 1992); extrapolating to the industrial capitalist countries as a group (United Nations Development Programme, 1992), we might estimate they have about thirty-five million children in poverty, which might be regarded as the potential target group for compensatory education.[2] The great disadvantages of the poverty-line approach are that it ignores important dimensions of deprivation and inequality, and that it readily leads to political misperceptions of poverty, as I explain below.

The second form of complexity is that economic deprivation, however defined, is shared by people who are very different in other respects. Ethnic background is far from homogeneous. The poverty of indigenous peoples, still grappling with the consequences of invasion and colonization, is different from the poverty of recent immigrant groups. Political debate on poverty in the United States mainly addresses African-American urban "ghettos," but the majority of the people marked off by the poverty line in the United States are White. In a disadvantaged inner-city Australian school, there may be ten or twelve languages spoken on the playground. Further, poor people are not all of one gender. To note this is not merely to say we must count women as well as men. As with race relations, gender relations affect the creation of poverty and affect people's responses to poverty. Thus, women's overall economic disadvantage vis-à-vis men shapes the demography of poverty: female-headed households have higher poverty rates than male-headed households. The ways children and teenagers deal with gender affect their schooling. This is a familiar general point (Thorne, 1993). It should not be forgotten that it applies to children and teenagers in poverty; for both girls and boys, gender relations shape their difficult relationships with their schools (Anderson, 1991; Walker, 1988).

Schooling designed specifically for the poor dates back to the charity schools of the eighteenth century, and to the ragged schools of the nineteenth century that were established to tame the children of "the perishing and dangerous classes" (Clark, 1977). Modern compensatory programs date from the 1960s and have a specific history. Earlier in this century, most educational systems were sharply and deliberately stratified: they were segregated by race, by gender, and by class; tracked into academic and technical schools; divided among public and private, Protestant and Catholic. A series of social movements expended enormous energy to desegregate schools, establish comprehensive secondary systems, and open universities to excluded groups. As a result of this pressure, the expanding educational systems of the mid-century generally became more accessible. The idea of education as a right, which was crystallized in the 1959 United Nations Declaration of the Rights of the Child, was interpreted internationally as implying equal access to education (with notable exceptions like South Africa).

Yet equal access was only half a victory. Children from working-class, poor, and minority ethnic families continued to do worse than children from rich and middle-class families on tests and examinations, were more likely to be held back in grade, to drop out of school earlier, and were much less likely to enter college or university (for example, Curtis, Livingstone, & Smaller, 1992; Davis, 1948). Documenting this informal segregation within formally unsegregated institutions was the main preoccupation of educational sociology in the 1950s and 1960s. A mass of evidence built up, ranging from national surveys like the 1966 Coleman report in the United States (see his retrospective account in Coleman, 1990) to case studies like Ford's (1969) *Social Class and the Comprehensive School in Britain*. The evidence of socially unequal outcomes continues to mount; it is one of the most firmly established facts about Western-style educational systems in all parts of the world.

Compensatory education programs were designed in response to this specific historical situation: that is, the failure of postwar educational expansion, despite its principle of equal access, to deliver substantive equality. The educational movement occurred within a broader context of social welfare reform. In the United States, the civil rights movement, the rediscovery of poverty by the intellectuals, and the political strategies of the Kennedy and Johnson administrations led to the War on Poverty. Its main designers were welfare economists, and its main success was the reduction of poverty among the elderly — not among children (Katz, 1989).

Education was brought into the welfare picture through the correlation between lower levels of education on the one side, and higher rates of unemployment and lower wages on the other. The idea of a self-sustaining "cycle of poverty" emerged, where low aspirations and poor support for children led to low educational achievement, which in turn led to labor market failure and poverty in the next generation. Compensatory education was seen as a means to break into this cycle and derail the inheritance of poverty.[3] Thus the failure of equal access was read outward from the institutions to the families they served. Families and children became the bearers of a deficit for which the institutions should compensate. This maneuver protected conventional beliefs about schooling; indeed, a wave of optimism about the power of schooling and early childhood intervention accompanied the birth of compensatory education.

With this rationale, publicly funded programs were set up in the 1960s and 1970s in a number of wealthy countries, starting with the United States and including Britain, the Netherlands, and Australia.[4] While the details of these programs vary from country to country, they do have major design elements in common. They are "targeted" to a minority of children.[5] They select children or their schools by formulae involving a poverty-line calculation. They are intended to compensate for disadvantage by enriching the children's educational environment, which they do by grafting something on to the existing school and pre-school system. And, finally, they are generally administered separately from conventional school funding.

The False Map of the Problem

The circumstances of the birth of compensatory programs and the political means by which some have survived — not all did — produced a false map of the problem. By this I mean a set of assumptions that govern policy and public discussion but are factually wrong, doubtful, or profoundly misleading. Three are central: that the problem concerns only a disadvantaged minority; that the poor are distinct from the majority in culture or attitudes; and that correcting disadvantage in education is a technical problem requiring, above all, the application of research-based expertise.

The Disadvantaged Minority

The image of a disadvantaged minority is built into compensatory education via the poverty line by which target groups are identified. Whatever the formulae used to measure disadvantage (they vary from country to country, from state to state, and from time to time, with a running controversy over the method), the procedure always involves drawing a cut-off line at some point on a dimension of advantage and disadvantage. Where the cut-off comes is fundamentally arbitrary. This is a familiar problem with defining poverty lines. In compensatory programs, determining the cut-off point leads to unending dispute over which children or schools should be on the list for funds. The procedure could label 50 percent of the population "disadvantaged" as logically as it could 10 percent or 20 percent. In practice, however, the cut-off point is always placed so as to indicate a modest-sized minority. This demarcation is credible because of the already existing political imagery of poverty, in which the poor are pictured as a minority outside mainstream society.[6] The policy implication is that the other 80 or 90 percent, the mainstream, are all on the same footing.

However, this is not what the evidence shows. Regardless of which measures of class inequality and educational outcomes are used, gradients of advantage

17

and disadvantage typically appear across the school population as a whole (for one example among hundreds, see Williams, 1987). We can identify an exceptionally advantaged minority as well as an exceptionally disadvantaged one, but focusing on either extreme is insufficient. The fundamental point is that class inequality is a problem that concerns the school system as a whole. Poor children are not facing a separate problem. They face the worst effects of a larger pattern.

The Distinctiveness of the Poor

That the poor are not like the rest of us is a traditional belief of the affluent. This belief affected the design of compensatory education mainly through the "culture of poverty" thesis, where the reproduction of poverty from one generation to another was attributed to the cultural adaptations poor people made to their circumstances (Lewis, 1968; for a later review see Hoyles, 1977).

Though framed within the discourse of anthropology, this idea was immediately given a psychological twist. Cultural difference in the group meant psychological deficit in the individual; that is, a lack of the traits needed to succeed in school. With this twist, a very wide range of research could be read as demonstrating cultural deprivation, from studies of linguistic codes to occupational expectations to achievement motivation to IQ, and so on. In the 1960s and 1970s, the cultural deficit concept became folklore among teachers as well as policymakers (Interim Committee for the Australian Schools Commission, 1973; Ryan, 1971).

It was this tendency to reduce arguments about different situations to the idea of a cultural deficit that Bernstein (1974) protested against in a famous critique of compensatory education. Culture-of-poverty ideas were strongly criticized by anthropologists, linguists, and teachers, not to mention poor people themselves, yet these ideas have had tremendous resilience, persisting through two decades of changing rhetoric, as Griffin (1993) has recently shown in a detailed survey of youth research. The ideas survive partly because they have become the organic ideology of compensatory and special education programs. The very existence of such programs now evokes the rationale of deficit, as Casanova (1990) illustrates in heartbreaking case studies of two Latino children in a U.S. school system: battered by the system's languages policy, inserted into "special education" programs — with mandated, rigid, teacher-centered methods — these children's education was massively disrupted and their social selves assaulted with labels like "learning-disabled." More broadly, deficit ideas also survive because they fit comfortably into wider ideologies of race and class difference.

But the facts of the matter do not require us to adopt cultural deficit concepts. The bulk of evidence points to cultural similarity between the poorest groups and the less poor. This might be expected from facts about the demography of poverty not widely known to educators. Studies such as the U.S. Panel Study of Income Dynamics (PSID), which has followed the same families since 1968, show large numbers of families moving into and out of poverty (as measured by the poverty-line approach). Over a twenty-year period, nearly 40 percent of the families in the PSID spent some period in poverty, when the rate of poverty in any one year was only 11 percent to 15 percent (Devine & Wright, 1993). We should, then, expect those in poverty at any one time to have a lot in common with the broader working class, including their relations with schools. For example, attitude surveys produce little evidence that the poor lack other people's interest in education or in children (for a recent example in England, see Heath, 1992).

In the United States, the argument over cultural deficit has been refocused by the concept of the "underclass," which is defined as inhabitants of urban centers marked by massive unemployment, environmental decay, high numbers of births to single mothers, community violence, and the presence of the drug trade. It is clear that the most severe concentrations of poverty have the most severe impact on education (for statistical evidence, see Orland, 1990). Ethnographies in inner-city settings (Anderson, 1991) and in communities of the rural poor (Heath, 1983) show ways of life that do not mesh with the practices of mainstream schooling. Ogbu's (1988) argument that this bad mesh has roots in the history of imperialism, with "involuntary minorities" such as conquered indigenous peoples and enslaved labor forces resisting the institutions of White supremacy, is attractive.

But ethnography may not be the best guide to this issue. As a research method, it assumes the coherence of the group being studied, and ethnographic writing understandably tends to emphasize what is unique or distinctive about its subjects' way of life. We must counter-balance this by considering the interplay and interconnection of poor people with other groups. The cultural inventiveness of poor people (including the American "underclass"), and their interplay with wider popular culture, is hardly to be denied — witness music from jazz to rap, new wave rock, punk fashion, contemporary street styles, and so on. And further, close-focus research on schooling, using interviews and participant observation, documents a vigorous desire for education among poor people and ethnic minorities (for example, Wexler, 1992, from the United States; Angus, 1993, from Australia). Yet there is massive educational failure. Something is malfunctioning, but hardly the culture of the poor.

The Nature of Reform

The belief that educational reform is, above all, a technical question, a matter of assembling the research and deducing the best interventions, is embedded in the education world through the very hierarchy of teaching institutions. At the apex of this hierarchy are the universities, which both produce education research and train administrators for the schools in education studies programs. The dominant ideology in education studies is positivist. The 1966 Coleman Report (Coleman, 1990) was a monument to technocratic policy research, and the "effective schools" and national testing movements continue to promote the belief that quantitative research will generate good policy more or less automatically. Teachers are defined within this framework as receiving guidance from educational science, rather than as producing fundamental knowledge themselves. The structure of educational funding in federal systems, where local institutions provide bread-and-butter school finance while higher level institutions fund policy innovation, further encourages a view of school reform as based on outside expertise.

While these are general conditions in educational policymaking, their effect on policy about poverty is especially strong. The poor are precisely the group with the least resources and the least capacity to contest the views of policymaking elites. Social movements of the poor can win concessions, but only by widespread mobilization and social disruption, as shown in the classic study by Piven and Cloward (1979). Mobilization and disruption do not generally develop around the education of the poor.

As a consequence, policy discussions about education and poverty have frequently been conducted in the absence of the two groups most likely to understand the issues: poor people themselves, and the teachers in their schools. A striking example is the 1986 conference held by the U.S. Department of Education to reconsider Chapter I programs, which was entirely composed of academics, administrators, and policy analysts (Doyle & Cooper, 1988). Teachers are expected to implement policies, but not to make them, while poor people are defined as the objects of policy interventions rather than as the authors of social change.

The broad effect of this "map" of the issues has been to locate the problem in the heads of the poor and in the errors of the particular schools serving them. Meanwhile, the virtues of other schools are taken for granted. The consequences of this policy, as Natriello et al. (1990) have perceptively pointed out, has been an oscillation among strategies of intervention that are mostly technocratic, all narrowly focused, all within a context of massive under funding, and none making a great difference to the situation.

Re-Mapping the Issues

What can we offer instead — "we" meaning researchers, teacher educators, students, and administrators, the typical audience for academic journals in education? We cannot continue to offer what we usually do: proposals for fresh, expert interventions and for more research to support them. The exemplary research by Snow, Barnes, Chandler, Goodman, and Hemphill (1991) shows the limits that have been reached by this approach. This careful and compassionate study, which sought practical lessons for literacy teaching by comparing good and bad readers among poor children in a U.S. city, found on returning four years later that hopeful differences were overwhelmed by what one can only read as the structural consequences of poverty. The enrichments these researchers proposed certainly improved the children's quality of life, but they were not capable of altering the forces shaping the children's educational fates.

There are no great surprises in the research on poverty and education, no secret keys that will unlock the solution. If there is a mystery, it is the kind that Sartre (1958) called a "mystery in broad daylight," an un-knowing created by the way we frame and use our knowledge. Descriptive research on poor children by psychologists, sociologists, and educators will certainly continue — spiced by occasional claims from biologists to have found the gene for school failure. But that kind of research is no longer decisive. What we need, above all, is a rethinking of the pattern of policy, a reexamination of the way the issues have been configured.

This rethinking should start with the theme that comes through insistently when poor people talk about education: power. This issue leads to the institutional form of mass education, the politics of the curriculum, and the character of teachers' work. I develop each of these themes in the discussion that follows.

Power

Educators are uncomfortable with the language of power; to talk of "disadvantage" is easier. But schools are literally power-full institutions. Public schools exercise power, both in the general compulsion to attend and in the particular decisions they make. School grades, for instance, are not just aids to teaching. They are also tiny judicial decisions with legal status, which cumulate into large authoritative decisions about people's lives — progression in school, selection into higher education, employment prospects.

Poor people, like the rest of the working class, by and large understand this feature of schools. It is central to their more dire experiences of education. An example is Wexler's (1992) description of students' experiences at Washington High, where tardiness is policed by an intrusive patrolling of corridors, leading to the bureaucratic processing of students for expulsion.

Once again we must recognize that what students in poverty experience is not unique. Mass schooling systems were created in the nineteenth century as state intervention into working-class life, to regulate and partly take over the rearing of children. Legal compulsion was needed because this intervention was widely resisted.

From this history, public schools and their working-class clientele inherit a deeply ambivalent relationship. On the one hand, the school embodies state power; hence the most common complaint from parents and students is about teachers who "don't care" but cannot be made to change. On the other hand, the school system has become the main bearer of working-class hopes for a better future, especially where the hopes of unionism or socialism have died. Hence the dilemma, poignantly described by Lareau (1987), of working-class parents who want educational advancement for their children but cannot deploy the techniques or resources called for by the school. The extent to which school routines presuppose a gender pattern based on a certain level of affluence, the unpaid labor of a mother/housewife, is particularly noteworthy.

To deal with powerful institutions requires power. Some of the resources that families need to handle contemporary schools are the bread and butter of positivist research on children: adequate food, physical security, attention from helpful adults, books in the home, scholastic know-how in the family, and so on. Generally absent from positivist research (because they are hard to quantify as attributes of a person) are the collective resources that produce the kind of school system that favors a particular home environment for success. These resources are put into play when property owners cap taxes supporting public schools; or when university faculty dominate curriculum boards and corporations create textbooks; or when the professional parents at an upper income school meet with routine responsiveness from principal and teachers.

In the false map already discussed, poverty is constantly taken as the sign of something else, such as cultural difference, or psychological or genetic deficit. Educators need to be more blunt and see poverty as poverty. Poor people are short of resources, individually and jointly, including many of the resources that are deployed in education. The scale of material shortages is easily shown. For instance, an Australian study of household expenditure in families with dependent children found high-income couples spending an average of $8.82 per week on books and periodicals, while sole-parent pensioners (roughly equivalent to AFDC recipients in the United States) spent $2.06 (Whiteford, Bradbury, & Saunders, 1989).

Such differences in income and expenditure, not to mention the greater inequalities of wealth, mean both shortages of resources in the home and vulnerability to institutional power — such as derogatory labelling in the welfare system, and streaming or tracking in the education system. There is no mystery about this to poor people. As an activist in a Canadian immigrant women's group put it:

> Streaming of low income, immigrant children is obvious. More well-to-do parents make sure their children are directed in the proper direction, they have much more pro-active involvement in the school system. Poor working-class families don't have the time or the wherewithal to fight. (quoted in Curtis et al., 1992, p. 23)

Poverty and alienation are likely to mean material disruptions of life, one of the points emphatically made in the "underclass" discussion. Disruptions can also be seen outside the United States: witness Robins and Cohen's *Knuckle Sandwich* (1978), about youth and violence in England, and Embling's look at *Fragmented Lives* (1986) in Australia. We do not need to assume cultural difference to understand the damaging effects of poverty on young people's lives. We certainly need to think carefully about power in order to understand the violence that has long been an undercurrent in schools for the urban poor, and which has taken a dramatic turn with the advent of guns in U.S. high schools.

Serious violence is more common from boys than from girls, not because of their hormones, but because Western masculinities are socially constructed around claims to power. Where this claim is made with few resources except physical force, and where boys have been habitually disciplined by force, "trouble" in the form of violence is eminently likely. A familiar course of events frequently develops where boys' masculinity comes to be defined or tested in their conflict with the state power embodied in the school, a conflict that can turn violent. Losing this conflict, which is inevitable, is likely to end the boys' formal education.[7] The power relations of gender thus play out paradoxically in a context of poverty. To grapple with such a process means directly addressing the politics of masculinity — an issue, as Yates (1993) notes at the end of her review of the education of girls, still absent from educational agendas.

The School as an Institution

The young people who fight the school and find themselves bounced out on the street are meeting more than the anger of particular teachers and principals. They are facing the logic of an institution embodying the power of the state and the cultural authority of the dominant class. Fine's (1991) study of a New York inner-city school shows the dull bureaucratic rationality of encouraging students to drop out. In a school facing great difficulties in teaching and establishing its legitimacy, and with no prospect of the resources it needs or a change in its working methods, "discharge" of a student becomes the routine solution to a wide range of problems.

The role of institutional power in shaping pupil-teacher interactions has been clear in close-focus studies of schools for some time. It was vividly portrayed, for instance, in Corrigan's (1979) study of the struggle for control in two schools in a declining industrial area of England. What "school ethnographies" cannot show, however, is the institutional shape of the education system as a whole. Selectiveness at upper levels (selection cuts in at different ages in different countries) means a narrowing offer of learning that forces unequal outcomes, whether or not the system attempts to equalize opportunity. For instance, if a university system trains only one in ten of a particular age group, which is the current average for industrial countries (United Nations Development Programme, 1992), then nine must go without degrees. If unequal outcomes are forced, a struggle for advantage results, and the political and economic resources that can be mobilized in that struggle become important. The poor are precisely those with the least resources.

Policies to increase competitive pressures within the school system — including mandatory objective testing, parental choice plans, and "gifted and talented" programs — have a transparent class meaning, reinforcing the advantages of the privileged and confirming the exclusion of the poor. The fact that such policies deliver class advantages is not new knowledge; similar observations on the class meaning of testing programs have been made for half a century (for example, Davis, 1948). It seems to be a fact that has to be constantly rediscovered.

The legitimacy of educational competitions depends on some belief in level playing fields. Economic facts have been marginal in discussions of educational disadvantage, though educators periodically justify compensatory programs as contributing to a well-trained work force. In the United States, however, Kozol (1991) has recently made an issue of differences in school funding. Taylor and Piché (1991), in a study of per-pupil expenditure by U.S. school boards, found a range from $11,752 in the richest district to $1,324 in the poorest, with many states having a 2.5-to-1 or 3-to-1 ratio between high-expenditure and low-expenditure groups of districts. Further, current per-capita spending is likely to understate differences, because background capital expenditure has also been unequal. And beyond public finance, as already noted, there are stark inequalities in what can be privately spent on educational resources.

Other wealthy countries have more centralized, and thus more uniform, funding of schools than the United States, but a more exclusive system of student selection for higher education. This, being more costly, weights overall per-capita expenditure back in favor of advantaged groups who enter higher education in greater proportions. On the face of it, differences in the total social investment in the education of rich children and poor children appear to be much larger than any redistributive effect of compensatory education funds.

Curriculum

The importance of curriculum for issues of educational inequality has long been argued by Apple (1982, 1993), and the point is highly relevant to strategy about poverty. Compensatory programs were intended to lever disadvantaged children back into mainstream schooling. The success of these programs is conventionally measured by pupil progress in the established curriculum, especially as evidenced by the closing of gaps to system norms. This logic has been taken to a startling extreme in a program in Cleveland, Ohio, which consists of awarding pupils $40 for getting an A, $20 for a B, and $10 for a C (Natriello et al., 1990).

When progress in the mainstream curriculum is taken as the goal of intervention, that curriculum is exempted from criticism. However, the experience of teachers in disadvantaged schools has persistently led them to question the curriculum. Conventional subject matter and texts and traditional teaching methods and assessment techniques turn out to be sources of systematic difficulty. They persistently produce boredom. Enforcing them heightens the problem of discipline, and so far as they are successfully enforced, they divide pupils between an academically successful minority and an academically discredited majority. (Connell, Johnston, & White, 1992; Wexler, 1992).

To teach well in disadvantaged schools requires a shift in pedagogy and in the way content is determined. A shift towards more negotiated curriculum and more participatory classroom practice can be seen in compensatory education in Australia, where it is a broad tendency in disadvantaged schools, not just a matter of isolated initiatives (Connell, White, et al., 1991). The effectiveness of similar practice in U.S. elementary classrooms is demonstrated by Knapp, Shields, and Turnbull (1992). However, such practices do not seem to be the main tendency in the United States. A survey of U.S. middle schools by MacIver and Epstein (1990) suggests a more conventional pedagogy, with less commitment to active learning methods and exploratory courses in disadvantaged schools than in advantaged schools. The push for "standards" and "basic skills" has fostered a rigid, teacher-centered pedagogy in compensatory and special education programs (for a striking illustration, see Griswold, Cotton, & Hansen, 1986).

To see "mainstream" curriculum as a key source of educational inequality raises the question of where it comes from. We are beginning to get an answer from the new social history of the curriculum produced by Goodson (1985,

1988) and others. The very concept of "mainstream" must be called into question, as it suggests reasoned consensus. What we are dealing with, rather, is a dominant, or hegemonic, curriculum, derived historically from the educational practices of European upper class men. This curriculum became dominant in mass education systems during the last hundred and fifty years, as the political representatives of the powerful succeeded in marginalizing other experiences and other ways of organizing knowledge. It has been reorganized from time to time by struggles among interest groups; thus classics was replaced by physical science as the highest prestige knowledge, without disturbing the "subject" organization of knowledge. The competitive academic curriculum sits alongside other kinds of curriculum in the schools — such as practical knowledge in music or in manual arts — but remains hegemonic in the sense that it defines "real" knowledge, is linked to teacher professionalism, and determines promotion in the education system (Connell, Ashenden, Kessler, & Dowsett, 1982).

The apparently remote discipline of curriculum history has made a key contribution to rethinking the issues of poverty and education. It has de-mythologized the hegemonic curriculum and shown it to be only one among a number of ways knowledge could have been organized for the schools (Whitty, 1985; Whitty & Young, 1976). Without this historical perspective, proposals for alternative curricula are easily discredited as abandoning real knowledge and educational quality. Different versions of this claim were made in turn by the "Black Papers" neoconservatives in England in the 1960s and 1970s, cultural literacy entrepreneurs in the United States in the 1980s, and professors attacking assessment reform in Australia in the 1990s. We can now see that the work of teachers in disadvantaged schools implies not a shift to different content (though there will be some of that), but, more decisively, a different organization of the field of knowledge as a whole.

Teachers' Work

Teachers are strikingly absent from much of the policy debate about schooling and poverty (so much so that a recent book reviewing the subject does not even list teachers in its index). This absence is an important consequence of the deficit interpretation of disadvantage and the technocratic style of policymaking.

But teachers are the front-line workers in schools. If exclusion is accomplished by schools, it is certainly in large measure through what teachers do. We may not wish to blame teachers, but we also cannot ignore them. Education as a cultural enterprise is constituted in and through their labor. Their work is the arena where the great contradictions around education and social justice condense.

Teachers' work has been studied in an international literature (surveyed by Ginsburg, forthcoming; Seddon, forthcoming), which, like curriculum history, has been little noticed in discussions of poverty. Nevertheless, its significance is clear. Lawn (1993), for example, shows the complexity of teachers' relationships to state power and the importance of teacher professionalism as a system of indirect control. Professionalism is an important factor attaching teachers to the hegemonic curriculum. The question of the "de-skilling" of teachers through tighter management control and packaged curricula is highly relevant to the prospects for good teaching in disadvantaged schools, which requires maximum flexibility and imagination.

Some activities included under the name "compensatory education" expand teachers' options and call for higher levels of skill. Others, as a condition of funding, constrict methods and de-skill teachers, generally pushing them towards more authoritarian styles. Where compensatory programs are accompanied by an active testing program, for example, a familiar pressure is created to teach to the test and thus narrow the curriculum. "Pull-out" classes are likely to disrupt the supportive classroom dynamics that good teachers try to establish. The whole model of expert intervention tends to disempower teachers. Given all these effects, it is likely that some compensatory interventions have worsened the educational situation in disadvantaged schools, not improved it. It is almost impossible for embattled schools to resist offers of resources, but the consequences are not always beneficial. (See the uneasy discussions in Doyle & Cooper, 1988; Knapp, Shields, & Turnbull, 1992; Savage, 1987; Scheerens, 1987.)

By looking at the industrial conditions of teachers' work, we might also begin to understand the paradox of the evaluations of compensatory education (for example, Glazer, 1986). In a nutshell, most intervention projects produce little change when measured in conventional ways, while those that do produce change follow no clear pattern. The technocratic approach to policymaking should be deeply embarrassed by this situation, though the usual reaction is to call for more research.

I suspect these findings reflect a Hawthorne effect in poverty programs, along the following lines.[8] Teaching practice is governed mainly by the institutional constraints of the school as a workplace. Compensatory interventions are generally far too small to change these constraints, a point that has been made throughout their history (see, for example, Halsey, 1972; Natriello et al., 1990). Accordingly, most educational practice in disadvantaged schools is routinely like practice in other schools (for evidence, see Connell, 1991), and produces the usual socially selective effects. Those programs that do produce changes happen to have found one of the variety of ways — which may be situational and temporary — of bolstering teachers' agency, increasing their capacity to maneuver around constraints and grapple with the contradictions of the relationship between poor children and schools.

Towards a Strategy of Change

Given a remapping of the issues along these lines, our concept of what constitutes a solution must also change. Solutions cannot consist of expert interventions from a central place. The educational authority that defines "expertise" must itself be contested. People in disadvantaged schools and poor communities do not lack knowledge. They do, however, often lack ways of putting their knowledge to use.

Does this mean that academics should simply get out of the way? There is a lot to be said for breaking the routines by which science legitimates intrusions in the lives of the poor. Nevertheless, researchers often do have information, resources, and skills that poor people and their teachers can use.

Rather than vacate the field, then, we should rethink the relationship between professional intellectuals and disadvantaged communities — as is done, for instance, in participatory action research in the welfare field (Wadsworth, 1983). It is possible to support strategic thinking in the schools rather than substitute for it, though the balance is not an easy one. That is to say, it is possible for researchers to refine, criticize, inform, and disseminate attempts to achieve educational purposes defined from below. In this spirit, I will briefly explore four issues that necessarily arise for democratic education strategies concerned with poverty: the goals of action, the direction of change in curriculum, the work force, and the political conditions of change.

Formulating Goals

Most statements of purpose for educational reform treat justice in distributional terms. That is, they treat education in much the way arguments about economic justice treat money: as a social good of standard character that needs to be shared more fairly. Even if the criteria for fair shares vary from one policy sphere to another, as in Walzer's (1983) sophisticated model of justice, the distributional approach governs the discussion of education.

If we have learned one thing from research on the interaction of curriculum and social context, it is that educational processes are not standard in this sense. Distributing equal amounts of the hegemonic curriculum to girls and boys, to poor children and rich children, to Black children and White children, to immigrants and native-born, to indigenous people and their colonizers, does not do the same thing for them — or to them. In education, the "how much" and the "who" cannot be separated from the "what."

The concept of distributive justice certainly applies to material resources for education, such as school funds and equipment. But we need something more to deal with the content and process of education: a concept of curricular justice (Connell, 1993). This idea is closely connected to the lesson curriculum history teaches: that there are always multiple ways to organize the knowledge content of schooling.

Each particular way of constructing the curriculum (i.e., organizing the field of knowledge and defining how it is to be taught and learned) carries social effects. Curriculum empowers and disempowers, authorizes and de-authorizes, recognizes and mis-recognizes different social groups and their knowledge and identities. For instance, curriculum developed from academic institutions controlled by men has, in a variety of ways, authorized the practices and experiences of men and marginalized those of women.[9] Curriculum defined by representatives of a dominant ethnic group is liable to exclude or de-authorize the knowledge and experience of dominated groups, or to incorporate them on terms that suit the dominant group.[10] Curricular justice concerns the organization of knowledge, and, through it, the justice of the social relations being produced through education.

There is nothing exotic about this idea. It is implied in a great deal of practical teaching that goes on in disadvantaged schools, teaching that contests the disempowering effects of the hegemonic curriculum and authorizes locally produced knowledge. This is the kind of "good teaching" Haberman (1991) has recently contrasted with the "pedagogy of poverty." As he observes, the challenge is how to institutionalize "good teaching" in disadvantaged schools. Initiatives of this kind remain marginal and are easily dismantled, unless they can be linked to larger purposes.

I think a concept of curricular justice makes the link to larger purposes possible and should be at the heart of strategic thinking on education and disadvantage. It requires us to think through curriculum-making from the point of view of the least advantaged, not from the standpoint of what is currently authorized. It requires us to think about how to generalize the point of view of the least advantaged as a program for the organization and production of knowledge in general.

Taking an educational view of poverty and education thus pushes us beyond the goal of "compensation" and towards the goal of reorganizing the cultural content of education as a whole. This goal is intimidating, given the difficulties encountered with much more limited goals. Yet clear thinking is helped if we put local initiatives in the perspective of the larger agenda they imply.

The Direction of Curriculum Change

Compensatory programs have mainly supplemented the hegemonic curriculum, adding extra activities or small group instruction in core areas of conventional teaching — principally, mathematics and language skills. Add-on programs do not change the main patterns of teaching and learning in the school. A strategy that takes curriculum change seriously would base itself on another approach found in compensatory programs, the whole-school change approach, which uses compensatory funds to redesign the major activities of the school.

How we understand curricular change depends on what we take the basic social effects of education to be. Wexler (1992) sees the main effects as the discursive formation of identities. This would focus strategies for justice on respect for diversity, and on producing identities that are rich and solid — not far, indeed, from the concerns of multicultural education. I would argue, however, for a broader conception of educational effects as the development of capacities for social practice (Connell, forthcoming). The social practices addressed by schooling include the winning of livelihood, a theme whose importance for youth still in school is documented by Wilson and Wyn (1987); the construction of gender and negotiation of sexuality (Frank, 1993); and the mobilization of social power, which is a familiar theme in adult literacy work (see Lankshear, 1987). Perhaps learning how to mobilize and use power is the clearest example of how a course of learning can open up ways of transforming the situation of the poor. The same point was made by the Australian Schools Commission, in stating objectives for its national compensatory education program; the objectives included:

> To ensure that students have systematic access to programs which will equip them with economic and political understanding so that they can act individually or together to improve their circumstances. (Australian Schools Commission, 1985, p. 98)

The idea of helping the poor "act . . . together" to change things is directly opposed to the divisive effects of a competitive assessment system. The link between exclusionary curricula and competitive assessment is very close. It is no accident that the Blackburn report on post-compulsory education in the Australian state of Victoria, which pursued the principle of a socially inclusive curriculum, also laid the groundwork for an important democratic reform of secondary assessment (Ministerial Review, 1985). This report drew on the experience of disadvantaged schools to formulate a policy for the state's school system as a whole.

Curriculum and assessment reforms are not cheap, especially in the time and human energy they require. The level of material resources for schools serving the poor still matters, even if one agrees that the quality of education does not depend on the freshness of paint on the school buildings. Measures of current per-capita funding are, as I have already suggested, inadequate measures of total social investment in the education of different groups of children. Given the educationally relevant inequalities of resources around schools, the consequences of unequal family and community wealth and income, distributive justice would require much higher levels of funding to the schools of the poor, and higher funding to working-class schools in general.

A curriculum focus, similarly, does not erase issues about the school as an institution. The curriculum as it is taught and learned, not just as it is in the manual, is the labor process of pupils and teachers, and, like other forms of labor, is powerfully affected by the surrounding social relations. Expanding the agency of teachers means moving towards industrial democracy at the level of the school. This is not easily achieved, as teachers' unions know; for a situation like that found in Britain after a decade of new-right government, it may sound utopian. But if we are serious about educational enrichment, then we need to produce the industrial conditions for richer forms of teaching.

The students, too, are working in more than a metaphorical sense. Democratization means expanding the agency of those normally overwhelmed by the agency of others or immobilized by current structures. Good teaching does this in an immediate, local way — as is vividly shown in the adult education for empowerment described by Shor (1992), where the teacher functions as problemposer and a critical dialogue replaces teacher-talk. An agenda for change must concern itself with how this local effect can be generalized.

The Work Force

Given the institutional and cultural forces that make for inequality in education, the case can be made that more can be done outside schools than inside them. This seems to be implied by postmodernist readings of educational politics by authors such as Giroux (1992). Acknowledging the cultural changes to which this reading responds, I would nevertheless argue that the profoundly ambivalent relationship between working-class people and educational institutions is central to contemporary cultural politics in industrial countries. This relationship has grown in importance with the growing weight of education as a part of the economy and the culture. Teachers in schools are the workers most strategically placed to affect the relationship. I have argued already for bringing teachers' work to the center of discussions of disadvantage. If the education of children in poverty is to be changed, teachers will be the work force of reform. This conclusion has two important corollaries.

First, teachers should be centrally involved in the design of reform strategies. Giroux (1988) earlier called our attention to the sense in which teachers are intellectuals. A capacity for strategic thinking certainly exists among the teachers of the poor. The Disadvantaged Schools Program in Australia, partly because of its decentralized design, encouraged the growth of an activist network that included teachers' unions and a group of experienced teachers in poor districts. This informal network, more than any formal agency, has transmitted experience and provided the forum for intense policy debates (White & Johnston, 1993). Such groups exist in other countries, too. A notable example is the network around the magazine *Our Schools/Our Selves,* which has brought teachers across Canada into a series of debates about educational reform. An intelligent approach to policymaking would regard such teacher networks as a key asset.

Second, a reform agenda must concern the shaping of this work force: the recruitment, training, in-service education, and career structures of teachers in disadvantaged schools. The 1966 Coleman report, to its credit, raised this issue and collected data on teacher training, but the issue almost vanished from later discussions of disadvantage. In a recession, where education budgets are under pressure, funds for teacher preparation, and especially for in-service training, are likely to be cut. To an extent, compensatory programs themselves function as teacher educators. A potentially cost-effective reform would be to expand these programs' capacities to train teachers, to circulate information, to pool knowledge, and to pass on expertise.

The work force is not static. Families move into and out of poverty, and teachers move into and out of disadvantaged schools. For both reasons, issues about poverty should concern teachers in all parts of a school system. I would argue that these issues should be major themes in initial teacher training, and that competence in work with disadvantaged groups should be central to the idea of professionalism in teaching.

Political Conditions: The Poor and the Less Poor

Targeted compensatory education programs are based on definitions of disadvantage, which are always to some degree arbitrary and may also be stigmatizing — especially where, as in the United States, issues about poverty are interwoven with a volatile politics of race.

Special programs for the disadvantaged are most easily accepted where inequalities can be seen as accidental, or as consequences of neglect. They are not so easily accepted where the inequalities are intended. A recent court case showed the school system in Rockford, Illinois, to have been operating a covert system of racial segregation — via tracking, scheduling, and special programs — that subverted official desegregation policies to a startling degree ('Integrated' Schools," 1993). This is a conspicuous example, but institutional racism is, of course, not unusual (for a recent British example, see Tomlinson, 1992.) We also cannot ignore the intention behind other forms of inequality and exclusion, whether along lines of class or gender or nationality.

Disadvantage is always produced through mechanisms that also produce advantage. The institutions that do this are generally defended by their beneficiaries. The beneficiaries of the current educational order are, broadly speaking, the groups with greater economic and institutional power, greater access to the means of persuasion, and the best representation in government and in professions. No one should imagine that educational change in the interests of the poor can be conflict-free.

That change happens at all is due to two facts. First, advantaged groups are far from monolithic. They are internally divided in a number of ways: for example, professionals versus capitalists, regional elites versus multinational elites, elite women versus elite men, new wealth versus old. These divisions affect educational stances, such as support for public expenditure on schooling. Members of advantaged groups differ in their judgments of short-term versus long-term interests, and in their willingness to take stances based on a notion of the common good. Their views of long-term interests are affected by pressure from below. United States elites, as Domhoff (1990) argues, conceded reforms in the 1960s and early 1970s — including compensatory education — under pressure of social disruption from the civil rights and other social movements. The reassertion of conservatism in U.S. public policy followed the decline of this pressure.

Second, the interests of the poor are not isolated. I emphasized earlier the statistical evidence that the most severe disadvantage is part of a much broader pattern of class exclusion. The poorest groups share an interest in educational reform with a broader constituency in the working class, even in very wealthy countries. However, it is not automatic that shared interest will be turned into any kind of practical alliance. Racism, regionalism, the weakening of the union movement, and the impact of new-right educational politics all stand in the way.

Targeted programs, however well-designed and lively, are unlikely to have a major impact unless they are part of a broader agenda for social justice. The problem of breadth is familiar in debates over social policy (see, for example, Skocpol, 1991). Narrowly targeted benefits appear more cost-effective than universal benefits, especially in a context of budget-cutting. But narrow targeting is likely to stigmatize the targeted group; the current political hostility to welfare dependents in the United States is a prime example. Because their beneficiaries are stigmatized minorities, the programs are politically weak, and the level of benefits is held down to a minimum. Continuing poverty is a common result. Broad entitlements to benefits (as illustrated by age pensions and health insurance in countries with universal systems) create larger constituencies and mobilize more political strength. Paradoxically, then, less targeted benefits (including universal benefits) are often more effective in producing redistribution: they "level up."

In education the case is somewhat different because the universal benefit already exists — compulsory schooling. The problem, as I have argued throughout this article, is that this universal benefit contains powerful mechanisms of privilege and exclusion; it does not function in a universal way. A social justice program in education must attempt to reconstruct the service that is formally available to everyone. Once we recognize this, the same strategic principle applies as in welfare politics: the broader the agenda, the more chance of a social justice outcome. The task is easier than welfare reform in that the idea of common schooling is well established, and more difficult in that the unequal functioning of education systems is defended by a formidable combination of class interest, professional routine, and institutional hierarchy.

To accomplish the institutional change needed by children in poverty requires greater social forces than poverty programs themselves generate. At the end of the day, then, the educational problems of compensatory education are political problems. Their long-term solution involves social alliances whose outlines are still, at best, emerging. Yet work on education can be one of the ways these very alliances are created.

Notes

1. The term "compensatory" has been rightly criticized for its association with deficit notions about the poor. However, it is the only common term for the special-purpose programs that are the focus of the policy discussion. It continues in official use, so I, too, use it.
2. I have counted the U.N. Development Programme's group of "industrial countries," excluding the communist or former communist countries. A more sophisticated calculation could adjust for known differences in the rates of child poverty — the United States appears relatively high — but a poverty line in any case has an element of arbitrariness; the order of magnitude would remain the same.
3. Useful histories of the compensatory idea have been written by Jeffrey (1978) and Silver and Silver (1991).
4. For their stories see Connell, White, and Johnston (1991); Halsey (1972); Peterson, Rabe, and Wong (1988); and Scheerens (1987).
5. In Australia, which is particularly explicit on this point, national compensatory education funds reach about 15 percent of school-age children. In the United States, where the situation is more complex, the figure appears to be about 11 percent, according to a careful estimate of the early 1980s (Kennedy, Jung, & Orland, 1986).
6. The emergence of the modern concept of poverty is traced by Dean (1991), and its impact on welfare policy by Katz (1989).
7. See, for example, the life histories of unemployed young men discussed in Connell (1989).
8. The "Hawthorne effect" is named for the factory where a famous experiment found industrial workers increasing output no matter how their work was arranged by the experimenters. The researchers finally realized that it was the experiment itself, not the

manipulations within it, that was creating a supportive group and boosting the workers' morale.

9. For an excellent account of this process and the complexities of contesting it, see chapter five in Yates (1993).
10. For a striking historical example of debate within the dominant group about this issue, see Ball (1984).

References

Anderson, E. (1991). Neighborhood effects on teenage pregnancy. In C. Jencks & P. E. Peterson (Eds.), *The urban underclass* (pp. 375–398). Washington, DC: Brookings Institution.

Angus, L. (Ed.) (1993). *Education, inequality and social identity*. London: Falmer Press.

Apple, M. W. (1982). *Education and power.* Boston: Routledge & Kegan Paul.

Apple, M. W. (1993). *Official knowledge: Democratic education in a conservative age.* New York: Routledge.

Australian Schools Commission. (1985). *Quality and equality.* Canberra: Commonwealth Schools Commission.

Avalos, B. (1992). Education for the poor: Quality or relevance? *British Journal of Sociology of Education, 13,* 419–436.

Ball, S. J. (1984). Imperialism, social control and the colonial curriculum in Africa. In I. F. Goodson & S. J. Ball (Eds.), *Defining the curriculum: Histories and ethnographies* (pp. 117–147). London: Falmer Press.

Bernstein, B. B. (1974). A critique of the concept of "compensatory education." In D. Wedderburn (Ed.), *Poverty, inequality and class structure* (pp. 109–122). Cambridge, Eng.: Cambridge University Press.

Casanova, U. (1990). Rashomon in the classroom: Multiple perspectives of teachers, parents and students. In A. Barona & E. E. Garcia (Eds.), *Children at risk: Poverty, minority status, and other issues in educational equity* (pp. 135–149). Washington, DC: National Association of School Psychologists.

Clark, E. A. G. (1977). The superiority of the "Scotch system": Scottish ragged schools and their influence. *Scottish Educational Studies, 9,* 29-39.

Coleman, J. S. (1990). *Equality and achievement in education.* Boulder: Westview.

Connell, R. W. (1989). Cool guys, swots and wimps: The interplay of masculinity and education. *Oxford Review of Education, 15,* 291–303.

Connell, R. W. (1991). The workforce of reform: Teachers in the disadvantaged schools program. *Australian Journal of Education, 35,* 229–245.

Connell, R. W. (1993). *Schools and social justice.* Philadelphia: Temple University Press.

Connell, R. W. (forthcoming). Transformative labor: Theorizing the politics of teachers' work. In M. B. Ginsburg (Ed.), *The politics of educators' work and lives.* New York: Garland.

Connell, R. W., Ashenden, D. J., Kessler, S., & Dowsett, G. W. (1982). *Making the difference: Schools, families and social division.* Sydney: Allen & Unwin.

Connell, R. W., Johnston, K. M., & White, V. M. (1992). *Measuring up: Assessment, evaluation and educational disadvantage.* Canberra: Australian Curriculum Studies Association.

Connell, R. W., White, V. M., & Johnston, K. M. (1991). *"Running twice as hard": The disadvantaged schools program in Australia.* Geelong, Australia: Deakin University.

Corrigan, P. (1979). *Schooling the Smash Street kids.* London: Macmillan.

Curtis, B., Livingstone, D. W., & Smaller, H. (1992). *Stacking the deck: The streaming of working-class kids in Ontario schools.* Toronto: Our Schools/Our Selves Education Foundation.

Davis, A. (1948). *Social-class influences upon learning.* Cambridge, MA: Harvard University Press.

Dean, M. (1991). *The constitution of poverty: Toward a genealogy of liberal governance.* London: Routledge.

Devine, J. A., & Wright, J. D. (1993). *The greatest of evils: Urban poverty and the American underclass.* New York: Aldine de Gruyter.

Domhoff, G. W. (1990). *The power elite and the state: How policy is made in America*. New York: Aldine de Gruyter.

Doyle, D. P., & Cooper, B. S. (Eds.). (1988). *Federal aid to the disadvantaged: What future for Chapter 1?* London: Falmer Press.

Embling, J. (1986). *Fragmented lives: A darker side of Australian life*. Ringwood, Australia: Penguin.

Fine, M. (1991). *Framing dropouts: Notes on the politics of an urban public high school*. Albany: State University of New York Press.

Ford, J. (1969). *Social class and the comprehensive school*. London: Routledge & Kegan Paul.

Frank, B. (1993). Straight/strait jackets for masculinity: Educating for "real" men. *Atlantis, 18*(1–2), 47–59.

Ginsburg, M. B. (Ed.). (forthcoming). *The politics of educators' work and lives*. New York: Garland.

Giroux, H. A. (1988). *Teachers as intellectuals: Toward a critical pedagogy of learning*. Granby, MA: Bergin & Garvey.

Giroux, H. A. (1992). *Border crossings: Cultural workers and the politics of education*. New York: Routledge.

Glazer, N. (1986). Education and training programs and poverty. In S. H. Danziger & D. H. Weinberg (Eds.), *Fighting poverty: What works and what doesn't* (pp. 152–173). Cambridge, MA: Harvard University Press.

Goodson, I. F. (Ed.). (1985). *Social histories of the secondary curriculum: Subjects for study*. London: Falmer Press.

Goodson, I. F. (1988). *The making of curriculum: Collected essays*. London: Falmer Press.

Griffin, C. (1993). *Representations of youth: The study of youth and adolescence in Britain and America*. Cambridge, Eng.: Polity Press.

Griswold, P. A., Cotton, K. J., & Hansen, J. B. (1986). *Effective compensatory education sourcebook*. Washington, DC: U.S. Department of Education.

Haberman, M. (1991). The pedagogy of poverty versus good teaching. *Phi Delta Kappan, 73*, 290–294.

Halsey, A. H. (Ed.). (1972). *Educational priority: Vol. I. E. P. A. Problems and policies*. London: Her Majesty's Stationery Office.

Harrington, M. (1962). *The other America*. New York: Macmillan.

Heath, A. (1992). The attitudes of the underclass. In D. J. Smith (Ed.), *Understanding the underclass* (pp. 32–47). London: Policy Studies Institute.

Heath, S. B. (1983). *Ways with words: Language, life and work in communities and classrooms*. Cambridge, Eng.: Cambridge University Press.

Hoyles, M. (1977). Cultural deprivation and compensatory education. In M. Hoyles (Ed.), *The politics of literacy* (pp. 172–181). London: Writers and Readers Publishing Cooperative.

"Integrated" schools kept races separate. (1983, November 9). *San Francisco Chronicle*.

Interim Committee for the Australian Schools Commission. (1973). *Schools in Australia*. Canberra: Australian Government Publishing Service.

Jeffrey, J. R. (1978). *Education for children of the poor: A study of the origins and implementation of the Elementary and Secondary Education Act of 1965*. Columbus: Ohio State University Press.

Katz, M. B. (1989). *The undeserving poor: From the War on Poverty to the war on welfare*. New York: Pantheon.

Kennedy, M. M., Jung, R. K., & Orland, M. E. (1986). *Poverty, achievement and the distribution of compensatory education services: An interim report from the national assessment of Chapter I*. Washington, DC: U.S. Department of Education, Office of Educational Research and Improvement.

Knapp, M. S., Shields, P. M., & Turnbull, B. J. (1992). *Academic challenge for the children of poverty: Summary report*. Washington, DC: U.S. Department of Education, Office of Policy and Planning.

Korbin, J. E. (1992). Introduction: Child poverty in the United States. *American Behavioral Scientist, 35*, 213–219.

Kozol, J. (1991). *Savage inequalities: Children in America's schools*. New York: Crown.

Lankshear, C. (1987). *Literacy, schooling and revolution*. New York: Falmer Press.

Lareau, A. (1987). Social class differences in family-school relationships: The importance of cultural capital. *Sociology of Education, 60*(2), 73–85.

Lawn, M. (1993, April). *The political nature of teaching: Arguments around schoolwork.* Paper presented at American Educational Research Association Conference, Atlanta, 1993.

Lewis, O. (1968). *La vida: A Puerto Rican family in the culture of poverty — San Juan and New York.* London: Panther.

MacIver, D. J., & Epstein, J. L. (1990). *How equal are opportunities for learning in disadvantaged and advantaged middle grade schools?* Baltimore: Johns Hopkins University, Center for Research on Effective Schooling for Disadvantaged Students.

MacPherson, S. (1987). *Five hundred million children: Poverty and child welfare in the Third World.* Brighton, Eng.: Wheatsheaf.

Ministerial Review of Postcompulsory Schooling (Blackburn Committee). (1985). *Report.* Melbourne: Education Department, Victoria.

Natriello, G., McDill, E. L., & Pallas, A. M. (1990). *Schooling disadvantaged children: Racing against catastrophe.* New York: Teachers College Press.

Ogbu, J. U. (1988). Cultural diversity and human development. In D. T. Slaughter (Ed.), *Black children and poverty: A developmental perspective* (pp. 11–28). San Francisco: Jossey-Bass.

Orland, M. E. (1990). Demographics of disadvantage: Intensity of childhood poverty and its relationship to educational experience. In J. I. Goodlad & P. Keating (Eds.), *Access to knowledge: An agenda of our nation's schools* (pp. 43–58). New York: College Entrance Examination Board.

Peterson, P. E., Rabe, B. G., & Wong, K. K. (1988). The evolution of the compensatory education program. In D. P. Doyle & B. S. Cooper (Eds.), *Federal aid to the disadvantaged: What future for Chapter I?* (pp. 33–60). London: Falmer Press.

Piven, F. F., & Cloward, R. A. (1979). *Poor people's movements: Why they succeed, how they fail.* New York: Vintage.

Riley, R. W. (1994, January 27). Reinventing Chapter I deserves full support. *San Francisco Chronicle,* op ed page.

Robins, D., & Cohen, P. (1978). *Knuckle sandwich: Growing up in the working-class city.* Harmondsworth, Eng.: Penguin.

Ryan, W. (1971). *Blaming the victim.* New York: Vintage Books.

Sartre, J. P. (1958). *Being and nothingness.* London: Methuen.

Savage, D. G. (1987). Why Chapter I hasn't made much difference. *Phi Delta Kappan, 68,* 581–584.

Scheerens, J. (1987). *Enhancing educational opportunities for disadvantaged learners: A review of Dutch research on compensatory education and educational development policy.* Amsterdam: North-Holland Publishing.

Seddon, T. (forthcoming). Teachers' work and political action. In N. Postlethwaite & T. Husen (Eds.), *International encyclopedia for educational research.* Oxford, Eng.: Pergamon.

Shor, I. (1992). *Empowering education: Critical teaching for social change.* Chicago: University of Chicago Press.

Silver, H., & Silver, P. (1991). *An educational war on poverty: American and British policy-making, 1960–1980.* Cambridge, Eng.: Cambridge University Press.

Skocpol, T. (1991). Targeting within universalism: Politically viable policies to combat poverty in the United States. In C. Jencks & P. E. Peterson (Eds.), *The urban underclass* (pp. 411–436). Washington, DC: Brookings Institution.

Snow, C. E., Barnes, W. S., Chandler, J., Goodman, I. F., & Hemphill, L. (1991). *Unfulfilled expectations: Home and school influences on literacy.* Cambridge, MA: Harvard University Press.

Taylor, W. L., & Piché, D. M. (1991). *A report on shortchanging children: The impact of fiscal inequity on the education of students at risk.* Washington, DC: U.S. House of Representatives, Committee on Education and Labor.

Thorne, B. (1993). *Gender play: Girls and boys in school.* New Brunswick, NJ: Rutgers University Press.

Tomlinson, S. (1992). Disadvantaging the disadvantaged: Bangladeshis and education in Tower Hamlets. *British Journal of Sociology of Education, 13,* 437-446.

United Nations Development Programme. (1992). *Human development report 1992*. New York: Oxford University Press.

U.S. Bureau of the Census. (1992). *Poverty in the United States: 1991*. Washington, DC: Government Printing Office.

Wadsworth, Y. (1983). *Do it yourself social research*. Melbourne: Allen & Unwin.

Walker, J. C. (1988). *Louts and legends: Male youth culture in an inner-city school*. Sydney: Allen & Unwin.

Walzer, M. (1983). *Spheres of justice: A defense of pluralism and equality*. New York: Basic Books.

Weinberg, M. (1981). *The education of poor and minority children: A world bibliography*. New York: Greenwood.

Wexler, P. (1992). *Becoming somebody: Toward a social psychology of school*. London: Falmer Press.

White, V., & Johnston, K. (1993). Inside the disadvantaged schools program: The politics of practical policy-making. In L. Angus (Ed.), *Education, inequality and social identity* (pp. 104–127). London: Falmer Press.

Whiteford, P., Bradbury, B., & Saunders, P. (1989). Inequality and deprivation among families with children: An exploratory study. In D. Edgar, D. Keane, & P. McDonald (Eds.), *Child poverty* (pp. 20–49). Sydney: Allen & Unwin.

Whitty, G. (1985). *Sociology and school knowledge: Curriculum theory, research and politics*. London: Methuen.

Whitty, G., & Young, M. (Eds.). (1976). *Explorations in the politics of school knowledge*. Driffield, Eng.: Nafferton Books.

Williams, T. (1987). *Participation in education*. Hawthorn: Australian Council for Educational Research.

Wilson, B., & Wyn, J. (1987). *Shaping futures: Youth action for livelihood*. Sydney: Allen & Unwin.

Yates, L. (1993). *The education of girls: Policy, research and the question of gender*. Hawthorn: Australian Council for Educational Research.

My thinking on these issues has been profoundly influenced by my colleagues on the national study of the Disadvantaged Schools Program in Australia, Ken Johnston and Viv White, and by the other contributors to that project. This article is based on the 1992 Paul Masoner International Education Lecture; I am grateful to the University of Pittsburgh for the invitation to deliver this lecture and thus bring these ideas together for a North American audience.

"Improve the Women"

Mass Schooling, Female Literacy, and Worldwide Social Change

ROBERT A. LEVINE
SARAH E. LEVINE
BEATRICE SCHNELL-ANZOLA*

> That spring [1838] Darwin was in his deepest radical phase (p. 249). . . . It was essential to educate working men and women — which would double the benefits passed on to the children. "Educate all classes," he scribbled amid the evolutionary notes, "improve the women (double influence) & mankind must improve." (Desmond & Moore, 1991, p. 252)

The young Charles Darwin gave voice in his notebook to views that were then current among progressive intellectuals and which have proved remarkably durable: that universal education is the pathway to "human improvement," and that sending women to school is a particularly sound social policy because of women's presumed role in the rearing of children. These ideas are part of the Enlightenment project of human improvement that arose in its modern form in the eighteenth century, inspired the British reform movement of the 1830s (which influenced Darwin), and has continued to inspire reformers and revolutionaries to the present day. Darwin and the active reformers of that time could hardly have imagined the worldwide spread of schooling during the next 150 years. At the beginning of the twenty-first century, a majority of children in most regions of the world attends school, and although the formal education of girls and women long lagged behind that of boys and men, it has by now caught up in many countries. International declarations, focusing attention on those countries in which school enrollments, and those of females in particular, remain behind, put women's schooling high on the policy agenda for immediate action.

The social science disciplines, like mass schooling, developed during the nineteenth and twentieth centuries. Questions of what part schooling has played in the social transformation of that period, and whether its effects were positive or negative, have been extensively considered and debated in the so-

*This article was originally published under the name Beatrice Schnell.

Harvard Educational Review   Vol. 71   No. 1   Spring 2001, 1–50

cial sciences. During the last twenty years, however, an international consensus has emerged, based on large-scale survey research conducted in the developing or low-income countries that embraced mass schooling after 1950: Schooling, particularly that of females, has beneficial effects, and more schooling brings more benefits to individuals, families, and society at large. A vast body of empirical evidence assembled by economists, demographers, epidemiologists, and other social scientists points to this conclusion. Observational research on childhood environments tends to support the idea that maternal schooling is beneficial to children's development. In other words, empirical studies seem to have confirmed the Enlightenment conception of formal education as a major pathway for human improvement, and the schooling of women as the most potent ingredient in the pervasive influence of mass education.

These conclusions have formed the basis for the policy recommendations of numerous United Nations declarations and reports during the 1990s: the World Conference on Education for All (WCEFA, 1990), the World Bank (1993), the United Nations Population Fund (UNFPA, 1994), and the United Nations Children's Fund (UNICEF, 1998), among others. There would seem to be no need for further research into a set of generalizations that has perhaps broader empirical support than any policy-relevant findings in modern history (Caldwell, 1994). In some respects, however, the international evidence concerning school effects is very thin. It lacks the perspectives of history, social anthropology, and — most remarkably — educational research. It also offers no view of education beyond years of school (or highest level) attended and rarely includes direct data on what skills, attitudes, or other tendencies boys and girls acquire in school. The "black box" of imputed links between school attendance and its socially beneficial "outcomes" remains large and murky, as do the institutional and cultural contexts that selectively facilitate or block the processes of individual development. Thus, the taint of speculation clings to the voluminous findings of school effects, raising the suspicion that researchers and policymakers have jumped to conclusions they were predisposed to accept as ideological heirs to the Enlightenment legacy.

In this article we reexamine the problem of school effects from a multidisciplinary perspective, providing an overview of the evidence, building a theoretical model of the institutional and psychosocial processes that might be involved, and presenting relevant findings from our own research on maternal literacy in culturally diverse settings. Our central question is whether and to what extent education, in the sense of socially organized learning, is actually involved in the processes linking women's schooling to falling birth and child mortality rates and, if so, how it can be measured.

The State of Knowledge: Empirical Evidence and Its Interpretation

Demographic theory and research since at least the middle of the twentieth century have suggested that women's schooling has an influence on the widespread trends toward lower birth and child mortality rates (e.g., Davis & Blake, 1956; Notestein, 1945). It was only in the late 1970s, however, that syntheses of large-scale studies across the developing world showed women's schooling to be positively related to child survival and inversely related to fertility, even when other socioeconomic factors were controlled for (Caldwell, 1979, 1982; Cochrane, 1979; Cochrane, O'Hara, & Leslie, 1980). In the 1970s, many developing countries were facing two major population problems, namely infant mortality and population growth. Infant mortality rates dropped sharply between 1950 and 1970, but had stabilized at levels far above those of the developed industrial countries. Furthermore, the earlier declines in mortality, combined with rising fertility, had created very high rates of population growth that threatened long-term survival. Many countries, including China, India, and Mexico, instituted family-planning programs to curtail fertility, and many others put in place primary health-care programs as well, with a special focus on maternal and child health in order to reduce the mortality of infants, children, and mothers. In this context, the findings concerning female schooling as a factor in reducing child mortality and fertility were of direct policy relevance. There was a continuing debate among demographers and health-policy analysts as to whether declining fertility and mortality rates were due to the efforts of family-planning and primary health-care programs or to the processes of socioeconomic development, including mass schooling. Even among those on the development side of this issue, there was disagreement concerning whether demographic change was due simply to increased income and access to resources or to education-based changes in the ways people used income and resources. The findings from Caldwell and Cochrane that women's school attainment was not just a proxy for household socioeconomic status but played a crucial role of its own in the demographic transition were interpreted as supporting a policy of expanding female schooling in order to reduce mortality and fertility (World Bank, 1980).

Twenty years later, the developing world context is different, but some issues remain. Birth and death rates have come down almost everywhere, though they are still relatively high in sub-Saharan Africa, South Asia, and some Middle Eastern countries. Analyses of massive datasets from the World Fertility Survey and the more recent Demographic and Health Surveys have confirmed the importance of women's schooling as an influence in demographic transition, at least before 1990. The policy question driving recent demographic research on the effects of female schooling has been whether and to what extent low-income countries should invest in the further expansion of women's school attendance as a means of improving the survival, health, and welfare of children and families. Despite an international consensus on the value of gender equality in access to education and on the assumption that mass schooling for girls is generally beneficial to society, nagging issues of causal inference, as described below, continue to divide those who interpret the evidence for policy purposes.

The notion that educational policy should rely on empirical research is relatively recent; in fact, the universal schooling of girls, as well as boys, was adopted by the countries of Europe, North America, and Japan in the nineteenth century, and by many Latin American, Asian, and African countries in the third quarter of the twentieth century, *without* empirical evidence to prove its efficacy. In the last quarter of the twentieth century, however — and particularly after publication of the *World Development Report 1980* (World Bank, 1980) that summarized evidence that schooling had a positive impact on agricultural production, child survival, and fertility decline — the consideration of school expansion as a policy for developing countries was reframed for national policymakers in those countries as a means of achieving these (and other) demonstrable outcomes. This view has been attractive to public decisionmakers, as it offers them the option of expanding schools, and especially female school enrollments, as an accessible policy lever for attacking social problems. Differences of opinion concerning how tightly schooling is tied to demographic change, economic productivity, and social inequality now generate much of the interest in this topic for policy researchers.

There is more to schooling than its effects on health and population. Research on the effects of schooling is not needed to justify gender equality in access to education, which can be treated (properly, in our view) as a matter of fundamental values rather than simply a means to other ends. Our goal in this article is not to resolve debates over values or policy issues but to further our understanding of the processes of worldwide social change resulting from past and present policies of institutional transformation. The question of how education and learning might be implicated in these processes is important in itself and significant for both theory and practice.

The largest and most important body of evidence concerning the beneficial effects of women's schooling comes from national censuses and demographic surveys that indicate a relationship between female school attendance and falling birth and death rates in the countries of Latin America, Asia (outside of Japan), and Africa during the second half of the twentieth century. In these countries, fewer than half of the children aged six to eleven were enrolled in primary school in 1960, and girls' schooling was rare; by the mid-1990s, 81 percent of *girls* aged six to eleven were attending primary school. This figure conceals enormous disparities among regions, as well as the fact that, for these countries as a whole, only about 75 percent of those who enter school complete five years, but it does indicate that much expansion occurred in mass schooling for females between 1960 and 1995 (UNICEF, 1998).

Major socioeconomic and demographic changes occurred in the same countries during the same period: growth in economic infrastructure, output, income, and consumption; urbanization; expansion of transportation networks and health and family-planning services; and reduction in mortality and fertility rates. As data concerning these trends became available, social scientists examined the interrelations among them and attempted to explain change and variation. Women's schooling emerged from these analyses as an important factor in, and perhaps a determinant of, demographic transition and other social changes. The sheer magnitude of the demographic transition was enormous: for the developing countries as a whole, mortality among children under age five was 216 per thousand live births in 1960 and 96 in 1997; total fertility (the number of children born alive to the average woman in a population during her reproductive years, ages 15–49) declined from 6.0 in 1960 to 3.1 in 1997 (UNICEF, 1998). In Mexico, for example, the under-five mortality rate dropped from 134 in 1960 to 35 in 1997, and the total fertility rate declined from 6.9 in 1960 to 2.8 in 1997. A wealth of evidence shows that the rising level of women's schooling was related to these trends (LeVine et al., 1991).

The facts concerning the relationships between women's schooling and demographic change are not in serious dispute and can be summarized briefly. Demographers have found that women's school attendance (from none at all through the tertiary level) is negatively associated with child mortality and fertility and positively associated with use of health and contraceptive services, even when statistically controlling for other socioeconomic factors (urban or rural residence, household income, and husband's schooling and occupation).[1] The major accomplishment of these statistical analyses has been to demonstrate that, although women's schooling is associated with indicators of socioeconomic advantage, it is not simply a proxy for these indicators but has independent relationships with health behaviors and reproductive change. These relationships are usually stronger than those of men's schooling and are frequently the strongest associations at the household level.

These relationships are not identical for all demographic and health outcomes. Maternal schooling is more consistently related to child mortality than to fertility, and it is more robustly related to post-infancy child mortality (13–48 months) than to infant mortality (first 12 months). Thus, in many countries, the association between infant mortality and maternal schooling disappears when the family's current socioeconomic status is controlled for, but post-infancy mortality remains significantly related. Furthermore, while a mother's preventive health behavior (immunization, prenatal care) is almost always robustly associated with her schooling, the child's survival during infancy and early childhood may still be jeopardized by inadequate diet or exposure to infections such as HIV, hepatitis B, and drug-resistant malaria, for which no vaccines or cures exist. Maternal schooling alone does not guarantee child survival. Consistently and robustly, however, it is associated with some of the key components of child survival.

A widely replicated but less consistent pattern holds for fertility, which tends to be inversely related to women's schooling when other socioeconomic factors are controlled for at the individual level, within national populations. In the poorest countries, particularly those of sub-Saharan Africa, a curvilinear rather than linear relationship exists between fertility and maternal schooling; in other words, women with primary schooling bear more children than unschooled women, and only those who attended to the secondary level or higher show the effects of contraception or delayed onset of childbearing. When economic conditions improve, this U-shaped pattern changes to a linear one, as it did in some African countries between the World Fertility Survey of the 1970s and the Demographic and Health Surveys a decade later. Furthermore, the mass sterilization of unschooled rural women in parts of South Asia indicates that school attendance is not a necessary condition for effective contraception there (Cleland & Kaufman, 1998). These variations raise questions concerning attitudes toward "contraception," which in one context refers primarily to sterilization and in others to reversible methods such as the pill. There are, in other words, enough exceptions and qualifications to the inverse relationship between women's schooling and fertility to make the point that it is a contingent, context-dependent relationship rather than a uniform and universal one. At the level of cross-national variations, the average female schooling of a national population is inversely related to its total fertility rate, but regional variations exist in the strength of the relationship, suggesting that cultural influences are at work (Cleland & Kaufman, 1998; United Nations, 1995).

The relationships between maternal schooling (separated from other socio-economic factors) and child mortality and fertility, examined through cross-sectional surveys, are clearly dependent on support from variable economic, social, and cultural conditions, and they may also be relatively weak in magnitude (though consistent and robust) in the short run. Historical time-series analyses suggest, however, that women's schooling has been an important condition of *long-term* reductions in child mortality and fertility among developing countries during the period from 1960 to 1995 (Caldwell, 1986; Mehrotra & Jolly, 1997; Schultz, 1993). Furthermore, contraceptive prevalence, a strong predictor of lower fertility at the cross-national level, is also positively related to the average level of women's schooling across developing countries (United Nations, 1995). Thus, there is little doubt that women's schooling is implicated in the social processes of demographic transition (Cleland & Jejeebhoy, 1996), but the evidence can be read in different ways — like the glass that is half full or half empty. Those claiming the necessity and potency of women's schooling in demographic transition find an overwhelming pattern of recurrent, supportive findings, though with some exceptions. Those casting doubt on the importance of women's schooling point to the exceptions as disproving claims of universality, to the increasing number of exceptions concerning fertility, and to problems with the evidence, particularly as a basis for causal inference (Bledsoe, Casterline, Johnson-Kuhn, & Haaga, 1999).

There is doubt among investigators as to whether the evidence shows maternal schooling to be a *cause* of change in demographic and health variables or merely a concomitant of such changes. Two primary factors arouse skepticism concerning the causal inference: selection bias and ignorance of the causal links that may be connecting school experience to reproductive change. The problem of selection bias arises because the available evidence comes from cross-sectional sample surveys and population censuses that were not designed to answer causal questions about the effects of school experience. Schooling as an independent variable is not randomly assigned, as it would be in an experiment, so the possibility of selection bias exists from the start. Might not the factors causing differential durations of school attendance also cause its alleged effects? A survey designed to mitigate this problem would involve a longitudinal study of girls beginning before school entry and continuing until the end of their childbearing years (about 40 years), so that a direct assessment of their differential starting points (parental advantages, preschool ability), reasons for leaving school at different levels, learning influences, marriages, and other life events could be made. Several successive birth cohorts would have to be studied to disentangle cohort-specific historical factors from those at the level of individual differences. No study that was designed in advance to identify the causal impact of schooling has been conducted. From the viewpoint of school effects, the available worldwide evidence is deficient and results from post hoc analyses of cross-sectional datasets that indirectly and retrospectively assess a process that should be studied directly, intensively, and prospectively.

Until longitudinal research is launched, the problem of selection bias will have to be addressed through statistical controls and ethnographic examination. Elo (1992), for example, examined the question of whether the associations of maternal schooling with utilization of health-care services (prenatal care and medically attended delivery) in the 1986 Demographic and Health Survey of Peru were due to familial advantage by controlling for background characteristics (childhood place of residence, ethnicity, and age). She found that the effects of maternal schooling on use of health services were attenuated when the controls were included in the regression model, but that schooling was still a significant predictor of health-care utilization. We have adopted this approach in our community-level studies, using the mother's parents' schooling as a control for background advantages.

Another problem with the causal hypothesis is that the links between school experience and its hypothesized reproductive and health outcomes are unknown. More precisely, such links have been the focus of abundant speculation and a modest amount of research. Without a model of the intervening processes that is both plausible *and* supported by empirical findings, the credibility of women's schooling as a causal influence on social change is always in jeopardy. Our approach has been to begin with the most common patterns of demographic findings from across the world and attempt to fit explanatory models to those patterns. Even highly sophisticated syntheses, however, remain speculations until direct assessment of the pathways sheds light into the "black box" of intervening processes. This has been the goal of our research program, as presented below.

The existing evidence does indicate that some pathways from schooling to reproduction are more probable avenues of influence than others. The relationship of women's schooling to reduced fertility, for example, although partly reflecting the later marriage of those who have spent more time in school, is largely accounted for by the use of contraception of one sort or another, with or without organized family-planning programs (United Nations, 1995). This finding narrows the range of possible explanatory models: the primary problem is to explain why women who have attended school longer are more likely to use contraception with the intention of limiting births. Similarly, many studies have shown that women with more schooling are more likely to use maternal and child health services (immunization and prenatal care) more frequently and effectively, to adhere to domestic dietary and sanitary practices recommended by health authorities, and to attend to the mass media in countries ranging from Bangladesh and the Philippines to Egypt and Brazil (e.g., Cebu Study Team, 1991; Cleland, 1990; Guldan et al., 1993; Peña, Wall, & Person, 2000; Tekce, Oldham, & Shorter, 1994; Thomas, Strauss, & Henriques, 1991). All of these findings suggest that maternal participation in bureaucratic health services is a path through which schooling influences reproduction and health — in the clinic, through the public health information media, or through social contacts with those who have been directly influenced by clinic or media exposure.

This pattern of evidence concerning maternal schooling has led us to propose "bureaucratization of the life course" as a process through which school experience influences reproduction and child care. Such a process implies that individuals spend an increasing portion of their lives in the settings of bureaucratic institutions, such as government offices, health services, or corporate employers, either as workers or as clients. School attendance introduces girls to the communicative activities characteristic of bureaucratic institutions, thus facilitating their later responsiveness as mothers to authoritative guidance from clinics and public health messages in the media (LeVine, LeVine, Richman, Tapia Uribe, & Sunderland Correa, 1994).

Recent studies also point to the role of literacy practices in this process. In national surveys of mothers in Morocco (Glewwe, 1999) and South Africa (Thomas, 1999), directly assessed maternal literacy skills predicted better child health (less likelihood of chronic malnutrition) and lower fertility, with socioeconomic factors controlled for. The skills assessed through a brief test of health-related literacy (reading a medicine label) in the Morocco study, and one of reading comprehension in the South African study, point to a literacy pathway from school to the kinds of bureaucratic participation that affect health and reproduction.

The Spread and Expansion of Schooling

The spread of schooling throughout the world during the nineteenth and twentieth centuries was due largely to nation-building efforts by political leaders seeking to establish their peoples and geographical territories as modern nation-states. While it is true that Christian missionaries had first introduced schools in many of the countries under European colonial rule, when these countries became independent in the mid-twentieth century, their leaders — like the Japanese of the 1870s — tended to see universal schooling as an advantage held by the more powerful nations that they wanted for their own people. A nation, as it was increasingly conceptualized, had to have a school system as much as it did a government, an army, a civil service, a postal system, and hospitals. Competitive nationalism fostered hasty imitation of other countries, and since no other way existed of determining which school systems were best, those systems associated with the most powerful and prestigious were also most imitated (Meyer, Kamens, & Benavot, 1992). Meyer and his colleagues have shown a remarkable similarity in the structure of schools and the content of their curricula across the countries of the world. Few national or culture-specific experiments in formal education were conducted, as national policymakers sought conformity with emerging "international standards" based on Western models (Meyer, Kamens, & Benavot, 1992; Meyer, Ramirez, & Soysal, 1992).

The global popularity and spread of the Western school were facilitated by its attractiveness to leaders and people alike. Schools were seen by political leaders and presented to their constituents as the universal equipment of a modern bureaucratic state, as well as an import from the West. Bureaucratic schooling could be adopted as the means of realizing differing ideological visions: liberal democracy, Marxist and social-democratic socialism, militant nationalism, laissez-faire capitalism. The rhetoric linking mass schooling to these ideologies could be used to build popular support for a regime; thus the school became the major symbol of hope in much of the world. Furthermore, leaders saw bureaucratic schooling as a way to create loyal citizens, effective soldiers, productive workers — all essential to the growth of a powerful nation-state. The emphasis on one or another of these goals varied across countries and historical periods — across what Hobsbawm and Ranger (1983) have called the shift from an "operatic to a prosaic" mode of nationalism, as the construction of national myths, symbols, and monuments gave way to "the prosaic work of institution building based on internationally available models, such as setting up health care systems, mass schooling and pension funds" (Meyer, Kamens, & Benavot, 1992, p. 77).

Thus schooling has been a universal entailment of nation-building over the last 150 years, and school expansion has formed part of each plan for establishing a nation-state as the primary institution for collective action, citizen responsiveness, and national growth and development, however conceptualized. The diffusion of organizational models of nation-building and schooling from the West to other countries is a historical fact. It is not an essential or intrinsic feature of cultural evolution or human progress, but rather the outcome of a particular history that might have taken a different turn. Schools, as we know them, caught on among nineteenth-century nation builders as an extremely convenient way of harnessing people on a large scale to the nation-state in order to fulfill a national agenda. As with the proliferation of nation-states themselves in the world during the twentieth century, the expansion of formal education has continued at a rapid pace.

Nation-building has increasingly involved the average person's participation in bureaucratic institutions, that is, corporate organizations with a hierarchical structure of (nonkinship) roles and relationships and a standardized set of goals, recruitment and operating procedures, and roles and relationships. Bureaucracies are designed for expansion by replicating standard units and coordinating their operations under hierarchical control. Standardization of explicit rules for all activities, including communication, is central to the values of efficiency and equal treatment built into bureaucracies, which generate formal codes of conduct and discourse that deliberately transcend local customs and vernaculars of their participants. Schools (like the local branches of corporations and government health services) are units in bureaucracies, and our hypothesis is that schools prepare children, deliberately or not, to participate in other bureaucratic organizations by providing them with the skills, aspirations, and models of interaction appropriate for such participation. In the following section we examine the distinctive features of schools as conceptualized in educational research.

Properties of the School

Educational theory and research have identified certain properties of the school as an institutional environment that shapes children's social participation and the subjective meanings they acquire. These properties include group membership, age-grading, status hierarchy, intensified social comparison, adult-child interaction, verbal communication, and formal participation structure.

Group membership. Schools constitute membership in communities outside the family (Meyer & Hannan, 1979). At school entry, children learn that they belong to a community beyond the boundaries of the village and kin network, of which the nation-state is most important and has the right to claim loyalty and obedience and to confer the identity and privileges of a citizen. For children in rural villages of developing countries, this can be an important discovery. For example, a girl may learn for the first time that there are authorities higher than her parents whose demands for homework supersede her parents' commands for domestic labor.

Age-grading. Schools typically organize children into age-segregated groupings (Aries, 1962), creating peer reference groups. In the homes and communities of many agrarian societies without schools, a child grows up as part of a multi-age, often hierarchical, group of siblings and other children (Weisner & Gallimore, 1977). By putting children of the same age in a class segregated from those older and younger, schools make children more dependent on the teacher for their learning, since they are isolated from other examples of more mature practice (Lave & Wenger, 1991). But this segregation also establishes the conditions for childhood social relations to develop through peer groups, which can affect a child's attitudes. As girls who attend school reach adolescence, their models of marriage and fertility are influenced by the ideas and practices of their peer networks.

Status hierarchy. Schooling introduces the child to the ladder-like series of age-graded statuses in school that maps onto the ranked status system of adults in a socially stratified urban society, that is, the *academic-occupational hierarchy* in which level of school attainment is associated with occupational status, as opposed to the age-gender hierarchies of local communities without schools (LeVine & White, 1986). Children learn through years in school that those with more schooling are entitled to jobs with higher income and social power than those with lower levels of educational attainment. This message embodied in schooling provides awareness of the incentives embodied in socioeconomic standing and acts to motivate status-seeking behavior during and after the school years.

Social comparison. School attendance involves public evaluation of individual performance, legitimizing and intensifying social comparisons, invidious distinctions, and competitive pressures (LeVine, 1978). This practice often contrasts with the indigenous values of agrarian communities in which personal advantages are kept from public view in the interests of reducing interpersonal competition and promoting harmony and cooperation. Schools force a child to work for herself rather than helping others and to endure being publicly compared to others, in the classroom and outside. In this sense, schools promote individualism (Meyer, 1977). Whatever culture-specific impact this might have — and it can provoke stress and anxiety — it inevitably supports a conception of learning and performance as personal attributes related to a woman's future and that of her children.

Adult-child interaction. The school classroom can be a unique setting in many agrarian communities by its dedication of the full-time attention and activities of an adult to interacting with children for purposes of instruction. Classroom interaction in schools everywhere consists of an adult expert dedicating his attention to child novices (LeVine, LeVine et al., 1994; Wertsch, Minick, & Arms, 1984). Such an interaction pattern is taken for granted in societies with schools, but in many agrarian communities children grow up in interactive settings where they are peripheral to the activities of adults — in other words, where they are never the centers of adult attention or interaction for more than a few moments at a time (Lave & Wenger, 1991; Rogoff, Mistry, Goncu, & Mosier, 1993). The adult-expert/child-novice structure is an institutionalized instructional format that can become prototypical for other teaching and learning interactions in a population.

Verbal communication. The central activity of the classroom is verbal communication, not economic production or consumption (Scribner & Cole, 1973). Such communication is an aspect of the institutional format of adult-child instruction, but it deserves to be emphasized. In the rural communities of many largely agrarian countries, the school classroom may be the only place in a child's experience where words — in speech, reading, and writing — are treated as primary objects of attention themselves rather than as means to other ends. The school classroom, in its literacy instruction and in other ways, also promotes a unique self-consciousness about language, or metalinguistic awareness, that is a highly salient aspect of the school environment for its pupils (Scribner & Cole, 1981).

Participation structure. Classroom interaction has a highly scripted, formal participation structure such as the I-R-E (initiation-reply-evaluation) pattern of American instruction (Cazden, 1988; Phillips, 1983; Wells, 1999). Children acquire the script as part of their behavioral repertoire and may use it later in other settings. Middle-class American children may acquire the I-R-E script at home *before* going to school, as Heath found in her study of middle-class families in the southeastern United States: "Before the age of 2, the child is socialized into the initiation-reply-evaluation sequences repeatedly described as the central structural feature of classroom lessons" (Heath, 1986, p. 99). For others not so advantaged, the sequence must be learned in school. Classroom participation structure is undoubtedly influenced by local conversational norms and local conceptions of hierarchical and other social relationships; it is thus culturally diversified, rather than a uniform feature of schooling. Classrooms outside the United States and Canada may not follow the I-R-E sequence but are equally scripted and standardized according to other cultural formulas. Since all pupils participate in these interactional structures not once but innumerable times in the course of their schooling, it is plausible that these structures have an impact, that the pupil learns not just the script as a sequence of actions but also the code that lies behind it. It may be that the formality of the participation structure — in other words, its standardization and control of attention in a learning situation — has a similar impact everywhere regardless of the particular script for participation.

These findings, observations, and hypotheses suggest a variety of pathways through which prolonged school attendance might reshape the behavioral development of girls who attend school for a certain period of years in comparison with those from the same background who drop out or do not attend at all. As properties of schools and classrooms that could be universal, these structural features can be plausibly hypothesized to have cumulative effects on a woman's reproductive and health behavior with additional years of school attendance, through secondary school and beyond, rather than effects specific to the curricular content of a particular level.

A Theoretical Model of Schooling

We propose that mass schooling operates to change a population's behavior not only through the structural transformation of institutions (Meyer, 1977), but also through the reshaping of the social participation of individuals through school attendance. More specifically, nation-building includes social processes — recruitment to an urban-industrial occupational structure, the construction and operation of a state administrative bureaucracy, and continual social change — that influence a girl's school-based acquisition of aspirations, identity, skills, and models of learning that eventually affect her reproductive, child-rearing, and health behavior. Our formulation linking the microgenesis of individual dispositions with the macrosocial world of institutional history is based on premises well stated by Scribner and Cole (1973):

> Every theory of education clearly requires a theory of society as a whole and of how social processes shape education. A theory of formal education also requires a theory of how learning and thinking skills develop in an individual member of society, and how educational processes contribute to the shaping of these skills. (p. 553)

Our reading of the demographic evidence leads us to focus on four pathways through which schooling might affect a women's reproductive and health behavior: 1) aspirations influenced by the occupational structure; 2) identity formation and empowerment; 3) communications skills influenced by bureaucratic language; and 4) models of learning and teaching as adaptive strategies, influenced by the instructional relationship with an expert.

Aspirations

Schooling influences the motivations of girls in low-income countries, leading them to desire improvement in their own and their children's lives according to the standards of an urban-industrial occupational order (Kasarda, Billy, & West, 1986; LeVine et al., 1991). This type of influence operates through the academic-occupational hierarchy mentioned above, in which it becomes clearer to girls the longer they remain in school that higher levels of formal education can qualify students for higher status positions in society and access to material and social advantages. Where women are barred from higher occupational positions (or from all employment), prolonged schooling may nonetheless qualify them (according to local standards) for marriage to men of higher status who can provide them and their children with access to more advantages. Where women select their own mates, their school-heightened desires for personal and filial improvement may lead them to marry men of higher status. Surveys of poor and developing countries typically find that the schooling of husbands and wives are positively correlated (between .40 and .60), reflecting the impact of this mate-selection preference in current cohorts of childbearing women (LeVine et al., 1991). Women with more schooling often want smaller families and more schooling for their children than they themselves had, similarly reflecting their elevated aspirations for improvement according to contemporary standards. The impact of schooling on aspirations is a socialization effect in which school experience motivates women to seek higher status. Such a conceptualization is a standard sociological view of schooling.

One problem with this view, particularly in many agrarian communities, is the assumption that women gain access to higher status and the advantages that go with it through their own motivation and efforts, rather than through those of their parents and husbands. In societies where marriages are arranged by kin, the woman's marriage to a man with more schooling is likely to reflect her parents' status-seeking rather than her own, and once she has an advantageous marriage, her access to better health and contraceptive services and information may simply reflect her husband's social location. Insofar as this situation holds, one need not posit that school has a socialization effect on the female pupil's aspiration level, only that she is willing to follow her parents' desires and use advantages that accrue to her from marriage. This reasoning represents another common sociological view of schooling, in which behavior is explained in terms of social conditions, both constraints and opportunities, in the adult environment rather than in terms of the influence of earlier learning and socialization.

When the hypothesized outcomes of socialization are confounded with those of external constraints and opportunities, as in the case of marrying to enhance status, the question of whether schooling has an educational socialization effect may not be answerable without additional ethnographic or attitudinal evidence that specifically addresses that question. If ethnographic description of the context in which marriages are arranged indicates that brides are not permitted to choose their mates, then the educational effect on marital choice is rendered improbable. However, if women express preferences for fewer children than their husbands do, an educational effect on those preferences is suggested. One must not confuse improved access to advantages with the effects of learning; access and other environmental variables must be measured and controlled for in the search for educational processes that influence reproductive and health outcomes.

Identity Formation and Empowerment

The belief that girls in developing countries are positively transformed by schooling, gaining psychological attributes that enhance their health behavior as mothers, is widely held by policy analysts and international agencies but is controversial among social scientists. There are many variants of this notion, to which we refer as identity formation and empowerment, but most of them posit that schooling increases the self-confidence, assertiveness, and autonomy needed to use reproductive health services effectively; some formulations include an increase in rational judgment, knowledge, sophistication, and personal efficacy (Jejeebhoy, 1995). The concept of identity means that specific attributes form part of the girl's subjective sense of self in relation to the public world of social roles and relationships. *Empowerment* is the term most widely used at present, often with an emphasis on the social rather than on the psychological — in other words, on the freeing of the woman from the constraints of "traditional" women's roles. This proposed pathway between schooling and health behavior brings into focus the sharp differences in views about women's education that characterize policy-relevant social science at present. Our analysis of the theory and state of the evidence is summarized in the following four points:

Empowerment (and related) models of women's education are versions of an Enlightenment narrative that has been an established Western ideology for two centuries. In the Enlightenment narrative, schooling liberates children from the shackles of superstition and archaic customs so that they can think rationally and act autonomously. This powerful moral story has inspired social reform and school expansion from the eighteenth century to the present day, and it is enshrined in recent declarations of the United Nations. As an ideology, it predisposes those influenced by it to believe that schooling is a universally positive process associated with rationality and freedom. Like other ideologies it tends to foreclose or bias empirical inquiry, establishing truth by presumption rather than by open-ended investigation. It is important to treat its application to women's schooling in developing countries with skepticism and to ask, what evidence exists to support or falsify its premises?

Empowerment models have been criticized on the basis of anthropological perspectives and evidence. A cultural relativist framework prevalent among anthropologists makes them suspicious of claims of universality, such as Kant's universal human reason unfolding in the course of child development or the assumption that personal autonomy (another Kantian concept) is a universal human value. These anthropologists are particularly suspicious of claims that worldwide institutions of Western origin, like the school, are necessary for individuals to reach higher stages of intelligence, rationality, and freedom. Their field experience tells them that the unschooled people with whom they have worked have alternative standards of personal maturity and interpersonal effectiveness that are unknown to those who assume modern Western standards to be superior. Contemporary formulations concerning the psychological and social benefits of women's schooling in developing societies, then, insofar as they imply that unschooled women are lacking in rationality and social competence, arouse criticism from anthropologists, who see Western cultural superiority emerging once again in the guise of science and well-intentioned policy.

Anthropological research has also uncovered instances of communities in which the schooling of women does not empower them. Working in northern India, for example, Jeffery and Jeffery (1997) find that the actualities of women's lives in a situation of educational transition do not resemble the Enlightenment narrative with its liberationist model of schooling. Such cases, in which the more privileged segments of the population, whose daughters go further in Western-style education, are also those that have embraced religious orthodoxy (in the Hindu case, "Sanskritization") — including its greater restrictions on women at and during marriage (Jeffery & Basu, 1996) — demonstrate, at the very least, that female empowerment as conceptualized in Western thought is not a universal consequence of schooling worldwide.

Ethnographic and survey evidence do indicate, however, that women who have attended school shows signs of feeling empowered and efficacious. In our own earlier studies in urban Mexico (S. LeVine, 1993) and rural Nepal (Joshi, 1994), we found such evidence. Among the residents of a low-income neighborhood in urban Cuernavaca, Mexico, many of whom were migrants from rural villages, Sarah LeVine (1993) reported the following:

> Mothers stressed that their own parents had believed education was wasted on a girl who would "only get married"; in contrast, they themselves were convinced that education was essential both for self-respect and for the economic opportunities it provided. (p. 78)

> Though literacy skills poorly mastered in overcrowded schools may deteriorate through lack of practice, the social experience of schooling fosters a self-confidence that remains throughout life. In the classroom, where she is expected to apply herself *for her own benefit*, a girl who at home is being raised within a male-dominated structure to be compliant and to work for the good of the family, undergoes a process of resocialization. School is a new universe that operates according to different rules. . . . A girl can — and frequently does — beat out the boys for first place. The longer she stays in school, the more likely she is to be convinced of her own efficacy — vis à vis males in particular — a conviction that stays with her into adulthood, marriage and motherhood. She is likely to discuss family problems and make decisions jointly with her husband, rather than her husband keeping his own counsel and making decisions on his own. (pp. 196–197, italics in original)

Our small-scale survey of mothers in the same working-class neighborhood from 1983 to 1985 also found associations between maternal schooling and (reported) egalitarianism in the husband-wife relationship, (reported) less harsh discipline of children and knowledge of news events in the mass media — as proposed by theories of "psychological modernity" (Smith & Inkeles, 1974) and other liberationist models of change (LeVine et al., 1991). These findings came from an urban population with employment opportunities for women, in which schooling was expected to launch adolescent girls into jobs for a few years before marriage and to help them support their children after marriage should their husbands fail to do so (S. LeVine, 1993). This economic context is clearly part of the girl's acquisition of self-respect, operating along with effects attributable to the classroom.

In rural Nepal, on the other hand, among the high-caste Hindu farmers studied by Joshi (1994) in 1989–1990, women devoted their lives to domestic work (cultivation, food processing, gathering firewood, and household tasks), with no opportunities for formal employment outside the home. Those who had attended school were a minority and were seen as different from the norm by the older generation, especially their parents-in-law, who feared that school would make women less compliant workers. A time-allocation study suggested that the in-laws' apprehensions were correct, in the sense that mothers who had been to school spent less time doing the arduous cultivation assigned them and more time in child care (a task cherished by their mothers-in-law) than those who had not attended school. Furthermore, the mothers who had been to school were judged to be more confident by health-care workers. Here the situation is characterized by an early stage of the educational transition in which female schooling is still unusual and is subversive of young married women's roles as the most obedient workers in the family and the most self-effacing adults outside it. Although the socioeconomic and cultural situations are very different in Cuernavaca and rural Nepal, the evidence in both cases points to empowerment and perhaps identity transformation as an effect of women's schooling.

Empowerment and identity transformation as the result of schooling are context-dependent phenomena that must be demonstrated in particular cases. This conclusion, calling for much more evidence than is currently available, flows from a literature suggesting that empowerment and related effects of schooling vary by the economic opportunity structure for women, by other social and cultural contexts of women's roles, and by the specific moment in the history of women's education in a particular community. Women's schooling can be a liberating force and be experienced as such by girls in school and thereafter; it can also have other, even opposed, meanings and consequences. It would be premature to conclude from the evidence that empowerment and identity formation simply explain the widespread effects of schooling on demographic outcomes. Yet the role of empowerment and identity formation as a pathway of influence between schooling and demographic change cannot be ignored.

Skills

Do skills acquired in school (through deliberate instruction) play any role in the process by which women's school attendance leads to change in reproductive and health behavior? We shall argue that they do, but first we review the extremely varied positions on this question in population studies and psychology.

Some social scientists (e.g., Jain & Nag, 1986; Mayer, 1999) have presumed that schools automatically and universally confer the literacy and numeracy skills they are officially intended to transmit. This presumption is embedded in the conventions of censuses and statistical yearbooks that report female literacy figures based entirely on years of school attendance. According to a standard international convention, any woman fifteen years or older who attended school for five years is presumed literate; in the censuses of India and Nepal, any female six years old or older who is currently attending school is classified as literate, just as are adult women who attended school. This equivalence of schooling and literacy is incompatible with contemporary conceptions of literacy in educational research (Lockheed & Verspoor, 1991; Wagner, Venezky, & Street, 1999), but the demographic analysts who adopt the equivalence notion apparently believe they are following a respectable precedent. Thus the equivalence position, though obsolete from the perspective of educational research, has not died out in demographic and economic analyses of women's schooling.

At the other extreme, demographic analysts who explicitly consider the social contexts of schooling and women's lives in developing countries (e.g., Caldwell, 1982, 1994; Cleland, 1990) have tended to assume that the acquisition of skills such as literacy and numeracy — or knowledge gained through health and population curricula — could not account for the impact of school on reproduction and health, for three reasons. First, the global relationships of maternal schooling to child survival and fertility do not exhibit the kinds of discontinuities across countries, communities, and levels of schooling that would be expected if they reflected the impact of school quality or particular curriculum contents. Second, school expansion has reduced school quality in many countries so much that it would be foolhardy to assume that "years of school attendance" accurately measures skill acquisition (Fuller & Heyneman, 1989). Given the fact that there are functionally illiterate high school graduates in the United States, it is easy to imagine that women who have attended primary school in rural Kenya or Bangladesh might have acquired little skill in reading, writing, or calculation. Third, in many low-income countries, few post-schooling supports exist for the literacy of married women, who are rarely exposed to printed materials after leaving school. Thus, it has seemed likely to these analysts that even if rudimentary literacy skills had been acquired in school, they would have been lost afterwards for lack of practice. Yet it is a fact that in such populations even a few years of primary schooling is associated with improved child survival. On these grounds, it seems impossibly naive to assume a literacy pathway from school attendance to demographic change in poor countries. The socialization of women in school — increasing their sense of self-worth, autonomy, and empowerment — rather than their learning is more promising as an explanation.

Neither of these contrasting positions takes account of psychological research on the cognitive consequences of schooling (Cole, 1996; Rogoff, 1981, 1989; Scribner & Cole, 1981; Serpell, 1993; Sharp, Cole, & Lave, 1979; Stevenson, 1982; Wagner, 1974). These studies, conducted in Latin America, Africa, and other parts of the world where mass schooling is recent, by psychologists and anthropologists skeptical of school effects on cognition, are relevant to the demographic debate. One of their conclusions has been that schooling does not bring about a general cognitive transformation but, rather, enhances specific abilities. As Brown and French (1979) stated, commenting on the Yucatan (Mexico) research by Cole and his research group:

> Schooling, like tailoring or carpentry, promotes certain *task-specific* skills. The particular skills engendered by school experience involve the ability to apply a specific set of strategies to the task of solving decontextualized academic problems commonly encountered in school curricula. (p. 102)

In these studies, years of school experience is associated with the tendencies to use deliberate memory strategies, name superordinate categories in free associating to nouns (e.g., *animal* in response to the noun *dog*), use formal reasoning in verbal problem-solving, and other verbal skills that the investigators related to tasks learned and rehearsed in school. Sharp, Cole, and Lave (1979) also found in their Yucatan research that

> more highly educated subjects more readily engage in intellectual activities which are not rigidly predetermined by the structure of the task and which promote efficient performance. It is not differences in the information about the stimuli per se but differences in what people do with commonly available information that is critical. (p. 77)

They argue further that what differentiates the subjects by schooling is not their familiarity with the content of the tests but familiarity with the task structure of the assessment procedures, which simulate tasks learned in school. Sharp, Cole, and Lave (1979) analyzed in detail the selective bias in school attendance in the Yucatan and concluded that it did not account for the performance differences by level of formal education. Pointing out that only a longitudinal study could demonstrate the causal influence of schooling, they nevertheless conclude that schools augment performance on those cognitive tests that most resemble school tasks. They question the relevance of learning such tasks to the real-world tasks faced by adults in the Yucatan or elsewhere, yet reluctantly concede that

> the information-processing skills which school attendance seems to foster could be useful in a variety of the tasks demanded by modern states, including clerical and management skills in bureaucratic enterprises, or the lower-level skills of record keeping in an agricultural cooperative or a well-baby clinic. These activities may well be facilitated by skills currently transmitted in schools. (p. 84)

At the end, in asking, "Do rural Yucatecans who have been to school . . . engage in better health care practices?" (p. 112), they independently raise the question that was affirmatively answered in subsequent demographic and health research.

An important point about this body of psychological evidence from the point of view of maternal behavior is that it included adults as well as children in its samples and demonstrated repeatedly that — contrary to the expectations of the demographic analysts mentioned above — skills apparently acquired in school were retained in adulthood. Wagner's (1993) longitudinal study of Moroccan school dropouts lends additional support to the retention hypothesis: When children who left school after fifth grade were followed up three years later, they were found to have lost skill on math tests, remained stable on nonverbal cognitive tasks, and *gained* in their scores on both Arabic and French literacy tasks (pp. 222–232). This suggests that literacy may be an area particularly susceptible to retention.

The study of Scribner and Cole (1981) among the Vai of Liberia helped to reconceptualize the question of how literacy relates to schooling. Comparing three groups of Vai — (a) those who acquired Arabic literacy in Quranic school, (b) those who acquired literacy in the Vai script at home from kin, and (c) those who attended Western-type schools — Scribner and Cole found that only the latter were proficient in the verbal explanation of their own problem-solving processes — a *metacognitive* skill taught in school. One could learn to read and write, up to a point, without acquiring this skill. This finding suggests that literacy in the narrow sense must be distinguished from the "literacy practices" that are often part of learning to read and write in the classrooms of Western-type schools.

Thus, cross-cultural research on the cognitive consequences of schooling has shown that school experience affects proficiency in a variety of specific verbal skills, that these skills tend to be retained into adulthood, and that literacy practices in the broad sense are involved.

Our own approach to the skill question has been empirical. We initially agreed with the skeptical demographers who saw literacy as an unlikely pathway through which schooling could influence reproductive and health behavior, but we decided it was a hypothesis worth testing. Turning to two of our colleagues at the Harvard Graduate School of Education, the late Jeanne Chall (1983) and Catherine Snow (1990), we borrowed methods of assessing reading and other school-based language skills that could be adapted for use with mothers in Mexico, Nepal, and Zambia. We learned first that literacy itself, as conceptualized by specialists, is not confined to the decoding and inscribing of text — or to any simple dichotomy that could support a distinction between literates and illiterates — but includes comprehension, discourse processes, metalinguistic awareness. These last three abilities are often referred to as "cognitive" by psychologists, but they are also communication skills that grow and develop with years of schooling. No general agreement exists as to how many skills should be included under the rubric of "literacy," but experts do agree that its definition has varied with its social functions — across historical periods, cultures, and communities with different levels of formal education (Street, 1993, 1995; Wagner et al., 1999).

When we conducted direct assessments of literacy and language skills among mothers who varied in amount of schooling in Mexico, Nepal, and Zambia, the findings from correlational and multiple regression analyses showed that the mothers of young children retained such skills and that the skills were related to their health behavior, even with other socioeconomic factors controlled for (LeVine, Dexter, et al., 1994; Dexter, LeVine, & Velasco, 1998; Joshi, 1994;

Stuebing, 1997). These surprising results led us to formulate a new theory of how women in poor countries might acquire in school and retain into adult-hood literacy and associated language skills that could influence their repro-ductive and health behavior as mothers.

In school, girls (including those in agrarian communities and especially those whose parents are not literate) acquire a set of communication skills that they would be unlikely to learn in other settings: reading (including the com-prehension of increasingly complex written texts), writing (the production of written texts), and academic language proficiency. The last refers to mastery of the discourse skills taught in school classrooms, in other words, skills in us-ing the language characteristic of written texts for purposes of comprehending and producing oral communications. This type of oral language skill has been conceptualized by Snow (1990) as "decontexualized language ability," and it has syntactic, pragmatic, and lexical features that distinguish its use from or-dinary vernacular conversation in most speech communities. In contrast with conversation, this mode of speaking assumes less shared context, involves the frequent use of abstract nouns, and explicates particulars that are taken for granted among familiar conversational partners. Cummins (1984) refers to this kind of academic communication as "context-reduced," and Wells (1999) calls it "the synoptic mode of speaking and construing experience." Valdes and Geoffrion-Vinci (1998) have argued that it constitutes an academic "register," or an institutionalized situation-specific use of language with distinctive lin-guistic features. Children are exposed to academic language in school, often for the first time if they have been raised by parents with little schooling, and their mastery of it influences their performance on school tasks involving ver-bal communication. Since academic language is used throughout the years of schooling, proficiency in it could plausibly increase with years of attendance and help explain the linear relationship between school attendance and health behavior.

We propose that the academic register, with its features of formality, imper-sonality, explicitness, and abstractness, is the official language of all bureau-cracies, including health and family-planning clinics as well as schools. Chil-dren of university-educated parents begin learning this language during their preschool years; other children who attend school begin learning it at school entry; and those who do not attend school may never learn it at all. The lon-ger the child attends school, the more practice she gets in using the academ-ic register and the more proficient in it she can be expected to be. Proficien-cy in using the academic register is advantageous in oral communication with the health bureaucracy — for example, in understanding public health mes-sages in the media and medical instructions in the clinic, and in giving a co-herent account of symptoms and their emergence to a doctor or nurse. Thus, women who have spent more time in school know *in advance* much of the lan-guage used in public health and clinical settings — not the technical vocabu-lary but the use of general terms, forms of interrogation, and forms of expla-nation. This knowledge enables the mothers to learn from professional verbal communications about health, making it more likely that they will take preventive measures, recognize emergencies, and act promptly in health crises. Furthermore, women who lack the language skills expected are more likely to suffer frustration in seeking treatment and suffer humiliation at the hands of officious medical staff, leading these women to avoid going to the hospital or clinic until disaster is imminent. In their world, academic language proficiency and other communication skills acquired in school are the passports to maternal and child health.

Academic language proficiency as mastery of the academic register is a literacy skill. Indeed, it has been referred to as "oral literacy," the borrowing of written forms into oral communication (Tannen, 1982). Empirical research on the impact of schooling on maternal behavior must be concerned with a range of literacy and language skills — including reading comprehension and functional literacy as well as mastery of the academic register — and their relations to each other.

Models of Learning and Teaching

Every child who goes to school experiences and participates in the heavily scripted instructional performances of the classroom repeatedly during each year of schooling. It is plausible to assume that something is learned, or rather overlearned, in this massively redundant environment. We propose that, regardless of curricular content and the idiosyncrasies of the teacher, children learn something about how to learn and how to teach in a context structured by unequal authority and knowledge, and that the longer they attend school, the more they internalize the instructional schema of the classroom and spontaneously use it in other expert-novice settings involving unequal authority (LeVine et al., 1991). When women who have attended school longer are in the subordinate position, they are more likely to assume the role of the pupil seeking to learn; when they have greater authority than the other, they are more likely to assume the role of the teacher seeking to instruct. Since classroom instruction is primarily verbal interaction, those with more schooling are more inclined to prefer verbal communication in their adult learning and teaching behavior.

This process of internalization can be understood in terms of Vygotsky's concept of movement from the interpsychological (or interactional and interpersonal) arena to the intrapsychological (or intrapsychic) realm (Cole, 1996; Wertsch, 1985). The child acquires an instructional schema from scripted social experience that provides a model for future authority relations in terms of the teacher-pupil relationship (D'Andrade, 1995; Strauss & Quinn, 1999). The practical consequences for a woman's relations with health experts and her own children are enormous.

In a changing society, we hypothesize, one needs information but never has enough of it, and those who have new and valuable information become authoritative experts. Nation-building, often based on a metaphor of development, almost always entails rapid social and technological change that renders most of the population novices in the face of new conditions. Health care offers an extreme case of this phenomenon, with a small corps of professionally trained experts using a mysterious technology of potential benefit to all. In this situation, mothers who have gone further in school tend to act more like pupils than those with less schooling — paying closer attention to public health messages in the mass media, following medical advice more obediently, attempting to gain access to health information they believe will help their children, and, above all, using health services more frequently so as to bring themselves into closer contact with the experts. Much evidence supports the idea that mothers with more schooling do behave this way, and even opt for measures that carry the authority and prestige of modern medicine (reducing their breast-feeding, undergoing caesarian sections) but that actually elevate health risks. School experience has taught these mothers how to be novices who learn from experts, and the mothers then apply their knowledge and skills in the novel health situations they face as childbearing women.

School also teaches women how to act like experts when they are responsible for and in a position of authority over novices, as in child care. Women who attended school longer are more likely to structure the care of infants and young children as pedagogical interaction, taking the role of the teacher in talking frequently to the preverbal child, responding contingently to the child's initiatives with speech, tutoring the child, scaffolding the child's learning (e.g., by recasting and extending the child's speech, or breaking down a task into smaller units the child can understand), and interrogating the child about lessons previously taught. Our research in Mexico converges with a wealth of evidence from U.S. studies to show that a mother's verbal responsiveness to children under two years of age is associated with her years of schooling, with other socioeconomic factors controlled for (Richman, Miller, & LeVine, 1992). Similar findings with children in the same age range come from the comparative study of Rogoff et al. (1993) in Guatemala, Turkey, India, and the United States. These studies support the notion that more schooling increases a woman's tendency to assume a teaching role with her young children. The idea that women acquire an instructional schema in school that leads them to act like pupils in relation to health experts and like teachers in caring for their children helps make sense of the survey data on utilization of health and contraceptive services and the child development data on verbal responsiveness to preschool children. It suggests a process of learning through which a girl's social experience in the classroom influences her subsequent maternal behavior.

In this section, we have outlined a theoretical model of the pathways through which aspirations, identity changes, skills, and models of learning and teaching acquired in school may influence the reproductive and health behavior of women during their childbearing years. Figure 1 summarizes the model graphically, displaying four separate routes of influence converging on maternal health behavior, including the use of maternal and child health and family-planning services (MCH/FP) and domestic sanitary and dietary practices, which are assumed to affect child mortality and fertility rates. The figure does not show the political history that has established these pathways or the institutional environment that supports their operation. It should be borne in mind,

FIGURE 1   *Hypothetical Pathways from Women's Schooling to Health Behavior*

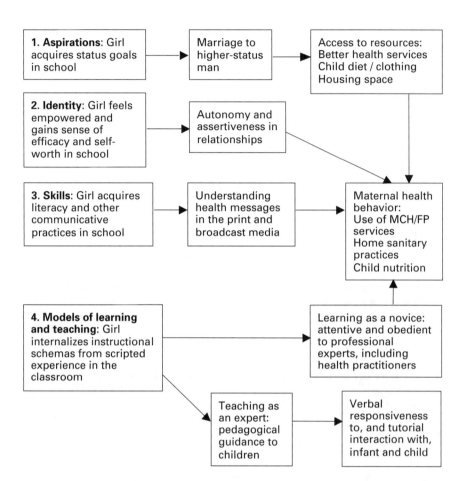

however, that the health and family-planning services and the public health system must reach some minimal level of accessibility and effectiveness for these pathways to have any influence at all.

The pathways may converge in ways not shown in the figure; for example, the first two pathways, Aspirations and Identity, may supply the motivation for use of the capacities of the second two, Skills and Models of Learning and Teaching, or the second two could provide the sense of efficacy that supports a girl's Identity and sense of empowerment. Furthermore, the pathways may operate synergistically on maternal health behavior, such that their combined effects may be greater than the sum of their separate effects. A large research program is implied here; our own research is only a beginning. In the following section we present our findings on the skill component of this model, the third pathway in Figure 1, focusing on communication skills and their relationship to health and reproductive behavior.

FIGURE 2   *Hypothetical Influences of Maternal Literacy on Health and Child Development*

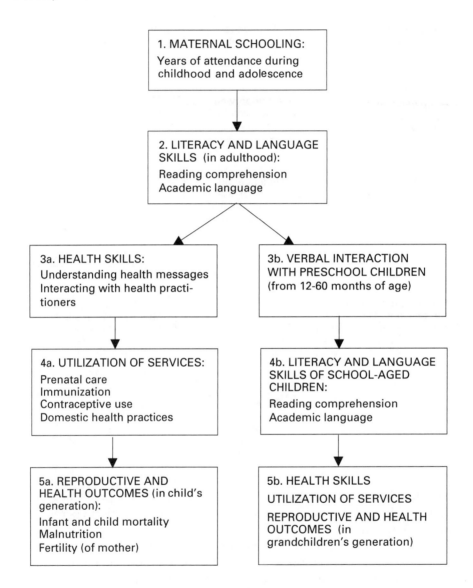

Testing the Model: Maternal Literacy and Health Care

We developed the theoretical model outlined above in the course of a program of research in diverse countries. The research began with a review of the literature twenty years ago (LeVine, 1980) that was followed by a series of community-level field studies in Mexico, Nepal, Zambia, and Venezuela conducted between 1983 and 1998. From 1990 onward we have focused on the assessment of maternal literacy and language skills as a means of answering the question of whether education and learning are actually involved in the pathways between schooling and population change. Here we shall describe what we have found so far, presenting new findings from Nepal and Venezuela. Figure 2 displays graphically the hypotheses to be tested and other hypotheses for future research. We ask the following questions:

- Do women retain school-acquired literacy and language skills into adulthood? More specifically, do a woman's years of schooling predict her adult level of reading comprehension and proficiency in academic language? (Boxes 1 and 2)
- Do women's school-acquired literacy and language skills influence their health-care skills as mothers? Specifically, do a mother's adult level of reading comprehension and her proficiency in academic language predict her ability to gain access to health information through the broadcast and print media? (Boxes 2 and 3a)

Boxes 4a and 5a show the behavioral and demographic/health factors that are influenced by health skills, according to this model, and Boxes 3b through 5b on the right-hand side of Figure 2 indicate how maternal schooling and literacy affect children's learning and transmit health skills to the next generation. These hypotheses are not tested in the present article.

Our research strategy involved multiple replications in maximally diverse samples, in which the same hypotheses were tested at the individual level in communities differing widely in culture, phase of demographic transition, and recency of mass schooling. We assumed that the most important common factors in women's school effects would be identifiable through replicated statistical relationships across diverse conditions. The first three studies, in Mexico (Dexter, 1994; Dexter et al., 1998), Nepal (Joshi, 1994, 1998), and Zambia (Stuebing, 1996, 1997), provided consistent empirical support for the predicted relationships among maternal schooling, directly assessed literacy skills (reading comprehension and academic language proficiency), and the ability to comprehend public health messages in the print and broadcast media (LeVine, Dexter, et al., 1994) — with relevant socioeconomic controls. These studies, conducted on three continents, in differing cultures and phases of educational and demographic transitions, and in different community settings — rural (Nepal), small town (Mexico), and urban (Zambia) — strongly suggested that the literacy pathway of Figure 2 was worthy of further investigation. Thus, we embarked upon more ambitious replications in Venezuela (1993–1995) and Nepal (1996–1998). All of the field investigations consisted of cross-sectional studies that lasted 18 to 36 months; it was not possible, due to budgetary constraints, to approximate the optimal longitudinal research design mentioned above. In each case, we collected ethnographic and individual data on the socioeconomic contexts of the women who were studied, while also setting our small-scale study in the context of demographic findings from the larger area in which the research community was embedded.

The Nepal and Venezuela Studies

Nepal and Venezuela provide an extreme contrast as settings for women's schooling and social change. Nepal, a predominantly rural country (15% urban) of about twenty million people that was almost completely isolated from the outside world until 1951, is a Hindu monarchy in the Himalayas, and is currently one of the poorest countries in the world. Venezuela, an urbanized (92%), resource-rich Latin American country of about twenty-two million people, is one of the major oil exporters in the world. In Nepal, only about 14 percent of adult women have ever attended school; in Venezuela, over 90 percent have. Despite its wealth, however, Venezuela has an impoverished majority whose conditions have been worsened further by recent economic and political crises. Our sample was drawn from a local population of the urban poor.

Table 1 shows how Nepal and Venezuela compare on indicators of demographic change over the past forty years. Both have changed considerably toward lower fertility and child mortality, but Venezuela began this period with a far lower under-five mortality rate — about a quarter of Nepal's — and remains at the same proportion in relation to Nepal at the end of the century. Venezuela's fertility rate was higher than Nepal's in 1960, but is lower in 1997. The populations of both countries were clearly undergoing demographic transition when we studied them during the 1990s. The transition in Venezuela began much earlier and has proceeded at a more rapid rate than that in Nepal. Evidence indicates that Nepal is now undergoing a relatively rapid decline in fertility as well as in child mortality (Thapa, Neidell, & Dahal, 1998).

The local populations we chose to sample in Nepal and Venezuela were selected for having variations in school attainment among current cohorts of childbearing women. They may not be typical of their national populations in terms of the average mortality figures of Table 1. In Nepal we worked in an area below the national average in child mortality, and in Venezuela we studied an area estimated to be higher in child mortality than the national average, for reasons indicated below.

In Nepal we selected two communities in the Kathmandu Valley for field research, Patan and Godavari. Kathmandu is the capital and principal city of Nepal, and the valley in which it is located is far more developed in socioeconomic terms and in demographic transition than the rest of the country. It is the only region that has a substantial proportion of adult women who have been to school, which is why we chose to work there. Both communities are located in Lalitpur District (1991 population: 257,000), which encompasses an urban segment, Patan, located just across the river from Kathmandu and effectively part of the city, and a rural segment of forty-one villages and small towns. In the district as a whole, approximately 31 percent of women aged fifteen to forty-nine had attended school as of 1991, but the proportion has been growing rapidly and was estimated at close to half only five years later. Like the Kathmandu Valley in general, Lalitpur District is complex in its social, cultural, religious, and linguistic composition, reflecting a history of ancient settlement and conquest.

TABLE 1   *Demographic Change in Nepal and Venezuela, 1960–1997*

	1960	1990	1997
Nepal			
Infant mortality rate	199	101	93
Under-5 mortality rate	297	138	104
Total fertility rate	5.8	5.6	4.6*
Venezuela			
Infant mortality rate	56	34	21
Under-5 mortality rate	75	27	25
Total fertility rate	6.6	3.5	3.0

Note: Infant mortality rate = number of deaths during the first 12 months per 1,000 live births. Under-5 mortality rate = number of deaths during the first 5 years per 1,000 live births. Total fertility rate = number of children born to average woman during her reproductive years (age 15–49).
Source: The State of the World's Children, 1999 (UNICEF, 1998).
* Corrected figure from the 1996 Nepal Family Health Survey.

The urban sample was drawn from a single neighborhood in central Patan, largely inhabited by Buddhist Newars whose ancestors have lived there for many centuries. Their native language is Newari, a Tibeto-Burman language, though many also speak the official national language, Nepali, a Sanskritic language. The Newars are segmented into their own ranked endogamous occupational groups, or castes. We sampled from four upper and middle castes, the only ones in this particular neighborhood of Patan that contained sufficient numbers of married women who had attended school. Even in this population, the two highest castes of Buddhists, Vajracaryas and Shakyas, had been slow to send children to school, as their sons could support themselves in traditional occupations (as household priests and goldsmiths, respectively) without gaining school credentials. Since brides were expected to have less schooling than their husbands, parents tended not to let their girls attend school for more than a few years, if at all. This situation contrasts with another high caste of Newars, the Shresthas, who, as Hindus traditionally employed by the monarchy, sought and gained advantage from Western-type education — and consequently permitted girls to attend school. During the 1970s and 1980s, when the women in our sample were children, all caste groups increasingly sent their children to school. Nevertheless, more schooling among Shrestha women, and less among those from the middle-status Maharjan caste, was still evident. In interviews, mothers reported that their length of school attendance depended on their parents' caste-based perception of whether more schooling would hurt their chances of a good marriage at that time, plus situational factors such as the need for them to take care of younger siblings, rather than their own preferences concerning, or performance in, school.

The rural sample was drawn from the village area of Godavari, where our previous study had been conducted in 1989–1990 (Joshi, 1994). Roughly eight miles south of Patan, Godavari is a fertile agricultural area set against the low-lying mountains bordering the southern edge of the Kathmandu Valley. Like the urban site, the area is inhabited by several ethnic and caste groups, but only among the high-caste Nepali-speaking Parbatiya Hindus (Brahmins and Chet-ris), who own and farm the land, did the women attend school. These small-scale farmers live in dispersed homesteads, with the houses of each patriarchal joint family adjoining its own cultivated fields. The fields are irrigated and produce three crops — wheat, rice, and mustard seed — each year, but families are no longer able to live by agriculture alone, so many of the men commute to town for employment. Meanwhile, shops and factories spread along the paved road nearby, bringing the city closer to Godavari each year.

Like the populations of northern India to whom they are related in language, religion, and other aspects of culture, the Brahmin-Chetris of Godavari practice a form of patrilocal residence at marriage in which brides of the same caste from other communities move to the homes of their husbands' fathers. Thus, the married women of Godavari did not grow up there, and many come from rural areas distant from the city, where schools are still rare or nonexistent. Only 43 percent of the rural sample mothers had attended school, and the distribution of school attendance among them reflects whether or not a school existed in their village, parental apprehensions about their marriages (as in Patan), and (also as in Patan) the need for their contribution to the family as infant caregivers. Once again, the mothers' personal preferences about and performances in school were reported to be largely irrelevant to their school attendance. Evidence is presented in S. LeVine (n.d.).

In Patan as well as in Godavari, most married women live in patrilineal extended families, with their parents-in-law, their husbands' brothers, and the brothers' wives and children. Their obligations to work and carry out rituals are specified by institutionalized norms and enforced by the older generation. Tasks are generally shared among the women of the house, but the pressures on young wives are somewhat different in rural Hindu Godavari versus urban Newar Patan. In Godavari, as mentioned above, the women come from far away, and they are expected to be dominated by their mothers-in-law, who are particularly concerned that the young women work hard in the fields and the home. If a mother-in-law makes unreasonable demands, the wife has no one to turn to but her husband. In Patan, however, wives often come from nearby families with whom they have daily contact after marriage. This social context and the smaller work burden for women in the city operate to protect Newar mothers from the kind of domination and restrictions that can affect their Parbatiya counterparts in Godavari.

Tables 2a and 2b include demographic characteristics of the urban sample in Patan and the rural sample in Godavari, respectively. As might be expected in a country where socioeconomic change is recent, the two samples are much more similar in levels of schooling and current and desired fertility than is usually manifest in urban-rural comparisons. The only notable difference is that 12.8 percent of the urban women's mothers had been to school, whereas only 3.7 percent of the rural women's mothers had.

TABLE 2a   *Demographic Characteristics of Women in Patan (Urban Nepal sample) (n = 86)*

	Mean (SD)	Range
Woman's Age	30.8 (4.9)	22–49
Woman's Schooling (years)	6.2 (5.0)	0–16
Husband's Schooling (years)	9.0 (4.5)	0–16
Children Living (number)	2.4 (1.0)	1–7
Desired Number of Children	2.3 (0.7)	1–5
Women Living in Joint Households	60.0%	
Woman's Mother Had Formal Schooling	12.8%	
Woman's Mother Could Read	18.6%	
Woman's Father Had Formal Schooling	53.5%	
Woman's Father Could Read	73.3%	

TABLE 2b   *Demographic Characteristics of Women in Godavari (rural Nepal sample) (n = 81)*

	Mean (SD)	Range
Woman's Age	28.1 (3.8)	20–38
Woman's Schooling (years)	4.1 (4.7)	0–12
Husband's Schooling (years)	9.9 (3.2)	0–16
Children Living (number)	2.7 (1.0)	1–7
Desired Number of Children	2.2 (.7)	1–5
Women Living in Joint Households	51.2%	
Woman's Mother Had Formal Schooling	3.7%	
Woman's Mother Could Read	14.6%	
Woman's Father Had Formal Schooling	53.7%	
Woman's Father Could Read	84.1%	

In Venezuela, the community studied was the *barrio* of La Silsa, a squatter settlement of some 30,000 people located on a steep hillside in Caracas, the large capital city of about 2.3 million. Like other barrios in which the poor live in the Caracas metropolitan area, La Silsa is on the outskirts of the city, though not in a remote area. Its settlement began around 1960, with the earliest residents living at the bottom of the hill and the more recent, and more impoverished, living near the top. In comparison with other such settlements, it is socially heterogeneous, with households ranging from extreme poverty to lower middle class, and a range in women's school attainment as well. A majority (52.4%) of the mothers sampled live with their children's grandparents, either paternal or maternal. Many live in female-headed households.

Table 3 indicates some demographic characteristics of the La Silsa sample mothers. They are somewhat younger on average than the Nepalese mothers but have slightly more schooling than their urban Nepalese equivalents. They have roughly the same number of children and desire more children (on average) than do the mothers in Nepal. About the same number live in joint or extended households as do in Nepal. Their own mothers had an average of four years of schooling and their fathers five, an indication that they are at least the second generation to experience mass schooling, whereas the Nepalese mothers are predominantly the first.

A large majority (82%) of the sample mothers in La Silsa had completed primary school, and while only four had never attended school, the others' schooling ranged from leaving primary school without completing to attending through secondary school and beyond. These variations in amount of schooling were due to a number of factors. In some cases, the eldest daughter was withdrawn from primary school to take care of younger children while the mother worked. Some girls became pregnant in school and had to leave. Some had grown up in villages distant enough from the nearest secondary school that they were never enrolled, and others moved with their families to the city right after primary school and never gained entrance to a secondary school. Although school attainment in this sample is moderately correlated with women's childhood socioeconomic status ($r = .39$, $p < .001$), these reasons for leaving school do not simply reflect variations in the parents' economic situation or the girl's school performance; rather, they reveal an environment in which numerous fortuitous factors can derail a girl's educational career at different points along the way.

In both Nepal and Venezuela, all sample mothers were interviewed and their literacy and language skills were assessed. The maternal interview covered the woman's socioeconomic and educational background, the schooling of her parents and siblings, the current socioeconomic conditions in which she is raising her children, her reproductive and health behavior, her knowledge of child development, and her attitudes toward her own children. The assessment of maternal literacy and language skills included reading comprehension, academic language proficiency (noun definitions), comprehension of health messages in both print and broadcast media, functional literacy, and

TABLE 3 *Demographic Characteristics of Women in La Silsa, Venezuela (urban sample) (n = 161)*

	Mean (SD)	Range
Woman's Age	26.6 (6.9)	14–46
Woman's Schooling (years)	7.4 (3.0)	0–14
Husband's Schooling (years)	7.8 (2.6)	0–14
Children Living (number)	2.4 (1.5)	1–9
Desired Number of Children	2.7 (1.3)	1–9
Percentage of Women Living in Joint Households	54	
Woman's Mother's Schooling (years)	4.1 (3.1)	0–13
Woman's Father's Schooling (years) (n = 98)*	5.1 (3.1)	0–11

*Data on father's schooling were only available for the 98 women who had not been abandoned by their fathers in early childhood.

ability to provide a health narrative in an interview situation resembling that used in clinics.[2]

We constructed separate indices of socioeconomic status (SES) for Nepal and Venezuela that were designed to be locally meaningful. The SES index for Nepal was composed of the following variables: husband's schooling and ownership of selected home appliances (radio, television, Star cable television, motorcycle, gas stove). In Venezuela, the SES index was composed of having health insurance, employment, crowding (number of people living in the home), source of water supply, and ownership of selected home appliances (video cassette recorder, automobile, refrigerator, washing machine). Husband's schooling was not included in the Venezuela index, as numerous mothers without resident husbands were in the sample.

Our first question must be whether our investigation of the intervening processes between maternal schooling and health behavior (Boxes 1 and 4a in Figure 2) is based on evidence that these two variables are actually related in these samples. In other words, do mothers who have been to school longer use health services more effectively? Evidence exists that they do: the partial correlations of mother's schooling with the key factor of earliness of her prenatal care, controlling for maternal age and SES, was .26 ($p < .001$) in the combined Nepal samples and .25 ($p < .01$) in Venezuela. In addition, regression analysis showed maternal schooling to remain a significant predictor of early prenatal care, with age and childhood SES as well as current SES controlled for, in Nepal and Venezuela. In both samples, then, mothers who have had more schooling use health services earlier in their pregnancy — an important safeguard against infant mortality (see Luther & Thapa, 1999) — controlling for access factors. It makes sense, then, to investigate the pathways that might connect schooling with health and reproductive outcomes in these samples.

Figures 3a, 3b, and 3c show how the mothers' current academic skills of reading and defining nouns for common objects (like "table" or "dog") are distributed across four levels of school attendance in the three samples. There was a clear positive relationship between schooling and scores on reading and noun definitions in both Nepal and Venezuela. The figures suggest that both reading and noun definitions may improve with a small amount of schooling and may continue to improve throughout a range that includes secondary and postsecondary school. This overall pattern corresponds to the pattern observed in many populations for the relations of maternal schooling to child mortality and fertility, providing a preliminary basis for further exploration of whether or not literacy variables are involved in demographic transition.

Table 4 presents the correlations between years of mother's schooling and a number of academic, health, and socioeconomic variables. As can be seen, when maternal schooling was treated as a continuous variable, its simple correlations with reading and noun definitions were high (over .50) and highly significant (p < .001) in the Nepal and Venezuela samples. Schooling also has significant relationships with other variables that indicate health skills and socioeconomic status. The coefficients are higher in Nepal than Venezuela, reflecting the greater variation in schooling among the Nepalese mothers (standard deviations of 5 and 4.7 years in the urban and rural samples, respectively, compared with 3 years for the Venezuelans), and also that 35 percent of the Nepalese women but hardly any of the Venezuelans had never attended school.

Maternal schooling was also correlated with Listening Comprehension (of radio health messages) and Print Comprehension (of written health messages) in all three samples, and in each one, the correlation with print was higher than that with listening. This difference suggests that print comprehension of health messages, like Reading Comprehension, may be more tightly connected with school learning, while proficiency in understanding radio messages may be more influenced by experience outside of school, though still reflecting school experience as well. The relatively low, though significant, correlation of maternal schooling with Listening Comprehension in Venezuela could reflect this phenomenon, in that La Silsa mothers inhabit a media-saturated environment compared with their counterparts in Patan and Godavari.[3]

Maternal schooling was significantly positively related to indicators of present and past socioeconomic status (SES), suggesting the possibility that the correlations of schooling with skill variables could reflect the constraints and opportunities of SES rather than learning that took place in school (see Table 4, Rows 3b, 3c, and 3d). The correlation between a woman's schooling and that of her husband was positive, though higher in urban Patan, where there was greater variation in husband's schooling (SD = 4.5 as opposed to 3.2 for rural Nepal); this degree of correspondence reflects the marital choices of kin rather than the women themselves, as most marriages are arranged by parents or

FIGURE 3   *Mean Maternal Reading Comprehension and Noun Definition Test Scores by Level of Schooling in Urban Nepal (top). Rural Nepal (middle), and Venezuela (bottom).*

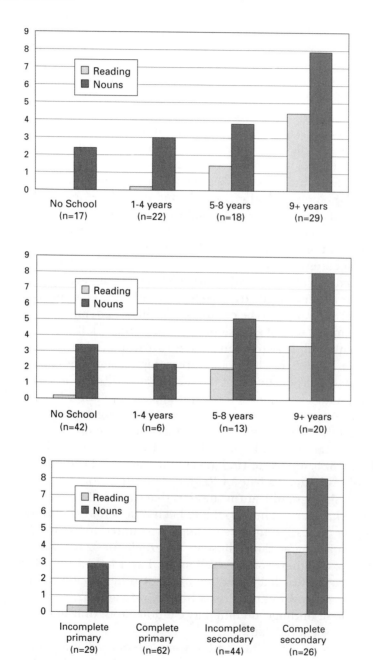

Note: Scores on the reading comprehension task were scaled from 0 to 6 in Nepal and 0 to 5 in Venezuela. Scores on the noun definition taks were scaled from 0 to 10 in both countries. See endnote 2 for a more detailed description of the tasks and scale points.

their surrogates in both Patan and rural Nepal. No corresponding correlation was estimated for the Venezuela sample, as the mothers in La Silsa were either unmarried or not living with their husbands (and typically did not know the father's level of formal education). In the Nepal samples, then, the relationship of a woman's schooling to that of her husband was strong enough to suggest that her social experience since marrying may be attributable to her husband's social position rather than the influence of her prior learning, making it necessary to control for husband's education in further analysis. Likewise, positive correlations existed between estimates of household wealth (current SES) and woman's schooling in all three samples (see Row 3c). In sum, higher levels of schooling were associated with higher levels of current advantages; these variables must be controlled for to determine if there is an education effect separate from current socioeconomic advantage.

Finally, Table 4 includes the significant correlations between women's schooling and their childhood socioeconomic advantages, indicating that women whose parents had had more formal education went further in their own schooling. This is our best quantitative estimate of the selection bias through which the amount of a woman's schooling might be influenced by being raised in an advantaged environment that may have deliberately kept her in school longer, married her to a man with more advantages, and even given her direct access to material and social advantages in adulthood. Like husband's schooling, childhood SES must also be controlled for in any attempt to determine the effects of a woman's school experience on her literacy skills.

Results from multiple regression analyses are displayed in Tables 5 and 6. As can be seen in Table 5, in all three samples, higher levels of maternal schooling continued to be associated with higher literacy skills (Noun Definitions and Reading) when all the socioeconomic variables were controlled for. The relationship of a woman's schooling to her academic language proficiency as assessed through the Noun Definitions test was not, therefore, simply due to the noneducational variables of her age, husband's schooling (in Nepal), current and childhood SES, and caste (in Patan), but may have been due to her learning in school. The same is true of Reading; in other words, maternal schooling remained highly significant in models that included all the controls, suggesting that a skill learned in school had been retained in adulthood. As Table 5 indicates, the regression models in Nepal accounted for 45 to 71 percent of the variation in academic skills, those in Venezuela for 32 to 36 percent. Thus, the question of whether women's schooling has a long-term effect on their academic literacy skills that is independent of other socioeconomic factors, as posited by the arrow linking Boxes 1 and 2 on Figure 2, receives a positive answer from these findings, qualified by caution about drawing causal conclusions from cross-sectional data.

The next question is whether and to what extent academic skills are linked with the understanding of media messages concerning child health, as the link between Boxes 2 and 3a in Figure 2 proposes. In other words, does proficiency in the literacy skills acquired in school enhance a woman's ability to under-

TABLE 4   *Simple Correlations (Pearson's r) of Mother's Schooling with Academic, Health, and Socioeconomic Variables in Nepal and Venezuela Samples*

	Nepal Urban (n = 86)	Nepal Rural (n = 81)	Venezuela (n = 161)
1. Academic Skills			
a. Reading Comprehension	.79***	.72***	.58***
b. Noun Definitions	.77***	.66***	.54***
2. Health Skills			
a. Listening Comprehension	.63***	.56***	.21**
b. Print Comprehension	.79***	.81***	.53***
3. Socioeconomic Variables			
a. Age	−.24***	.10	−.41***
b. Husband's Schooling	.68***	.41***	N.A.
c. Current SES	.68***	.60***	.31***
d. Childhood SES	.37***	.45***	.39***

*p < .05   **p < .01   ***p < .001

stand the bureaucratic language of public health messages, as we have argued above? To answer this question, we selected the comprehension of radio health messages for special attention because such messages are used in all developing countries, do not require the reading of written texts, and might indicate an effect of school literacy that transfers to oral communication. To conduct the analysis shown on Table 6, we created a Literacy Composite from the scores on Reading and Noun Definitions (which were highly correlated), merged the two Nepal samples (to augment sample size), and examined comprehension of radio health messages as predicted by maternal literacy, with socioeconomic controls included. For both Nepal and Venezuela, we compared a *First Model* predicting radio comprehension from maternal schooling alone (with the controls) with a *Final Model* in which the Literacy Composite was included in the regression equation. The results were dramatic in both samples: the effects of maternal schooling, which had been significant in the First Model, were sharply attenuated and rendered insignificant when the Literacy Composite was included, and the proportion of variation explained by the model jumped substantially (from 40% to 52% in Nepal and from 6.5% to 19% in Venezuela). These findings indicate that Maternal Schooling predicts much of the same variation in radio comprehension as Literacy, but the latter predicts additional variation in comprehension unaccounted for by schooling. This relationship would be expected if literacy and language skills were mediating the effects of schooling on health skills, as displayed in the flow chart of Figure 2.

71

TABLE 5 *Regression Models Predicting Literacy Skills (Formal Noun Definitions, Reading Level) on the Basis of Maternal Schooling Controlling for Socioeconomic Status (SES). Nepal and Venezuela Samples*

	β-Coefficient (Standard Error)					
	Academic Language (Noun Definitions)			Reading Level		
Predictors	Nepal Urban (n=86)	Nepal Rural (n=81)	Vene- zuela (n=161)	Nepal Urban (n=86)	Nepal Rural (n=81)	Vene- zuela (n=161)
Intercept	3.87* (1.20)	3.88~ (2.33)	−0.43 (1.20)	1.45 (1.24)	−1.70 (1.45)	0.34 (0.65)
Maternal Schooling	0.42*** (0.07)	0.39*** (0.07)	0.54*** (0.08)	0.23** (0.05)	0.24*** (0.05)	0.30*** (0.04)
Childhood SES	0.45 (0.36)	−0.35 (0.39)	0.14* (0.07)	0.24 (0.26)	0.18 (0.25)	0.02 (0.04)
Age	−0.03 (0.05)	−0.02 (0.07)	0.06 (0.03)	−0.05 (0.03)	0.03 (0.04)	−0.02 (0.02)
Current SES	−0.25 (0.21)	0.24 (0.24)	−0.25 (0.21)	0.25 (0.17)	0.34* (0.15)	0.09 (0.11)
Husband's Schooling	0.01 (0.07)	−0.01 (0.09)	n/a	0.08 (0.05)	0.04 (0.06)	n/a
Caste 1	−1.14 −(0.70)	n/a	n/a	−1.17* (0.50)	n/a	n/a
Caste 2	−1.80** (0.66)	n/a	n/a	−1.53** (0.48)	n/a	n/a
Caste 3	−1.42* (0.71)	n/a	n/a	−0.05 (0.03)	n/a	n/a
R^2-stat. (Error df)	.6481 (77)	.4518 (75)	.3173 (156)	.7061 (77)	.5592 (75)	.3546 (156)

Note: Background variables, despite statistical nonsignificance, are retained to show the controlled effects of maternal years of schooling on each outcome. In addition, two-way interaction effects models were fit, but no interaction effects were found.

~ p < .10; * p < .05; ** p < .01; *** p < .001

n/a = not applicable for the site

TABLE 6 *Regression Models Predicting Comprehension of Radio Messages on the Basis of Maternal Schooling and Socioeconomic Controls, with and without Literacy Skills, Nepal and Venezuela Samples*

	β-Coefficient (Standard Error)			
	Comprehension of Radio Messages			
	Nepal (n = 167)		Venezuela (n = 161)	
Predictors	First Model	Final Model	First Model	Final Model
Intercept	0.12	1.56	−0.33	0.95
	(1.03)	(0.95)	(0.74)	(0.74)
Maternal Schooling	0.25***	0.06	0.13**	−0.02
	(0.04)	(0.05)	(0.05)	(0.05)
Childhood SES	0.58*	0.42~	−0.01	−0.03
	(0.27)	(0.25)	(0.04)	(0.04)
Age	−0.07*	−0.07*	−0.01	−0.01
	(0.03)	(0.03)	(0.02)	(0.02)
Current SES	−0.32~	−0.44**	−0.19	−0.19
	(0.16)	(0.15)	(0.13)	(0.12)
Husband's Schooling	0.08~	0.05	n/a	n/a
	(0.05)	(0.05)		
Urban/Rural Dummy	−0.28	0.04	n/a	n/a
	(0.37)	(0.33)		
Literacy Composite		1.11***		0.61***
		(0.18)		(0.13)
R -stat.	.4039	.5230	.0652	.1870
(Error df)	(160)	(159)	(152)	(151)

Note: Background variables, despite statistical nonsignificance, are retained to show the controlled effects of maternal years of schooling and literacy skills on the outcome. In addition, interaction effects models were fit, but no interaction effects were found.

~ $p < .10$; * $p < .05$; ** $p < .01$; *** $p < .001$

n/a = not applicable for the site

This evidence is consistent with an affirmative answer to our second question: academic skills learned in school do predict the comprehension of health information through the radio, even after controlling for socioeconomic factors, and seem to play an intervening role in the influence of schooling on comprehension. Evidence exists, then, that the skills a woman acquires in school provide an *educational* pathway to better health care, and are not due simply to the status advantages or sense of empowerment that come from joining the ranks of the "educated."

Conclusions

In this article we used educational research to help explain how school learning by rural and urban women in developing countries might have contributed to the major changes in child survival and fertility rates that have been documented by demographic research. We began with the findings that variations in women's schooling at the individual and cross-national levels are related to birth and death rates and to the use of health and contraceptive services in much of the world during the last half of the twentieth century. We constructed a theoretical model that might explain how the expansion of mass schooling has contributed to this alteration in basic population parameters through an *educational* pathway that includes learning and is not restricted to status enhancement or personal empowerment. Our model assumes that, in the actual lives of women who have attended school, learning, status strivings, and empowerment are often combined; in theory and research we seek to disentangle them and examine their separate effects. We took as our starting point a skeptical attitude toward the idea that education, and specifically the acquisition of literacy skills, was involved in this process at all, given the poor quality of schools in low-income and developing countries and the apparent lack of opportunities for ordinary women to practice such skills. As results of our research began to show that literacy and language skills were implicated, we constructed a detailed model (Figure 2) of how a girl might acquire communication skills in school that would affect her later reproductive and health behavior in adulthood.

This model is embedded in a theory of bureaucratization, positing that schools are the institutional settings in which children learn the communication skills required for effective use of services offered by the bureaucratic organizations of a contemporary nation-state. As nationalism swept through many parts of the world during the last two centuries, and models of bureaucratic organization diffused from West to East and North to South, regardless of political ideology or traditional culture, the role of schools in reshaping public communication became equally widespread. The increased role of schools meant not only the spread of reading and writing but also the imposition of standard forms of discourse for both oral and print communication. In schools, children undergo a *communicative socialization* as they learn these new forms of discourse. Acquiring this new kind of communicative competence does not necessarily entail change in personality traits or other broad psychological dispositions, although it can be accompanied by such change. It does not necessarily make one more autonomous, although in specific contexts where women have been extremely restricted, schooling for girls may represent a break with the past and may facilitate the emergence of new forms of autonomy for girls. Finally, the acquisition of literacy and language skills in school does not necessarily signal a higher level of cognitive development or intelligence for those who attend than for those who do not, as in the "autonomous model" of literacy discussed by Street (1984); rather, it represents the learning of specific skills that are advantageous in communicating with bureaucratic organizations.

From this perspective, the organizational entailments of nation-building policies have created a social tautology for individual development in which only those who have learned the norms of bureaucratic communication in school can be effective in the new, bureaucratized world of the nation-state. Those who do not attend school find that the standards of competence have been changed so that their skills and intellectual capacities — shaped by indigenous education and once valued socially and rewarded economically — cannot lead to success unless reshaped through bureaucratic schooling. To most poor and unschooled adults, the tide of school expansion cannot be opposed; their only hope is to make sure their children go as far in school as they can.

Our theory differs from the economics of human capital (Becker, 1964), though some overlap exists. The overlap lies in the proposition that duration of schooling leads to greater proficiency in some useful skills that schools teach. But insofar as human capital models make the blanket assumption that schooling realizes the individual's general capacity to make rational choices in an environment of incentives and disincentives, our model is different. We assume, to the contrary, that schooling can foster uncritical obedience to the authority of experts so long as the experts are presented as modern, scientific, or endorsed by government officialdom. Accordingly, women with more schooling in the developing world tend to be more ready than those with less schooling to accept novel practices, such as the use of synthetic milk formula that they believe to be associated with medical authority, even when those practices actually elevate the health risks for their children. Human capital theorists might argue that it is rational *on balance* for a mother to follow medical authority uncritically, even though such obedience occasionally results in taking the wrong advice. They might also argue that rational choice depends on access to knowledge about the consequences of a behavior, and in the case of milk formula, mothers do not have the knowledge to connect the subsequent disease or death of their children to the contaminated feeding. Both of these arguments make sense but do not explain why mothers with schooling are more likely to follow medical advice in the first place. Our model posits that mothers are applying the schema of teacher and pupil they have internalized from a classroom script in which the teacher is an authoritative adult and the pupil is an ignorant child following instructions. The application of such a schema is not the exercise of individual rationality but the repetition of a formulaic prescription for behavior. We believe it is the automatic following of authoritative medical instructions that accounts for the consistency of the statistical relationship between schooling and health care, even in comparisons of unschooled mothers with those who attended school for only a few years. A woman's obedience to medical authority does not preclude her subsequent acquisition of rational strategies and critical responses to health care, but it is mass obedience that has the most powerful effects in an environment of bureaucratized services.

Another difference between our own approach and that of human capital formulations is our focus on situated learning in the school (Bransford, Brown, & Cocking, 1999; Lave & Wenger, 1991; Scribner & Cole, 1973; Sharp et al., 1979). From the situated learning perspective, human learning occurs through participation in institutionalized situations, but the participation structures of schools can, and often do, differ from those of work situations and other settings of learning for children and adults. This makes the links between school learning of literacy and language skills and their uses in later situations of adult life problematic rather than — as represented by the economic metaphor of school experience as *human resource development* — a default assumption or even an article of faith. Our concept of the links as problematic led us to the questions for empirical research: Do women retain literacy skills into their childbearing years, and do these skills influence their health behavior?

The research findings from our Nepal and Venezuela studies reported in this article suggest affirmative answers to both questions. The schooling of women in these two diverse countries appears to have left them with skills that could be used in their interactions with the bureaucratized health and family-planning services of their urban or rural environments. More specifically, the amount of maternal schooling predicted proficiency on tests of reading and academic language, controlling for current and childhood socioeconomic factors, in urban and rural sites in Nepal and in an urban site in Venezuela. A composite literacy variable predicted the comprehension of radio health messages in both countries, controlling for the same SES factors, indicating that literacy may be a pathway through which schooling improves health skills, including the ability to understand oral messages. The direct assessment of literacy skills in these studies thus provides some empirical evidence supporting the model shown in Figure 2, which specifies a literacy pathway intervening between schooling and health. The pathway is further supported by recent direct assessments of literacy skills in national samples in Morocco (Glewwe, 1999), where mothers' functional literacy predicted better child health (as measured by height for age, an inverse indicator of chronic malnutrition among children three years or younger), and in South Africa (Thomas, 1999), where mothers' reading comprehension predicted their reduced fertility (controlling for socioeconomic factors in both studies). These studies from the African continent together with our own in Asia and Latin America represent the beginnings of a new body of evidence showing literacy skills to be implicated in the processes by which schooling affects mothers' "uptake" of health and contraceptive services. The strength of this evidence is that it measures — in samples that include unschooled women as well as those with a wide range of schooling — some of the links between amount of school experience and its hypothesized population outcomes, establishing a plausible basis for causal interpretations. The evidence from these studies indicates that an educational pathway from schooling to reproductive and health change may indeed exist and that literacy may be part of that pathway.

This new evidence does not settle once and for all the issues of credibility concerning the impact of schooling and literacy on reproduction and health. Selection bias has been measured crudely and needs to be addressed through longitudinal research on particular birth cohorts of women and across cohorts in historical time. The question of whether a historical rise in women's literacy skills in a population results in more effective use of health care in the aggregate, and a consequent change in population parameters, requires a baseline assessment of female literacy skills as the beginning of a historical time series. Such an analysis could be aided by the addition of literacy assessment to the Demographic and Health Surveys and other large-scale surveys conducted repeatedly in countries that have expanding female school enrollments and are undergoing demographic change.

More research is also needed on the microsocial processes through which specific literacy skills are connected with patterns of maternal health behavior. Questions of the relations between literacy skills and motivational factors — aspirations, identity, and empowerment — also need to be studied at this level. Finally, and perhaps most importantly from the perspective of educators, the question of school quality must be addressed: if attending what we assume to be low-quality primary and secondary schools results in such long-lasting and positive effects throughout the world, does school quality make a difference to maternal reproductive and health behavior — or is the quality of schooling unimportant?

We cannot say on the basis of the evidence to date how important school quality is. If instruction were better in the schools our sample mothers attended, they might have even better skills for participating in the health-care system. We find it plausible that improved instruction would result in better health outcomes, but we cannot know this without studying variations in school quality and health behavior comparatively and over time. This topic should be high on the agenda for future research.

The findings reported in this article open the door to a new field for investigation at the boundaries of education and health care and propose directions for future research. Women's schooling as an instrument of human improvement is appealing to reformers today, as it was in Darwin's youth. Its continuing spread throughout the world, however, gives us unprecedented opportunities to deepen our understanding of the part education plays in social transformation.

Notes

1. The influential analyses by Caldwell (1979) and Cochrane (1979; Cochrane, O'Hara, & Leslie, 1980) initiated two decades of research leading to these conclusions. Their hypotheses were examined, debated, and extended using data from the World Fertility Survey (WFS) of the 1970s (Cleland & Hobcraft, 1985; Cleland & van Ginneken, 1988; Kasarda, Billy, & West, 1986; United Nations, 1987) and from the Demographic and Health Surveys (DHS) of the 1980s and 1990s (Bicego & Boerma, 1993; Cleland & Kaufman, 1998; Desai & Alva, 1998; Diamond, Newby, & Varle, 1999; Jejeebhoy, 1995; United Nations, 1995). The demographic literature covers a massive amount of evidence, including country-specific census analyses and surveys, as well as the WFS and DHS, both conducted in dozens of countries around the world.

2. In this article we present findings from the reading comprehension, noun definition, and media health message tasks; findings on functional literacy and health narratives will appear in future publications. The reading-comprehension task used health passages from texts graded by difficulty of comprehension according to level of schooling. We selected materials related to common child illnesses or accidents (diarrhea, burns) in order to keep the task as similar as possible across cultures and to provide a situational context for the readings that is potentially relevant to the contexts in which women would use their reading skills as mothers. We realize that the use of this task could be construed as biasing the data collection in favor of finding relationships between reading skill and health behavior, but we believe literacy practices to be situated in particular tasks and contexts rather than generic capacities, particularly at the lower levels of literacy we were trying to assess, and that it is more valid to have responses given in a known context than in a supposedly generic context, the meanings of which are unknown. The reading-comprehension task thus assessed ability to read and understand in a health context, a context in which we were particularly interested. The noun definitions task, on the other hand, included common objects of various content domains from the domestic and community environment, and thus tested a skill selected from the situational contexts of schools, that is, that of defining words.

   In both countries the reading-comprehension task consisted of six health-related texts corresponding to school grade levels 1, 3, 5, 7, 9, and 11. The woman's score on this task was the grade level at which she was able to answer 50 percent of the questions in Nepal, and 50 percent of the idea units (units of information determined by the investigators), aided by questions if mothers did not recall idea units on their own, in Venezuela.

   The scores were converted into a continuous scale of 0 through 5 in Venezuela and 0 through 6 for Nepal. The Venezuela scale is smaller because there mothers who could not read and those who could only decode the text for grade level one were given a score of zero. In Nepal, however, we differentiated those who were able to read at grade level one from those who could not read at all. Thus the mean scores for reading shown on Figure 3 are based on the scales for the two countries and do not represent the actual grade or class levels in school of the mothers' performance.

   The noun definition task followed Snow (1990) and our own previous field studies. Each mother was asked to define ten nouns for common things (different ones for Nepal and Venezuela), such as "knife," "thief," and "dog," with the question, "What is a ____? Their responses were scored for the presence or absence of superordinate category membership ("a dog is an animal . . .") as an indicator of decontextualized language use. Future analyses will include additional indicators, such as the explicit mention of distinctive characteristics, such as "four legs, barks, domesticated." Decontextualization in this sense refers to the ability to communicate meaning through words alone to someone who does not share the same context in background knowledge or current experience; it does not mean that any verbal communication is entirely free of context. The ability to use the less contextual, more abstract, and more explicit language taught in schools to define a noun is our measure of academic language proficiency.

3. Regarding the socioeconomic variables listed in Table 4, a mother's schooling was not related to her age in Patan but it was negatively correlated with age in Godavari and Venezuela. The significant negative correlations are usual in populations that have un-

dergone expansion of school enrollment, because they indicate simply that a greater proportion of younger women than older women have attended school and have done so for longer periods of time than older women in the same locality. Patan, with its nonsignificant coefficient of .10, is the anomaly here. In Patan, female school enrollment historically varied by caste, with upper-caste girls going to school at a time when the lower castes did not. Our sample contained unschooled younger women from the lower castes and schooled older women from the higher ones, eliminating the usual inverse relationship between age and school attendance. (By 1996, all young girls attended school, regardless of caste.) Controlling for age in a multivariate analysis, therefore, is not sufficient; for Patan, the variable indicating caste must also be included as a control.

References

Aries, P. (1962). *Centuries of childhood*. New York: Vintage.

Becker, G. (1964). *Human capital*. New York: Columbia University Press.

Bicego, C. T., & Boerma, J. T. (1993). Maternal education and child survival: A comparative study of survey data from 17 countries. *Social Science and Medicine, 36,* 207–228.

Bledsoe, C., Casterline, J. B., Johnson-Kuhn, J., & Haaga, J. G. (Eds.). (1999). *Critical perspectives on schooling and fertility in the developing world*. Washington, DC: National Academy Press.

Bransford, J., Brown, A. L., & Cocking, R. R. (1999). *How people learn: Brain, mind, experience and school*. Washington, DC: National Academy Press.

Brown, A. L., & French, L. (1979). Comment. In D. Sharp, M. Cole, & C. Lave (Eds.), Education and cognitive development: The evidence from experimental research. *Monographs of the Society for Research in Cognitive Development, 44* (1-2, Serial No. 178), 101–109.

Caldwell, J. C. (1979). Education as a factor in mortality decline: An examination of Nigerian data. *Population Studies, 33,* 395–413.

Caldwell, J. C. (1982). *Theory of fertility decline*. New York: Academic Press.

Caldwell, J. C. (1986). Routes to low mortality in poor countries. *Population and Development Review, 12,* 171–214.

Caldwell, J. C. (1994). How is greater maternal education translated into lower child mortality? *Health Transition Review, 4,* 224–229.

Cazden, C. (1988). *Classroom discourse*. Portsmouth, NH: Heinemann.

Cebu Study Team. (1991). Underlying and proximate determinants of child health: The Cebu longitudinal health and nutrition study. *American Journal of Epidemiology, 133,* 185–201.

Chall, J. C. (1983). *Stages of reading development*. New York: McGraw-Hill.

Cleland, J. (1990) Maternal education and child survival: Further evidence and explanations. In J. Caldwell, S. Findley, P. Caldwell, G. Santow, W. Cosford, J. Braid, & D. Broers-Freeman (Eds.), *What do we know about health transition? The cultural, social and behavioural determinants of health* (pp. 400–419). Canberra: Australian National University Health Transition Centre.

Cleland, J., & Hobcraft, J. (Eds.). (1985). *Reproductive change in developing countries: Insights from the World Fertility Survey*. New York: Oxford University Press.

Cleland, J., & Jejeebhoy, S. (1996). Maternal schooling and fertility: Evidence from censuses and surveys. In R. Jeffrey & A. M. Basu (Eds.), *Girls's schooling, women's autonomy and fertility change in South Asia* (pp. 72–106). New Delhi: Sage.

Cleland, J., & Kaufman, G. (1998). Education, fertility and child survival: Unraveling the links. In A. Basu & P. Aaby (Eds.), *The methods and uses of anthropological demography* (pp. 128–152). Oxford, Eng.: Clarendon Press.

Cleland, J., & van Ginneken, J. (1988). Maternal education and child survival in developing countries: The search for pathways of influence. *Social Science and Medicine, 27,* 1357–1368.

Cochrane, S. H. (1979). *Fertility and education: What do we really know?* Baltimore, MD: Johns Hopkins University Press.

Cochrane, S. H., O'Hara, D. J., & Leslie, J. (1980). *The effects of education on health* (World Bank Working Paper No. 405). Washington, DC: World Bank.

Cole, M. (1996). *Cultural psychology: A once and future discipline.* Cambridge, MA: Harvard University Press.

Cummins, J. (1984). Wanted: A theoretical frame for relating language proficiency to academic achievement among bilingual students. In C. Rivera (Ed.), *Language proficiency and academic achievement* (pp. 2–19). Clevedon, Eng.: Multilingual Matters.

D'Andrade, R. G. (1995). *The development of cognitive anthropology.* New York: Cambridge University Press.

Davis, K., & Blake, J. (1956). Social structure and fertility: An analytic framework. *Economic Development and Cultural Change, 4*(3).

Desai, S., & Alva, S. (1998). Maternal education and child health: Is there a strong causal relationship? *Demography, 35,* 71–81.

Desmond, A., & Moore, J. (1991). *Darwin: The life of a tormented evolutionist.* New York: W. W. Norton.

Dexter, E. R. (1994). *Women's schooling, language, and literacy skills, and use of formal health care services: Evidence from rural Mexico.* Unpublished qualifying paper, Harvard University.

Dexter, E., LeVine, S., & Velasco, P. (1998). Maternal schooling and health-related language and literacy skills in rural Mexico. *Comparative Education Review, 42,* 139–162.

Diamond, I., Newby, M., & Varle, S. (1999). Female education and fertility: Examining the links. In C. Bledsoe, J. B. Casterline, J. A. Johnson-Kuhn, & J. G. Haaga (Eds.), *Critical perspectives on schooling and fertility in the developing world* (pp. 23–48). Washington, DC: National Academy Press.

Elo, I. T. (1992). Utilization of maternal health-care services in Peru: The role of women's education. *Health Transition Review, 2,* 49–69.

Fuller, B., & Heyneman, S. (1989). Third World school quality: Current collapse, future potential. *Educational Researcher, 18,* 12–19.

Glewwe, P. (1999). Why does mother's schooling raise child health in developing countries? Evidence from Morocco. *Journal of Human Resources, 34,* 124–159.

Guldan, G., Zeitlin, M., Beiser, A., Super, C., Gershoff, S., & Datta, S. (1993). Maternal education and child feeding practices in rural Bangladesh. *Social Science and Medicine, 36,* 925–935.

Heath, S. B. (1986). What no bedtime story means: Narrative skills at home and school. In B. Schieffelin & E. Ochs (Eds.), *Language socialization across cultures* (pp. 97–124). New York: Cambridge University Press.

Hobsbawm, E. J., & Ranger, T. (1983). *The invention of tradition.* New York: Cambridge University Press.

Jain, A., & Nag, M. (1986). Importance of female primary education for fertility reduction in India. *Economic and Political Weekly, 21,* 1602–1608.

Jeffery, R., & Basu, A. M. (Eds.). (1996). *Girl's schooling, women's autonomy and fertility change in South Asia.* New Delhi: Sage.

Jeffery, R., & Jeffery, P. (1997). *Population, gender and politics: Demographic change in rural north India.* Cambridge, Eng.: Cambridge University Press.

Jejeebhoy, S. (1995). *Women's education, autonomy, and reproductive behaviour: Experience from developing countries.* Oxford, Eng.: Clarendon Press.

Joshi, A. (1994). Maternal schooling and child health: Preliminary analysis of the intervening mechanisms in rural Nepal. *Health Transition Review, 4,* 1–28.

Joshi, A. (1998). *Maternal schooling, maternal behavior and child health: A Nepalese case study.* Unpublished doctoral dissertation, Harvard University.

Kasarda, J. D., Billy, J., & West, K. (1986). *Status enhancement and fertility: Reproductive responses to social mobility and educational opportunity.* Orlando, FL: Academic Press.

Lave, J., & Wenger, E. (1991) *Situated learning: Legitimate peripheral participation.* New York: Cambridge University Press.

LeVine, R. A. (1978). Western schools in non-Western societies: Psychosocial impact and cultural response. *Teachers College Record, 80,* 749–755.

LeVine, R. A. (1980). Influence of women's schooling on maternal behavior in the Third World. *Comparative Education Review, 24* (Suppl.), 78–105.

LeVine, R. A., LeVine, S., Richman, A., Tapia Uribe, M. F., Sunderland Correa, C., & Miller, P. (1991). Women's schooling and child care in the demographic transition: A Mexican case study. *Population and Development Review, 17,* 459–496.

LeVine, R. A., Dexter, E., Velasco, P., LeVine, S., Joshi, A., Stuebing, K., & Tapia Uribe, M. F. (1994). Maternal literacy and health care in three countries: A preliminary report. *Health Transition Review, 4,* 186–191.

LeVine, R. A., LeVine, S., Richman, A., Tapia Uribe, M. F., & Sunderland Correa, C. (1994). Schooling and survival: The impact of maternal education on health and reproduction in the Third World. In L. Chen, A. Kleinman, & N. Ware (Eds.), *Health and social change in international perspective* (pp. 303–338). Boston: Harvard School of Public Health.

LeVine, R. A., & White, M. I. (1986). *Human conditions: The cultural basis of educational development.* London: Routledge.

LeVine, S. (n.d.). *Getting in, staying on, and dropping out: Determinants of school attendance among Nepali and Newar girls in the Kathmandu Valley of Nepal.* Unpublished manuscript.

LeVine, S. E. (1993). *Dolor y alegría: Women and social change in urban Mexico.* Madison: University of Wisconsin Press.

Lockheed, M., & Verspoor, A. (1991). *Improving primary education in developing countries.* New York: Oxford University Press.

Luther, N., & Thapa, S. (1999). *Infant and child mortality in Nepal* (East-West Center Working Paper: Population Series No. 105). Honolulu: East-West Center Press.

Mayer, P. (1999). India's falling sex ratios. *Population and Development Review, 25,* 323–343.

Mehrotra, S., & Jolly, R. (Eds.). (1997). *Development with a human face.* Oxford, Eng.: Clarendon Press.

Meyer, J. (1977). The effects of education as an institution. *American Journal of Sociology, 83,* 55–77.

Meyer, J., & Hannan, M. (1979). *National development and the world system.* Chicago: University of Chicago Press.

Meyer, J. W., Kamens, D. W., & Benavot, A. (1992). *School knowledge for the masses: World models and national primary curricular categories in the twentieth century.* London: Falmer Press.

Meyer, J. W., Ramirez, F. O., & Soysal, Y. (1992). World expansion of mass education, 1870–1980. *Sociology of Education, 65,* 128–149.

Notestein, F. W. (1945). Population: The long view. In T. W. Schultz (Ed.), *Food for the World* (pp. 36–57). Chicago: University of Chicago Press.

Peña, R., Wall, S., & Person, L. (2000). The effect of poverty, social inequality, and maternal education on infant mortality in Nicaragua, 1998–1993. *American Journal of Public Health, 90,* 64–69.

Phillips, S. U. (1983). *The invisible culture: Communication in classroom and community on the Warms Springs Indian Reservation.* New York: Longman.

Richman, A., Miller, P., & LeVine, R. A. (1992). Cultural and educational variations in maternal responsiveness. *Developmental Psychology, 28,* 614–621.

Rogoff, B. (1981). Schooling and the development of cognitive skills. In H. Triandis & A. Heron (Eds.), *Handbook of cross-cultural psychology* (vol. 4, pp. 233–294). Boston: Allyn & Bacon.

Rogoff, B. (1989). *Apprenticeship in thinking.* New York: Oxford University Press.

Rogoff, B., Mistry, J., Goncu, A., & Mosier, C. (1993). Guided participation in cultural activity by toddlers and caregivers. *Monographs of the Society for Research in Child Development, 58* (8, Serial No. 236).

Schultz, T. P. (1993). Investments in the schooling and health of women and men: Quantities and returns. *Journal of Human Resources, 28,* 694–725.

Scribner, S., & Cole, M. (1973). Cognitive consequences of formal and informal education. *Science, 182,* 553–559.

Scribner, S., & Cole, M. (1981). *The psychology of literacy.* Cambridge, MA: Harvard University Press.

Serpell, R. (1993). *The significance of schooling: Life-journeys in an African society.* New York: Cambridge University Press.

Sharp, D., Cole, M., & Lave, C. (1979). Education and cognitive development: The evidence from experimental research. *Monographs of the Society for Research in Child Development, 44* (1-2, Serial No. 178).

Smith, D., & Inkeles, A. (1974). *Becoming modern.* Cambridge, MA: Harvard University Press.

Snow, C. E. (1990). The development of definitional skill. *Journal of Child Language, 17,* 697–710.

Stevenson, H. W. (1982). Influences of schooling on cognitive development. In D. Wagner (Ed.), *Cultural perspectives on child development* (pp. 208–224). San Francisco: W. H. Freeman.

Strauss, C., & Quinn, N. (1999). *A cognitive theory of cultural meaning.* New York: Cambridge University Press.

Street, B. (1984). *Literacy in theory and practice.* New York: Cambridge University Press.

Street, B. (Ed.). (1993). *Cross-cultural approaches to literacy.* New York: Cambridge University Press.

Street, B. (1995). *Social literacies.* London: Longman.

Stuebing, K. (1996). *Educational and religious factors in maternal verbal responsiveness and child health in urban Zambia.* Unpublished doctoral dissertation, Harvard University Graduate School of Education.

Stuebing, K. (1997). Maternal schooling and comprehension of child health information in urban Zambia: Is literacy a missing link in the maternal schooling-child health relationship? *Health Transition Review, 7,* 151–172.

Tannen, D. (1982). The oral/literate continuum in discourse. In D. Tannen (Ed.), *Spoken and written language: Exploring orality and literacy* (pp. 7–35). Norwood, NJ: Ablex.

Tekce, B., Oldham, L., & Shorter, F. (1994). *A place to live: Families and child health in a Cairo neighborhood.* Cairo: American University in Cairo Press.

Thapa, S., Neidell, S. G., & Dahal, D. R. (Eds.). (1998). Fertility transition in Nepal [Special Issue]. *Contributions to Nepalese Studies, 25.*

Thomas, D. (1999). Fertility, education and resources in South Africa. In C. Bledsoe, J. B. Casterline, J. A. Johnson-Kuhn, & J. G. Haaga (Eds.), *Critical perspectives on schooling and fertility in the developing world* (pp. 138–180). Washington, DC: National Academy Press.

Thomas, D., Strauss, J., & Henriques, M. (1991). How does mother's education affect child height? *Journal of Human Resources, 26,* 183–211.

UNICEF. (1998). *The state of the world's children 1999.* New York: Author.

United Nations. (1987). *Fertility behaviour in the context of development: Evidence from the World Fertility Survey.* New York: Author, Population Division.

United Nations. (1995). *Women's education and fertility behaviour: Recent evidence from the Demographic and Health Surveys.* New York: Author, Population Division.

United Nations Population Fund. (1994). *Programme of action of the International Conference of Population and Development (ICPD) in Cairo, Egypt.* New York: Author.

Valdes, G., & Geoffrion-Vinci, M. (1998). Chicano Spanish: The problem of the "underdeveloped" code in bilingual repertoires. *Modern Language Journal, 82,* 473–501.

Wagner, D. (1974). The development of short-term and incidental memory: A cross-cultural study. *Child Development, 45,* 389–396.

Wagner, D. A. (1993). *Literacy, culture, and development: Becoming literate in Morocco.* New York: Cambridge University Press.

Wagner, D., Venezky, R., & Street, B. (Eds.). (1999). *Literacy: An international handbook.* Boulder, CO: Westview Press.

WCEFA. (1990). *World conference on education for all: Final report.* New York: UNICEF.

Weisner, T., & Gallimore, R. (1977). My brother's keeper: Child and sibling caretaking. *Current Anthropology, 18,* 169–180.

Wells, G. (1999). *Dialogic inquiry: A sociocultural practice and theory of education.* New York: Cambridge University Press.

Wertsch, J. (1985). *Vygotsky and the social formation of mind.* Cambridge, MA: Harvard University Press.

Wertsch, J., Minick, N., & Arms, F. (1984). The creation of context in joint problem-solving. In B. Rogoff & J. Lave (Eds.), *Everyday cognition: Its development in social context* (pp. 151–171). Cambridge, MA: Harvard University Press.

World Bank. (1980). *World development report 1980.* New York: Oxford University Press.

World Bank. (1993). *World development report 1993.* New York: Oxford University Press.

The Project on Maternal Schooling at the Harvard Graduate School of Education has received support from private foundations, government organizations, and international agencies. The Nepal field study and the analyses of data from Nepal and Venezuela reported in this article were funded by an award from the William T. Grant Foundation. The Venezuela field study was funded by contracts from the United States Agency for International Development (USAID) to the Academy for Educational Development and from the United Nations Population Fund (UNFPA) to World Education, Inc. Earlier support was provided by the Spencer Foundation, the National Science Foundation, the Ford Foundation, the Rockefeller Foundation, and the Population Council (under its program on The Determinants of Fertility in Developing Countries, funded by USAID).

The field study in Nepal was conducted by Sarah LeVine, with the assistance of Deepa Pokharel, Jyoti Tiwari, and Saruna Amatya. Beatrice Schnell designed and pretested the literacy instruments for both Nepal and Venezuela and codirected the Venezuela field study with Ileana Recagno-Puente, the collaboration of Cristina Otalora and Zulme Lomelli, and the research assistance of Denis Martinez, Maria Mercedes Mercado, Yuruany Moreno, and Zoraida Rodriguez. Binayak Dungana entered the Nepal data for analysis at Harvard. Beatrice Schnell and Claudia Ordonez coded the Venezuela literacy data. Alina Martínez, Meredith Rowe, and Seeta Pai conducted the data processing and analysis. Emily Dexter made valuable suggestions for the data analysis.

We are very grateful to Daniel A. Wagner for his valuable comments on the first draft of this article.

Cognitive Skill and Economic Inequality

Findings from the National Adult Literacy Survey

STEPHEN W. RAUDENBUSH

RAFA M. KASIM

In all modern societies, differences in social origins (e.g., social class, gender, and ethnic, cultural, or linguistic background) predict inequalities in adult employment and earnings. The sources of such inequality have received enormous attention in economics and sociology (see reviews by Carnoy, 1995; Ferber, 1995; Ganzeboom, Treiman, & Ultee, 1991; Kerckhoff, 1995). Research in many countries shows that social origins are related to schooling experience, which, in turn, is related to employment and earnings. Thus, unequal educational attainment is a crucial link between inequality of social origin and inequality of adult economic status. A question of fundamental and enduring interest, therefore, is whether and to what extent investments in schooling can equalize economic opportunity.

U.S. policymakers, journalists, and educators, in particular, have long claimed that improvement of educational opportunity holds the key to reducing inequality of economic opportunity (see reviews by Bowles & Gintis, 1976; Levin & Kelley, 1994), and decades of research provide some support for that argument. While it is well known that the socioeconomic status (SES) of the family at birth is statistically related to adult SES, this relationship has, in many studies, been largely "explained" by unequal access to schooling (Blau & Duncan, 1967; Duncan, Featherman, & Duncan, 1972; Sewell & Hauser, 1975). Thus, the statistical evidence suggests that two individuals of different SES at birth could nonetheless expect nearly equal access to jobs and earnings as adults if they had obtained the same level of schooling and credentials. Levin and Kelley (1994) wisely warn us not to extrapolate the longitudinal consequences of public investments in education from such research;[1] nevertheless, this finding provides encouragement to the claim that understanding social inequality in access to schooling is crucial to understanding social inequality in adult economic status.

Harvard Educational Review   Vol. 68   No. 1   Spring 1998, 33–79

Despite this link between educational opportunity and adult economic status, gender and ethnicity inequities continue to be a puzzle. Gender and ethnic gaps in economic outcomes remain large even after controlling for inequality in access to schooling (Card & Krueger, 1993; Carnoy, 1995; Rivera-Batiz, 1992). Levels of educational attainment are now similar for men and women, yet the gender gap in earnings remains large. Furthermore, although on average African Americans and Hispanic Americans attain fewer years of schooling and fewer degrees than do European Americans, large ethnic gaps in access to employment and earnings remain even after taking into account such differences in educational attainment. For example, African Americans and Hispanic Americans can expect lower pay than can European Americans who have the same gender and educational background. In fact, gender and ethnic inequality are inextricably linked, with the magnitude of these "ethnic gaps" varying by gender, and the ethnic gaps remaining considerably larger for men than for women (Carnoy, 1995).

In this article, we consider alternative explanations for this puzzle. The first contends that quantitative measures of education, such as years of schooling and degrees obtained, inadequately capture the cognitive knowledge and skills that have become decisive in the modern labor market. An extreme version of this view, popularized especially by Herrnstein and Murray (1994), claims that inherited differences in cognitive ability have created an aristocracy of intelligence, and that such differences explain ethnic differences in economic success. A more mainstream view accepts the centrality of cognitive skill in the modern labor market, but takes a more environmental viewpoint. In this view, educational policy should equalize the quality of schooling and not just the quantity. Such educational equalization would presumably eliminate gender and ethnic inequality in access to good jobs and high pay.[2]

If one accepts the proposition that cognitive skill is important to labor market success and the key to understanding current group inequality, then the role for affirmative action in the labor market is diminished or nonexistent. Few would hold employers responsible for rectifying inequality in cognitive skills. Thus, the main target for affirmative action policy would be the educational system, which is primarily responsible for producing cognitive skill.

A second explanation for gender and ethnic inequality in economic success emphasizes preferences rather than skills as the active ingredient. According to this view, people vary in their preferences for different kinds of work, and therefore select occupations that have varied job security and earnings. In particular, women are widely held to select occupations that pay less than do occupations preferred by men. These gender differences in preference are believed to constitute an important part of the gender gap in earnings (Ferber, 1995). If true, the "preference explanation" is likely to be more important for understanding gender inequality than for understanding ethnic inequality.

The emphasis on gender differences in occupational preference implies a small or nonexistent need for affirmative action in the workplace, as it is plausible to expect parents and teachers to broaden the occupational aspirations of girls. Asking employers to reshape the occupational aspirations of their female workers appears a less promising strategy for reform.

We see, then, that an emphasis on either cognitive skills or preferences as keys to understanding ethnic and gender inequality tends to erode the basis for affirmative action in the workplace. Both explanations, however, are based on assumptions that can, to some degree, be tested empirically. In this article, we examine these assumptions. To the extent that the evidence contradicts these assumptions, alternative explanations for persistent inequality must be considered, including those based on social competition, labor market discrimination, residential segregation, and noncognitive skill. These alternative explanations have quite different implications for educational and economic policy.

Assumptions Underlying the Emphasis on Cognitive Skill

Several key assumptions underlie the premise that differences in cognitive skill underlie group differences in employment and pay. First, there must be a single meritocratic labor market, one that distributes jobs and pay strictly on the basis of worker qualifications. If the labor market is not meritocratic — for example, if it distributes rewards partly on the basis of ascriptive characteristics such as gender or ethnicity — the benefit to currently disadvantaged groups of equalizing cognitive skills would be limited. Moreover, this explanation assumes that cognitive skills are of preeminent importance in the modern labor market. Finally, it assumes that disadvantaged groups, in particular ethnic minorities, suffer from deficits in such cognitive skills. In sum, according to this reasoning, the importance of cognitive skills in a meritocratic labor market, combined with inequalities in access to cognitive skills, accounts for the lion's share of inequality in economic outcomes. Critics of this view would reject one or more of these assumptions.

Is There a Single, Meritocratic Labor Market?

According to human capital theory (Becker, 1964), wage offers in a competitive market equal a worker's marginal productivity, which is determined by job-related knowledge and skill (Velloso, 1995). A prominent criticism of the human capital view denies that there is a single labor market in which all workers freely compete to sell their human capital. Rather, critics have argued, the labor market is subdivided as a function of occupations and industries into sectors or "segments" with varying pay and benefits (Doeringer & Piore, 1971); a worker's productivity and pay are determined more by the job and its technology than by the human capital of the worker (Velloso, 1995); and social groups compete to control access to scarce and favored jobs (Tomaskovic-Devey, 1993). Moreover, these critics contend that residential segregation based on race may spatially separate minority groups from the primary labor market, creating a secondary labor market consisting primarily of low-paying and insecure jobs (Kain, 1968; Massey & Denton, 1993; Wilson, 1996). In sum, it can be argued that economic inequalities, as a function of social origin, arise because disadvantaged groups are systematically denied access to the better jobs via occupational, industrial, and residential segregation. In addition, it may be argued that disadvantaged groups are denied equal access to promotions and pay raises within a given occupation (Carnoy, 1995).

Are Cognitive Skills of Preeminent Importance in the Labor Market?

Many studies have indicated that cognitive skills, as measured by scores on IQ or achievement tests, are only modestly helpful in predicting labor-force outcomes once years of education are controlled (see reviews by Bowles & Gintis, 1996; Levin & Kelley, 1994). Moreover, cognitive skills have accounted for only part of the contribution of education and credentials to employment and earnings in prior research. In their review of thirteen studies of the relationship between cognitive skills and earnings, Bowles and Gintis (1996) found that cognitive skills accounted, on average, for only about 25 percent of the contribution of education to earnings. The implication is that skills not measured by cognitive tests, such as noncognitive skills, attitudes, and habits, may be highly significant in determining the productivity of the worker, and therefore may be strongly rewarded in a labor market operating on the human capital model.[3] If so, one would not expect social inequality in cognitive skill to account for social inequality in economic outcomes, even in a meritocratic labor market.

Do Economically Disadvantaged Social Groups Lag Far Behind More Advantaged Groups in Job-Related Cognitive Skills?

Although many studies have found ethnic differences in cognitive test scores (Coleman, Hoffer, & Kilgore, 1982; Lee & Bryk, 1989), it is not clear that such differences are sufficiently large to account for large observed ethnic differences in employment and earnings, even under the assumption that such skills are of great importance to productivity. Moreover, gender differences in cognitive skill are typically found to be very small (often favoring women); thus, cognitive skill gaps cannot account for gender gaps in economic outcomes. If social inequality in cognitive skill is not sufficiently large to account for social inequality in employment and earnings, some other explanation is required.

Assumptions Underlying the Emphasis on Preferences

If cognitive skill differences cannot plausibly explain gender differences in earnings, gender differences in occupational preference may provide a more promising explanation (Ferber, 1995). Ethnic differences in occupational preference may exist as well, and these differences may help explain ethnic inequality, though that idea is not prominent in the research literature.

It is difficult to distinguish occupational segregation that arises from preference from occupational segregation that arises because of discriminatory hiring practices. In 1940, 60 percent of all Black women in the U.S. labor force worked as domestic servants, and 40 percent of the Black men worked as agricultural laborers (Allen & Farley, 1986). These facts are incomprehensible without understanding the pervasive racial and gender discrimination characterizing the economy at that time. It is far more difficult in the 1990s to disentangle preference and discrimination. It is quite clear, however, that occupational preference cannot explain gender and ethnic inequalities that lie within occupations. We can, therefore, test the limits of the occupational-preference argument by examining within-occupation inequality in employment and pay by gender and ethnicity. Indeed, if gender and ethnic inequalities are found within occupations, and if these inequalities cannot be explained by differences in cognitive skill, then neither the cognitive skill explanation nor the occupational preference explanation will be adequate for understanding inequality. Other explanations, involving either discrimination in promotions and pay within occupations or group differences in noncognitive skills, would be required.

The National Adult Literacy Survey

The National Adult Literacy Survey (NALS), conducted by the U.S. National Center for Educational Statistics to describe job-related cognitive skills of the adult population, provides a unique opportunity to evaluate key assumptions underlying beliefs that job-related cognitive skills or occupational preferences are key to understanding persistent social inequalities in economic outcomes. The survey uses a sophisticated, individually administered, multifaceted assessment of adult literacy operationalized to tap key aspects of job-related cognitive knowledge and skill. In addition, it provides detailed information on the social background, educational experience, and occupations of a large, nationally representative sample of U.S. adults in 1992.

Using this data source, we addressed the following empirical questions:

1. How important is cognitive skill, as indicated by the literacy assessment in the NALS, in reducing the risk of unemployment and predicting earnings?

Even if gender or ethnic inequality in cognitive skills are large, such inequalities will translate into social inequality in economic outcomes only if these skills are important in the labor market.

Answering this question is vital not only for understanding economic inequality, but also for evaluating arguments about the centrality of cognitive skills in improving worker productivity more generally. It is widely asserted that improving the cognitive skills of the labor force by increasing the quantity and quality of education is the key to any nation's economic future (Johnston & Packer, 1987; National Commission on Educational Excellence, 1983; Statistics Canada, 1996). Yet research reviewed by Levin and Kelley (1994) and Bowles and Gintis (1996) suggests that the link between cognitive skills and earnings is modest and accounts for only a fraction of the association between education and earnings. The NALS data create the opportunity to assess the association between cognitive skills and earnings for a large, nationally representative sample of the entire adult work force in the United States.

2. How large are the differences in cognitive skills between groups?

No matter how important cognitive skills are in the labor market, inequality in these skills as a function of ethnicity and gender must be quite large if it is to account for the large gaps in economic outcomes among these groups.

3. How important is group inequality in cognitive skills for understanding social inequality in labor-force outcomes?

The answer to this question depends on the answers to the first two questions. If cognitive skills are sufficiently important in the labor market and if group inequality in these skills is sufficiently large, then inequality in cognitive skills will statistically "explain" economic inequality between groups.

Rivera-Batiz (1992) found that ethnic inequalities in the quantitative skills of young adults were sufficiently large to account for a large portion of the gap among ethnic groups in the risk of unemployment. The residual gap in the risk of unemployment between African Americans and European Americans remained ambiguous: though the estimated gap was fairly large, it was nonsignificant, and the results remained inconclusive because the sample size was small. The current study enlarges this inquiry in three ways: a) we include the entire adult labor force; b) the NALS data include a much larger sample, enabling us to estimate gaps unexplained by cognitive skills with more precision; and c) we are able to include earnings and unemployment as outcomes.

4. To the extent that cognitive skill differences do not account for ethnic and gender differences in economic outcomes, does the remaining inequality lie between occupations, within occupations, or both?

Recall that a prominent explanation of gender inequality in pay was based on gender differences in occupational preference. Gender differences in occupational preference would indeed lead to some degree of occupational segregation by gender, with disproportionate numbers of women located in occupations with low pay. Statistically, the gender gap in pay would be a between-occupation phenomenon. Such preferences would presumably have no impact on gender differences within occupations. Hence, if large gender differences in pay exist within occupations, the data will contradict the assertion that occupational preference accounts for gender inequality. Similarly, the existence of large ethnic gaps in outcomes within occupations would undermine the importance of occupational preference as an explanation of ethnic inequality.[4]

The partitioning of inequality between and within occupations can also partially test the theory that social groups struggle to control access to favored occupations. Under that theory, group membership, not job-related skill, would, to some degree, determine occupational access. If this is true, cognitive skill differences between social groups would not be adequate to account for group differences in access to favored occupations. Social segregation in the labor market would be pronounced, and the gender and/or ethnic composition of occupations would be related to outcomes even after controlling for worker cognitive skills. If we find, however, that group differences in cognitive skills do explain group differences in access to such occupations, then it becomes harder to argue that the job market is unfair in this way.[5]

Data and Methods

Sample and Measures

The target population of this study is all U.S. adults between the ages of twenty-five and fifty-nine who were in the labor force in 1992; that is, people working full time or who wished to work full time at the time of the interview. Our analytic sample included 12,492 people and is described in Table 1 (see the Appendix, which describes in detail the construction of the analytic sample). Key variables for the analysis were of four types: social origin, human capital, occupation, and labor force outcomes.

Social origins include age, parent education, gender, and ethnicity. Indicator variables were computed for each ethnic group;[6] thus, the means in Table 1 are proportions. We see, then, that 70.1 percent of the sample were European American, 16.9 percent African American, 10.4 percent Hispanic American, and 1.6 percent Asian American. Between occupations, the proportion female, proportion African American, and proportion Hispanic as compiled for each occupation by the U.S. Bureau of Labor Statistics reflect occupational segregation by gender and ethnicity.

Human capital includes educational attainment (years of schooling), credentials obtained (a "GED" or general education diploma equivalent to a high school degree, a regular high school degree, an associates degree [or some college experience], a bachelors degree, or a masters or higher); labor-force experience (age minus 5 minus years of schooling);[7] and a composite measure of adult literacy. Literacy in NALS is conceptualized as the ability to comprehend prose, extract and use information from documents, and draw inferences from quantitative information (Kirsch, Jungeblut, Jenkins, & Kolstad, 1993; Sum, 1994). Literacy was assessed individually in the homes of the sample adults.

Literacy NALS has adopted the view that literacy is neither a dichotomy (literate/nonliterate) nor a minimum competency, but, rather, that literacy "encompasses a broad range of skills that adults use in accomplishing the many different types of literacy tasks associated with work, home, and community contexts" (Kirsch et al., 1993, p. 3). The assessment involves three subscales: prose literacy (knowledge and skills involved in understanding editorials, news stories, prose, and fiction); document literacy (knowledge and skills needed for job applications, payroll forms, transportation schedules, maps, tables, and graphs); and quantitative literacy (arithmetic operations used alone or sequentially, using numbers embedded in printed materials, etc.). Tasks within each subscale vary widely in difficulty to allow classification at five levels. For example, a level-5 task in the prose subscale requires high-level inferences from complex information; tasks in the document subscale require a search of complex displays to make text-based inferences; and level-5 tasks in the quantitative sub-scale require the respondent to disembed features of a problem from text and to determine operations needed to solve it. To achieve these assessment goals, 165 literacy tasks were constructed. Most tasks require a brief written or oral response or require respondents to explain how they would set up and solve a problem. Of course, all 165 tasks could not be administered to every respondent because the time required per assessment would be excessive. (For additional information see the Appendix, which describes how the tasks were sampled for each respondent and how we analyzed the resulting data.)

Despite the sophistication of the literacy assessments in NALS, it could not have captured all aspects of job-related cognitive skills. We consider the resulting uncertainty in the Discussion section. Henceforth we refer to our measure of cognitive skills as "literacy," as measured by NALS.

Occupation Sample respondents were classified into occupations defined by the Dictionary of Occupational Titles (three-digit codes). Sample members were found to be in one of 460 distinct occupations. The three-digit codes produced a relatively fine-grained definition of occupations; our aim was to produce occupational classes that were as internally homogeneous as possible so that outcome variation could be partitioned between and within occupations. Nevertheless, some occupational heterogeneity remained within these 460 classes, and our interpretations regarding "within-occupation" variation must be qualified by recognizing this heterogeneity. We return to this issue in the Discussion section.

Labor-force outcomes include the natural logarithm of wages per week and employment status (1 = unemployed; 0 = employed). The relatively high rate of unemployment (8.4%) in Table 1 reflects the recessionary nature of the period during which the data were collected (early 1992) and the exclusion from the sample of individuals working part time who did not wish to work full time. The mean of log wages of 6.037 corresponds to a wage of $419 per week.[8]

Analytic Approach

Analyses using continuous outcomes (literacy and log earnings) were of two types. First, we estimated each model using ordinary least squares (OLS) regression. Each of the regression coefficients quantifies the overall advantage of a unit increment in one of the predictor variables, holding constant other predictors in the model. Of great importance, for example, is the estimated benefit of literacy, that is, the advantage of a unit increment in literacy with respect to log-wages, holding constant education, labor-force experience, gender, ethnicity, and parent education. Similarly, OLS regression enabled us to estimate the mean difference in outcomes between any pair of ethnic or gender groups, holding constant literacy as well as education, labor-force experience, and parent education.

However, as noted previously, we were interested in partitioning ethnic and gender gaps into their between-occupation and within-occupation components (Burstein, 1980; Cronbach, 1976). Such partitioning is critical in testing explanations based on occupational preference and between-occupation discrimina-

TABLE 1
Description of the Sample

		n	*Mean*	*Standard Deviation*
Social Origin	Age	12492	38.970	9.152
	Parent Education (Yrs.)	12492	10.932	3.532
	Female	12492	0.482	0.500
	African American	12492	0.169	0.375
	Asian American	12492	0.016	0.126
	European American	12492	0.701	0.458
	Hispanic American	12492	0.104	0.306
	Other	12492	0.010	0.099
Human Capital	Educational Attainment (Yrs.)	12492	13.275	0.777
	GED	12492	0.874	0.332
	High School Diploma	12492	0.836	0.370
	Associates Degree	12492	0.398	0.490
	Bachelors Degree	12492	0.268	0.443
	Masters Degree	12492	0.093	0.290
	Log Labor-Force Experience	12492	2.907	0.519
	Average Literacy	12492	286.108	60.958
Occupational Segregation	Proportion Female	460	0.35	0.29
	Proporton Black	460	0.09	0.06
	Proportion Hispanic	460	0.08	0.06
Labor-Force Outcomes	Log Wages	11912	6.037	0.710
	Unemployment	12492	0.084	0.28

tion. For this purpose, we estimated a two-level hierarchical linear regression model or "HLM" (Raudenbush & Bryk, 1986). Using this approach, any difference between two groups can be separated into a component representing the contribution of between-occupation segregation on the basis of group membership and a second component attributable to gaps between groups within occupations.

Two analyses using the binary unemployment variable as an outcome were also conducted. A standard logistic regression model enabled us to estimate the relationship between literacy and the risk of unemployment, holding constant social background and education. It also enabled us to estimate ethnic and gender gaps in the risk of unemployment, holding constant other personal characteristics such as literacy and education. Once again, however, we were interested in examining the extent to which ethnic and gender inequality in the risk of unemployment lay between versus within occupations. We achieved this goal by applying a two-level hierarchical logistic regression analysis.

The sample size for the log wage analysis was 11,912. The unemployment status analysis was based on 12,492 cases. The discrepancy represents missing data on log-wages.[9] The sampling plan, measures, and analytic approach are described in detail in the Appendix.

Findings

Before turning to the key questions for the analysis as stated earlier, we first consider relationships between pairs of variables. This preliminary examination and discussion will provide the reader some sense of the data and make clear why more complex multivariate and multilevel analyses were needed to avoid misleading conclusions.

Bivariate Relationships

An inspection of the relationships between pairs of variables makes a seemingly strong prima facie case that a) literacy is important for labor force outcomes; b) social background and ethnicity are related to inequality in literacy; and c) social and ethnic economic inequalities mirror these ethnic differences in literacy. Inequality in literacy thus becomes a plausible explanation for social and ethnic economic inequality. Let us consider the evidence for each assertion.

Relationship between literacy and labor-force outcomes We see from Table 2A that literacy is moderately correlated with log wages (r = .39): individuals with higher literacy scores earn more than do individuals with lower scores. Moreover, a large "literacy gap" exists between the employed and the unemployed (Table 2B). Clearly, literacy is related to labor-force outcomes.

Social and ethnic inequality in literacy We see that SES of family of origin, as indicated by years of parent education, is quite strongly positively correlated with literacy (r = .51; Table 2A). Also, a literacy gap exists between European Americans, m = 305.7, and African Americans, m = 247.3 (Table 3). The mean difference between these two groups of 58.4 is almost one standard deviation ("sd") (note, sd = 61.0 for literacy in Table 1). An even larger gap between European Americans and Hispanic Americans of 83.5 points is about 1.4 standard deviation units. Note, however, the similarity in literacy means of men and women. Thus, we see clear evidence of literacy inequality as a function of family SES and ethnicity (but not gender).

Social and ethnic inequality in labor-force outcomes Inspection of Tables 2 and 3 reveals that social and ethnic inequality in labor-force outcomes roughly parallel social and ethnic inequality in literacy. We see that parent education is positively associated with log wages (r = .22, Table 2A), and negatively associated with the probability of unemployment (note the positive mean difference in parent education between the employed and unemployed in Table 2B). Table 3 shows large log wage differentials among ethnic groups. The mean difference between European Americans and African Americans (6.13-5.83 = .30) is more than .40 standard deviation units,[10] while the mean difference between

TABLE 2A
Bivariate Correlations

	Log Wages	*Parent Education*	*Educational Attainment*
Literacy	.39	.51	.66
Log Wages		.22	.41
Parent Education			.51

TABLE 2B
Literacy, Parent Education, and Educational Attainment by Employment Status

Total n = 12492	Unemployed			Employed		
	n	*m*	*sd*	*n*	*m*	*sd*
Literacy	1055	259.39	62.11	11437	288.57	60.26
Parent Education	1055	10.30	3.66	11437	10.99	3.51
Educational Attainment	1055	12.23	2.82	11437	13.37	2.75

European Americans and Hispanic Americans is somewhat larger. Ethnic differences in the probability of unemployment are more dramatic: note from Table 3 that the unemployment rate of African Americans is nearly double that of European Americans.

It is tempting to put these three pieces of evidence together into an interpretation of social and ethnic inequality in labor-force outcomes. According to this interpretation, literacy is critical for obtaining jobs and good pay, and large social and ethnic inequalities in access to good pay and job security are linked to similar inequalities in literacy. Although it is tempting to adopt this explanation based on the bivariate evidence, we must resist this temptation and consider why a deeper analysis is required. The required analysis is both multivariate and multilevel.

The multivariate character of the analysis is required in part because education can produce benefits in the labor market that are independent of the cognitive skills associated with higher levels of education. These benefits include noncognitive skills and credentials (Arrow, 1973; Berg, 1970; Bowles & Gintis, 1996). Note that in Table 2A education is highly correlated with log wages (r = .41), as is literacy (r = .39). Given that literacy and education are quite strongly related (r = .66), some attempt must be made to control for the noncognitive contributions of education when assessing the association between literacy and outcomes. Thus, we shall hold constant education when examining the association between literacy and outcomes. The multivariate character of the analysis is also needed because literacy and social origins are confounded; it is essential to sort out their independent effects, one controlling for the other, and, espe-

TABLE 3
Literacy, Log Wages, Unemployment, and Educational Attainment by Ethnicity and Gender

	n	Literacy[a]		Log Wages[b]		Proportion Unemployed [a]		Educational Attainment [a]		Parent Education[a]	
		m	sd	m	sd	m	sd	m	sd	m	sd
Ethnicity											
European American	8751[a] 8443[b]	305.7	46.7	6.13	.70	.069	.253	13.73	2.38	11.68	2.92
African American	2113[a] 1931[b]	247.3	52.0	5.83	.68	.137	.344	12.73	2.38	10.14	3.32
Hispanic American	1302[a] 1229[b]	222.2	79.4	5.74	.66	.094	.293	10.91	4.09	7.34	4.67
Asian American	203[a] 194[b]	267.7	66.1	6.21	.75	.094	.292	14.81	2.84	10.53	4.73
Others	123[a] 115[b]	263.5	65.7	5.78	.71	.179	.385	12.70	3.02	9.90	3.92
Gender											
Female	6027[a] 5708[b]	286.7	57.0	5.85	.68	.088	.284	13.29	2.59	10.93	3.45
Male	6465[a] 6204[b]	285.5	64.4	6.21	.79	.081	.272	13.26	2.94	10.93	3.61

[a] Statistics for literacy, proportion unemployed, educational attainment, and parent education are based on the entire sample, n = 12,492.
[b] Statistics for log wages are based on those who had worked at least one week during the prior year, n = 11,912.

cially, to assess the magnitude of ethnic and gender inequality after controlling for education and literacy.

The multilevel character of the analysis is required to test explanations for ethnic and gender inequality that are based on gender and ethnic occupational segregation. These explanations include those based on occupational preference and the very different explanation based on social group competition for control of access to favored occupations. The multilevel analysis considers participants to be nested within occupations. It separates ethnic and gender gaps into a part lying within occupations, thus comparing people who share the same occupation, and a second piece lying between occupations. The analysis appropriately adjusts all estimates for the similarities among individuals working in the same occupation. Given these advantages to multilevel modeling, we now turn to multivariate and multilevel analyses tailored to answer our key questions.

1. How important is adult literacy in predicting earnings and the risk of unemployment?

Our aim in this analysis was to estimate the association between literacy and outcomes, holding constant social origins, labor-force experience, and educational attainment. Social origins include parent education, gender, and ethnicity indicators. We found that ethnic differences varied by gender, and therefore included the gender-by-ethnicity interaction effect in the model.[11] We also found that the effect of labor-force experience varied by gender. Specifically, labor-force experience had a stronger positive effect on wages for men than for women. We therefore included the relevant interaction term.[12]

To represent the contribution of education to earnings, we created a "years-of-education" variable that took on a value equal to the number of years of schooling of each individual, with a maximum value of twelve. In addition, we included as explanatory variables indicators for degrees obtained (GED, high school, associates, bachelors, and masters or more). This representation enabled us to estimate the expected benefit of each year of education for those without degrees, as well as the value added by each degree obtained.[13]

Literacy and earnings Table 4, part A, reproduces that part of the OLS results relevant to understanding the relationship between literacy and earnings, controlling for the other predictors. (Complete results are reported in Table I in the Appendix.) We see a highly significantly positive relationship, b = .002672. Given the standard deviation of literacy at 61.0 (Table 1), we can interpret this result by saying that a one standard deviation unit difference in literacy is associated with a difference in log-wages of 61.0*.002672 = .163, equivalent to a wage gain of about 17.7 percent,[14] controlling for educational attainment, type of degree obtained, parent education, gender, ethnicity, and labor-force experience.

This contribution of literacy to earnings is a bit larger than that estimated in past studies (Bowles & Gintis, 1996; Levin & Kelley, 1994; Murnane, Willett, & Levy, 1995). Interestingly, the benefit of a one standard deviation increase in literacy is about the same as the benefit to a twelfth-grader of receiving a high school diploma (b = .168), holding constant literacy and controlling for all other variables in the model. It has generally been found difficult to devise educational programs that boost cognitive skills such as those measured in this study by a full standard deviation. We can conclude that the independent contribution of literacy to earnings is of importance but is not of exceedingly large magnitude. Notice the large benefit of achieving a bachelors degree (b = .537), equivalent to a 71 percent jump in wages as compared to having no degree, and to a 46 percent jump compared to having only a high school degree, holding constant literacy and educational attainment, as well as gender, ethnicity, parental education, and labor-force experience.

To what extent does literacy account for the contribution of education to earnings? The answer to this question can be found by comparing the estimated effect of education in the first two columns of Table 4, part A; that is, the estimates with and without literacy. We see, first, that literacy accounts for most of the effect of years of schooling for those without degrees (compare b = .0410 to b = .0140). The independent effect of years of schooling, after controlling for literacy, is, in fact, very small and only marginally significant statistically.

Literacy accounts for only a modest portion of the benefit of obtaining credentials, however. Specifically, the coefficients for a high school diploma, associates degree, bachelors degree, and masters are each reduced by 21–23 percent, just what was found by Bowles and Gintis (1996) in their review of thirteen studies. Even after controlling for literacy and for educational attainment, the benefit of obtaining degrees remains large and highly significant. We can thus conclude that most of the effect of obtaining educational credentials operates independently of cognitive skills as indexed by adult literacy in this study.

The model controlling for social origins, labor-force experience, and education accounts for 29.1 percent of the variation in log wages. Adding literacy accounts for an additional 2.3 percent of the variation, so that the model including literacy accounts for 31.4 percent of the variation (see Appendix, Table I). A parallel HLM analysis (see Appendix Table II) showed that the model including all predictors accounted for 72.6 percent of the variation between occupations, but only 10.6 percent of the variation within occupations, indicating that the explanatory variables are quite strongly related to occupational status, but are only modestly helpful in accounting for wage differences among people who share the same occupation.

Literacy and unemployment   In assessing literacy's contribution to reducing the risk of unemployment, the story closely parallels that for earnings (see the first two columns of Table 4, part B). We see first that literacy is significantly negatively related to the log-odds of unemployment (b = −.00502) controlling for all other predictors. This coefficient is nearly identical to that found by Rivera-Batiz (1992), though he used a measure of quantitative literacy as a predictor. In our models, a one standard deviation unit difference in literacy is thus associated with a difference of −.306 units in the log-odds of unemployment, and this is equivalent to a 26.4 percent reduction in the odds of being unemployed,

TABLE 4

Regression Coefficients Relating Education and Literacy to Log Wages and Employment [a]

A. Log Wages

| | Ordinary Least Squares | |
Predictor	(1)	(2)
Educational Attainment (to 12 years)	.0410***	.0140*
GED	.0705	.0398
High School Diploma	.2248***	.1685***
Associates Degree	.4588***	.3467***
Bachelors Degree	.6893***	.5370***
Masters Degree or higher	.9152***	.7337***
Literacy		.002672***

B. Unemployment

| | Logistic Regressions | |
Predictor	(1)	(2)
Educational Attainment (to 12 years)	−.025	.023
GED	−.209	−.138
High School Diploma	−.680***	−.570***
Associates Degree	−.966***	−.750***
Bachelors Degree	1.325***	−1.039***
Masters Degree or higher	−1.777***	−1.427***
Literacy		−.00502***

*	$p < .05$
**	$p < .01$
***	$p < .001$

[a] These estimates are adjusted for gender, ethnicity, parent education, log labor-force experience and interactions between gender and ethnicity, and gender and log labor-force experience.

controlling for all other predictors. While certainly non-trivial, this benefit is not nearly as great as the benefit associated with a twelfth-grader finishing high school (b = −.570), which is associated with a 43.4 percent reduction in the odds of unemployment (holding all other predictors constant, including literacy).[15] We can conclude that the independent contribution of literacy to reducing the risk of unemployment is non-trivial, but it also cannot be viewed as an exceptionally large effect, given the degree of effort required to increase literacy by a full standard deviation.

TABLE 5
Social Inequality in Literacy (Net Labor-Force Experience, Education, and Credentials)

Predictor	Coefficient	Standard Error	t
Parent Education	2.42	0.171	14.200
African American	−49.16	1.928	−25.493
Hispanic American	−42.55	2.511	−16.942
Asian American	−46.41	5.674	−8.179
Female	−0.32	1.437	−0.226
Female by African American	9.05	2.433	3.720
Female by Hispanic American	4.12	3.505	1.176
Female by Asian American	3.89	7.578	0.514

To what extent does literacy account for the contribution of education to reducing the risk of unemployment? The answer is parallel to that found with respect to earnings. The coefficients associated with each credential are reduced only by between 20 percent and 33 percent when literacy is added to the model, and remain large and significantly greater than zero. The implication is that only a fraction of the benefit of obtaining credentials can be "explained" by literacy, closely paralleling our result for log wages.

2. How large are social, ethnic, and gender inequalities in literacy?

In order to address this equation, we fit an equation whose outcome is literacy; predictors include social origins, age, years of education, and credentials. Only the results relevant to the question at hand are provided in Table 5 (see the Appendix, Table V, for complete results). We see highly significant literacy gaps (p < .001) between African American and European American males (b = −49.16), between Hispanic American and European American males (b = −42.55), and between Asian American and European American males (b = −46.41), controlling for contributions of other predictors. In light of literacy's standard deviation of 61.0, these estimates represent differences of 70 percent to 80 percent of a standard deviation. These gaps are quite large. Ethnic gaps among females are estimated to be slightly smaller: −40.1 for African Americans, −38.4 for Hispanic Americans, and −42.52 for Asian Americans.

Family SES, as indicated by parent education, is modestly related to literacy (b = 2.42, p < .001), controlling for all other predictors. Thus, a unit standard deviation difference in parental education is associated with a predicted literacy difference of 8.54 points, less than one-seventh of a standard deviation. As indicated by a regression not reported in this article, most of the bivariate relationship between parent education and literacy is predicted by the respondent's education and credentials.

Gender gaps in literacy are uniformly small. Essentially nonexistent for European Americans, gender gaps favoring females are estimated at 9.05 points for African Americans, 4.12 points for Hispanic Americans, and 3.89 for Asian Americans. None of these exceeds 15 percent of a standard deviation unit.

The model (see the Appendix, Table V) accounts for 56.6 percent of the variation in literacy. A parallel HLM analysis showed that the model accounted for 95.4 percent of the variation in literacy between occupations and 40.5 percent within occupations. Thus, the model explains nearly all the variation between the literacy means of the 460 occupations represented in these data, as well as a substantial fraction of the literacy differences within occupations.

In sum, we found large literacy gaps between ethnic minority groups and European Americans after controlling for social origins, educational attainment and credentials, and age. Thus, literacy appears to be potentially important in understanding ethnic gaps in employment and earnings. Gaps associated with family of origin and gender were small.

3. How important is literacy inequality for understanding economic inequality as a function of social origins?

We now consider the extent to which social and ethnic inequality in literacy accounts for social ethnic gaps in earnings and employment. Again, we estimated an OLS model for earnings and a logistic regression model for unemployment. In each case, two models were estimated, one without and one with a control for literacy (Tables 6 and 7). The use of two models allowed an assessment of social inequalities in outcomes before and after controlling for literacy. The "before" results look much like many previous results controlling only for education and labor-force experience (Kerckhoff, 1995; Velloso, 1995). The "after" results give some sense of the "value added" of literacy for understanding social inequality in labor-force outcomes.

Correlates of Earnings

Complete results of the regressions are presented in the Appendix; only results relevant to the current question are provided in the tables of the text.

Parent education and earnings   In the model that includes all predictors except literacy, the parent education coefficient is b = .010, a small but statistically significant effect. Controlling for literacy reduces this coefficient to b = .004, a coefficient that is no longer significant (Table 6A). Thus, the evidence suggests that literacy is successful in accounting for the parent education contribution to log wages, controlling all other predictors.

Earnings gaps between African Americans and European Americans   The magnitude of this ethnic gap depends strongly on gender. In the model that does not control for literacy, the expected gap in log wages between African American males and European American males is b = −.292 and is statistically significant (p < .001). This gap implies that the African American male can expect to earn only 74.6 percent of that earned by a European American male with the same level of parent education, labor-force experience, education, and credentials. However, controlling for adult literacy reduces the coefficient to b = −.162, still highly significant (p < .001), but now associated with a wage gap of 15 percent

TABLE 6A
Social Inequality in Log Wages Before and After Adjusting for Literacy
(Net Effects of Labor-Force Experience, Education, and Credentials)

	Ordinary Least Squares		Hierarchical Linear Models	
	Without Literacy	With Literacy	Without Literacy	With Literacy
Parent Education	.010***	.004	.007***	.004*
Female	−.417***	−.416***	−.282**	−.280***
African American	−.292***	−.162***	−.176***	−.111***
Hispanic American	−.165**	−.053*	−.079**	−.021
Asian American	−.091	.030	−.032	.035
Female by African American	.287***	.262***	.246***	.234***
Female by Hispanic American	.148***	.140***	.109***	.106***
Female by Asian American	.154	.145	.129	.121
Literacy		.002672***		.001480***

*   p < .05
**   p < .01
***   p < .001

TABLE 6B
Selected Inequalities in Log Wages Based on Table 6A

		Without Literacy	With Literacy
Ethnicity Gap	African American Males – European American Males	−.292	−.162
	Hispanic American Males – European American Males	−.165	−.053
Gender Gap (Female-Male)	European American	−.417	−.416
	African American	−.130	−.154
	Hispanic American	−.269	−.276

(that is, an African American male can expect to earn 85 percent of what is earned by a European American male having the same values on other predictor variables). Clearly, cognitive skill levels, as indicated by our adult literacy measure, are quite helpful in explaining Black-White inequality among males.

TABLE 7A

Social Inequality in Log Odds of Unemployment Before and After Adjusting for Literacy (Net Effects of Labor-Force Experience, Education, and Credentials)

	Logistic Regression		Hierarchical Logistic Regression	
	Without Literacy	*With Literacy*	*Without Literacy*	*With Literacy*
Parent Education	−.002	.010	.003	.011
Female	.097	.109	.239**	.242**
African American	.679***	.430***	.591***	.433**
Hispanic American	−.093	−.332*	−.182	−.340
Asian American	.588	.333	.535	.354
Female by African American	−.174	−.125	−.162	−.129
Female by Hispanic American	.046	.066	.084	.096
Female by Asian American	−.172	−.167	−.280	−.276
Literacy		−.005		−.004

*	p < .05
**	p < .01
***	p < .001

TABLE 7B

Point Estimates of Selected Ethnic Gaps in Log Odds of Unemployment

	Without Literacy	With Literacy
African American Males – European American Males	.679	.430
African American Females – European American Females	.505	.305
Asian American Males – European American Males	.588	.333

This explanatory power is true in part because of the significant link between literacy and earnings, but even more importantly, because of the substantial ethnic difference in literacy. Nevertheless, it is disturbing to see that a non-trivial and highly significant wage gap remains to be understood even after controlling for literacy. In the Discussion section, we consider the implications of this finding for affirmative action policy.

Among females, the gap between African Americans and European Americans in log wages is non-significant. In essence, after controlling for parental education, labor-force experience, educational attainment, and degree obtained, no observable earnings gap for females existed that could be explained by literacy.

Earnings gaps between Hispanic Americans and European Americans Again, the magnitude of the gap depends on gender. In the model that does not control for literacy, the expected gap in log wages between Hispanic American males and European American males is b = −.165, and is highly statistically significant. This gap implies that the Hispanic American male can expect to earn only 84.8 percent of the earnings of a European American male with the same level of parent education, labor-force experience, education, and credentials. Controlling for adult literacy, however, reduces the coefficient to b = −.053. Marginally significantly different from zero (p < .05), this point estimate is associated with a wage ratio of 94.8 percent. Thus, the adult literacy measure predicts most of the earnings disparity between Hispanic American and European American males.

Other ethnic gaps in earnings As in the case of African American females, no gap between Hispanic American and European American females existed once education and credentials were controlled. Gaps involving Asian Americans and European Americans were estimated to be small, but to have wide confidence intervals, given the small number of Asian Americans in the sample.

Gender gaps in earnings Among European Americans, a large gap that favors males (b = −.417, which corresponds to females earning about 65 percent of what males earn) is hardly changed when literacy is added to the model (b = −.416). This result is not surprising, given that European American females and males have nearly identical literacy means.

Among African Americans, the story is somewhat different. A small gender gap in favor of males (b = −.130) becomes larger after controlling for literacy (b = −.154), a result that is not surprising, given that African American females score modestly higher in literacy than do African American males. Thus, controlling for literacy and background characteristics, an African American female can expect to earn about 85.7 percent of what her African American male counterpart earns.

Among Hispanic Americans, gender differences parallel those among European Americans, but are smaller. Control for literacy has essentially no discernible impact on the estimated gender gap for Hispanic Americans (b = −.269 before control for literacy and b = −.276 after). This "after" coefficient translates to a female earning of 75.9 percent of her male counterpart.

Summary

The results indicate that adult literacy is an important "explainer" of SES and ethnic inequality in earnings. That is, estimated inequalities associated with SES of family origin and ethnicity, inequalities not explained by labor-force experience, education, and credentials, are either partially or fully explained by adding literacy to the model. Nevertheless, a disturbing gap between African American males and European American males remains unexplained by literacy. To be sure, literacy has helped account for a good part of this gap, but the remaining gap is non-trivial.

In contrast to ethnic and SES gaps, important gender gaps, predictably, are not explained by literacy differences, simply because gender gaps in literacy are either small (in the case of African Americans) or virtually non-existent (in the case of European Americans and Hispanic Americans).

Correlates of Unemployment

When we examined inequality in the risk of unemployment, the results showed parallels to the findings for earnings, yet some important differences also emerge.

Parent education and unemployment   Controlling for gender and ethnicity, the link between parent education and unemployment was non-significant once education and credentials were also controlled; thus, there was little or no gap to be explained by adding literacy (Table 7A).

Unemployment gaps between African Americans and European Americans   The magnitude of this gap depends on gender. In the model that does not control for literacy, the expected gap in the log odds of unemployment between African American males and European American males is b = .679. This gap implies that an African American male faces almost twice the odds of unemployment faced by a European American male with the same level of parent education, labor-force experience, education, and credentials. Controlling for adult literacy reduces the coefficient to b = .430 (relative odds of 1.54). Clearly, literacy has accounted for a sizable chunk of the gap, but the remaining gap is still large.

Our point estimates are quite similar to those of Rivera-Batiz (1992). Consider the gap between African American males and European American males:

	Not including literacy	*Including literacy*
Rivera-Batiz	.659	.307
Current Study	.679	.430

While the Rivera-Batiz estimate of the gap after controlling for literacy was associated with a wide confidence interval and did not achieve statistical significance, our estimate is based on a much larger sample and is statistically significant (p < .001). The highly significant gap between European American and African American males underscores his caution that his findings should not be taken to indicate the absence of labor-market discrimination against African American males. Our findings strongly suggest that this gap is real and not an artifact of small sample size.

Among females, the gap between African Americans and European Americans in the log odds of unemployment is b = .505 (relative odds of 1.66). Control for literacy reduces the gap to .305 (relative odds of 1.36). Again, literacy is a potent explainer of the gap, but the magnitude of the remaining gap remains non-trivial.[16]

Unemployment gaps between Hispanic Americans and European Americans   Without control for literacy, no significant gap exists for males (b = −.093) or for females (b = −.047). Controlling for literacy in this case "creates" negative gaps (b =

−.332 for males and b = −.266 for females; relative odds of .717 and .766). In essence, Hispanic Americans have significantly lower employment rates than expected, given their comparatively low levels of literacy in English.

Unemployment gaps between Asian Americans and European Americans   Asian American males and females suffer higher than expected unemployment rates, given their comparatively high levels of education. Controlling for literacy reduces these somewhat. Nevertheless, the gaps of b = .333 for males and b = .166 for females imply that, even controlling for literacy, Asian Americans suffer higher unemployment rates than do European Americans. In this sense, the profile for Asian American males parallels that for African American males. However, the sample size of Asian Americans is too small for firm statistical inference.

Gender gaps in the risk of unemployment   Among European Americans, females have modestly higher unemployment rates than do males (b = .097, relative odds of 1.10), a gap that is not changed after controlling for literacy. Among Hispanic Americans, female-male gaps closely parallel those of European Americans and are also not affected by control for literacy. There is some suggestion among Asian Americans that gender gaps in the log odds of unemployment are different from those for European Americans, but again, the sample size of Asians is not large enough to make a reliable statistical inference about this ethnicity-by-gender interaction effect.

Finally, in contrast to the European American and Asian American cases, African American women have lower log odds of unemployment than do African American men, a difference that is virtually eliminated after literacy is controlled for. That is, the gender gap in literacy, which favors females, accounts for the corresponding gender gap in the risk of unemployment.

Summary

As in the case of earnings, the results indicate that adult literacy is an important "explainer" of ethnic inequality in the log odds of unemployment, even after education and credentials are controlled. However, the gap in the log odds of unemployment between African Americans and European Americans, while partially explained by literacy gaps between these groups, remains distressingly large. Similarly, Asian Americans appear to face elevated odds of unemployment controlling for literacy and all other predictors.

Again, as in the case of earnings, literacy is less helpful in understanding gender gaps than in understanding ethnic inequality in the risk of unemployment. In addition, these gaps are quite small. The exception is the case of African Americans, where a modest-sized gender gap (with females having the lower risk of unemployment) is accounted for by literacy.

4. Do gaps unexplained by literacy lie between or within occupations?

In one view, gender (or ethnic) differences in occupational preference are key in understanding gender (or ethnic) differences in pay and employment. To test this view, we considered the magnitude of gender and ethnic gaps within and between occupations.

Our focus was on those aspects of social inequality in economic outcomes that proved resistant to explanation on the basis of worker literacy. If we found this unexplained inequality to lie primarily between occupations, the implication is that members of the disadvantaged group have a smaller probability of entering favorable occupations than do members of the advantaged group, even when they share the same educational background and cognitive skill. As mentioned earlier, this between-occupation effect could represent either occupational segregation based on discrimination or occupational segregation based on differences in occupational preference. In contrast, if we found unexplainable inequality within occupations, the implication is that socially disadvantaged persons have less access to stable employment and good pay than do their more advantaged peers, even when they share the same educational background and cognitive skill and when they work in the same occupation. It would be difficult to argue, then, that either unwanted occupational segregation or differences in occupational preference are responsible for the observed inequality.

Inequality in Earnings

We focus on two aspects of inequality that remained large even after accounting for literacy: the gap between African American and European American males; and gender gaps among European Americans and Hispanic Americans. Table 8A shows the magnitude of these gaps before and after controlling for literacy. In each case the gap is partitioned into its within-occupation and between-occupation components. Also tabulated (see Table 8C) is the magnitude of the contribution of occupational segregation on the basis of ethnicity and gender before and after controlling for literacy.

African American versus European American male earnings Without controlling for literacy, about 40 percent of the gap (.116/.292) is between occupations. That is, about 40 percent of the expected difference in log wages between African American and European American males (given the same education, labor-force experience, and parent education) is attributable to the fact that African Americans are less likely than European Americans to be employed in favorable occupations. The remainder of the difference is within occupations. However, control for literacy explains over half of the between-occupation gap but less than half of the within-occupation gap. As a result, after control for literacy, most of the gap lies within occupations. Note that the evidence is consistent with the hypothesis that lower literacy denies African Americans access to favorable occupations and therefore helps explain wage inequality on the basis of ethnicity. This is not the most important story in the data, however. More important is the within-occupation gap, which is the largest part of the gap and the least explained by inequality in literacy. This gap is explained neither by literacy differences nor by differences in occupational preference. We consider alternative explanations in the Discussion section.

Gender gaps in earnings As mentioned, literacy is inconsequential as an "explainer" of gender gaps in log wages for both European Americans and Hispanic Americans. This finding is hardly surprising, given the absence of gender gaps in literacy. More interestingly, Table 8A tells us that most of the overall gender gaps (about two-thirds) lie within occupations. Neither theories of gender-based occupational preferences nor of discriminatory occupational segregation, then, can explain most of the gender gaps in log wages. Again, some other explanation is required.

Unemployment Now we focus on three aspects of inequality in the risk of unemployment unexplainable on the basis of literacy and all other predictors: African American versus European American gaps (for males and females) and the gap between Asian American and European American males (Table 8B). Unlike the case of earnings, we see in all three cases that control for literacy virtually eliminates the between-occupation component of these gaps. Ethnic inequality in employment opportunities, controlling for the effect of all predictors, is strictly a within-occupation phenomenon. Thus, theories of ethnic- or gender-based occupational preferences and theories of discriminatory occupational segregation are irrelevant in understanding ethnic and gender inequalities in the risk of unemployment once literacy is controlled. These inequalities become strictly within-occupational phenomena. Since explanations based on literacy, occupational preference, and occupational segregation are inadequate, other explanations are required.

In sum, for both earnings and unemployment, inequalities unexplainable on the basis of our human capital indicators lie primarily within occupations. In the face of this evidence, it is hard to maintain the view that gender or ethnic differences in occupational preference account for corresponding differences in access to jobs and good pay. An alternative explanation is required, and we consider the alternatives in the next section.

Discussion

The central aim of this inquiry has been to investigate those aspects of social inequality in adult economic outcomes that cannot be explained by social inequality in educational attainment. In particular, research reviewed earlier has consistently uncovered large ethnic and gender differences in access to jobs and pay, differences that could not be attributed to ethnic and gender differences in years of schooling and educational credentials. Our results replicate these findings: after controlling for educational attainment, labor-force experience, and social background, we found sizable gaps in log wages between men and women, between African American men and European American men, and between Hispanic American and European American men. Differences in social class background as indexed by parental education weakly predicted differences in log wages, controlling for other influences.[17] We also found that African Americans were at substantially higher risk of unemployment than were European Americans, even after taking into account all other factors, including educational attainment.[18]

TABLE 8A
Decomposition of Unexplained Inequality Within and Between Occupations

		Without Literacy	With Literacy
Ethnicity Gap			
African American Males –	Between Occupations	−.116	−.051
European American Males	Within Occupations	−.176	−.111
	Total	−.292	−.162
Gender Gap (Female – Male)			
European American	Between Occupations	−.135	−.136
	Within Occupations	−.282	−.280
Total		−.417	−.416
Hispanic American	Between Occupations	−.096	−.103
	Within Occupations	−.173	−.173
	Total	−.269	−.276

TABLE 8B
Ethnic Gaps in Log Odds of Unemployment

		Without Literacy	With Literacy
African American Males –	Between Occupations	.088	−.003
European American Males	Within Occupations	.591	.433
	Total	.679	.430
African American Females –	Between Occupations	.076	.001
European American Females	Within Occupations	.429	.304
	Total	.505	.305
Asian American Males –	Between Occupations	.053	.021
European American Males	Within Occupations	.535	.354
	Total	.588	.355

Having reproduced these essential findings of past research, our main aim was to evaluate the credibility of alternative explanations for these unexplained ethnic and gender gaps. The first explanation focused on inequality in cognitive skill; the second highlighted group differences in occupational preference. If gender and ethnic differences in these skills and preferences are key,

TABLE 8C

Occupational Segregation as Predictor of Log Wages and the Log Odds of Unemployment

	Log Wages		Log Odds of Unemployment	
	Without Literacy	*With Literacy*	*Without Literacy*	*With Literacy*
Percent Female	−.284***	−.204***	−.290	−.259
Percent African American	−.869***	−.764**	−.125	−.087
Percent Hispanic American	−2.60***	−2.38***	−5.34***	4.86***

*	$p < .05$
**	$p < .01$
***	$p < .001$

employers carry comparatively little responsibility for persistent inequality in economic outcomes. Rather, if such inequalities are to be eliminated, changes will have to occur in the homes and schools that socialize young people. If these two explanations are inadequate, however, other explanations, including those based on labor-market discrimination, become more plausible.

Inequality in Cognitive Skill as an Explanation for Economic Inequality

An increasingly prominent view is that group differences in cognitive skills of great value in today's labor market are primarily responsible for group differences in economic outcomes. This view recognizes that quantitative measures of educational attainment inadequately reflect the cognitive skills increasingly required in the labor force. Possibly because of unequal educational opportunities outside of school, unequal quality of schooling, and unequal aptitude, persons having the same educational attainment will nonetheless vary in cognitive skills that presumably are linked to productivity. If these skills are of preeminent importance at work, and if the labor market is meritocratic, then differences in cognitive skill should account for differences in economic outcomes left unexplained by differences in the quantity of education obtained. We found some evidence in favor of this explanation with respect to differences in earnings and unemployment associated with social background and ethnicity. Specifically, after controlling for education and credentials (in addition to parental education, ethnicity, gender, years of education, degrees obtained, and labor-force experience), literacy was moderately related to earnings and unemployment. Moreover, literacy depended quite strongly on social background and ethnicity, even after controlling for education. As a result, social class and ethnic differences in literacy become quite potent "explainers" of social class and ethnic differences in earnings and unemployment:

- *Social background and earnings* Even after taking education into account, we found social background as indicated by parental education to be weakly but statistically significantly related to adult earnings. This "social background gap" was essentially eliminated once we controlled for literacy.

- *Hispanic ethnicity and earnings* Controlling for education and all other predictors other than literacy, Hispanic males were found to earn significantly less than European American males. This "gap" essentially disappeared after controlling for literacy.
- *African American ethnicity and earnings* African American males were found to earn substantially less than European American males, controlling for education and all other predictors other than literacy. After controlling for literacy, this gap was smaller, but remained fairly large and highly statistically significant. In contrast to the cases of social background and Hispanic ethnicity, then, literacy was only partially successful in accounting for the earnings gap between African American and European American males.
- *Gender and earnings* Inequality in literacy did not provide a plausible explanation for gender gaps in earnings. Females did not lag behind males in adult literacy, but did earn substantially less.
- *Ethnicity and unemployment* After control for education, one source of inequality remained large and highly statistically significant: the gap between African Americans and European Americans. African American males were found to suffer about twice the odds of unemployment suffered by European American males having similar age, social background, and education. After controlling for literacy, the gap was substantially smaller but remained large. The same ethnic gap among women appeared smaller, though the sample sizes were not sufficiently large to allow a powerful test of the ethnicity-by-gender interaction effect in the case of unemployment. A similarly large, unexplained gap appeared between Asian Americans and European Americans, though the small sample size of Asian Americans precluded firm statistical inferences.

In sum, we found inequality in adult literacy to provide an important part of the explanation of inequalities in earnings and unemployment as a function of social background and ethnicity. Gaps not explainable by differences in education were in every case partly or completely explained by literacy. The most important exception involved inequalities in earnings and unemployment between African Americans and European Americans. Especially among males, large inequalities remained even after controlling for adult literacy. Nor was inequality in literacy a plausible explanation for gender differences in earnings. Other explanations, then, are required to understand inequality associated with African American ethnicity and female gender.

Differences in Occupational Preference as an Explanation of Economic Inequality

Gender and ethnic differences in occupational preference offer a possible explanation for corresponding gaps in economic outcomes. Persons having similar levels of adult literacy will choose occupations that vary in job security and earnings. If such differences in preference are associated with gender and ethnicity, they will produce differences in outcomes. Our data suggest, however, that such differences in preference are not powerful explainers of gender and ethnic differences in outcomes. This conclusion is based on three findings:

- about two-thirds of the gender gap in earnings lies within rather than between occupations;
- similarly, about two-thirds of the earnings gap between African American and European American males lies within occupations; and
- essentially all of the gap between African Americans and European Americans in unemployment lies within occupations.

Occupational preference cannot account for inequality within occupations. Because most inequality in outcomes lie within occupations (controlling for education, literacy, and the other predictors), occupational preferences can at most explain only a fraction of the inequalities in outcomes found in these data.

Alternative Explanations

To the extent explanations of inequality based on cognitive skill and occupational preference fail to account for manifest inequalities in earnings and unemployment, other explanations are required.

- *Social competition and occupational segregation*   Past research and theory reviewed earlier suggest that social groups may compete for control of access to favored occupations, leading to occupational segregation on the basis of ethnicity and gender and then to inequality in pay and job security. Our data cannot distinguish between the validity of this explanation and the validity of the explanation based on group differences in occupational preference. Both would lead to sizable gender and ethnic gaps associated with occupational segregation. While our data provide some evidence of such gender and ethnic segregation effects after controlling for literacy, most of the gender and ethnic inequality in earnings and all of the inequality in unemployment were found to lie within occupations. Thus, our data put a limit on the importance of theories that emphasize occupational discrimination.

- *Labor-market discrimination within occupations*   We have seen that substantial gaps between African American and European American men and between men and women remain unexplained by education, credentials, labor-force experience, and literacy, and that these gaps lie largely within occupations. Thus, our data are consistent with the hypothesis that gender and ethnic discrimination within occupations remain salient in the U.S. economy. Our data cannot readily distinguish, however, between such an explanation and alternatives, including those based on non-cognitive skills and residential segregation on the basis of ethnicity. Stronger evidence of discrimination comes from controlled experiments (Dickens, Kane, & Schultz, 1995), in which job candidates with identical resumes are dispatched to interviews.

Implications for Educational Policy and Affirmative Action

The findings of this study support the contention that understanding ethnic inequality in cognitive skills as indicated by the adult literacy assessment in NALS is vital to understanding corresponding inequality in employment and earnings. Equalizing access to years of schooling and even to educational credentials is not sufficient. There are clearly important differences in cognitive skills among persons sharing the same educational backgrounds, and these differences are linked to prospects for employment and earnings. This finding lends urgency to the task of improving the quality of schooling and of non-school educative environments, especially for Hispanic American and African American youth.

At the same time, we view these findings as lending support to continued vigorous affirmative action in the workplace. Inequality in literacy is far from sufficient for understanding ethnic and gender inequality in the labor market. Nor can theories of gender or ethnic differences in occupational preference provide powerful explanations of economic inequality. Even if parents and schools were successful in eliminating gender and ethnic differences in cognitive skills and occupational preferences, the evidence suggests that substantial inequality in employment and earnings would persist. Neither these data nor other available data can pinpoint the source of the unexplained inequality. We therefore face the familiar problem of decisionmaking under uncertainty. One might presume that labor-market discrimination is no longer prevalent, that unexplained differences between men and women and between African Americans and European Americans reflect unmeasured job-relevant differences, including non-cognitive skills. Given that labor-market discrimination based on gender and ethnicity has been pervasive throughout our history, however, it is much more defensible to assume that group differences not explained by literacy reflect, at least in part, the continuing effects of inequality of opportunity for females and for ethnic minorities.

A similar line of reasoning involves the limitations of our data. The adult literacy measure used in this study is probably the best available measure of job-related cognitive skills to date for a nationally representative sample, yet good reason certainly exists to seek improved measurement. In addition, a better measure may be more powerful in accounting for variation in outcomes. Thus, our study may have underestimated the importance of cognitive skills, though our findings about their relative importance replicate findings in many past studies reviewed earlier. Similarly, we may have erred in estimating the magnitude of inequality within occupations based on an imperfect measure of occupations. A more fine-grained classification than is possible based on the three-digit codes of the Dictionary of Occupational Titles may reveal a larger proportion of variation between occupations than that found here, thus lending some added credence to a theory based on occupational segregation. More research is certainly warranted.

Nevertheless, policy ought to attend to the best available evidence, and that evidence suggests that disturbingly large ethnic and gender inequalities in access to jobs and pay persist even after taking into account education, credentials, and cognitive skills. In light of historical inequalities, such evidence of current inequality supports a renewed and aggressive effort to secure opportunities for minorities and women in the workplace, as well as in school.

Notes

1. Studies such as those cited above, as well as the present study, can tell us little about how changes in educational policy would affect the future distribution of occupational and economic success. It is hard to predict, for example, how the labor market would respond to large changes in the schooling and credentials of the work force. These studies do a better job at estimating the expected consequences of a person's decision to obtain education, holding constant current labor-market conditions.
2. See review by Levin and Kelly (1994).
3. Following Parsons (1959) and Dreeben (1967), Bowles and Gintis (1996) theorize that educational persistence produces non-cognitive skills and orientations valuable to employers. Employers may view highly educated workers as well-socialized for work, or, in the words of P. Meyer, as "persistent, dependable, consistent, punctual, and tactful" (Bowles, Gintis, & Meyer, 1975). If education helps workers compete in the labor market primarily by inculcating such attitudes and values, it becomes less plausible to believe that increasing the quantity and quality of education for disadvantaged groups will have a major impact on inequality, or that such an effect could be explained by cognitive skills.
4. The occupational-preference argument predicts important differences in pay between occupations that vary in gender composition. However, a finding of such between-occupation differences does not validate the preferences argument because such differences could also reflect gender discrimination in access to better paying occupations.
5. Thus, a finding that literacy "explains" ethnic and gender differences between occupations would undermine the argument that occupational discrimination is key to understanding group differences. However, to the extent literacy cannot account for such differences between occupations, the results would be considered ambiguous (see prior note).
6. For example, the variable "female" = 1 if the respondent is female and 0 if male. The mean of this variable is therefore the proportion female in the sample, which, according to Table 1, is .482, or 48.2 percent.
7. In studies of wage differences among earners, labor-force experience is conventionally inducted by time elapsed since the completion of full-time schooling, unless more detailed information is available.
8. Thus, $\exp(6.037) = 418.63$; this number is close to the median wage per week in the sample and slightly underestimates the mean wage, given the positively skewed distribution of wages per week.
9. In many studies, unemployed persons do not provide information on wages because wages are conceived as current wages, which are absent for the unemployed. However, NALS enables one to define wages as "average weekly wages during the past year." Because most of the unemployed worked at least one week during the last year, log wages was missing for only a fraction of the unemployed. This completeness in the wage data is important because the smaller the fraction of unemployed excluded from the sample because of missing wage information, the less the selection bias in estimating correlates of wages.
10. This mean difference in log wages is equivalent to a weekly wage differential of $119 per week, and indicates that African Americans, on average, earn about 74 percent of what European Americans earn. This difference is highly statistically significant.
11. These interactions are represented by including as explanatory variables the product terms female-by-African American, female-by-Hispanic American, and female-by-Asian American.

12. Labor-force experience was found to have a slightly curvilinear relationship with the outcomes; a logarithmic transformation of this predictor proved helpful in simplifying this relationship. We also included as an explanatory variable a product term female-by-log-labor-force experience. All comparisons involving gender and ethnicity were evaluated at the sample mean value of log-labor-force experience.
13. Under this representation, a quadratic representation of years of education, which is sometimes used in log wage equations, was not needed.
14. With log wages as the outcome, the percent difference in wages associated with a one unit difference in the predictor of interest is exp{b}, where b is the coefficient in the log wages equation and "exp" is the exponential function.
15. The difference in the odds ratio associated with a unit difference in a predictor is exp{b}, where b is the coefficient in the equation predicting the log odds of unemployment.
16. Our sample is not large enough to allow a powerful test of the difference between males and females in the magnitude of this gap between African Americans and European Americans.
17. These differences are found in Tables 6 and 7 in the OLS model "without literacy."
18. See Table 7A "Logistic Regression" results "without literacy."

References

Allen, W., & Farley, R. (1986). The shifting social and economic tides of Black America, 1950–1980. *Annual Review of Sociology, 12,* 277–306.

Arrow, K. (1973). Higher education as a filter. *Journal of Public Economics, 2,* 193–216.

Becker, G. (1964). *Human capital.* New York: Columbia University Press.

Berg, I. (1970). *Education and jobs: The great training robbery.* New York: Praeger.

Blau, P., & Duncan, O. (1967). *The American occupational structure.* New York: John Wiley.

Bowles, S., & Gintis, H. (1976). *Schooling in capitalist America.* New York: Basic Books.

Bowles, S., & Gintis, H. (1996). *Productive skills, labor discipline, and the returns to schooling.* Unpublished manuscript.

Bowles, S., Gintis, H., & Meyer, P. (1975). The long shadow of work: Explaining the economic return to education. *Insurgent Sociologist* (Summer).

Burstein, L. (1980). *The analysis of multi-level data in educational research and evaluation. Review of Research in Education, 8,* 158–233.

Card, D., & Krueger, A. (1993). Trends in relative Black-White earnings revisited. *American Economical Review, 83*(2), 85–91.

Carnoy, M. (1995). Race earnings differentials. In M. Carnoy (Ed.), *International encyclopedia of economics of education* (2nd ed., pp. 235–242). New York: Elsevier Science.

Coleman, J., Hoffer, T., & Kilgore, S. (1982). *High school achievement: Public, Catholic and other schools compared.* New York: Basic Books.

Cronbach, L. (1976). *Research on classrooms and schools: Formulation of questions, design and analysis* (Occasional paper of the Stanford Evaluation Consortium). Palo Alto, CA: Stanford University.

Dickens, W., Kane, T., & Schultz, C. (1995). Does 'The Bell Curve' ring true? Brookings Review, 12(3), 18–23.

Doeringer. P., & Piore, M. (1971). *Internal labor markets and manpower analysis.* Lexington, MA: D. C. Heath.

Dreeben, R. (1967). *On what is learned in school.* Reading, MA: Addison-Wesley.

Duncan, O., Featherman, D., & Duncan, B. (1972). *Socioeconomic background and achievement.* New York: Seminar Press.

Ferber, M. (1995). Gender differences in earnings. In M. Carnoy (Ed.), *International encyclopedia of economics of education* (2nd ed., pp. 242–247). New York: Elsevier Science.

Ganzeboom, H., Treiman, D., & Ultee, W. (1991). Comparative intergenerational stratification research: Compensation, reinforcement, or neutrality? *Annual Review of Sociology, 17,* 277–302.

Herrnstein, R. J., & Murray, C. (1994). *The bell curve: Intelligence and class structure in American life.* New York: Free Press.

Johnston, W. B., & Packer, A. (1987). *Workforce 2000: Work and workers for the 21st century.* Indianapolis, IN: Hudson Institute.

Kain, J. F. (1968). Housing segregation, Negro employment, and metropolitan decentralization. *Quarterly Journal of Economics, 82,* 175–197.

Kerckhoff, A. (1995). Institutional arrangements and stratification processes in industrial societies. *Annual Review of Sociology, 21,* 175–197.

Kirsch, I., Jungeblut, A., Jenkins, L., & Kolstad, S. (1993). *Adult literacy in America: A first look at the results of the National Adult Literacy Survey.* Washington, DC: U.S. Department of Education, National Center for Education Statistics.

Lee, V. E., & Bryk, A. S. (1989). A multilevel model of the social distribution of educational achievement. *Sociology of Education, 62,* 172–192.

Levin, H. M., & Kelly, C. (1994). Can education do it alone? *Economics of Education Review, 13*(2), 97–108.

Massey, D., & Denton, N. (1993). *American apartheid: Segregation and the making of the underclass.* Cambridge, MA: Harvard University Press.

Murnane, R. J., Willett, J. B., & Levy, F. (1995). The growing importance of cognitive skill in wage determination. *Review of Economics and Statistics, 77,* 251–266.

National Commission on Educational Excellence. (1983). *A nation at risk.* Washington, DC: U.S. Government Printing Office.

Parsons, T. (1959). The school class as a social system. *Harvard Educational Review, 29,* 297–318.

Raudenbush, S., & Bryk, A. (1986). A hierarchical model for studying school effects. *Sociology of Education, 59,* 1–17.

Rivera-Batiz, F. L. (1992). Quantitative literacy and the likelihood of employment among young adults in the United States. *Journal of Human Resources, 27,* 313–328.

Sewell, W. H., & Hauser, R. M. (1975). *Education, occupations, and earnings: Achievement in the early career.* New York: Academic Press.

Sum, A. (1994). *Literacy in the labor force: A report on the results of the National Adult Literacy Survey.* Washington, DC: U.S. Department of Education, National Center for Education Statistics.

Statistics Canada. (1996). *Reading the future: A portrait of literacy in Canada.* Ottawa: Human Resources Development Canada.

Tomaskovic-Devey, D. (1993). The gender and race composition of jobs and the male/female, White/Black pay gaps. *Social Forces, 72*(1), 45–76.

Velloso, J. (1995). Income distribution and education. In M. Carnoy (Ed.), *International encyclopedia of economics of education* (2nd ed., pp. 230–234). New York: Elsevier Science.

Wilson, W. J. (1996). *When work disappears: The world of the new urban poor.* New York: Knopf.

We wish to express thanks to Marilyn Binkley, Douglas Giddings, Alan Kerckhoff, Henry Levin, Scott Murray, Lars Osberg, Craig Riddel, and Trevor Williams for their helpful comments on an earlier draft. Suwanna Eamsukkawat, Yasuo Miyazaki, and Marjorie Wallace contributed significantly to the analysis of the data. Research reported here was funded by Statistics Canada and the U.S. National Center for Education Statistics (NCES) under a contract to Michigan State University. The views expressed herein do not represent the positions or policies of Statistics Canada or NCES.

Appendix

Sample

The NALS sample of 24,944 U.S. adults is composed of two sub-samples: a national sample of 13,600, supplemented by samples of approximately 1,000 each from eleven states electing to enhance their samples to facilitate state-level generalizations.[1] The design of the national sample and each of the eleven supplemental state samples involved four stages. At stage 1, primary sampling units (PSU's) were stratified on the basis of region, metropolitan status, percent Black, percent Hispanic, and, where possible, per capita income. Eight to twelve PSU's per state were selected, with probability proportional to population size as measured by the 1990 decennial census. Within each PSU, segments (census blocks or block groups) were selected with probability proportional to size, except that segments with large Black and Hispanic populations were over-sampled to insure adequate sub-sample sizes of these sub-groups for precise statistical estimation. Within each segment, all dwelling units were listed and households were sampled with equal probability. Finally, within each household, one or two adults (depending on household size) were selected at random from all eligible adults age sixteen to sixty-four in the household. Sample design weights were constructed so that data from the entire sample of 24,944 could produce unbiased national estimates.

Data for the analyses described herein were based on all adults between twenty-five and fifty-nine who were in the labor force; that is, persons working full time or who wished to work full time at the time of the interview. This age range was chosen to insure that only very small fractions of the analytic sample were persons who were primarily in school or retired.[2]

The survey questions that determine work-force participation include: Does the subject 1) work full time or 2) have two or more part-time jobs? Is the subject 3) unemployed or laid off and looking for work? Does the subject 4) have a job but is not currently working due to illness or 5) have a job but is out on leave? Is the subject 6) working part time but not keeping house, in school, volunteering, or other? It is not possible using NALS to determine with certainty whether a part-time worker wishes to work full time. We have kept in our sample those part-time people who are not doing volunteer work, keeping house, or caring for children during the work day. Nevertheless, some of the remaining part-timers may not wish to work full time. Key analyses regarding income were computed with and without this part-time group to assess the sensitivity of our findings to these ambiguities.

The sample selected for study included 12,492 persons.

Assessment of Literacy

NALS has adopted the view that literacy is neither a dichotomous variable (literate/not literate) nor a minimum competency, but, rather, that literacy "encompasses a broad range of skills that adults use in accomplishing the many different types of literacy tasks associated with work, home, and community contexts."[3] The assessment involves three sub-scales: prose literacy (knowledge and skills involved in understanding editorials, news stories, poems, and fiction), document literacy (knowledge and skills needed for job applications, payroll forms, transportation schedules, maps, tables, and graphs), and quantitative literacy (arithmetic operations used alone and sequentially, using numbers embedded in printed materials, balancing a checkbook, completing an order form, determining the amount of interest from a loan advertisement). Items in each sub-scale vary widely in difficulty as scaled using item response models, so that few examinees "hit the ceiling" of the scale. Indeed, the assessment was designed to allow classification at five levels, including a level 5 that requires "high-level inferences from complex information" (prose sub-scale), "a search of complex displays involving multiple distractors to make text-based inferences and to use specialized knowledge" (document sub-scale), and performance of "multiple operations sequentially . . . that require the examinee to disembed features of the problem from text and to rely on background knowledge to determine the quantities or operations needed" (quantitative literacy). To achieve these assessment goals, 165 tasks were administered, with an emphasis on tasks that require brief written and/or oral responses and those that require respondents to explain how they would set up and solve a problem.

Of course, it would be impossible to administer all 165 tasks during the 45-minute assessment time available per respondent. The assessment was therefore organized so that every respondent encountered a representative sub-sample of the 165. This approach ensured that precise information on the entire 165 tasks would be available for each of the participating states, all of the key sub-groups, and the nation as a whole. To generate comparable proficiency results for each respondent on each sub-scale, five "plausible values" per sub-scale per person were computed. The plausible values are drawn randomly from the conditional distribution of the person's true score on the sub-scale, given that person's actual item responses and given all other measured characteristics of the person. The existence of five plausible values, while complicating the analysis (see below), insures unbiased estimation of relationships between literacy proficiency and other variables and, provided the appropriate adjustments are made, facilitates consistent estimates of standard errors of all regression coefficients.

Analytic Approach

After exploratory analysis, continuous outcome data (educational attainment, literacy) were analyzed by means of ordinary least squares (OLS) and in a hierarchical linear model (HLM) as described, for example, by Goldstein (1987), Longford (1993), or Bryk and Raudenbush (1992), with persons nested within states. This approach assured consistent estimation of within-state parameters and allowed examination of variability across states in adjusted mean outcomes and in specific regression coefficients, for example, those representing sex differences associated with racial/ethnic groups. The OLS and HLM produced nearly identical results. Therefore, the simple OLS results are presented in the tables. However, it was necessary to make provision for the special character of the outcome variable used in NALS as a result of the matrix sampling scheme in which each respondent was assessed on only a subset of the 165 literacy tasks. As mentioned, rather than yielding a single measured variable, NALS produces five "plausible values" — random draws from the posterior distribution of each student's "true" outcome, given the subset of items observed on that student (Johnson, Mazzeo, & Kline, 1993). To cope with this problem, Arnold, Kaufman, and Sedlacek (1992) modified the HLM program (Bryk, Raudenbush, Congdon, & Seltzer, 1994) to compute a separate analysis for each of the five plausible values and then to synthesize the results via an adaptation of Rubin's (1987) recommended approach to the analysis of multiply imputed data. This approach, described in detail in Little and Schenker (1994) and Mislevy (1992), takes into account the extra uncertainty that arises because multiple plausible values rather than a single observed outcome were available.

Key analyses were also repeated using HLM with persons nested within occupations. An adaptation of the hierarchical linear model was used for unemployment as outcome. The initial estimates use penalized quasi likelihood estimation (Breslow & Clayton, 1993) to estimate parameters of a hierarchical logistic regression for Bernoulli data with a logit link function. However, the variance-components estimates from this analysis are then used to obtain population-average estimates and robust standard errors via generalized estimating equations (Zeger, Liang, & Albert, 1988). This analysis enabled a partitioning of the relationships between personal background and outcomes into two components: a within-occupation component and a between-occupation component. Occupations were defined using the three-digit codes of the Dictionary of Occupational Titles. All reported standard errors, whether based on OLS or HLM, were robust standard errors as described by Zeger et al. (1988).

The sample size for these analyses was 12,492. There were minimal losses of sample from missing data. Methods of imputation were highly effective in reducing missing data, and the amount of imputation was small.[4] Cases in the analyses of log wages and literacy were weighted to reflect their varying probabilities of selection so that results would generalize to the corresponding national population of adults.

Person Level Indicators and Constructs

Social Origin   The indicators used were age, years of parent education, and gender.

- *Age:* The indicator of age is the NALS variable, derived age, measured in years. Our sample includes only people from age twenty-five to fifty-nine, those available for the work force.
- *Parent Education (yrs.):* Variables available in the NALS data set included mother/stepmother's highest grade completed, mother/stepmother's highest educational level completed (degree/certificate), father/stepfather's highest grade completed, and father/stepfather's highest educational level completed (degree/certificate). These variables were combined to create the continuous variable of years of parent education. If both moth-

er's and father's information was available, they were averaged. If information existed on only one parent, it was used by itself. If the information was completely missing for both parents, the variable was imputed.
- *Female:* An indicator of gender. (Female = 1, Male = 0)

Ethnicity/Race Dichotomous variables were created from the NALS derived race variable.
- *African American:* An indicator for African American ethnicity. (African American = 1, Other = 0)
- *Asian American:* An indicator for Asian American ethnicity. (Asian American = 1, Other = 0)
- *Hispanic American:* An indicator for Hispanic American ethnicity. (Hispanic American = 1, Other = 0)
- *European American:* An indicator of European American ethnicity. (European American = 1, Other = 0)
- *Other:* An indicator of Other ethnicity. (Other = 1, Otherwise = 0)

Ethnicity/Race by Gender Interaction These interactions were set up as products of pairs of dichotomous variables. One reflects ethnicity, the other reflects gender.
- *African American by Female:* The product of African American and female.
- *Asian American by Female:* The product of Asian American and female.
- *Hispanic American by Female:* The product of Hispanic American and female.
- *European American by Female:* The product of European American and female.
- *Other by Female:* The product of Other and female.

Human Capital This category combines years of education, degree obtained, and literacy — the qualities that the individual brings to the labor market.
- *Educational Attainment:* Years of education.
- *GED:* Yes = 1, No = 0.
- *High School:* 1 if highest degree is high school, 0 if not.
- *Associates Degree:* 1 if highest degree is associates or if college experience, 0 if not.
- *Bachelors Degree:* 1 if highest degree is bachelors, 0 if not.
- *Masters Degree or Higher:* 1 if highest degree is masters or higher, 0 if not.
- *Labor-Force Experience:* This variable is measured by using the log of (age minus years of education minus 5).

Occupational Segregation Ethnicity/race and gender proportions by occupation were gathered from the 1993 U.S. Census report, "Employed Civilians by Occupation, Sex, Race and Ethnicity." These proportions were then assigned to the occupational and industrial sector using the occupational codes.
- *Proportion Female:* Proportion female in each occupation.

- *Proportion African American:* Proportion African American in each occupation.
- *Proportion Hispanic American:* Proportion Hispanic American in each occupation.

Outcome Variables
- *Log Wages:* Natural log of the average weekly wages received when working over the past year.
- *Unemployment:* The NALS variable included those subjects who reported that they were unemployed, laid off, and looking for work. (1 = unemployed, 0 = employed)
- *Literacy:* The three sub-scales of literacy are document, prose, and quantitative literacy. Each of these sub-domains has five plausible values. The first plausible value for document, the first plausible value for prose, and the first plausible value for quantitative have been totaled and divided by three to create Average Literacy 1. This process was also used to create the other four average literacies. These average literacies were then treated as five plausible values.
  - *Average Literacy 1:* The average of the first plausible values for document, prose, and quantitative.
  - *Average Literacy 2:* The average of the second plausible values for document, prose, and quantitative.
  - *Average Literacy 3:* The average of the third plausible values for document, prose, and quantitative.
  - *Average Literacy 4:* The average of the fourth plausible values for document, prose, and quantitative.
  - *Average Literacy 5:* The average of the fifth plausible values for document, prose, and quantitative.

Appendix Notes

1. Detailed descriptions of the sample are provided by Kirsch, Jungeblut, Jenkins, and Kolstad (1993, pp. 5–8), and Sum (1994), Appendix B. The latter provides technical details on the sample design and weighting.
2. For example, persons of age twenty who are in the labor force represent a highly selected sub-population within the overall population of twenty-year-olds, and this population tends to be disadvantaged to an unknown degree on a variety of social origin and human capital characteristics. Similarly, persons over sixty in the labor force are not representative of their age group, many of whom are retired.
3. Kirsch et al. (1993) p. 3; see also Sum (1994), Appendices A, B, and C.
4. As expected, income had the largest amount of missing data. Missing incomes were imputed from occupation (socioeconomic index) education, and employment status using the regression method with addition of a randomly sampled residual to control variance deflation. The variance-covariance matrix was examined before and after imputation. Changes were trivial.

Appendix References

Arnold, C. L., Kaufman, P. D., & Sedlacek, D. S. (1992). *School effects on educational achievement in mathematics and science: 1985–1986* (Research and Development Report). Washington, DC: U.S. Department of Education, National Center for Education Statistics.

Breslow, N., & Clayton D. G. (1993). Approximate inference in generalized linear mixed models. *Journal of the American Statistical Association, 88,* 9–25.

Bryk, A. S., & Raudenbush, S. W. (1992). *Hierarchical linear models in social and behavioral research: Applications and data analysis methods.* Beverly Hills, CA: Sage.

Bryk, A. S., Raudenbush, S. W., Congdon, R. T., & Selzer, M. (1994). *An introduction to HLM: Computer program and users' guide* (Version 2). Chicago: University of Chicago, Department of Education.

Goldstein, H. (1987). *Multilevel models in educational and social research.* London: Oxford University Press.

Johnson, E. G., Mazzeo, J, & Kline, D. L. (1993). *Technical Report of the NAEP 1992 Trial State Assessment Program in Mathematics.* Washington, DC: U.S. Department of Education, National Center for Education Statistics.

Kirsch, I., Jungeblut, A., Jenkins, L., & Kolstad, S. (1993). *Adult literacy in America: A first look at the results of the National Adult Literacy Survey.* Washington, DC: U.S. Department of Education, National Center for Education Statistics.

Little, R. J. A., & Schenker, N. (1994). Missing data. In G. Arminger, C. C. Clogg, & M. E. Sobel (Eds.), *Handbook of statistical modeling for the social and behavioral sciences* (pp. 39–75). New York: Plenum Press.

Longford, N. (1993). *Random coefficient models.* Oxford, Eng.: Clarendon Press.

Mislevy, R. J. (1992). Scaling procedures in NAEP. Special Issue: National Assessment of Educational Progress. *Journal of Educational Statistics, 17,* 131–154.

Rubin, D. B. (1987). *Multiple imputation for nonresponse in surveys.* New York: Wiley.

Sum, A. (1994). *Literacy in the labor force: A report on the results of the National Adult Literacy Survey.* Washington, DC: U.S. Department of Education, National Center for Education Statistics.

Zeger, S., Liang, K., & Albert, P. (1988). Models for longitudinal data: A likelihood approach. *Biometrics, 44,* 1049–1060.

TABLE I

Ordinary Least Squares Regressions, Log Wages as Outcome

| | A | | | B | | |
| | Without Literacy | | | With Literacy | | |
	Co-efficient	Standard Error	t	Co-efficient	Standard Error	t
Social Origin						
Parent Education (Yrs.)	0.010	0.002	4.851	0.004	0.002	1.902
Female	−0.417	0.030	−13.905	−0.416	0.029	−14.346
African American	−0.292	0.029	−10.203	−0.162	0.026	−6.313
Hispanic American	−0.165	0.027	−6.239	−0.053	0.026	−2.022
Asian American	−0.091	0.066	−1.390	0.030	0.062	0.487
Other	−0.334	0.070	−4.751	−0.252	0.068	−3.730
Female by African American	0.287	0.035	8.191	0.262	0.034	7.752
Female by Hispanic American	0.148	0.040	3.739	0.140	0.038	3.668
Female by Asian American	0.154	0.080	1.915	0.145	0.079	1.839
Female by Other	0.282	0.108	2.609	0.232	0.104	2.224
Human Capital						
Educational Attainment (Yrs.)	0.041	0.007	6.257	0.014	0.006	2.260
GED	0.070	0.044	1.620	0.040	0.042	0.953
High School Diploma	0.225	0.034	6.652	0.168	0.032	5.274
Associates Degree	0.459	0.052	8.802	0.347	0.050	6.980
Bachelors Degree	0.689	0.050	13.729	0.537	0.046	11.695
Masters Degree	0.915	0.066	13.783	0.734	0.062	11.917
Literacy				0.003	0.0002	14.647
Log Labor-Force Experience	0.326	0.023	14.006	0.331	0.023	14.699
Female by Log Labor-Force Experience	−0.182	0.024	−7.634	−0.177	0.023	−7.776
R^2		29.1%			31.4%	

TABLE II
Hierarchical Linear Regressions, Log Wages as Outcome

	A Without Literacy			B With Literacy		
	Co-efficient	Standard Error	t	Co-efficient	Standard Error	t
Social Origin						
Parent Education (Yrs.)	0.007	0.002	3.789	0.004	0.002	2.055
Female	−0.282	0.017	−16.615	−0.280	0.017	−16.691
African American	−0.176	0.021	−8.312	−0.111	0.022	−5.064
Hispanic American	−0.079	0.022	−3.544	−0.021	0.023	−0.944
Asian American	−0.032	0.046	−0.682	0.035	0.046	0.764
Other	−0.270	0.066	−4.092	−0.227	0.065	−3.468
Female by African American	0.246	0.028	8.720	0.234	0.028	8.368
Female by Hispanic American	0.109	0.027	4.045	0.106	0.027	3.985
Female by Asian American	0.129	0.068	1.892	0.121	0.069	1.770
Female by Other	0.216	0.102	2.123	0.189	0.100	1.880
Human Capital						
Educational Attainment (Yrs.)	0.035	0.006	6.136	0.021	0.006	3.676
GED	−0.007	0.036	−0.183	−0.018	0.035	−0.501
High School Diploma	0.102	0.026	3.914	0.082	0.026	3.212
Associates Degree	0.207	0.031	6.733	0.165	0.030	5.445
Bachelors Degree	0.336	0.031	10.701	0.280	0.031	9.119
Masters Degree	0.483	0.040	12.101	0.414	0.040	10.434
Literacy				0.001	0.0001	10.167
Log Labor-Force Experience	0.257	0.015	17.200	0.263	0.015	17.539
Female by Log Labor-Force Experience	−0.120	0.018	−6.588	−0.119	0.018	−6.524
Occupational Segregation						
Proportion Female	−0.284	0.053	−5.319	−0.294	0.052	−5.624
Proporton Black	−0.862	0.256	−3.370	−0.764	0.249	−3.075
Proportion Hispanic	−2.596	0.329	−7.898	−2.379	0.312	−7.614
R^2						
Level 1		9.7%			10.6%	
Level 2		70.6%			72.6%	

TABLE III
Logistic Regressions, Unemployment as Outcome

	A			B		
	Without Literacy			With Literacy		
	Co-efficient	Standard Error	t	Co-efficient	Standard Error	t
Social Origin						
Parent Education (Yrs.)	−0.002	0.0112	−0.201	0.010	0.012	0.891
Female	0.098	0.101	0.962	0.109	0.100	1.087
African American	0.679	0.122	5.574	0.430	0.120	3.593
Hispanic American	−0.093	0.183	−0.511	−0.332	0.184	−1.811
Asian American	0.588	0.303	1.942	0.333	0.295	1.127
Other	0.576	0.371	1.551	0.416	0.366	1.135
Female by African American	−0.174	0.165	−1.053	−0.125	0.166	−0.755
Female by Hispanic American	0.046	0.203	0.226	0.066	0.206	0.321
Female by Asian American	−0.172	0.469	−0.366	−0.167	0.475	−0.351
Female by Other	0.496	0.440	1.129	0.570	0.438	1.304
Human Capital						
Educational Attainment (Yrs.)	−0.025	0.027	−0.902	0.023	0.030	0.772
GED	−0.209	0.164	−1.276	−0.138	0.164	−0.844
High School Diploma	−0.680	0.113	−6.023	−0.570	0.116	−4.909
Associates Degree	−0.966	0.157	−6.156	−0.750	0.164	−4.584
Bachelors Degree	−1.325	0.164	−8.080	−1.039	0.170	−6.129
Masters Degree	−1.777	0.225	−7.883	−1.427	0.237	−6.015
Literacy				−0.005	0.001	−7.172
Log Labor-Force Experience	−0.251	0.095	−2.634	−0.263	0.095	−2.760
Female by Log Labor-Force Experience	−0.259	0.125	−2.073	−0.266	0.126	−2.108

125

TABLE IV
Hierarchical Logistic Regressions, Unemployment as Outcome

| | A | | | B | | |
| | Without Literacy | | | With Literacy | | |
	Co-efficient	Standard Error	t	Co-efficient	Standard Error	t
Social Origin						
Parent Education (Yrs.)	0.003	0.012	0.274	0.011	0.011	0.988
Female	0.239	0.086	2.767	0.242	0.087	2.775
African American	0.591	0.120	4.914	0.433	0.119	3.625
Hispanic American	−0.182	0.177	−1.024	−0.340	0.178	−1.914
Asian American	0.535	0.286	1.872	0.354	0.285	1.242
Other	0.514	0.369	1.394	0.403	0.369	1.092
Female by African American	−0.162	0.161	−1.006	−0.129	0.162	−0.798
Female by Hispanic American	0.084	0.203	0.415	0.096	0.206	0.468
Female by Asian American	−0.280	0.471	−0.594	−0.276	0.481	−0.574
Female by Other	0.473	0.447	1.057	0.533	0.447	1.191
Human Capital						
Educational Attainment (Yrs.)	−0.008	0.029	−0.280	0.023	0.031	0.763
GED	−0.106	0.165	−0.643	−0.068	0.166	−0.409
High School Diploma	−0.495	0.120	−4.140	−0.441	0.122	−3.623
Associates Degree	−0.590	0.155	−3.804	−0.479	0.161	−2.984
Bachelors Degree	−0.771	0.153	−5.044	−0.629	0.158	−3.982
Masters Degree	−1.124	0.203	−5.549	−0.946	0.213	−4.442
Literacy				−0.004	0.001	−5.114
Log Labor-Force Experience	−0.140	0.096	−1.450	−0.157	0.096	−1.631
Female by Log Labor-Force Experience	−0.343	0.122	−2.813	−0.340	0.123	−2.776
Occupational Segregation						
Proportion Female	−0.270	0.157	−1.715	−0.259	0.157	−1.656
Proporton Black	0.125	0.767	0.163	−0.087	0.746	−0.117
Proportion Hispanic	5.341	0.951	5.616	4.859	0.949	5.118

TABLE V
OLS Regression, Literacy as Outcome

	Coefficient	Standard Error	t
Social Origin			
Parent Education (Yrs.)	2.424	0.171	14.200
Female	−0.325	1.437	−0.226
African American	−49.155	1.928	−25.493
Hispanic American	−42.552	2.511	−16.942
Asian American	−46.413	5.674	−8.179
Other	−32.609	6.815	−4.785
Female by African American	9.051	2.433	3.720
Female by Hispanic American	4.122	3.505	1.176
Female by Asian American	3.892	7.578	0.514
Female by Other	17.373	9.831	1.767
Human Capital			
Educational Attainment (Yrs.)	10.033	0.518	19.386
GED	11.136	3.012	3.698
High School Diploma	20.968	2.325	9.017
Associates Degree	41.727	2.463	16.944
Bachelors Degree	56.853	2.694	21.104
Masters Degree	67.777	2.740	24.738
Log Labor-Force Experience	−1.681	1.270	−1.323
Female by Log Labor-Force Experience	−2.225	1.673	−1.329
R^2		56.6%	

Part Two

The Interactions
among Schools, Students,
and Communities

Part Two

Introduction

Educational opportunity is to a significant extent a product of the interactions among administrators, teachers, students, parents, and communities. The authors in Part Two examine the dynamics among key actors
in education, and how individual and group behavior fosters or denies
educational opportunities for students. A salient theme of each of the three
chapters is the different treatment shown to students based on race and class.
Although the politics of tracking is the explicit focus of one chapter, the separation of students, whether in a school or a classroom, serves as the back-
drop for all three. Whether due to teacher expectations, community norms,
or school culture, some groups of students, often those poor and of color, are
never given opportunities to learn, excel, or achieve postsecondary academic
success. The authors discuss some factors that contribute to a richness of opportunity for some and a dearth of it for others.

In "The Politics of Culture: Understanding Local Political Resistance to Detracking in Racially Mixed Schools," Amy Stuart Wells and Irene Serna examine how elite parents, most of whom are well-to-do and White, resist detracking
efforts in economically and racially diverse public schools, thus securing educational opportunities for their children while undermining those of less privileged students. They present data from a three-year study of ten high schools
across the nation, which include observational field notes and interviews of
more than four hundred school community members, including administrators, teachers, parents, and students. Referring to social reproduction theory and Pierre Bourdieu's work on cultural capital, Wells and Serna argue that
schools often cater to the demands and expectations of elite parents, which allows these parents to wield their influence on matters that affect entire school
communities. The elite and the culture of the elite affect detracking reform.
Parents may threaten to remove their children from school, causing fear in
district and school administrators and quelling detracking efforts. Their influence may be more subtle, as indicated by "not-quite-elite" parents' support for
or silence toward the resistance to detracking. Wells and Serna state that their
objective is not simply to expose how elite parents contribute to social reproduction in schools, but also to demonstrate how the larger social and educational systems in the United States encourage the privileged few to act in their
own children's perceived interests, which has consequences for all children.

131

In "Structuring Failure and Success: Understanding the Variability in Latino School Engagement, " Gilberto Q. Conchas examines the institutional mechanisms and culture of school programs that mediate student engagement and affect students' perceptions of a school's opportunity structure. His chapter is the result of a two-year study of one low-income, racially diverse comprehensive high school in the western United States. The school features four programs that offer a wide range of academic experiences for students. Latino students in the general academic program lacked academic confidence and expressed general dissatisfaction with school. Conchas attributes this to the absence of social scaffolding efforts, such as academic advising, administrative support, and the creation of a high-achieving setting. While two other programs, the Graphics Academy and the Advanced Placement program, boasted high graduation rates, they were not as successful as the Medical Academy (which also featured a high graduation rate) in fostering student confidence, positive teacher-student relations, and interracial and interethnic bonding. It was the only specialized program in the school that closely reflected the racial proportions of the larger school community, as program staff made an explicit effort to enroll Black and Latino males. Students who graduated from the Medical Academy believed that they would not only attend college, but that they would go on to become doctors. Conchas's article demonstrates that teachers and administrators play an active role in increasing student confidence and ambition by offering students academic and social support.

The final chapter in Part Two, "Student Social Class and Teacher Expectations: The Self-Fulfilling Prophecy in Ghetto Education" by Ray C. Rist, is now considered to be an *HER* classic. Although it first appeared in 1970, the implications of the study for urban education are relevant today, noted by Rist in his 2000 commentary on his then 30-year-old article. Rist observed a group of students in an all-Black school from kindergarten through second grade. Despite a shared racial identity, the teacher differentiated the students by social class and seated them accordingly. Rist observed the teacher giving preferential treatment to the students who came from middle-class homes, while she treated students whose families earned less money as slow learners and did not engage them in learning. When the students entered the second grade, Rist discovered that the "ability" groupings the kindergarten teacher had created had essentially remained the same, possibly due to conversations between teachers and a school culture that reinforced teachers' practice of within-classroom ability grouping. Rist concludes that student performance is a result of teachers' expectations, which determine how they will teach and engage children. As he notes, the teachers offered high-quality instruction only to the students of high socioeconomic backgrounds, thus excluding and alienating the other children. In essence, the teachers created a sort of caste system in the classroom that reflected and perpetuated the class system of the United States.

The Politics of Culture

Understanding Local Political Resistance to Detracking in Racially Mixed Schools

AMY STUART WELLS
IRENE SERNA

Research on tracking, or grouping students into distinct classes for "fast" and "slow" learners, has demonstrated that this educational practice leads to racial and socioeconomic segregation within schools, with low-income, African American, and Latino students frequently placed in the lowest level classes, even when they have equal or higher test scores or grades (see Oakes, 1985; Welner & Oakes, 1995). Furthermore, being placed in the low track often has long-lasting negative effects on these students, as they fall further and further behind their peers and become increasingly bored in school. Partly in response to this research and partly in response to their own uneasiness with the separate and unequal classrooms created by tracking, educators across the country are beginning to respond by testing alternatives to tracking, a reform we call "detracking."

Over the last three years, our research team studied ten racially and socio-economically mixed schools undergoing detracking reform, and attempted to capture the essence of the political struggles inherent in such efforts.[1] We believe that an important aspect of our qualitative, multiple case study is to help educators and policymakers understand the various manifestations of local political resistance to detracking — not only who instigates it, but also the ideology of opposition to such reforms and the political practices employed (see Oakes & Wells, 1995).

This article focuses on how forces outside the school walls shaped the ability of educators to implement "detracking reform" — to question existing track structures and promote greater access to challenging classes for all students. More specifically, we look at those actors whom we refer to as the "local elites" — those with a combination of economic, political, and cultural capital that is highly valued within their particular school community.[2] These elites are most likely to resist detracking reform because their children often enjoy privileged

Harvard Educational Review   Vol. 66   No. 1   Spring 1996, 93–118

status in a tracked system. The capital of the elites enables them to engage in political practices that can circumvent detracking reform.

In order to understand the influence of local elites' political practices on detracking reform, we examine their ideology of entitlement, or how they make meaning of their privilege within the educational system and how others come to see such meanings as the way things "ought to be." According to Gramsci (cited in Boggs, 1984), insofar as ruling ideas emanating from elites are internalized by a majority of individuals within a given community, they become a defining motif of everyday life and appear as "common sense" — that is, as the "traditional popular conception of the world" (p. 161).

Yet we realize that the high-status cultural capital — the valued tastes and consumption patterns — of local elites and the resultant ideologies are easily affected by provincial social contexts and the particular range of class, race, and culture at those sites (Bourdieu, 1984). In a study of social reproduction in a postmodern society, Harrison (1993) notes that "the task is not so much to look for the global correspondences between culture and class, but to reconstruct the peculiarly local and material micrologic of investments made in the intellectual field" (p. 40). Accordingly, in our study, we particularize the political struggles and examine the specific ideologies articulated at each school site. Because we were studying ten schools in ten different cities and towns, we needed to contextualize each political struggle over detracking reform within its local school community. These local contexts are significant because the relations of power and domination that affect people most directly are those shaping the social contexts within which they live out their everyday lives: the home, the workplace, the classroom, the peer group. As Thompson (1990) states, "These are the contexts within which individuals spend the bulk of their time, acting and interacting, speaking and listening, pursuing their aims and following the aims of others" (p. 9).

Our research team used qualitative methods to examine technical aspects of detracking — school organization, grouping practices, and classroom pedagogy — as well as cultural norms and political practices that legitimize and support tracking as a "commonsense" approach to educating students (Oakes & Wells, 1995). Our research question was, What happens when someone with power in a racially mixed secondary school decides to reduce tracking? Guided by this question, we selected ten sites — six high schools and four middle schools — from a pool of schools that were undergoing detracking reform and volunteered to be studied. We chose these particular schools because of their diversity and demonstrated commitment to detracking. The schools we studied varied in size from more than three thousand to less than five hundred students. One school was in the Northeast, three were in the Midwest, one in the South, two in the Northwest, and three in various regions of California. Each school drew from a racially and socioeconomically diverse community and served significant but varied mixes of White, African American, Latino, Native American/Alaska Native, and/or Asian students. We visited each school three times over a two-year period. Data collection during our site visits included in-depth, semi-structured tape-recorded interviews with administrators, teachers, students, parents, and community leaders, including school board members. In total, more than four hundred participants across all ten schools were interviewed at least once. We also observed classrooms, as well as faculty, PTA, and school board meetings. We reviewed documents and wrote field notes about our observations within the schools and the communities. Data were compiled extensively from each school to form the basis of cross-case analysis. Our study ran from the spring of 1992 through the spring of 1995.[3]

Descriptions of the "Local Elites"

The struggles over tracking and detracking reforms are, to a large extent, concerned with whose culture and lifestyle is valued, and, thus, whose way of knowing is equated with "intelligence." Traditional hierarchical track structures in schools have been validated by the conflation of culture and intelligence. When culturally biased "truths" about ability and merit confront efforts to "detrack," political practices are employed either to maintain the status quo or to push toward new conceptions of ability that would render a rigid and hierarchical track structure obsolete (see Oakes, Lipton, & Jones, 1995).

While we acknowledge that many agents contribute to the maintenance of a rigid track structure, this article examines the political practices of local elites in the school communities we studied. The elites discussed here had children enrolled in the detracking schools and thus constitute the subgroup of local elites active in shaping school policies. Their practices were aimed at maintaining a track structure, with separate and unequal educational opportunities for "deserving" elite students and "undeserving" or non-elite students. Our analysis of elite parents' ideology of privilege and the resultant political practices therefore includes an examination of "corresponding institutional mechanisms" (Bourdieu & Wacquant, 1992, p. 188) employed to prevent structural change that would challenge their status and privilege.

Our intention is not to criticize these powerful parents in an unsympathetic manner. Yet, we believe that too often the cultural forces that shape such parents' agency as they try to do what is best for their children remain hidden from view and thus unquestioned. Our effort to unpack the "knapsack" of elite privilege will expose the tight relationship between the "objective" criteria of the schools and the cultural forces of the elite (McIntosh, 1992).

Detracking, or the process of moving schools toward a less rigid system of assigning students to classes and academic programs, is a hotly contested educational reform. In racially mixed schools, the controversy surrounding detracking efforts is compounded by beliefs about the relationship among race, culture, and academic ability. In virtually all racially mixed secondary schools, tracking resegregates students, with mostly White and Asian students in the high academic tracks and mostly African American and Latino students in the low tracks (Oakes, 1985; Oakes, Oraseth, Bell, & Camp, 1990). To the extent that elite parents have internalized dominant, but often unspoken, beliefs about race and intelligence, they may resist "desegregation" within racially mixed schools — here defined as detracking — because they do not want their children in classes with Black and Latino students.

Efforts to alter within-school racial segregation via detracking, then, are generally threatening to elites, in that they challenge their position at the top of the hierarchy. The perceived stakes, from an elite parent's perspective, are quite high. They argue, for instance, that their children will not be well served in detracked classes. And while these stakes are most frequently discussed in academic terms — for example, the dumbing down of the curriculum for smart students — the real stakes, we argue, are generally not academics at all, but, rather, status and power. For example, if a school does away with separate classes for students labeled "gifted" but teachers continue to challenge these students with the same curriculum in a detracked setting, the only "losses" the students will incur are their label and their separate and unequal status. Yet in a highly stratified society, such labels and privileged status confer power.

In looking at the ability of the upper strata of society to maintain power and control, Bourdieu (1977) argues that economic capital — that is, income, wealth, and property — is not the only form of capital necessary for social reproduction. He describes other forms of capital, including political, social, and cultural (Bourdieu & Wacquant, 1992). In our analysis of resistance to detracking reforms, we focus on cultural capital and its relationship to dominant ideologies within our school communities because of the explicit connections between cultural capital and educational achievement within Bourdieu's work. According to Bourdieu (1984), cultural capital consists of culturally valued tastes and consumption patterns, which are rewarded within the educational system. Bourdieu discusses "culture" not in its restricted, normative sense, but rather from a more anthropological perspective. Culture is elaborated in a "taste" for refined objects, which is what distinguishes the culture of the dominant class or upper social strata from that of the rest of society. In order for elites to employ their cultural capital to maintain power, emphasis must be placed on subtleties of taste — for example, form over function, manner over matter. Within the educational system, Bourdieu argues, students are frequently rewarded for their taste, and for the cultural knowledge that informs it. For instance, elite students whose status offers them the opportunity to travel to other cities, states, and countries on family vacations are often perceived to be more "intelligent" than other students, simply because the knowledge they have gained from these trips is reflected in what is valued in schools. When high-status, elite students' taste is seen as valued knowledge within the educational system, other students' taste and the knowledge that informs it is devalued (Bourdieu & Passeron, 1979). In this way, high-status culture is socially constructed as "intelligence" — a dubious relationship that elites must strive to conceal in order to legitimize their merit-based claim to privileged status. In other words, what is commonly referred to as "objective" criteria of intelligence and achievement is actually extremely biased toward the subjective experience and ways of knowing of elite students. Similarly, Delpit (1995) describes the critical role that power plays in our society and educational system, as the worldviews of those in privileged positions are "taken as the only reality, while the worldviews of those less powerful are dismissed as inconsequential" (p. xv). The education system is the primary field in which struggles over these cultural meanings take place and where, more often than not, high-status cultural capital is translated into high-status credentials, such as academic degrees from elite institutions (Bourdieu & Passeron, 1977).

Thus, socially valuable cultural capital — form and manner — is the property many upper class and, to a lesser extent, middle-class families transmit to their offspring that substitutes for, or supplements, the transmission of economic capital as a means of maintaining class, status, and privilege across generations (Bourdieu, 1973). Academic qualifications and high-status educational titles are to cultural capital what money and property titles are to economic capital. The form and manner of academic qualifications are critical. Students cannot simply graduate from high school; they must graduate with the proper high-status qualifications that allow them access to the most selective universities and to the credentials those institutions confer.

Through the educational system, elites use their economic, political, and cultural capital to acquire symbolic capital — the most highly valued capital in a given society or local community. Symbolic capital signifies culturally important attributes, such as status, authority, prestige, and, by extension, a sense of honor. The social construction of symbolic capital may vary from one locality to another, but race and social class consistently play a role, with White, wealthy, well-educated families most likely to be at the top of the social strata (Harrison, 1993).

Because the cultural capital of the elite is that which is most valued and rewarded within the educational system, elite status plays a circular role in the process of detracking reform: parents with high economic, political, and cultural capital are most likely to have children in the highest track and most prestigious classes, which in turn gives them more symbolic capital in the community. The elite parents can then employ their symbolic capital in the educational decisionmaking arena to maintain advantages for their children. Educational reforms that, like detracking, challenge the advantages bestowed upon children of the elite are resisted not only by the elites themselves, but also by educators and even other parents and community members who may revere the cultural capital of elite families. The school and the community thus bestow elite parents with the symbolic capital, or honor, that allows them political power.

The status of the local elites in the ten school communities we studied derived in part from the prestige they and their children endowed to public schools simply by their presence. The elite are the most valued citizens, those the public schools do not want to lose, because the socially constructed status of institutions such as schools is dependent upon the status of the individuals attending them. These are also the families most likely to flee public schools if they are denied what they want from them. For example, at Grant High School, an urban school in the Northwest, the White, upper-middle-class parents who sent their children to public schools held tremendous power over the district administration. Many of them were highly educated and possessed the economic means to send their children to private schools if they so chose.

While the elites at each of the schools we studied held economic, social, and political capital, the specific combination of these varied at each site in relation to the cultural capital valued there. Thus, who the elites were and their particular rationale for tracking varied among locations, based on the distinctive mix of race, class, and culture. For instance, at Liberty High School, located in a West Coast city, many of the White parents were professors at a nearby university. As "professional intellectuals," they strongly influenced the direction of Liberty High; although they were generally not as wealthy as business executives, they were nevertheless imbued with a great deal of high-status cultural capital. Meanwhile, educators and White parents at Liberty noted that most of the Black and Latino students enrolled in the school came from very low-income families. Many of the people we interviewed said there was a sizable number of middle-class Black families in this community, but that they did not send their children to public schools. This school's social class divide, which some educators and Black students argued was a caricature, allowed White parents to blame the school's resegregation through tracking on the "family backgrounds" of the students, rather than on racial prejudice.

In the midwestern town of Plainview, the local White elites worked in private corporations rather than universities. Here, the high-status cultural capital was, in general, far more conservative, pragmatic, and less "intellectual" than at Liberty. Nonetheless, the elite parents here and at each of the schools we studied strove for the same advantages that the elite parents at Liberty High demanded for their children.

The African American students in Plainview comprised two groups — those who lived in a small, working-class Black neighborhood in the district and those who transferred into Plainview from the "inner city" through an inter-district desegregation plan. At this site, however, the social class distinctions between the two groups of Black students were blurred by many White respondents, particularly in their explanations of why Black students from both groups were consistently found in the lowest track classes. For instance, teachers could not tell us which Black students lived in Plainview and which rode the bus in from the city. Some teachers also spoke of Black students' — all Black students' — low levels of achievement as the result of their families' culture of poverty, and not the result of what the school offered them. Despite the relative economic advantages of many African American students who lived in the Plainview district as compared to those who lived in the city, all Black students in this mostly White, wealthy suburban school were doing quite poorly. While African Americans constituted 25 percent of the student population, less than 5 percent of the students in the highest level courses were Black. Furthermore, a district task force on Black achievement found that more than half of the Black students in the high school had received at least one D or F over the course of one school year.

In other schools, the interplay between race and class was more complex, especially when the local elite sought to distinguish themselves from other, lower income Whites. For instance, in the small midwestern Bearfield School District, which is partly rural and partly suburban, wealthy, well-educated, White suburban parents held the most power over the educational system because they possessed more economic and highly valued cultural capital than rural Whites or African Americans. When a desegregation plan was instituted in the 1970s, it was Black and poor rural White children who were bused. As the Bearfield Middle School principal explained, "As our business manager/superintendent once told me, the power is neither Black nor White; it's green — as in money. And that's where the power is. Rich people have clout. Poor people don't have clout."

Still, the less wealthy and less educated rural Whites in Bearfield, while not as politically powerful as the suburban Whites, remained more influential than the African American families. When the two middle schools in the district were consolidated in 1987, Whites — both wealthy suburban and poor rural — were able to convince the school board to close down the newly built middle school located in the African American community and keep open the older middle school on the White side of the town.

Although the interplay between class and culture within a racially mixed community is generally defined along racial lines, we found that was not always the case. For example, King Middle School, a magnet school in a large northeastern city, was designed to attract students of many racial groups and varied socioeconomic status. A teacher explained that the parents who are blue-collar workers do not understand what's going on at the school, but the professional and middle-class parents frequently call to ask for materials to help their children at home. Educators at King insisted that middle-class and professional parents were not all White, and that there was very little correlation between income and race at the school, with its student body composed of more than twenty racial/ethnic groups, including Jamaican, Chinese, Armenian, Puerto Rican, African American, and various European ethnic groups. While we found it difficult to believe that there was no correlation between race/ethnicity and income in this city with relatively poor African American and Latino communities, it is clear that not all of the local elites at King were White.

Thus, the layers of stratification in some schools were many, but the core of the power elite in all ten communities consisted of a group of parents who were more White, wealthy, and well-educated relative to others in their community. They were the members of the school communities with the greatest economic and/or high-status cultural capital, which they have passed on to their children. The schools, in turn, greatly rewarded the children of these elite for their social distinctions, which were perceived to be distinctions of merit (DiMaggio, 1979).

The Political Ideology of Tracking and Detracking: "Deserving" High-Track Students

Bourdieu's concepts of domination and social reproduction are particularly useful in understanding the education system, because education is the field in which the elite both "records and conceals" its own privilege. Elites "record" privilege through formal educational qualifications, which then serve to "conceal" the inherited cultural capital needed to acquire them. According to Harrison (1993), "What is usually referred to as equality of opportunity or meritocracy is, for Bourdieu, a "sociodicy"; that is, a sacred story that legitimates the dominant class' own privilege" (p. 43).

The political resistance of the local elite to detracking reforms cannot, therefore, be understood separately from the "sociodicy" or ideology employed to legitimize the privileged place elites and their children hold in the educational system. Ideology, in a Gramscian sense, represents ideas, beliefs, cultural preferences, and even myths and superstitions, which possess a certain "material" reality of their own (Gramsci, 1971). In education, societal ideas, beliefs, and cultural preferences of intelligence have found in tracking structures their own material reality. Meanwhile, tracking reinforces and sustains those ideas, beliefs, and cultural preferences.

According to Thompson (1990), ideology refers to the ways in which meaning serves, in particular circumstances, to establish and sustain relations of power that are systematically asymmetrical. Broadly speaking, ideology is meaning in the service of power. Thompson suggests that the study of ideology requires researchers to investigate the ways in which meaning is constructed and conveyed by symbolic forms of various kinds, "from everyday linguistic utterances to complex images and texts; it requires us to investigate the social contexts within which symbolic forms are employed and deployed" (p. 7).

The ideology of the local elites in the schools we studied was often cloaked in the "symbolic form" that Thompson describes. While the symbols used by politically powerful people to express their resistance to detracking differed from one site to the next, race consistently played a central, if not explicit, role. Although local elites rarely expressed their dissatisfaction with detracking reform in overtly racial terms, their resistance was couched in more subtle expressions of the politics of culture that have clear racial implications. For example, they said they liked the concept of a racially mixed school, as long as the African American or Latino students acted like White, middle-class children, and their parents were involved in the school and bought into the American Dream. At Central High, a predominantly Latino school on the West Coast with a 23 percent White student body, the local elite consisted of a relatively small middle class of mostly White and a few Latino families. No real upper middle class existed, and most of the Latino students came from very low-income families; many were recent immigrants to the United States. A White parent whose sons were taking honors classes explained her opposition to detracking efforts at Central, exposing her sense of entitlement this way:

> I think a lot of those Latinos come and they're still Mexicans at heart. They're not American. I don't care what color you are, we're in America here and we're going for this country. And I think their heart is in Mexico and they're with that culture still. It's one thing to come over and bring your culture and to use it, but it's another thing to get into that . . . and I'm calling it the American ethic. They're not into it and that's why they end up so far behind. They get in school, and they are behind.

This construct of the "deserving minority" denies the value of non-White students' and parents' own culture or of their sometimes penetrating critique of the American creed (see Yonesawa, Williams, & Hirshberg, 1995), and implies that only those students with the cultural capital and underlying elite ideology deserve to be rewarded in the educational system. Yet because the political arguments put forth by powerful parents in the schools we studied sounded so benign, so "American," the cultural racism that guided their perspective was rarely exposed. Consequently, both the racial segregation within the schools and the actions of parents to maintain it were perceived as natural.

We found many instances in which elite parents attempted to distance their children from students they considered to be less deserving of special attention and services. For instance, at Rolling Hills Middle School, located in a southeastern metropolitan area with a large, county-wide desegregation plan, one wealthy White parent said she and her husband purchased a home in the nearby neighborhood because Rolling Hills and its feeder high school are two of the handful of schools in the district that offer an "advanced program." She said several people had told her that in the advanced program the curriculum was better, fewer behavior problems occurred in the classes, and students received more individualized attention from teachers. She also said that had her children not been accepted into the advanced program, she and her family would not have moved into this racially mixed school district, but would have purchased a home in one of the Whiter suburbs east of the county line. Interestingly enough, this parent did not know whether or not the White suburban schools offered an advanced program. Also of interest in this district is the creation of the advanced program in the same year as the implementation of the desegregation plan.

The White, well-educated parents at Grant High School often stated that the racial diversity of the student body was one characteristic they found most appealing about the school. They said that such a racially mixed environment better prepared their children for life in "the real world." One parent noted that "the positive mixing of racial groups is important to learning to live in society." But some teachers argued that while these parents found Grant's diversity acceptable — even advantageous — their approval was conditioned by their understanding that "their children [would] only encounter Black students in the hallways and not in their classrooms." Grant's assistant principal noted that "many upper class, professional parents hold occupational positions in which they work toward equity and democracy, but expect their children to be given special treatment at Grant."

This ideology of "diversity at a distance" is often employed by White parents at strategic moments when the privileged status of their children appears to be threatened (Lareau, 1989). In our study, the parents of honors students at Grant successfully protested the school's effort to eliminate the "tennis shoe" registration process by which students and teachers jointly negotiated access to classes.[4] Some of the faculty had proposed that the school switch to a computer registration program that would guarantee Black and Latino students greater access to high-track classes. The parents of the honors students stated that they were not protesting the registration change because they were opposed to having their children in racially mixed classes, but because "they [felt] that their children [would] learn more in an environment where all students are as motivated to learn as they are — in a homogeneous ability classroom."

Respondents at Grant said that parents assumed that if any student was allowed into an honors class, regardless of his or her prior track, it must not be a good class. The assumption here was that if there was no selectivity in placing students in particular classes, then the learning and instruction in those classes could not be good. Parents of the most advanced students "assumed" that since the language arts department had made the honors and regular curriculum the same and allowed more students to enroll in honors, the rigor of these classes had probably diminished, despite the teachers' claims that standards had remained high.

At Liberty High School, where the intellectual elite were more "liberal" than the elite in most of the other schools, parents also frequently cited the racial diversity of the school as an asset. For instance, one parent commented that it was the racial and cultural mix — "the real range of people here" — that attracted her to Liberty High. She liked the fact that her daughter was being exposed to people of different cultures and different socioeconomic backgrounds: "We took her out of private school, where there's all these real upper middle-class White kids." Yet, despite this espoused appreciation for diversity among White liberal parents at Liberty, they strongly resisted efforts to dismantle the racially segregated track system. According to another White parent of a high-track student at Liberty:

> I think the one thing that really works at Liberty High is the upper track. It does. And to me, I guess my goal would be for us to find a way to make the rest of Liberty High work as well as the upper track. But it's crucial that we not destroy the upper track to do that, and that can happen . . . it really could. . . . I feel my daughter will get an excellent education if the program continues the way it is, if self-scheduling continues so that they aren't all smoothed together.

In all of the schools we studied, the most interesting aspect of elites' opposition to detracking is that they based their resistance on the symbolic mixing of high "deserving" and low "undeserving" students, rather than on information about what actually happens in detracked classrooms. For instance, an English teacher at Plainview High School who taught a heterogeneous American Studies course in which she academically challenged all her students said that the popularity of the Advanced Placement classes among the elite parents was in part based upon a "myth" that "they're the only classes that offer high standards, that they're the only courses that are interesting and challenging. And the myth is that that's where the best learning takes place. That's a myth."

At Explorer Middle School, located in a mid-sized northwestern city, the identified gifted students — nearly all White, despite a school population that was 30 percent American Indian — were no longer segregated into special classes or teams. Rather, "gifted" students were offered extra "challenge" courses, which other "non-gifted" students could choose to take as well. The day after a grueling meeting with parents of the "gifted" students, the designated gifted education teacher who works with these and other students in the challenge classes was upset by the way in which the parents had responded to her explanation of the new challenge program and the rich educational opportunities available in these classes:

> And they didn't ask, "Well what are our kids learning in your classes?" Nobody asked that. I just found that real dismaying, and I was prepared to tell them what we do in class and here's an example. I had course outlines. I send objectives home with every class, and goals and work requirements, and nobody asked me anything about that . . . like they, it's . . . to me it's like I'm dealing with their egos, you know, more than what their kids really need educationally.

What this and other teachers in our study told us is that many elite parents are more concerned about the labels placed on their children than what actually goes on in the classroom. This is a powerful illustration of what Bourdieu (1984) calls "form over function" and "manner over matter."

Notions of Entitlement

Symbols of the "deserving," high-track students must be juxtaposed with conceptions of the undeserving, low-track students in order for strong protests against detracking to make sense in a society that advocates equal opportunity. Bourdieu argues that "impersonal domination" — the sociocultural form of domination found in free, industrial societies where more coercive methods of domination are not allowed — entails the rationalization of the symbolic. When symbols of domination are rationalized, the entitlement of the upper strata of society is legitimized, and thus this impersonal domination is seen as natural (Harrison, 1993, p. 42).

In our study, we found that elite parents rationalized their children's entitlement to better educational opportunities based upon the resources that they themselves brought to the system. For instance, parents from the White, wealthy side of Bearfield Middle School's attendance zone perceived that the African American students who attended the school and lived on the "other" side of town benefited from the large tax burden shouldered by the White families. One White parent noted, "I don't feel that our school should have, you know, people from that far away coming to our school. I don't think it's right as far as the taxes we pay. . . . They don't pay the taxes that we pay, and they're at our schools also. Um, I just don't feel they belong here, no." According to the superintendent of the school district, this statement reflects the widely held belief among Whites that they are being taxed to pay for schools for Black students, "and therefore, the White community . . . should make the decisions about the schools . . . because they are paying the bill." These perspectives explain in part why the consolidation of the district's two middle schools resulted in the closing of the mostly Black but much more recently built school, and favored the old, dilapidated Bearfield building as the single middle school site.

At the same time, these parents balked at the suggestion that their own social privilege and much of their children's advantages had less to do with objective merit or intellectual ability than it had to do with their families' economic and cultural capital. Harrison (1993) expands upon Bourdieu's notion that culture functions to deny or disavow the economic origins of capital by gaining symbolic credit for the possessors of economic and political capital. Harrison argues that the seemingly legitimate and meritocratic basis upon which students "earn" academic credentials is an important aspect of the dominant class' denial of entitlement as a process in which inherited economic and political power receives social consecration. In other words, the elite parents must convince themselves and others that the privileges their children are given in the educational system were earned in a fair and meritocratic way, and are not simply a consequence of the parents' own privileged place in society. "The demonstration that the belief of merit is a part of the process of social consecration in which the dominant class's power is both acknowledged and misrecognized, is at the core of Bourdieu's analysis of culture" (Harrison, 1993, p. 44).

There is strong evidence from the schools we studied that students frequently end up in particular tracks and classrooms more on the basis of their parents' privilege than of their own "ability." A school board member in the district in which Rolling Hills Middle School is located explained that students are placed in the advanced program depending on who their parents happen to know. Because the advanced program was implemented at the same time as the county-wide desegregation plan, it has become a sophisticated form of resegregation within racially mixed schools supported by conceptions of "deserving" advanced students. The school board member said that parents of the advanced students are very much invested in labels that their children acquire at school. When children are labeled "advanced," it means their parents are "advanced" as well. In fact, said the board member, some of these parents refer to themselves as the "advanced parents": "There is still an elitist aspect as far as I am concerned. I also think it is an ego trip for parents. They love the double standard that their children are in Advanced Placement programs."

Similarly, several elite parents of students in the advanced program at Grant High School expressed regret that the school had such a poor vocational education department for the "other" students — those who were not advanced. Their lament for vocational education related to their way of understanding the purpose of the high school in serving different students. One of these parents, for example, stated that the role of the honors classes was to groom students to become "managers and professionals" and that something else should be done for those kids who would grow up to be "workers."

According to Harrison (1993), the elite seek to deny the arbitrary nature of the social order that culture does much to conceal. This process, which he calls "masking," occurs when what is culturally arbitrary is "essentialized, absolutized or universalized" (p. 45). Masking is generally accomplished via symbols — culturally specific as opposed to materially specific symbols (Bourdieu & Wacquant, 1992). For example, standardized test scores become cultural symbols of intelligence that are used to legitimize the track structure in some instances while they are "masked" in other instances.

An example of this "masking" process was revealed to us at Grant High School, where elite parents of the most advanced students approved of using test scores as a measure of students' intelligence and worthiness to enroll in the highest track classes. But when children of the elite who were identified as "highly able" in elementary school did not make the test score cutoffs for high school honors classes, the parents found ways to get their children placed in these classes anyway, as if the tests in that particular instance were not valid. The educators usually gave in to these parents' demands, and then cited such instances as evidence of a faulty system. The so-called faults within the system, however, did not lead to broad-based support among powerful parents or educators to dismantle the track structure.

Similarly, at Explorer Middle School, where the wealthy White "gifted" students were all placed in regular classes and then offered separate challenge classes along with other students who chose to take such a class, the principal collected data on the achievement test scores for the identified gifted students and other students in the school. She found huge overlaps in the two sets of scores, with some identified "non-gifted" students scoring in the 90th percentile and above, and some "gifted" students ranking as low as the 58th percentile. Yet, when the mostly White parents of children identified by the district as "gifted" were presented with these data, they attributed the large number of low test scores among the pool of gifted students to a handful of non-White students participating in that program, although the number of non-White "gifted" students was far lower than the number of low test scores within the gifted program. The White parents simply would not admit that any of their children did not deserve a special label (and the extra resources that come with it). According to the teacher of the challenge classes, one of the most vocal and demanding "gifted" parents was the mother of a boy who was not even near the top of his class: "I still can't figure out how he got in the gifted program; he doesn't perform in any way at that high a level. . . . She is carrying on and on and on . . ."

Despite evidence that the "gifted" label may be more a form of symbolic capital than a true measure of innate student ability, the parents of students who had been identified as gifted by this school district maintained a strong sense of entitlement. For instance, a White, upper middle-class father of two so-called gifted boys told us he was outraged that the "gifted and talented" teacher at Explorer spent her time teaching challenge classes that were not exclusively for gifted students. This father was adamant that the state's special funding for gifted and talented (G/T) programs should be spent exclusively on identified G/T students. He noted that at the other middle school in the district, the G/T teacher worked with a strictly G/T class, "whereas at Explorer, the G/T teacher works with a class that is only 50 percent G/T." In other words, "precious" state resources for gifted and talented students were being spent on "non-deserving" students — many of whom had higher middle school achievement test scores than the students who had been identified by the school district as gifted many years earlier.

At Plainview High School, the English teacher who created the heterogeneous American Studies class began reading about the social science research on intelligence, and concluded that our society and education system do not really understand what intelligence is or how to measure it. When the principal asked her to present her research to parents at an open house, her message was not well received, particularly by those parents whose children were in the Advanced Placement classes. According to this teacher, "If you were raised under the system that said you were very intelligent and high achieving, you don't want anyone questioning that system, OK? That's just the way it is." She said that what some of the parents were most threatened by was how this research on intelligence was going to be used and whether the high school was going to do away with Advanced Placement classes. She recalled, "I used the word `track' once and debated whether I could weave that in because I knew the power of the word, and I didn't want to shut everyone down. It was very interesting."

Political Practices: How the Local Elite Undermined Detracking

The ideology and related symbols that legitimate local elites' sense of entitlement are critical to educational policy and practice. As Harrison (1993) and Harker (1984) note, Bourdieu's work is ultimately focused on the strategic practices employed when conflicts emerge. In this way, Bourdieu identifies "practices" — actions that maintain or change the social structures — within strategically oriented forms of conflict. These strategic actions must be rooted back into the logic or sense of entitlement that underlies these practices. In other words, we examined political practices that are intended to be consistent with an ideology of "deserving" high-track students. These practices were employed by elite parents when educators posed a threat to the privileged status of their children by questioning the validity and objectivity of a rigid track structure (Useem, 1990).

According to Bourdieu, when seemingly "objective" structures, such as tracking systems, are faithfully reproduced in the dispositions or ways of knowing of actors, then the "arbitrary" nature of the existing structure can go completely unrecognized (Bourdieu & Wacquant, 1992). For instance, no one questions the existence of the separate and unequal "gifted and talented" or "highly advanced" program for children of the local elites, despite the fact that the supposedly "objective" measures that legitimize these programs — standardized tests scores — do not always support the somewhat "arbitrary" nature of student placement. This arbitrary placement system is more sensitive to cultural capital than academic "ability."

In the case of tracking, so-called objective and thus non-arbitrary standardized tests are problematic on two levels. First, the tests themselves are culturally biased in favor of wealthy, White students, and therefore represent a poor measure of "ability" or "intelligence." Second, scores on these exams tend to count more for some students than others. Elite students who have low achievement test scores are placed in high tracks, while non-White and non-wealthy students with high test scores are bound to the lower tracks (see Oakes et al., 1995; Welner & Oakes, 1995). Still, test scores remain an undisclosed and undisputed "objective" measure of student track placement and thus a rationale for maintaining the track structure in many schools.

When these undisclosed or undisputed parts of the universe are questioned, conflicts arise that call for strategic political practices on the part of elites. As Harrison (1993) states, "Where the fit can no longer be maintained and where, therefore, the arbitrary nature of the objective structure becomes evident, the dominant class must put into circulation a discourse in which this arbitrary order is misrecognized as such" (p. 41). When the arbitrary nature of the "objective" tracking structure becomes evident, detracking efforts are initiated, often by educators who have come to realize the cultural basis of the inequalities within our so-called meritocratic educational system.

Within each of our ten schools, when educators penetrated the ideology that legitimizes the track structure (and the advantages that high-track students have within it), elite parents felt that their privileges were threatened. We found that local elites employed four practices to undermine and co-opt meaningful detracking efforts in such a way that they and their children would continue to benefit disproportionately from educational policies. These four overlapping and intertwined practices were threatening flight, co-opting the institutional elites, soliciting buy-in from the "not-quite elite," and accepting detracking bribes.

Threatening Flight

Perhaps nowhere in our study was the power of the local elite and their ideology of entitlement more evident than when the topic of "elite flight" was broached, specifically when these parents threatened to leave the school. Educators in the ten schools we studied were acutely aware that their schools, like most institutions, gain their status, or symbolic capital, from the social status of the students who attend (Wells & Crain, 1992). They know they must hold onto the local elites in order for their schools to remain politically viable institutions that garner broad public support. As a result, the direct or indirect threat of elite flight can thwart detracking efforts when local elite parents have other viable public or private school options.

At Liberty High School, the liberal ideals and principles that are the cornerstone of this community were challenged when local elites were asked to embrace reforms that they perceived to be removing advantages held by their children. In fact, discussions and implementation of such reforms — for example, the creation of a heterogeneous ninth-grade English/social studies core — caused elite parents to "put into circulation a discourse" that legitimized their claim to something better than what other students received. Without this special attention for high-track students, elite parents said, they had little reason to keep their children at Liberty. As one parent of a high-track student noted in discussing the local elite's limits and how much of the school's equity-centered detracking reforms they would tolerate before abandoning the school:

> I think it happens to all of us; when you have children, you confront all your values in a totally different way. I mean, I did all this work in education; I knew all these things about it, and it's very different when it's your own child 'cause when it's your own child your real responsibility is to advocate for that child. I mean, I might make somewhat different decisions about Liberty High, though probably

not terribly different, because as I say, I would always have in mind the danger of losing a big chunk of kids, and with them the community support that makes this school work well.

The power of the threat of elite flight is evident in the history of the creation of tracking structures in many of our schools, where advanced and gifted programs began to appear and proliferate at the same time that the schools in these districts were becoming more racially mixed, either through a desegregation plan or demographic shifts. This shift toward more tracking as schools became increasingly racially mixed follows the long history of tracking in the U.S. educational system. Tracking became more systematized at the turn of the century, as non-Anglo immigrant students enrolled in urban high schools (Oakes, 1985). At Grant High School, which is located in a racially diverse urban school district surrounded by separate Whiter and more affluent districts, the highly advanced and "regular" advanced programs were started shortly after desegregation at the insistence of local elite parents who wanted separate classes for their children. One teacher noted that the advanced programs were designed to respond to a segment of the White community that felt, "Oh, we'll send our kids to public school, but only if there's a special program for them."

At Grant, the chair of the language arts department, an instigator of detracking reform efforts, said that the parents of the "advanced" students run the school district:

> They scare those administrators the same way they scare us. They're the last vestiges of middle-class people in the public schools in some sense. And they know that. And they flaunt that sometimes. And they scare people with that. And the local media would spit [the deputy superintendent] up in pieces if she did something to drive these parents out of the school district. So, yeah. I'm sure she's nervous about anything we're doing.

Similarly, at Rolling Hills Middle School, where the Advanced Program began in the late 1970s, shortly after the county-wide desegregation plan was implemented, the mother of two White boys in the program noted, "If I heard they were going to eliminate the Advanced Program, I would be very alarmed, and would seriously consider if I could afford a private school." She indicated that she thought that most parents of students at Rolling Hills felt this way.

At Central High School, White flight consistently paralleled the influx of Latino immigrant students into the school. Administrators said they hoped that the relocation of the school to a new site in a more middle-class area of the district would allow Central to maintain its White population. But many educators said they felt that what keeps White students at Central is the honors program, which would have been scaled back under detracking reform. This reform effort has been almost completely derailed by political roadblocks from both inside the school and the surrounding community.

Suburban, midwestern Plainview High School was the school in which we perhaps noted the perceived threat of elite flight to be most powerful. There, the concept of "community stability" was foremost on the minds of the educators. Many of the teachers and administrators in the Plainview district, particularly at the high school, came to Plainview from the nearby Hamilton School District, which experienced massive White flight two decades earlier. Essentially, the population of the Hamilton district shifted from mostly White, upper middle class to all Black and poor in a matter of ten years — roughly between 1968 and 1978. According to these educators and many other respondents in Plainview, the status of the Hamilton district and its sole high school plummeted, as each incoming freshman class became significantly darker and poorer. Once regarded as the premier public high school in the metropolitan area, Hamilton suddenly served as a reminder of the consequences of White flight. The large numbers of White residents and educators who came to Plainview after fleeing Hamilton kept the memory of White flight alive, and used Hamilton as a symbol of this threat.

Of all the educators in the district, it was the Plainview High School principal, Mr. Fredrick, who appeared most fixated on issues of community "stability" and the role of the schools in maintaining it:

> Here's my problem, what I'm doing at Plainview High School is essentially trying to make it stable enough so that other people can integrate the neighborhood. Now if other people aren't integrating the neighborhood, I'm not doing it either. I'm not out there working on that, I don't have time to be out there working on that, I've got to be making sure that what we're doing in Plainview High School is strong, we're strong enough, and have the reputation of, so that as we integrate, which I'm hoping is happening, that Whites won't get up and flee . . . when they come in and say, I hope you're here in eight years, that is a commitment those White people are gonna be there in eight years.

Fredrick argues that an academically strong high school led by a principal who maintains a good relationship with the community will help stabilize the whole community. As he explains, "I believe we can keep stability in Plainview while still being out in front of education. Now that's what I feel my job is." Fredrick's goal of maintaining racial stability in the community is noble in many respects, but we learned during our visits to Plainview that his focus on White flight has resulted in intense efforts to please the elite White parents. These efforts to cater to elite parents have consistently worked against detracking reforms in the school. While some of the teachers and other administrators continued to push for more innovative grouping and instructional strategies, Fredrick has advocated more Advanced Placement courses and encouraged more students to take these classes. In this way, the threat of White elite flight has helped maintain the hierarchical track structure and an Advanced Placement curriculum that many teachers, students, and less elite parents argue is not creative or instructionally sound.

Co-opting the Institutional Elites

The threat of flight is one of the ways in which local elites provoke responses to their institutional demands. This threat, and the fear it creates in the hearts of educators, is related to the way in which the "institutional elites" — that is, educators with power and authority within the educational system — become co-opted by the ideology of the local elites. Both Domhoff (1983, 1990) and Mills (1956) write about institutional elites as "high-level" employees in institutions (either private corporations or governmental agencies, such as the U.S. Treasury Department) who see their roles as serving the upper, capitalist-based class. At a more micro or local level, we find that the institutional elites are the educational administrators who see their roles as serving the needs and demands of the local elites. Indeed, in most situations, their professional success and even job security depend on their ability to play these roles.

For instance, in small-town Bearfield, the new superintendent, who is politically very popular with elite parents and community members, has developed a less than positive impression of detracking efforts at the middle school. Yet his view is based less on first-hand information about the reform through visits to the school or discussions with the teachers than on the input he has received from White parents who have placed their children in private schools. To him, the educators at Bearfield Middle School have "let the academics slide just a little bit." Because of the superintendent's sense of commitment to the powerful White, wealthy parents, the principal of Bearfield indicated that he feels intense pressure to raise standardized test scores and prove that academics are not sliding at the school. Thus, some degree of "teaching to the test" has come at the expense of a more creative and innovative curriculum that facilitates detracking efforts by acknowledging, for example, different ways of knowing material. In a symbolic move, the teaching staff has rearranged the Black History Month curriculum to accommodate standardized test prepping in the month of February.

The relationship among the institutional elites at urban Grant High School, its school district office, and the local elite parents, however, demonstrates one of the most severe instances of "co-optation" that we observed. At the district's main office and at the high school, many of the educational administrators are African American. Still, these administrators frequently have failed to push for the kinds of reforms that would benefit the mostly African American students in the lowest track classes. Several respondents noted that Black educators who have been advocates for democratic reform have not survived in this district, and that those who cater to the demands of powerful White parents have been promoted within the system.

At the end of the 1993–1994 school year, the African American principal of Grant, Mr. Phillips, rejected the language arts department's proposal to detrack ninth-grade English by putting "honors" and "regular" students together in the same classes and offering honors as an extra credit option for all students. The principal claimed that it was not fair to do away with separate honors classes when the proposal had not been discussed with parents. His decision, he explained, was based on frequent complaints he received from the mostly White parents of high-track students that changes were being made at the school, particularly in the language arts department, without their prior knowledge or consent. According to the language arts department chair, when her department detracked twelfth-grade electives, it "really pissed people off." Also, when these elite parents were not consulted about the proposal to change the school schedule to an alternative four-period schedule, they protested and were successful in postponing the change.

Furthermore, a recent attempt by Grant's history department to do away with separate honors classes at the request of some students was thwarted by the parents of honors students, who, according to one teacher, "went through the roof." Some of the teachers in other departments indicated that they suspected that the history department's move to eliminate honors classes was not sincere, but rather a political tactic designed to generate support among powerful elite parents for the honors program. In fact, the history department chair, who opposes detracking, noted that his only recourse to stop the detracking reform was to go to the parents and get them upset "because they had the power to do things at school."

At Grant, administrators at the district office have historically been very responsive to the concerns of White parents, and thus regularly implement policies designed to retain the White students. For instance, the district leadership convened an all-White "highly capable parent task force" to examine issues surrounding the educational advanced programs for "highly capable" students. The task force strongly recommended self-contained classrooms for advanced students, making detracking efforts across the district more problematic. According to one of the teachers at Grant, school board members would not talk about the elitism around this program because they were "feeling under siege."

At several schools in our study, educational administrators, especially principals, have lost their jobs since detracking efforts began, in part because they refused co-optation and advocated detracking. At Liberty High School, despite the principal's efforts to make detracking as politically acceptable to the elite parents as possible, in the end he was "done in" by the institutional elites at the district office who would not give him the extra resources he needed to carry out detracking in a manner local elites would have considered acceptable.

Buy-in of the "Not-Quite Elite"

In an interesting article about the current political popularity of decentralized school governance and growth of school-site councils with broad decisionmaking power, Beare (1993) writes that the middle class is a very willing accomplice in the strategy to create such councils and "empower" parents to make important decisions about how schools are run. He notes that it is the middle-class parents who put themselves forward for election to such governing bodies. Yet he argues that in spite of this new-found participatory role for middle-class parents, they actually have little control over the course of their children's schools, because such courses are chartered by a larger power structure. As Beare states, "In one sense, then, participative decision-making is a politically diversionary tactic, a means of keeping activist people distracted by their own self-inflicted, busy work. The middle class are willing accomplices, for they think they are gaining access to the decision-making of the power structures" (p. 202).

The ideology of the local elite's entitlement is so pervasive and powerful that the elites do not necessarily have to be directly involved in the decisionmaking processes at schools, although they often are. But between the local elites' threats to flee, co-optation of institutional elites, and ability to make their privilege appear as "common sense," such school-site councils will most likely simply reflect, as Beare (1993) points out, the broader power structure. In this way, the "self-inflicted busy work" of the not-quite elites, which, depending on the context of the schools, tend to be the more middle- or working-class parents, is just that — busy work that helps the schools maintain the existing power relations and a highly tracked structure. This is what Gramsci (1971) would refer to as the "consensual" basis of power, or the consensual side of politics in a civil society (see Boggs, 1984).

We saw a clear example of how this co-optation plays out at Plainview High School, where a group of about thirty predominantly White parents served on the advisory board for the most visible parent group, called the Parent-Teacher Organization, or PTO (even though there were no teachers in this organization). The PTO advisory board met with the principal once a month to act as his "sounding board" on important school-site issues, particularly those regarding discipline. We found through in-depth interviews with many of the parents on the PTO board that these parents were not the most powerful or most elite parents in the one-high-school district. In fact, as the former president of the advisory board and the mother of a not-quite-high-track student explained, "The Advanced Placement parents don't run the president of the PTO. As a matter of fact, I'm trying to think when the last time [was] we had a president of the PTO whose kids were on the fast track in Advanced Placement. I don't think we've had one in quite a few years."

She did note, however, that there were "a lot of parents on the [district-wide] school board whose kids are in the Advanced Placement classes." Interestingly, in the Plainview school district, the school board and the central administration, and not the school-site councils such as the PTO advisory board, have the power to change curricular and instructional programs — the areas most related to detracking reform — in the schools.

Furthermore, despite the past president's assertion that the Advanced Placement parents do not run the PTO advisory board, the board members we interviewed told us they were unwilling to challenge the pro-Advanced Placement stance of the principal. Still, several of the PTO board members said they believed there was too much emphasis on Advanced Placement at Plainview, and that they were at times uncomfortable with the principal's constant bragging about the number of Advanced Placement classes the school offers, the number of students taking Advanced Placement exams, and the number of students who receive 3's, 4's, or 5's on these exams. Some of these parents said that, in their opinion, a heavy load of Advanced Placement classes is too stressful for high school students; others said the curriculum in the Advanced Placement classes is boring rote memorization. But none of these parents had ever challenged the principal in his effort to boost the number of Advanced Placement classes offered and students enrolling in them. According to one mother on the PTO board:

I think parents have seen that there are so many pressures in the world, they realize that this is high school and they're fed up with all the competition. At the
same time they know you have to play the game, you know. . . . And again, it's hard
to evaluate with some of the top, top students, you know, what's appropriate. . . .
I think a lot of this has to do with Plainview as a community, too. Now, for example, where I live right here is in Fillburn, and that is a more upscale community
[within the Plainview district]. Two houses from me is the Doner school district,
which is a community of wealthier homes, wealthier people, many of whom have
children in private schools.

During interviews, most of the not-quite-elite parents at all of the schools in
our study discussed their awareness of the demands that families with high economic and cultural capital placed on the schools. They cited these demands
as reasons why they themselves did not challenge the push for more Advanced
Placement or gifted classes and why they were not supporters of detracking efforts — even when they suspected that such changes might be beneficial for
their own children. For instance, at Grant High School, the chair of the language arts department formed a parent support group to focus on issues of
tracking and detracking. This group consisted mostly of parents of students
in the regular and honors classes, with only a handful of parents of very advanced students in the highest track. The department chair said she purposefully postponed "the fight" with more of the advanced parents. "We thought if
we could get a group of parents who are just as knowledgeable . . . as we were,
they should be the ones that become the advocates with the other parents. So
that's probably our biggest accomplishment this year is getting this group of
parents that we have together." But one of the few parents of advanced students
left the group because she said her concerns were not being addressed, and the
advisory group disbanded the following spring.

We saw other examples of "not-quite-elite" buy-in at schools where middle-
class minority parents had become advocates of tracking practices and oppo-
nents of detracking efforts, despite their lament that their children were often
the only children of color in the high-track classes. For instance, a Black professional parent at Rolling Hills Middle School, whose two children were in the
advanced program, noted that a growing number of African American parents
in the district were upset with the racial composition of the nearly all-White
"advanced" classes and the disproportionately Black "comprehensive" tracks
within racially mixed schools. He said, "So you have segregation in a supposedly desegregated setting. So what it is, you have a growing amount of dissatisfaction within the African American community about these advanced programs
that are lily White." Despite his dissatisfaction, this father explained that he
is not against tracking per se. "I think tracking has its merits. I just think they
need to be less rigid in their standards."

Similarly, at Green Valley High School, a rural West Coast school with a 43
percent White and 57 percent Latino student population, a professional, middle-class Latino couple who had sent their children to private elementary and
middle schools before enrolling them in the public high school said that the
students at Green Valley should be divided into three groups: those at the top,

those in the middle, and those at the bottom. The father added that those students in the middle should be given more of a tech prep education, and that an alternative school might be good for a lot of kids who won't go to college.

Detracking Bribes

Another political practice employed by local elites in schools that are attempting detracking reforms is their use of symbolic capital to bribe the schools to give them some preferential treatment in return for their willingness to allow some small degree of detracking to take place. These detracking bribes tend to make detracking reforms very expensive and impossible to implement in a comprehensive fashion.

Bourdieu (in Harrison, 1993) would consider such detracking bribes to be symbolic of the irreversible character of gift exchange. In exchange for their political buy-in to the detracking efforts, elite parents must be assured that their children are still getting something more than other children. In the process of gift exchange, according to Bourdieu, gifts must be returned, but this return represents neither an exchange of equivalents nor a case of cash on delivery:

> What is returned must be both different in kind and deferred in time. It is within this space opened up by these two elements of non-identity [of the gifts] and temporality [deferred time] that strategic actions can be deployed through which either one actor or another tries to accumulate some kind of profit. The kind of profit accumulated is, of course, more likely to be either symbolic or social, rather than economic. (p. 39)

In the case of the detracking bribes, the elite parents tend to profit at the expense of broad-based reform and restructuring. Yet, detracking bribes take on a different shape and character in different schools, depending upon the bargaining power of the local elite parents and the school's resources. As Bourdieu (in Harrison, 1993) notes, in the case of the gift exchange, it is the agent's sense of honor that regulates the moves that can be made in the game.

For instance, at King Middle School, located in a large northeastern city, the bribe is the school itself — a well-funded magnet program with formal ties to a nearby college and a rich art program that is integrated into the curriculum. Because King is a school of choice for parents who live in the surrounding area of the city, it is in many ways automatically perceived to be "better than" regular neighborhood schools, where students end up by default. Still, an administrator noted that King must still work at getting elite parents to accept the heterogeneous grouping within the school: "The thing is to convince the parents of the strong students that [heterogeneous grouping] is a good idea and not to have them pull children out to put them in a gifted program. It is necessary to really offer them a lot. You need parent education, along with offering a rich program for the parents so that they don't feel their children are being cheated."

At Rolling Hills Middle School, where African American students are bused to this otherwise White, wealthy school, the detracking bribe comes in the form of the best sixth-grade teachers and a "heterogeneous" team of students, which is skewed toward a disproportionate number of advanced program students. For instance, the heterogeneous team is comprised of 50 percent "advanced" students, 25 percent "honors" students, and 25 percent "regular" students, while the sixth grade as a whole is only about one-third "advanced" students and about one-half "regular" students. Thus, detracking at Rolling Hills is feasible when it affects only one of four sixth-grade teams, and that one team enrolls a disproportionate number of advanced students and is taught by the teachers whom the local elite consider to be the best. The generosity of the "gifts" that the school gives the elite parents who agree to enroll their children in the heterogeneous team are such that this team has become high status itself. The "parent network" of local elites at this school now promotes the heterogeneous team and advises elite mothers of incoming sixth-graders to choose that team. According to one wealthy White parent, "the heterogeneous team is `hand-picked'." Another White parent whose daughter is on the heterogeneous team noted, "It's also been good to know that it's kind of like a private school within a public school. And that's kind of fair, I hate to say that, but it's kind of a fair evaluation."

Of course, Rolling Hills does not have enough of these "gifts" to bribe all of the local elite parents to place their children on a heterogeneous team. In other words, Rolling Hills will never be able to detrack the entire school as long as the cost of the bribe remains so high and the elite parental profit is so great. By definition, the "best" teachers at any given school are scarce; there are not enough of them to go around. In addition, the number of Advanced Placement students in the school is too small to assure that more heterogeneous teams could be created with the same skewed proportion of advanced, honors, and comprehensive tracks.

At Grant High School, the bribe for detracking the marine science program consists of this unique science offering, coupled with the school's excellent science and math departments and one of the two best music programs in the city. These are commodities that elite parents cannot get in other schools — urban or suburban. As one teacher explained, "So what options do these parents have? Lift their kids out of Grant, which they love? They can't get a science program like this anywhere else in the city." Although the school itself is highly tracked, especially in the history department, the marine science classes enroll students from all different tracks. A marine science teacher noted that parents of the advanced students never request that their kids be placed in separate classes because curricula in this program are both advanced and unique.

Interestingly, the detracking bribe at Liberty High, as the school moved -toward the ninth-grade English/social studies core classes, was to be smaller class sizes and ongoing staff development. Unfortunately, the district administration withheld much of the promised funding to allow the school to deliver these gifts to the parents of high-track students. Whether or not these parents were ever committed to this bribe — whether they thought the school was offering them enough in return — is not really clear. What we do know is that the principal who offered the gift was, as we mentioned, recently "let go" by the district. His departure may have been the ultimate bribe with the local elites, because, as Bourdieu (in Harrison, 1993) argues, the kind of profit accumulated is, of course, more likely to be either symbolic or social, rather than economic.

Conclusions

When our research team began this study in 1992, we initially focused on what was happening within the racially mixed schools we were to study. Yet as we visited these schools, it became increasingly evident to us that the parents had a major impact on detracking reform efforts. Over the course of the last three years, we came to appreciate not only the power of this impact but its subtleties as well. In turning to the literature on elites and cultural capital, we gained a deeper understanding of the barriers educators face in their efforts to detrack schools.

As long as elite parents press the schools to perpetuate their status through the intergenerational transmission of privilege that is based more on cultural capital than "merit," educators will be forced to choose between equity-based reforms and the flight of elite parents from the public school system.

The intent of this article is not simply to point fingers at the powerful, elite parents or the educators who accommodate them at the ten schools we studied. We understand that these parents are in many ways victims of a social system in which the scarcity of symbolic capital creates an intense demand for it among those in their social strata. We also recognize the role that the educational system writ large — especially the higher education system — plays in shaping their actions and their understanding of what they must do to help their children succeed.

Still, we hope that this study of ten racially mixed schools undertaking detracking reform is helpful to educators and policymakers who struggle to understand more clearly the political opposition to such reform efforts. Most importantly, we have learned that in a democratic society, the privilege, status, and advantage that elite students bring to school with them must be carefully deconstructed by educators, parents, and students alike before meaningful detracking reforms can take place.

Notes

1 . Our three-year study of ten racially mixed secondary schools that are detracking was funded by the Lilly Endowment. Jeannie Oakes and Amy Stuart Wells were coprincipal investigators. Research associates were Robert Cooper, Amanda Datnow, Diane Hirshberg, Martin Lipton, Karen Ray, Irene Serna, Estella Williams, and Susie Yonezawa.

2 . By "school community," we mean the broad and diverse network of students, parents, educators, and other citizens who are connected to these schools as institutions.

3 . For a full description of the study and its methodology, see Oakes & Wells (1995).

4 . During the "tennis shoe" registration, teachers set up tables in the gymnasium with registration passes for each of the classes they will be offering. Students have an allocated time slot in which they are allowed into the gym to run from teacher to teacher and ask for passes for classes they want. Under this system, teachers are able to control who gets into their classes, and the children of the elite, who hold more political power in the school, are more likely to get the high-track classes that they want.

References

Beare, H. (1993). Different ways of viewing school-site councils: Whose paradigm is in use here? In H. Beare & W. L. Boyd (Eds.), *Restructuring schools: An international perspective on the movement to transform the control and performance of schools* (pp. 200–214). Washington, DC: Falmer Press.

Boggs, C. (1984). *The two revolutions: Gramsci and the dilemmas of western Marxism.* Boston: South End Press.

Bourdieu, P. (1973). Cultural reproduction and social reproduction. In R. Brown (Ed.), *Knowledge, education, and cultural change* (pp. 487–501). New York: Harper & Row.

Bourdieu, P. (1977). *Outline of a theory of practice.* Cambridge, Eng.: Cambridge University Press.

Bourdieu, P. (1984). *Distinction: A social critique of the judgment of taste.* Cambridge, MA: Harvard University Press.

Bourdieu, P., & Passeron, J. C. (1977). *Reproduction in education, society and culture.* Beverly Hills, CA: Sage.

Bourdieu, P., & Passeron, J. C. (1979). *The inheritors: French students and their relation to culture.* Chicago: University of Chicago Press.

Bourdieu, P., & Wacquant, L. J. D. (1992). *An invitation to reflexive sociology.* Chicago, IL: University of Chicago Press.

Delpit, L. (1995). *Other people's children: Cultural conflict in the classroom.* New York: New Press.

DiMaggio, P. (1979). Review essay: On Pierre Bourdieu. *American Journal of Sociology, 84,* 1460–1472.

Domhoff, W. G. (1983). *Who rules America now? A view for the 80s.* Englewood Cliffs, NJ: Prentice-Hall.

Domhoff, W. G. (1990). *The power elite and the state: How policy is made in America.* New York: A. deGruyter.

Gramsci, A. (1971). *Selections from the prison notebooks.* New York: International Publishers.

Harker, K. (1984). On reproduction, habitus and education. *British Journal of Sociology of Education, 5*(2), 117–127.

Harrison, P. R. (1993). Bourdieu and the possibility of a postmodern sociology. *Thesis Eleven, 35,* 36–50.

Lareau, A. (1989). *Home advantage.* London: Falmer Press.

McIntosh, P. (January/February, 1992). White privilege: Unpacking the invisible knapsack. *Creation Spirituality,* pp. 33–35.

Mills, C. W. (1956). *The power elite.* London: Oxford University Press.

Oakes, J. (1985). *Keeping track: How schools restructure inequalities.* New Haven, CT: Yale University Press.

Oakes, J., Oraseth, T., Bell, R., & Camp, P. (1990). *Multiplying inequalities: The effects of race, social class, and tracking on opportunities to learn mathematics and science.* Santa Monica, CA: Rand.

Oakes, J., Lipton, M., & Jones, M. (1995, April). *Changing minds: Deconstructing intelligence in detracking schools.* Paper presented at the annual meeting of the American Educational Research Association, San Francisco.

Oakes, J., & Wells, A. S. (1995, April) *Beyond sorting and stratification: Creative alternatives to tracking in racially mixed secondary schools.* Paper presented at the annual meeting of the American Educational Research Association, San Francisco.

Thompson, J. B. (1990). *Ideology and modern culture.* Stanford, CA: Stanford University Press.

Useem, B. (1990, April). *Social class and ability group placement in mathematics in transition to seventh grade: The role of parental involvement.* Paper presented at the annual meeting of the American Educational Research Conference, Boston.

Wells, A. S., & Crain, R. L. (1992). Do parents choose school quality or school status? A sociological theory of free-market education. In P. W. Cookson (Ed.), *The choice controversy* (pp. 65–82). Newbury Park, CA: Corwin Press.

Welner, K., & Oakes, J. (1995, April). *Liability grouping: The new susceptibility of school tracking systems to legal challenges.* Paper presented at the annual meeting of the American Educational Research Association, San Francisco.

Yonesawa, S., Williams, E., & Hirshberg, D. (1995, April). *Seeking a new standard: Minority parent and community involvement in detracking schools.* Paper presented at the annual meeting of the American Educational Research Association, San Francisco.

An earlier version of this article was presented at the American Educational Research Association's 1995 annual meeting in San Francisco.

Structuring Failure and Success

Understanding the Variability in Latino School Engagement

GILBERTO Q. CONCHAS

Children of immigrants now account for nearly one in five of all U.S. schoolchildren. There is increasing public debate about how best to educate these newest Americans. Most of the parents of these children arrived in the United States from Latin America and Asia. Although these newcomers have settled in all parts of the United States, the majority of immigrants are concentrated in California, Florida, Illinois, New York, and Texas (U.S. Bureau of the Census, 2001). California alone houses more than two-fifths of today's immigrant youth (Vernez & Abrahamse, 1996). Of these immigrant youth, Latinos[1] will represent 50 percent of the total school-age enrollment in California by the year 2005 (del Pinal & Singer, 1997). Within this growing population of Latino school-age children, low academic achievement and a high dropout rate persist (Trueba, 1998; U.S. Census Bureau, 2001). Thus, Latino students' school achievement should be among the top priorities of educational policymakers.

Some scholars attribute the low academic achievement among Latinos to segregation and neglect in a racially stratified society (Orfield, 1998). Research indicates that low-income minority students often encounter aesthetically unpleasant and ill-equipped learning environments, inadequate instructional materials, ineffective teachers, and defiant peer subcultures, such as youth gangs (Anyon, 1997; Orfield, 1998; Sánchez-Jankowski, 1991; Trueba, 1998; Vigil, 1988, 1997). These studies specifically point to school factors, such as teachers' low expectations and lack of cultural awareness, a curriculum that does not reflect the life experiences of minority youth, and the lack of institutional support systems, as contributing to low academic performance (Conchas, 1999; Gándara, 1999; Goyette & Conchas, 2002; McQuillan, 1998; Mehan, Villanueva,

Harvard Educational Review Vol. 71 No. 3 Fall 2001, 475–504

Hubbard, & Lintz, 1996). Other research links family background to lower levels of educational performance (Diaz Salcedo, 1996; Trueba, 1998). However, despite the overall poor performance of low-income Latino students, many of them are defying the odds and succeeding at school (Conchas, 1999; Conchas & Clark, 2002; Gándara, 1995, 1999; Gibson, 1997; Mehan et al., 1996).

While schools by themselves are hard pressed to circumvent structural inequality at the larger social and economic level, they can have a powerful effect on students' experience of social conditions. In this article, I describe the results of a study that examined how school programs construct school failure and success among low-income immigrants and U.S.-born Latino students. The findings from this study extend our understanding of the fluidity and nuance of Latino students' within-group variations in an urban school context. They specifically reveal that institutional mechanisms have an impact on Latino school engagement. By capturing the voices of both low-achieving and high-achieving low-income Latino students, this research shows promising ways that schools may begin to shape social and academic success.

Assessing Latinos' School Engagement

Many questions have been posed about the education of Latino youth. Why do some low-income immigrant and U.S.-born Latino students do well in school while others do not? Why are low-income Latino students generally not as successful in school as their White peers? What are the effects of institutional mechanisms on low-income Latinos' school engagement? For the past two decades, the most persuasive explanations for these questions have been advanced by the cultural ecologists, who suggest that academic achievement differences by race result from minority groups' perceptions of the opportunity structure — that is, social and economic institutions, including the work force, education, and other areas that influence social mobility (Fordham & Ogbu, 1986; Gibson & Ogbu, 1991; Matute-Bianchi, 1986; Ogbu, 1974, 1978, 1987, 1989, 1991; Weis, 1990).

The cultural ecological model suggested by Ogbu and his associates distinguishes between voluntary and involuntary minorities (Gibson & Ogbu, 1991; Ogbu, 1974, 1991; Ogbu & Matute-Bianchi, 1986). Voluntary minorities (such as Japanese, Koreans, Chinese, Cuban Americans, Filipino Americans, and West Indians) are immigrant groups who have historically moved to the United States of their own free will, usually for economic, social, or political reasons. Although voluntary minorities may face subordination and exploitation, they perceive and react to schooling positively because they regard their current situation in the United States more favorably than their situation in their country of origin. Their specific experiences in the United States relative to their native countries contribute to high levels of immigrant optimism that often results in higher levels of school achievement.

Involuntary minorities (African Americans, Mexican Americans, Puerto Ricans, and Native Americans), on the other hand, are groups who have historically been more or less involuntarily and permanently incorporated into U.S.

society through slavery, conquest, or colonization. Ogbu refers to these groups as "caste-like" because their incorporation often resulted in social and economic subordination. For instance, African Americans were enslaved through force and Mexican Americans were incorporated through conquest. Involuntary minorities, as the paradigm suggests, are unlikely to work hard in school because they do not wish to assimilate, and because they recognize that, relative to Whites, they have a limited chance of benefiting from education. These unique historical and social experiences relate to high levels of pessimism toward the opportunity structure and toward schooling in particular. Thus, involuntary minorities perceive a limited opportunity to attain school success. Ogbu (1987) concludes that "membership in a caste-like minority group is permanent and often arrives at birth" (p. 91). In general, involuntary minorities are believed to develop oppositional subcultures and identities resistant to the assimilation process prevalent in schooling.

The minority group categories depicted by the cultural ecologists, however, do not explain the variations in school experience that exist between and within racial minority groups. While many voluntary minority students attain school success, others do not; and while many involuntary minorities are academically "at risk," some do well (Gibson, 1997). For instance, Mehan, Hubbard, and Villanueva (1994) found academically successful involuntary minorities such as Mexican American and African American students in large urban high schools. Foley (1990, 1991) shows that middle-class Mexican American youth respond to schooling like voluntary minorities; that is, they do not resist the schooling process. Conversely, Lee (1996) depicts low-achieving behavior among some voluntary immigrant Asian students.

Research documenting generational influences on school engagement make the voluntary/involuntary immigrant dichotomy even more problematic. Specifically, Ogbu's typology does not take into consideration the variability in school performance from one generation to another. Several studies suggest that Latino school performance may decline with each successive generation (Gibson, 1997; Portes & Rumbaut, 1996; Suárez-Orozco & Suárez-Orozco, 1995; Vigil, 1997). In their comprehensive study of Latino immigration and school achievement, for instance, Suárez-Orozco and Suárez-Orozco (1995) report that newly arrived Mexican immigrants have a strong desire to learn English, acculturate, and partake in U.S. society, while subsequent generations of U.S.-born Mexican Americans develop an oppositional identity against "making it" in school. The researchers state that "many second-generation Latino youth reject . . . schools . . . that violently reject them, and they seek refuge with their peers" (p. 67), sometimes through youth gangs. The Suárez-Orozcos explain the achievement paradox between immigrant and U.S.-born Mexican Americans as a function of racial stratification in society. Mexican American youth become more ambivalent toward schooling as they become more acculturated and as they face greater levels of racial discrimination.

The aforementioned studies overlook the role of school processes and their influence on Latino students' varying academic trajectories. While many Latino youth perform poorly in school, many others attain success in urban schools with support from specific institutional processes. The Latino student population reflects not a monolithic entity in which all Latinos perform poorly, but a heterogeneous one in which some perform well and others do not (Conchas, 1999; Gándara, 1995; Gibson, 1997; Goyette & Conchas, 2002; Mehan et al., 1996; Vigil, 1997). Although research studies accurately present variability, the majority do not show how group differences in school engagement may be related to institutional factors within the school context.

Stanton-Salazar (1997, 2001; see also Stanton-Salazar & Dornbusch, 1995) begins to explore that relationship by studying the micro-process of information networks within the school as a source of social and cultural capital and eventual academic success. Stanton-Salazar and Dornbush (1995) argue "that supportive ties with institutional agents represent a necessary condition for engagement and advancement in the educational system and, ultimately, for success in the occupational structure" (p. 117). According to Stanton-Salazar, successful low-income youth of Mexican origin find supportive ties within schools. The development of a successful support network rests upon the youths' developing social consciousness in response to their assessment of the opportunity structure. In other words, once youth consciously recognize what it takes to be successful in school and in society in general, they will, on their own, seek the necessary avenues to attain social mobility. Those who are most successful seek out institutional agents who can help them. Consequently, it is up to Mexican American youth to forge the necessary relationships with key agents in the school.

While Stanton-Salazar's research advances our understanding of how some Mexican American youth become academically successful, we are still uncertain why some of them seek out institutional agents and form supportive relationships while others do not, and why some institutional agents are available while others are generally unreachable. A few studies have identified the key role of institutional support networks in promoting student engagement and achievement. Mehan et al. (1996), for instance, examined African American and Latino youth in an untracked college-bound program for low-income urban youth, called Advancement Via Individual Determination, better known by its acronym, AVID. The study investigated the features of AVID that make schools work for these youth, such as the curriculum, teachers, mentors, networking, and other social factors (Hubbard, 1995; Mehan et al., 1996).

Mehan et al. (1996) employ the term *social scaffolding* to describe the institutional support systems that AVID creates to increase school success for low-achieving students. They define these supports as "the practice of combining heterogeneous grouping with a uniform, academically rigorous curriculum enhanced with strong supports" (p. 78). Concentrating on the organizational arrangements provided through AVID, Mehan et al. demonstrate how social scaffolding can contribute to positive academic motivation and engagement. It is through social scaffolding that low-achieving youth can attain the socialization required for academic success. More specifically, the AVID program "explicitly teach[es] aspects of the implicit culture of the classroom and the hidden curriculum of the school" (p. 81). AVID provides low-achieving Mexican American and African American youth with the foundations essential for navigating the opportunity structure and achieving social mobility.

Mehan et al. (1996) argue that this organizational support must begin early in the high school experience and then be slowly removed as the students internalize "the help their guides provided" (p. 79). Once aware of these organizational supports, students are more capable of navigating the school system on their own. Mehan et al. demonstrate that the social scaffolding process fosters student identities and peer cultures oriented toward academic success. This study effectively shows how the school context contributes to academic engagement among involuntary U.S.-born Mexican Americans.

The cultural-ecological model provides a simplistic framework for understanding school engagement. According to the model, voluntary minorities are likely to succeed, while involuntary minorities are doomed to fail. However, the work of Suárez-Orozco and Suárez-Orozco, Stanton-Salazar, and Mehan et al. suggests that variations among minority school achievement do exist. In fact, some members of involuntary minorities, such as Mexican Americans and African Americans, can and do attain school success. Suárez-Orozco and Suárez-Orozco (1995) also show that differences in academic achievement exist between immigrant and U.S.-born Mexican Americans. Moreover, Stanton-Salazar (1997, 2001; see also Stanton-Salazar & Dornbusch, 1995) and Mehan et al. (1996) indicate the importance of institutional factors in understanding the educational plight of minority youth. Still, two issues remain unclear: the impact of institutional factors on both immigrant and U.S.-born low-achieving and high-achieving Latinos, and the relationship between cultural ecological explanations and institutional explanations.

This article explores these issues through a qualitative case study of low-income immigrant and U.S-born Latino students attending an urban high school. Some of these were low-achieving students, most of whom were enrolled in the general school program, while most of the high-achieving Latino students were enrolled in career academies and/or the Advanced Placement (AP) program.[2] The aim is to show how institutional mechanisms mediate school engagement. In the case of a specific urban high school, this study shows how school structures and practices can contribute to optimism and pessimism among immigrant and U.S.-born Latino students. Various institutional mechanisms create opportunity structures within a school that students navigate and interpret optimistically and pessimistically. These mechanisms also divide the students into different peer groups that have different subcultures and support networks. This study argues that particular units within the school may be reinforcing the patterns of student engagement laid out by the cultural ecological model, while others may be disrupting these patterns and accounting for some of the variation in Latino student engagement.

The Setting

Baldwin High School is located in a large, predominantly racial-minority city in the western United States.[3] According to the U.S. Bureau of the Census report

(1996), the city's racial and ethnic composition is 42.9 percent African American, 28.3 percent White, 14.3 percent Asian, 13.8 percent Latino, 0.5 percent Native American, and 0.3 percent Other. The city's household income ranges from $27,095 to $61,171. Baldwin High School is one of several comprehensive high schools serving a low-income and racially diverse student body that is reflective of the larger community. Baldwin High was built at the turn of the century, and is a large, three-story structure, now accompanied by portable classrooms.

At the time of this study, the Baldwin High School community of 1,817 students was richly diverse. Table 1 presents the high school's racial profile. Some of the Latino students at Baldwin High were immigrants, mostly from Mexico and Central and South America, while the majority were second- and third-generation Mexican Americans.

Baldwin High offered a full curriculum ranging from general classes to Advanced Placement. During the period of this study, the high school housed a Medical Academy for students who were interested in pursuing health-related occupations and a Graphics Academy, a magnet program specializing in computer-assisted graphics technology. The administration and teachers were also interested in establishing a Computer Academy and a Teacher Academy. Their goal was to restructure the high school into smaller, more intimate learning environments, each of which focused on a particular career theme. The school also housed an English as a Second Language (ESL) program and a highly reputable AP program that included five subject areas. It is important to note that the AP program had a strong relationship with the Graphics Academy, and that the majority of AP students were also in the Graphics Academy. This study concentrates on the experiences of students in the Medical Academy, Graphics Academy, and AP program, comparing them to the experiences of those in the general academic program. Table 2 profiles each program.

Methods

This case study is part of a larger comparative racial and ethnic research project of urban high school students' educational experiences.[4] Baldwin High School was chosen as a research site for a number of reasons. First, it represents a typical urban high school in California, with a majority of low-income minority students, both low and high achieving. Second, it houses unique schools-within-schools that attempt to shape school success. The aim was not to research career academies per se, but to understand the experiences of low- and high-achieving youth that happened to be enrolled in career academies. The focus here is on students' perspectives about the institutional processes that related to their motivation and academic engagement. This study, however, concentrates specifically on the variations among Latino students' experiences.

The data collection for this study consisted of two years of participant observation. Data consist of field notes on day-to-day student-student and student-teacher interactions, interviews with students and teachers, maps of seating arrangements, and site documents such as report cards, student work, teacher

TABLE 1
Baldwin High School Profile: 1997–1998

Race and Ethnicity	Socioeconomic Status	Limited English Proficiency	College Prospects
65% African American	More than 30% receive AFDC benefits	18% limited English proficiency	11% college attendance rate
20% Asian American			
10% Latino			The majority of college-bound students are enrolled in one of several school-within-school college preparatory programs
4% White	More than 50% are eligible for free or reduced lunch	More than a dozen different languages are taught at Baldwin	
1% Filipino, Native American, and Pacific Islander			

TABLE 2
Medical Academy, Graphics Academy, and Advanced Placement Program Profiles: 1997–1998 School Year

Medical Academy	Graphics Academy	Advanced Placement Program
School-within-school: 10th–12th grade (some start in the 9th grade)	School-within-school: 10th–12th grade	Blocked scheduling: 11th–12th grade
Voluntary enrollment: teachers place a high emphasis on recruiting at-risk youth, in particular African American and Latino males	Voluntary enrollment: teacher recruitment within AP pathway and outside of school, concentrating on high-achieving math students	Voluntary enrollment: counselor/teacher/ parent recommendation
267 students:	127 students:	64 students:
55% African American	25% African American	16% African American
32% Asian American	56% Asian American	66% Asian American
10% Latino	9% Latino	4% Latino
3% White	10% White	14% White
93% graduation rate	100% graduation rate	100% graduation rate
98% college enrollment:	100% college enrollment:	100% four-year colleges
77% four-year colleges	98% four-year colleges	
19% two-year colleges	2% two-year colleges	
2% transferred out of college		

evaluations, and announcement flyers. Social and academic events were close-ly observed before school, during lunch, and after school. Close attention was paid to the overall social organization of the school, but specific attention was given to one school-within-a-school's attempt to create a meaningful learning community within a racially polarized school setting.

This article focuses on the data collected in interviews, focus groups, and observations of twenty-six Latino students in the tenth through twelfth grades. Semi-structured protocols were used for the interviews and focus groups, which lasted one to two hours and were taped and transcribed verbatim. Eighteen of these students were enrolled in the three college preparatory programs (11 in the Medical Academy, 3 in the Graphics Academy, and 4 in the AP program), and eight were not part of any high-track grouping, but were instead enrolled in the general academic program. Fifteen of the students were female and eleven were male. Thirteen of the students were U.S-born Mexican Americans, six were Mexican immigrants, and seven were immigrants from Central America. The students self-identified their race and ethnicity and also reflected upon their generational status. The Latino students in the sample were from low-socioeconomic-status (SES) backgrounds that included intact families as well as single-female-headed households and foster families.

This sample is not entirely representative, for it does not include Limited English Proficient (LEP) Latino students. It reflects, nonetheless, the larger English-speaking and bilingual Latino population at the school. At the beginning of the study, Latinos were recruited to participate and all who volunteered were interviewed. The majority of these were followed for two years. Ultimately, this study endeavored to explore the origins of low-income Latino students' school failure and success in relationship to the school context.

School Opportunity Structure and Racial Perceptions

> Like, you got an all-Black class, or something, and if you are in there, [Black teachers] try to misplace you. . . . They take care of their own. . . . We are invisible.
> David, third-generation Mexican American sophomore

According to my observations, structural and cultural processes at Baldwin High School divided students by race and distributed opportunities among students in a way that reproduced social inequities. These racial hierarchies reinforced immigrant pessimism among involuntary minorities, such as U.S.-born Mexican American students. The high school, for instance, was segmented into various academic groupings, the structures of which contributed to an academically competitive school culture and, at times, hostile racial and ethnic relations.[5] Selection and instructional processes divided students and distributed opportunities along racial and ethnic lines. Latino students were among those who experienced, observed, and questioned these inconsistent racial and ethnic divisions. In turn, the majority of Latino students separated themselves within classrooms, during lunch, and after school. Distinct Latino subcultures existed that either perpetuated these racial and ethnic divisions or attempted to circumvent them.

The racial and ethnic divisions associated with the various subcultures are important to understand, for each reflects how immigrant and non-immigrant students engage in school. For instance, Stanton-Salazar (1997) suggests how different peer groups and support networks affect student optimism and pessimism. Those students who perceive stronger and healthier racial and ethnic relations are more motivated and more engaged in school, whereas those who feel more intimidated by the racial and ethnic climate suffer. Latino students' academic success is also associated with close relationships with other high-achieving peers outside of their own race and ethnic group. Those Latino students who forge relationships with non-Latino students build a stronger high-achieving peer network. This peer network in turn helps mediate immigrant and native-born differences as Latino students help each other engage and succeed in school.

Latino students at Baldwin were aware that most low-track classes were composed of Black and Latino students, whereas high-track classes were composed of primarily Asian and White students. Although the school's racial and ethnic demographic profile showed a majority of African American students, African Americans as well as Latinos were underrepresented in the AP program (see Table 2). The racial composition of the Graphics Academy, on the other hand, while not yet representative of the overall school population, was significantly improving because the director and staff were making a strong effort to recruit more non-White and non-Asian students. Nevertheless, these two programs enrolled a majority of Baldwin High's Asian students and a significant number of the White students.[6] Asians and Whites made up approximately 25 percent of the student population, yet represented 69 percent of the total enrollment in the Graphics Academy and the Advanced Placement program. Bill, a third-generation Mexican American AP student, commented that "there are mostly all Asians in the Advanced Placement program . . . and almost all Whites in school have Advanced Placement. Actually, a lot of students in the Advanced Placement are also in the [Graphics Academy]."

This structural racial and ethnic separation within the school was reflected in the ways students socialized and with whom they socialized at school. Ana, an immigrant from Mexico who was enrolled in the Medical Academy, explained that "students segregate themselves based on how they are treated. Like you go out for lunch . . . and you see . . . a group of Asian people right there in the classes with some Whites, and then you see a group of Blacks in the front, and then you see a group of Latinos by the gym." The same was true at school functions, where students were given a limited choice as to where and with whom they would sit; for example, during school assemblies students sat and spoke with students of their same racial and ethnic group. A common sight was that of Asians sitting on one side of the school auditorium, Blacks toward the front, and Latinos clustered together according to what academic program they belonged to. This pattern extended into the classroom, where students formed strong relationships with others of their own racial groups and sat together. It was not uncommon to observe a classroom with Blacks sitting on one side, Asians on another, and the few Latinos sitting together.

Students made strong links between the racial composition of the different academic programs and the racial stigma associated with each. Latino students clearly articulated how the racial and ethnic divisions within each program reflected the racial hierarchy present in the larger society. Consider, for example, a Salvadoran immigrant student's astute response when asked about the relationship between racial stereotypes and a program's academic image:

> *GC:* Is there a connection between race and ethnic perceptions and what programs are perceived to be the best?
>
> *Rocío:* Oh gosh! Yes, like AP. You walk in and you see order, you see hard-nose people working . . . and you see mostly Asian. That makes a difference! (Laughing) You know, if you walk into a regular class and see the majority African Americans and Mexicans, you know you would think it's bad. The messages we are told about African Americans and Mexicans are bad and we would think that was the case. Gosh! Our opinions about how good the programs are here are based on race. They are pretty heavily based on race.
>
> *GC:* Can you explain that for me?
>
> *Rocío:* Well, if society says that . . . you are Latino and lazy, that [if] you are Asian, you are smart, if you are White, Oh God, the best, and if you are Black, you are bad, horrific. If you walk into a class full of Asians and White students . . . you think that this is a really good class, because they are Asian and White. It must be a good class. If you walk into a class that is majority African American and Latino, you know it's bad, because they are lazy and dumb. . . . It is like a pyramid, you know, the supreme of the supreme on top and the rest down the way. The classes are set and they are there, who embodies them is different. That makes the difference.

Diego, a third-generation Chicano Medical Academy junior, and Ricardo, an immigrant Mexican sophomore in the Graphics Academy and AP program, commented on how the school programs reinforced racial and ethnic stereotypes:

> *Ricardo:* (Translated from Spanish) For instance, my teacher, and I'm in Graphics, he goes up to [an] Asian student, looks at his work and says, "You could do better." With me, however, he simply says . . . "It's all right." But he never says I can do better, right? He is like telling me, for me [as a Mexican], it is all right. Like if I cannot do better than that, that is the best I can do. And I do not like that.

While Ricardo thought racial stereotypes were an explicit part of school interaction, Diego saw it as more subtle:

> *Diego:* I don't think any of this is done directly, all this racial segregation in the school. I don't think there is any one person or group of people that are out to do this at this school, but I think just the ways things have shaped up, things that happen . . . are the way they are because [of] the stereotypes that people

hold and they get turned into who gets the best and most challenging things here. Teachers have also been influenced by this. . . . I think that over the years they have seen it over and over and over again, and after a while they help in making stereotypes come true.

Diego poignantly speaks to the institutionalized nature of racial and ethnic divisions. He explains how teachers are both passive and active agents in perpetuating these forms of inequality. Teachers are passive in that they adhere to common perceptions about race and ethnic groups, yet they also actively reinforce these forms of racial and ethnic divisions by following these traditions. In general, he locates teacher agency within a larger structural process that feeds into the school setting. Unfortunately, these actions affect student relations and, in turn, their academic engagement.[7]

Latino students' experiences and perceptions of schooling differed according to the programs in which they were enrolled, and the subsequent sociocultural processes to which they were exposed. The following section addresses how the distinct school programs mediated students' interactions with one another and with their teachers, and their overall school engagement.

Latino Responses to the Distinct School Programs

Latino students fell into distinct academic niches that corresponded to the school's stratification system. A continuum of academic programs reflected distinct processes and student actions. On one side of the continuum the general academic program served mostly U.S.-born Mexican American students. This academic niche corresponded to the lowest academic status on campus and mediated marginalization, pessimism, low achievement, and racial divisions.[8] On the other side of the continuum, academic programs like the Graphics Academy and AP catered to high-achieving immigrant and first-generation youth and provided rigorous academic training. The Latino students in these programs had a higher sense of anxiety and alienation from the general school body. Thus, they benefited from strong social scaffolding processes, but were at odds with themselves and with others around them. Nevertheless, these Latinos managed to succeed and were eager to conform to school processes.

Interspersed along this continuum were other high-achieving Latino youth, both immigrant and U.S.-born, who were both critical of the opportunity structure and academically successful. Their ideologies reflected direct knowledge of the institutional mechanisms at play, and their behavior closely resembled the "accommodation without assimilation" strategy suggested in previous studies on successful involuntary minorities (Gibson, 1988; Mehan et al., 1994, 1996). Accommodation without assimilation refers to minority students navigating between distinct cultural worlds, such as the home, community, and schools, but consciously assuming their native cultural point of reference. Baldwin's Medical Academy, in particular, attempted to enhance cultural awareness, promote racial diversity, create community, construct school success, and, in general, circumvent institutionalized inequality.

General School Program

> Mexicans at this school have like a 5 percent chance of graduating,
> man — no higher, and I'm not part of that 5 percent.
> Miguel, third-generation Mexican American sophomore

Baldwin High School strove to educate all students equally. The school envisioned a united community of educators that would enhance the motivation and expectations of urban youth. The Baldwin High vision statement in 1996 read:

> All members of the [Baldwin] community will work cooperatively, communicate respectfully in a peaceful, safe, and clean environment.

> All [Baldwin] students will strive to achieve high expectations, meet solid academic standards, and have equal access to an enriching curriculum that will enable them to reach their highest potential.

> All [Baldwin] students will graduate with transferable skills in academic, vocational, and social development for quality jobs, college, or career education.

Regrettably, the school fell short of its vision, especially in creating a larger sense of community and in equally educating all students.

Students in the general academic program did not benefit from these strong social and academic institutional mechanisms that promote school success (Mehan et al., 1996). Among these students were the majority of self-identified Chicanos at Baldwin High School. They were not enrolled in any alternative academic structure at school, nor did they express confident ideologies about school success. Instead, these students were enrolled in the lower-level track where they received little support from teachers and peers. These students were mostly third-generation Mexican Americans who hung out with their "homeboys" and "homegirls," smoking by the gym during lunch and after school. Several students in both the general track and in other academic programs reported that many of these Latinos may also have been involved in youth gangs. Interviews and observations suggest that these students found school boring and disengaging, and they cut classes because, as Blanca, a third-generation Chicana in the general track, explained, "there ain't nothing else to do." Most of them attributed their lack of academic motivation and achievement to their marginalized status and lack of guidance from adults and other students.

This group of Latino students was relegated to a position of invisibility within the larger high school setting. Most of these students felt that teachers and counselors only cared for the academic concerns of Black and Asian students. Marisa, a third-generation Mexican American student, stated that Latinos were treated differently from the rest of the students because teachers "think we're all the same, they think we don't exist." Jorge, an immigrant Mexican American student, shared this sentiment and explained that the school counselors did not care for his concerns:

> I don't think they care because I have been filling out slips to go see my counselor. I sent like four from September and they still have not called me. Every time

I go there, he's at lunch or is with other students and during class he has no time for me.

They also reported that other Latino students in the college preparatory programs on campus ignored their presence. "We see other Latinos around," said Bella, a third-generation Mexican American, "but they don't talk to us. Even the *recién llegados* [recent immigrants] stay away." Bella suggested that the recent Mexican immigrants were motivated to succeed in the United States and that these students viewed the Mexican Americans in the general program as unmotivated and undesirable peers.

The Mexican American students in the general program did have career goals and expectations, but they did not experience the social scaffolding available in the other school programs. For instance, data reveal that these students did not experience the unique peer group effect, the advising, a high-achieving setting, a homeroom system, more positive racial and ethnic relations, administrative support, and curricular focus available in the more demanding programs. These students were given little guidance and support from what Stanton-Salazar (1997, 2001; see also Stanton-Salazar & Dornbusch, 1995) calls key "institutional agents," such as peers and adult staff members. During interviews and informal conversations, some expressed interest in becoming computer technicians, nurses, doctors, astronauts, and small-business owners, but they did not know how to achieve these goals. Miguel, for example, wanted to eventually marry, have children, and run a small business. "I have lots of goals," Miguel explains. "I want to be a lot of people and do lots of things. . . . I want to have my own shop, like a high-performance shop dealing with engines. I know a lot about that." However, he articulated his awareness of the limitations schooling and society impose upon Latinos, believing that these obstacles would likely impede him from achieving his goals. "I have no support, man, no way of doing it."

These students had few positive role models to whom they could turn for help. They understood the importance of positive peer relationships and caring teachers in the schooling process but had little experience of either. Jorge, for example, stated that if he had had the positive influence of friends to push him, perhaps he would have done well. Miguel agreed with Jorge's opinion and explained that "good teachers and good school programs could help." Although there were plenty of good programs and teachers at Baldwin, these Latino students did not feel they had access to them. Their sense of alienation and invisibility translated into a lack of motivation, failure to plan for college, and pessimism about lifelong career goals (Conchas, 1999).

Graphics Academy and Advanced Placement Program

The Graphics Academy was a school-within-a-school magnet program specializing in computer-assisted graphics technology. This program had a reputation for catering to students with strong math and science backgrounds. Its aim was to prepare students to succeed in college and to pursue careers in computer technology. During their three years in the Graphics Academy, students took a variety of classes in physics, calculus, and chemistry, and in the summer following their junior year they participated in paid internships linked to their studies.

The Graphics Academy enrollment was about 127 during the two years of this study. Not surprisingly, enrollment was nearly two-thirds male (63%), reflecting a broader pattern in the United States of female under-enrollment in math and science. Although the academy's ethnic profile did not reflect the Baldwin student population, it did so more closely than the Advanced Placement program. During the 1996–1997 school year, enrollment in the Graphics Academy was 56 percent Asian, 26 percent Black, 10 percent Latino, and 8 percent White. Occasionally, program recruitment took place at other schools in the district, but at the time of this study, most students were recruits from Baldwin's ninth-grade AP track. The director hoped to keep enrollment as low as 150 to better serve the students in the future.

Graphics Academy students' experienced high levels of success. School records indicate that the Graphics Academy had a 100 percent graduation rate during the 1996–1997 school year, and nearly all graduates enrolled in top four-year universities. A majority of students in this academy also participated in the AP program.

Also geared toward high-achieving youth, the AP program began in the mid-1980s. The goal was to bring the instructional quality available in privileged private schools into an urban public school setting. The courses set rigorous reading, writing, and discussion standards. The Socratic method was the major pedagogical strategy, for the lead teachers felt this method prepared students better for college through class participation and discussion. AP classes were offered to tenth through twelfth graders in the humanities and social sciences, including world cultures; American, English, and world literature; political theory and U.S. government. A ninth-grade feeder course linked with the AP track, California history/literature, was also added. All of the courses in both the ninth-grade block and the AP program were classified as AP and/or Honors. There were also Advanced College Prep (ACP), junior history, and English classes for students who had been dropped from AP. The ACP tag carried no college credit significance, but guaranteed that these students would not be in class with the general school population.

The AP program also did not reflect the racial and ethnic composition of the high school. During the 1997–1998 school year, sixty-four students were enrolled in the AP program. Of them, 66 percent were Asian, 14 percent were White, 16 percent were African American, and 4 percent were Latino. Interestingly, most of the White and middle-class African American students at Baldwin were enrolled in this program.

AP students were required to take advanced placement examinations in history, government, and English. According to district data, AP students at Baldwin consistently scored above the national average on these exams and three times as many students scored a three or higher out of a five-point rating system than at the more affluent high schools in the district. In addition, many of the students enrolled in top four-year universities with twenty advanced place-ment units — that is, the equivalent of twenty college course units. School re-cords show that the majority of the AP students enrolled in four-year public universities as well as elite private colleges.

AP Program and Graphics Academy Student Responses

Latinos in the AP program and in the Graphics Academy were part of a very small and exclusive peer group of high achievers. In the eleventh and twelfth grades combined, there were three Latinos in the AP track and thirteen in the Graphics Academy, mostly immigrants, during the 1996–1997 academic year. The three Latino students enrolled in the AP classes were also in the Graphics Academy.

Teachers, administrators, and students perceived the two programs as the most rigorous and intellectually challenging structures in the school. School data revealed that both maintained a 100 percent graduation and college ac-ceptance rate. Students from these programs were accepted at Stanford Uni-versity, the University of California at Berkeley, Harvard, and Yale.

These thirteen Latinos were caught in an interesting paradox. While they were placed at a high academic level in school and were projected to enroll in top colleges, they marginalized themselves not only from the rest of the school but also from other youth in their program. These students were high-ly stressed as they strove to achieve academic excellence. Data from this study revealed high levels of Latino student alienation and depression within these two programs.

Unfortunately, the social bonds among the Latino students were fragment-ed. These Latino students made little effort to form relationships with other Latino students in other academic communities, in part because they felt that others did not share similar values. They exclusively befriended other high achievers who were predominantly Asian and White. Bill, an AP Chicano, for example, had no intention of congregating with other Latinos. He explained that his friends were "mostly Asian students because they are more [his] type, . . . unlike . . . the guys that hang out by the gym, . . . never go to class, have low grades, and tend to be different." Latinos in this setting simply had little desire to associate with students at the bottom of the academic track whether they were Latino or not. An AP student, a female immigrant from Peru, said, "I don't associate with those other Latinos because . . . they belong to this gang or that gang and they don't even go to class. I mean, they bring their mess to our school, they bring their mess to our learning environment."

Some students explained their isolation in terms of a structural phenom-enon. Ricardo, a Mexican immigrant, for instance, asserted that he had no choice with regard to peer relationships because "mostly all are Asians" in his academic program. The choice to form relationships with other Latinos was unavailable because this student community was separated from the rest of the Latino and general school culture through ability grouping within a distinct academic enclave. They also were physically located on another section of the campus and had minimal contact with the general high school environment.

While these two programs facilitated peer bonding through small class size, curricular focus, and strong teacher relationships, the demands placed on students resulted in social divisions. The AP program and Graphics Academy provided high academic standards for young intellectuals, but success came at a price. Students and teachers explained that the competitive spirit among the students resulted in extreme isolation and unhealthy relationships among Latino students. Some students resorted to creative strategies, such as cheating, to elevate their academic standing and simply pass. Several students divulged during interviews that some of their peers cheated to survive in a course. Rocío had this to say on this issue:

> *Rocío:* The Advanced Placement is kinda intimidating, pretty intimidating. I noticed that a lot of my friends . . . cheat and they still make good grades. It is so hard and stressful that a lot had to cheat. You know, . . . they got better grades while cheating . . . and [they were] praised for it.
> *GC:* Do students work together?
> *Rocío:* No, not really. . . . Students there did not because they had to prove that they are the most brilliant and don't need help. Yeah, it was really competitive. . . . In Advanced Placement you are striving to be the best for the teacher's attention. . . . If you are not putting your neck out there . . . you will not get noticed, you will just get passed by.

While Asian students at times assisted other Asian students who needed extra help, the few Blacks and Latinos fended for themselves. Other student interviews and observations confirmed that Asian students worked more closely with one another than with other racial groups. Flor, an AP third-generation Mexican American, had no problem with this arrangement and explained that it did no good to be in a top program if you were not going to be aggressive: "If you're not aggressive about doing good, then, oh well, you are not going to be the best." Thus, Flor felt that the most aggressive students did the best, irrespective of race and ethnic divisions.

The Latino students in these two programs conformed to the school processes and demonstrated competitive values that they believed led to academic success. Fordham and Ogbu (1986) argue that minority students believe that social mobility is possible with the adaptation of majority cultural traits that result in the burden of acting White. This requires successful minority students to resist developing a critical consciousness of the opportunity structure in favor of adaptation. The high-achieving Latino students in both the Graphics Academy and AP program acknowledged the need to repress their perceptions of inequality in favor of conformity and school success. "Oh my God," Rocío expresses, "me be in regular English? Forget that. That does not look good. What would that look like? I want to be tagged the best. The other programs are seen . . . as easy, that's why I'm in Advanced Placement." Despite feelings of isolation, competition, and racial and ethnic divisions, these Latino students adapted to these school processes in order to succeed.

These Latino students put themselves through this ordeal because they wanted to show everyone that they could "make it" in the most difficult of academic settings. These students felt a sense of academic pride in being in these two programs, but at a major social cost: stress and isolation. Ramon, a second-generation Chicano, affirmed that by being in the AP program he felt "damn proud, like [he was] actually someone in the school." However, he was quick to point out that the whole situation was unhealthy because "you're always trying . . . to catch up . . . and always comparing yourself to others. I always feel depressed."

Medical Academy

> That's the sort of magic that goes on inside the [Medical] Academy, the flag-ship of the . . . School District's eight high schools within a high school. Teachers ramble off personal incidents about their students' lives, students tell of working harder than they ever have and getting support from their teachers.
>
> ("'Disenchanted' Students," 1992)

Baldwin High School's Medical Academy, the first in the city, began in 1985 as an experimental program bridging classroom lessons with real-life experience. Since its inception, its focus has been to serve the district's many students who are likely to drop out of high school. One Baldwin English teacher designed and implemented the program, spending countless hours responding to the critical need to increase the number of inner-city students pursuing careers in the fields of health, medicine, life sciences, and biotechnology. According to a Medical Academy pamphlet,

> The goal of the Academy has been to capture the interest of students in health and bioscience careers and to provide students with the breadth and depth of educational experiences needed to be well prepared for high quality health/bioscience careers, for post secondary education, and for active (and healthy) citizenship.

The Medical Academy enrolled 267 students during the 1996–1997 academic year. Student composition more closely reflected the racial makeup of the overall Baldwin student community than did the Graphics Academy and AP program: 54 percent of the enrollees were African American, 32 percent were Asian, 10 percent were Latino, 2.5 percent were White, and 1.5 percent were Filipino. According to Medical Academy staff and research report evaluations, the academy's student body has historically been over 60 percent female.

Medical Academy students took interrelated academic and lab classes during 80 percent of their school day for three or four years. They typically joined the program in the ninth or tenth grade. The Medical Academy relied heavily on team teaching to link the curriculum along interdisciplinary lines. As the pamphlet explains, academy students participated in related "worksite learning, which includes volunteer experience, career explorations, clinical rotations, summer and senior year internships, career portfolios, senior projects, demonstrations of mastery, etc."

Although not the first to combine education with work, the Baldwin Medical Academy earned recognition as a national model (Stern et al., 1992). In

1995, a local newspaper wrote that "the [Medical] Academy was a leader in an apprenticeship movement long before then Labor Secretary Robert Reich recently declared it 'a success story we would like to replicate across the nation'" ("[Baldwin] Leads the Way," 1995). Capturing the sense of community that developed from the Medical Academy is at the heart of what school reformers seek to emulate.

Medical Academy teachers nurtured their students in many facets of school life, not only in the linkage between school and work. Every teacher knew each student by name. Teachers met regularly to devise better ways of improving individual student success. The program provided career mentors and postsecondary student coaches. Frequent contact was made between school and home, and there were tutors and workshop support services available. Further, a Student Peer Educator program helped link the academy students with other students, faculty, community members, and parents. Throughout the school year, special social and award activities highlighted the program's success and promoted the sense of community. Unlike large, comprehensive high schools in which students may feel like mere numbers, the academy sought to treat each student as an important and valuable individual. A very close sense of community seemed to result from being in the academy. Many academy students and teachers described the academy as a "family."

The graduating class of 1998 was remarkably successful, considering that many of the students enrolled as "at risk": 93 percent graduated, and the remaining 7 percent left the school district or enrolled in another high school. Of the graduates, 91 percent enrolled in college — 72 percent in four-year universities and 19 percent in two-year community colleges. Two students chose not to attend college: an Asian male decided to pursue a military career and a Latina decided to work to help her family financially.

Medical Academy Student Responses

Medical Academy students participated in a thriving school-within-a-school program where supportive institutional processes existed throughout.[9] These students felt close bonds with one another and their teachers, and they also formed relationships with non-Latino youth. As Diego passionately explained, "We are like a family. We know each other well and get along." The Medical Academy functioned differently from the Graphics Academy and AP program in eliciting student engagement. While the other two programs engendered competition, the Medical Academy built a sense of community among its students.

The Medical Academy also provided common visions and goals for the Latino youth. Latino students in the Medical Academy supported one another as they strove to succeed academically. Ana, a second-generation Chicana, reported that "the Medical Academy is like a community of a group of people that are working together . . . and if one is not doing good, the other helps . . . to make it better, to make everything better." Marisol, a Mexican immigrant, expressed similar feelings of affinity and emphasized that students united to meet common goals as future medical professionals: "We are like a community, because in the Medical Academy, they are always telling us to work together and more things are going on for us to unite. We help each other to fulfill our goals in school and go into health [professions]."

Latino students actively engaged in their schooling and worked toward careers in the medical profession. Juan, an immigrant from El Salvador, declared, "*Claro* [of course], we all help each other. *Todos queremos hacer bien* [We all want to do good]. We want to be in health." These students linked their career goals with what they saw around them on a daily basis; that is, they often witnessed and experienced poverty in their neighborhoods and acknowledged the great need for health care for their immediate families and those around them. Consider these statements by Latino students in the program:

> *GC:* Why did you choose the medical career?
> *Diego:* I want to help other people. It's because what I see around me. I've seen how in many cases Latinos don't have as much access to health care. That's one of my priorities. Not just becoming a doctor and forgetting about it, but thinking about my community. I have also spent a lot of time in the hospital so I understand what people go through. I think I can relate to people in need.
>
> . . . . .
>
> *GC:* Ana, what plans do you have for the future?
> *Ana:* I plan to be a pediatrician too, because I like to work with little kids. I have a lot of cousins and I've seen many people that are really in need of health care. Many children are sick . . . and the parents say, "Oh, we can't do that, we can't do that, we have no money." I see this all around me. I want to help, not because of money for me, but for helping kids out. To me money does not matter, it will matter to survive, but not to be happy.

The cultural and institutional mechanisms in the Medical Academy supported students' positive vision to do well in school and further enhanced Latino youths' desire to become health professionals. Table 3, modified from Stern et al. (1998), summarizes the key institutional practices that the Medical Academy students reacted and responded to.

Latino students were exposed to various careers in health through field trips, internships, and having mentors in the medical field. Ana, for example, explains that they "get to experience the different careers in health, have mentors, and have more real goals because we see it and they bring it to us." Monica, a second-generation Mexican American, similarly linked her desire to become a doctor with her personal and academic experiences:

> This past summer I interned with Children's Hospital . . . and I had the opportunity to see many things and learn about what went on around the hospital. It is sad how so many children need the help of others and how few people there are to help them. I thought so many times of a way that I could be of service to the children.

The same was true for Marisol, who shared that her summer internship experience led her to firm up her goal to become a medical doctor:

> During the summer of 1997, I had the honor of being a health intern in a well-known . . . medical hospital. I worked side by side with real doctors. This has forever inspired and encouraged me to pursue my lifelong career choice. . . . I observed the many doctors' professional expertise as they had to make vital life-saving decisions. Regrettably, I even witnessed a death while I was an intern in the emergency room. I have a strong academic background in science, and most importantly, I have hands-on experience in the world of health.

Marisol explained that the Medical Academy's science curriculum coupled with her internship experience in an emergency room gave her a solid foundation to pursue her career goal. In sum, the Medical Academy structured the opportunity for Latinos to experience real-life health professions while they were in high school by incorporating paid internships into the formal curriculum. These institutional mechanisms greatly affected Latino students' perceptions about the opportunity structure, which led to more optimism. Medical Academy Latino students did not only aspire to become professionals, they also expected to realize their college and career goals.

Additionally, the Medical Academy community instilled principles of inclusion and teamwork within students as a way for them to form relationships. Competition was experienced as "healthy." "We are always happy for other students who do well and we help one another out," stated Diego, "but, there is some healthy competition." Diego defined "healthy competition" as a form of competition that

> pushes you to work harder. It is not the kind of competition that makes you say, "Oh well, I'm the worst student and so and so always has the answer." And teachers encourage us to work in teams. . . . Like, I'm not worried about getting the best grades. I'm worried about getting good grades.

Latino students in the Medical Academy were encouraged to work in teams and help each other in times of need. This form of peer relationships often resulted in higher levels of academic success.

Veronica, a Chicana sophomore, also shared the view that she belonged to a community of learners who supported rather than competed with each other for the best grades. She said that "sometimes . . . students will be clapping for you, making big ol' sounds when you do good in class. . . . They're like, 'Oh good.'" Latino students reported a strong and supportive academic program and participated in a high-achieving peer group.

Most significantly, Latino students explained that the Medical Academy's racial and ethnic composition differed from the school's other special academic programs in that it was the only one that reflected the composition of the school as a whole. Juan stated that "in the Medical Academy everybody is in there. The largest group was African Americans, then Asian, then Latino, then a few White. The school looked like that. The Medical Academy looks like the school." While the numbers did not match exactly, the Medical Academy more or less paralleled the larger high school's race and ethnic composition.

Latino students in the Medical Academy reported that the racial and ethnic diversity of the program encouraged intergroup contact. Latino students became friends, colleagues, and, in many cases, the boyfriends or girlfriends

TABLE 3

The Medical Academy and Institutional and Cultural Processes

Small Learning Community	College-Prep, Career-Related Curriculum	Partnerships with Employers, Community, and Higher Ed.
Academy-only classes for 2-4 years	College-entrance academic classes	Steering committee to govern academy
Team of teacher-managers	Broadly defined career class	Parental involvement, support
Limited, voluntary enrollment	Contextual, applied, integrated curriculum	Business and community speakers, role models
Family-like atmosphere	Common teacher planning time	Field trips, job shadowing
Administrator and counselor support	Project-based learning	Mentor program
Other courses and activities outside the academy	College and career planning, articulation	Workplace internships, community service
School-within-school	Multicultural pedagogy	Articulation with post-secondary education

of individuals of different racial and ethnic backgrounds. The majority of the Latinos in the program credited the academy's diversity with debunking preconceived notions about other racial and ethnic groups. The Medical Academy took the initial step in forging racial and ethnic integration and breaking down segregation within the school. In addition, the curriculum and pedagogy reflected the various social and historical experiences of the student body. The following student comments on the issue of racial integration showed this clearly. We begin with Laura, a second-generation Mexican American:

> *Laura:* I guess I feel more comfortable talking to *Morenos* [African Americans]. Like, if you have regular classes . . . it's not easy to meet people, and then you can't have a friendship with them. At the academy, you have the same people in all your classes, so you get to talk to them more and become friends.
> *Marisol:* You know, also stereotypes we might have had are not true because we get to know people better. I don't look at Black people the same way. We have common goals.
> *Ana:* We change our thoughts and get to know people better.
> *GC:* Is this positive for students to get to know people who are different from them?
> *Diego:* Little by little people begin to change. Stereotypes begin to change.
> *Juan:* That's their strategy, *la meta* [the goal] — *trabajar con los demás, y no solo con tu propia raza* [to work with others and not just your own race].

Unlike the high-achieving Latino students in the Graphics Academy and AP program who did not seem preoccupied with racial and ethnic integration, Medical Academy students were cognizant of the changes occurring within themselves concerning racial and ethnic stereotypes. The strong social relationships that students formed, coupled with the program's institutional mechanisms, were strong mediating forces against the larger racialization in school and in society. Perhaps in the world of work or in the university setting these Latino students would be better able to work with individuals of different cultural backgrounds as a result of being in the Medical Academy. While these students acknowledged racial and ethnic differences, they worked together as a team for a common academic goal despite the differences. These students were fully aware of the racial and ethnic hierarchy at their school and simultaneously created and benefited from their own safe space (see Fine, Weis, & Powell, 1997).

Latino Medical Academy students affirmed that they expected to become medical professionals despite the racial, class, and gender obstacles they would confront all along the way. They did not suppress their critical consciousness in favor of academic success. The students in the Medical Academy continued to view a limited opportunity structure, but they remained optimistic. For example, the Latino young men acknowledged that race and class might affect their career expectations. "I'm sure I'll find racism and financial difficulty," declared Diego, "but race is no excuse though." Juan, who wanted to be a psychologist, and David, who wanted to be a doctor, also believed that race and class could impact their lives in one way or another. These students affirmed a strong determination to succeed through hard work, but they also suggested the importance of the academy structure.

These issues also relate to Latino students' expectations about attaining a professional career. Although many minority students had future aspirations, these students expected to realize them despite structural constraints. Asked about whether they would be practicing medicine in twenty years, Juan replied:

> *Sí* [Yes]. I know and I want to do this. The only thing I can say is that I will put everything possible to do it. No obstacles for me but myself. *Porque soy latino no es obstáculo* [Being Latino is no obstacle]. *Más difícil por ser pobre y latino, pero si puedo* [It is more difficult being poor and Latino, but I can do it]. *Pero ser latino será más difícil aquí* [But being Latino here will be more difficult].

As an immigrant from Central America, Juan realized that his class status might have affected him more than his race in his home country. He predicted, however, that in the United States being Latino would be the most difficult challenge to his life aspirations. David agreed that race and class are significant obstacles he must overcome in his journey to become a medical doctor:

> I want to be a doctor too. Not sure what kind, but I do. School will help and it's the only way to do it. I really believe this, and the Medical Academy is helping me. I expect to become a doctor. Nothing will stop me. Race might affect, but it will not stop me. Money too, but I'll work harder.

David viewed the interaction between race and class as a difficult barrier, but he fully expected to achieve his goals. If money became an issue, he stated, then he would simply have to work harder. For these Latino youth, it was difficult to separate issues of class and race, for they were critically aware of the impact both had and would continue to have in their lives. The same was true for the Latinas, who must also wrestle with sexism in society.

The majority of the Latina students also intended to be medical doctors. They felt that the Medical Academy (and education in general) would help them get into college and into medical school. However, they were acutely aware of racism, sexism, and classism in U.S. society. They understood that as Latinas they were stigmatized by not only their race and class, but by gender as well. For instance, Ana reported that "racism, money, and being a woman . . . is a lot of pressure." Similarly, María, a Chicana junior, affirmed that "being a Latina . . . makes it . . . really hard to accomplish your goals because of stereotypes of Latinas." On the other hand, Marisol explained that "being a woman is not as much as an obstacle as . . . being Mexican. Money too will be an obstacle, but racism because of being Mexican is the hardest. I can't erase being Mexican and what people think."

These young Latinas did not separate their racial and ethnic identity from their gender identity. As poor, racialized minorities and women, they did not distinguish among these three spheres of oppression. Juana, a second-generation Mexican American, eloquently explained that she could not decipher different forms of oppression and how each related to her experiences as a Latina because she was "all three."

Although these Latina students were aware of both the structural and the ideological influences in society, they were determined to become health professionals. These were articulate, critical, ambitious, and optimistic young women. Both Latinos and Latinas in the Medical Academy foresaw many challenges in their lives, but they were determined to achieve their goals. These Latino students were by all measures successful, and they managed to be critical of, yet not deterred by, the opportunity structure.

Discussion and Conclusion

This study suggests that institutional support systems, in relationship to cultural processes, have an impact on the daily lives of low- and high-achieving poor Latino students. In particular, immigrant and U.S.-born Latinos experienced distinct school structures that mediated school engagement and success. Latino students responded to institutional actions, and institutional actors responded to Latino students in distinct ways. Students became active agents in the creation of school success as they interacted with school structures and cultures. This simultaneous interplay of structure, culture, and agency was the proximate source of engagement and school success.

The structure of each of Baldwin High's special academic programs provided opportunities for Latino students to attach themselves to school and develop academically oriented forms of agency. This was possible for the Latino students in the Medical Academy, Graphics Academy, and AP program, whereas the students in the general program did not interact with academy structures at all. However, it was not just the structure that determined student experiences. As explained here, the culture of each program was also important in determining how students interacted with each other and how they viewed academic success. In sum, structure and culture are both in active interplay with student agency.

Many Latino students' actions in relationship to school structures reified failure while others navigated borders and achieved school success. The Latino students in the general program, for instance, represented the majority of the "invisible" students at Baldwin High School who shared in the weakest institutional processes and experienced lack of support from peers and teachers, low expectations, and low achievement. These students represented Chicanos as involuntary minorities who were not optimistic about their future and did not perceive schooling as important, while their Mexican immigrant counterparts embraced expectations of success. Suárez-Orozco and Suárez-Orozco (1995) explained the interesting paradox in motivation between recent Mexican immigrants and U.S.-born Mexican Americans as a function of racial and ethnic stratification in schooling. The general program students were predominantly second- and third-generation Mexican Americans whose experiences confirmed this finding and, in effect, produced and reproduced school failure (Ogbu & Matute-Bianchi, 1986; Obgu, 1987, 1989). This academic niche did not help to dismantle the negative effects of school inequality.

On the other hand, the Latino students in the Graphics Academy and AP program were the invisible students who were by all accounts doing exceptionally well academically. They were, however, highly stressed and mentally and physically alienated from the rest of the Latino students and the larger high school in general. Moreover, they were further marginalized within their own peer group in the two programs as they attempted to outdo one another. These students accommodated to school norms as a means of attaining academic success.

In contrast, the Medical Academy structured a positive learning environment that began to bind all its students and teachers across race, gender, and class. Most students in this academy strove toward a common goal and helped one another in the process. The cultural and institutional processes in the program were based on common visions and goals, difference, and cooperation among teachers and students. This combination of principles began to foster healthier and better integrated racial and ethnic relations, at least among students in the Medical Academy, that led to greater student optimism. This new racial formation promoted a stronger sense of social belonging and academic success for Latinos involved in the academy. This program's building of strong support mechanisms was the bridge that linked racial and ethnic minority youth with adults and other high-achieving peers, which was necessary for educational mobility (Stanton-Salazar, 1997, 2001). These students, both immigrant and U.S.-born, were successful and remained optimistic in spite of their critical consciousness of social inequality.

In general, this case study of Latino students shows the diversity of experiences in a large comprehensive high school. It suggests that, while schools often replicate existing social and economic inequality present in the larger society and culture, they can also circumvent inequality if students and teachers work in consort toward academic success. The distinct Latino voices in this study demonstrate the importance of school communities that structure learning environments that link academic rigor with strong collaborative relationships among students and teachers. In addition, the varied experiences of the Latino students reveal the necessity of establishing strong links between racial and ethnic minority youth and the institutional support necessary for academic engagement and success. Most importantly, the study illustrates that supportive institutional and cultural processes in schools can play a significant role in the formation of high-achieving Latino students.

Notes

1. The term *Latino*, for the purposes of this study, refers to Chicana/o and/or Mexican American, Central American, and South American.
2. In California, career academies grew out of the need to retain potential dropouts and prepare students for postsecondary education (Stern, Dayton, & Raby, 1992). Career academies are schools-within-schools that offer a career-related academic curriculum to students in the tenth through twelfth grades. Sometimes ninth graders are included. The number of career academies has increased dramatically in recent years. Stern, Dayton, and Raby (1998) suggest two reasons: 1) academies improve student achievement and 2) research shows the design of career academies is "strongly congruent with the widely accepted principles of high school reform" (p. 2). While Stern et al. write that it is not possible to suggest a definitive career academy model because of the many variations among them, they do outline several key features fundamental to all academies: small learning communities, college-preparatory curriculum with a career theme, and partnerships with employers and community.
3. Baldwin High School and student and teacher names are all pseudonyms.
4. The descriptions of the programs and students at Baldwin are based on data gathered during the 1996–1997 and 1997–1998 school years. As part of the larger study, I interviewed eighty high school students to assess their responses to the various school cultures at Baldwin. I interviewed an equal number of boys and girls, including twenty-six Latinos, twenty-seven African Americans, and twenty-seven Asian American students. In addition, I conducted focus groups and interviews with a total of forty-five teachers, administrators, and staff. While my focus was on the Medical Academy teachers (n=7), I sought interviews with teachers who reflected the staff composition at Baldwin High (n=38). I interviewed the director of each academic program, as well as various teachers throughout the school setting.
5. Following Deal and Peterson (1999), this study defines school culture as "the underground stream of norms, values, beliefs, traditions, and rituals that has built up over time as people work together, solve problems, and confront challenges. This set of informal expectations and values shapes how people think, feel, and act in schools" (p. 28).
6. The different approaches to recruitment in the two career academies in this study reflect two very different educational philosophies. From its inception, the Medical Academy was committed to the belief that all students can achieve to high standards and made a special effort to include those students who were not already succeeding in a traditional education setting. The Graphics Academy began as an honors AP program and continued to target those students who were already high-achieving, especially those students with demonstrated success in mathematics. While the Medical Academy did accept high-achieving students, its primary target population included "high-potential" students (students who have not yet demonstrated their excellence.)
7. This finding is similar to one that Lee (1996) found in her study of race and ethnic relations in her ethnography of Asian American students in an urban high school.
8. Fine (1991) also observed similar findings among the dropouts in her ethnography. Fine argued that the dropouts in her study developed an in-depth critique of class, gen-

der, and race, in contrast to the high school graduates, who accepted notions of hard work and meritocracy. The low-achieving Latinos in this study exhibited some of the dropout traits suggested by Fine (1991), such as non-engagement, truancy, and low achievement, but related their sense of alienation and failure almost exclusively to the lack of institutional support systems.

9. It is important to point out that Medical Academy students self-select into the program. Stern et al. (1992) argue that if academy students self-select into an academy, one does not have a true assessment of engagement and achievement. They therefore suggest a more systematic study that controls for self-selectivity bias. The Medical Academy director argues against this as an indicator of success because she makes tremendous strides, along with the other teachers, to recruit the most needy at-risk youth. While some students self-select, the director suggests that many others were "seduced" through intense recruitment efforts on behalf of the academy staff and other students.

References

Anyon, J. (1997). *Ghetto schooling: A political economy of urban educational reform.* New York: Teachers College Press.

[Baldwin] leads the way in business-school teamwork. (1995). *City Tribune,* p. B6.

Conchas, G. Q. (1999). *Structuring educational opportunity: Variations in urban school success among racial minority youth.* Unpublished doctoral dissertation, University of Michigan, Ann Arbor.

Conchas, G. Q., & Clark, P. A. (2002). Career academies and urban minority schooling: Forging optimism despite limited opportunity. *Journal of Education for Students Placed at Risk, 7,* 287–311.

Deal, T., & Peterson, K. D. (1999). *Shaping school culture: The heart of leadership.* San Francisco: Jossey-Bass.

del Pinal, J., & Singer, A. (1997). *Generations of diversity: Latinos in the United States.* Washington, DC: Population Reference Bureau.

Diaz Salcedo, S. (1996). *Successful Latino students at the high school level: A case study of ten students.* Unpublished doctoral dissertation, Harvard Graduate School of Education.

"Disenchanted" students turned on to science classes. (1992). *City Tribune,* p. A14.

Fine, M. (1991). *Framing dropouts: Notes on the politics of an urban public high school.* Albany: State University of New York Press.

Fine, M., Weis, L., & Powell, L. C. (1997). Communities of difference: A critical look at desegregated spaces for and by youth. *Harvard Educational Review, 67,* 247–284.

Foley, D. E. (1990). *Learning capitalist culture: Deep in the heart of Texas.* Philadelphia: University of Pennsylvania Press.

Foley, D. E. (1991). Reconsidering anthropological explanations of ethnic school failure. *Anthropology & Education Quarterly, 22,* 60–86.

Fordham, S., & Ogbu, J. U. (1986). Black students' school success: Coping with the burden of "acting White." *Urban Review, 18,* 176–206.

Gándara, P. (1995). *Over the ivy walls: The educational mobility of low-income Chicanos.* Albany: State University of New York Press.

Gándara, P. (1999). Staying in the race: The challenge for Chicanos/as in higher education. In J. F. Moreno (Ed.), *The elusive quest for equality: 150 years of Chicano/Chicana education.* Cambridge, MA: Harvard Educational Review.

Gibson, M. A. (1988). *Accommodation without assimilation: Sikh immigrants in an American high school.* Ithaca, NY: Cornell University Press.

Gibson, M. A. (1997). Conclusion: Complicating the immigrant/involuntary minority typology. *Anthropology & Education Quarterly, 28,* 431–454.

Gibson, M. A., & Ogbu, J. U. (1991). *Minority status and schooling: A comparative study of immigrant and involuntary minorities.* New York: Garland.

Goyette, K. A., & Conchas, G. Q. (2002). Family and nonfamily roots of social capital among Vietnamese and Mexican American children. In B. Fuller & E. Hannum (Eds.), *Schooling and social capital in diverse cultures* (pp. 41–72). London: Elsevier Service.

Hubbard, L. (1995). *Academic achievement among minority students: The effects of institutional mechanisms and student ideology.* Unpublished doctoral dissertation, University of California at San Diego.

Lee, S. J. (1996). *Unraveling the "model minority" stereotype: Listening to Asian American youth.* New York: Teachers College Press.

Matute-Bianchi, M. E. (1986). Ethnic identities and patterns of school success and failure among Mexican-descent and Japanese-American students in a California high school. *American Journal of Education, 95,* 233–255.

Matute-Bianchi, M. E. (1991). Situational ethnicity and patterns of school performance among immigrant and nonimmigrant Mexican-descent students. In J. U. Ogbu & M. A. Gibson (Eds.), *Minority status and schooling* (pp. 205–247). New York: Garland.

McQuillan, P. J. (1998). *Educational opportunity in an urban high school: A cultural analysis.* Albany: State University of New York Press.

Mehan, H., Hubbard, L., & Villanueva, I. (1994). Forming academic identities: Accommodation without assimilation among involuntary minorities. *Anthropology & Education Quarterly, 25,* 91–117.

Mehan, H., Villanueva, I., Hubbard, L., & Lintz, A. (1996). *Constructing school success: The consequences of untracking low-achieving students.* Cambridge, Eng.: Cambridge University Press.

Ogbu, J. U. (1974). *The next generation: An ethnography of education in an urban neighborhood.* New York: Academic Press.

Ogbu, J. U. (1978). *Minority education and caste: The American system in cross cultural perspective.* New York: Academic Press.

Ogbu, J. U. (1987). Variability in minority school performance: A problem in search of an explanation. *Anthropology & Education Quarterly, 18,* 312–334.

Ogbu, J. U. (1989). The individual in collective adaptation: A framework for focusing on academic underperformance and dropping out among involuntary minorities. In L. Weis, E. Farrar, & H. G. Petrie (Eds.), *Dropouts from school* (pp. 181–204). Albany: State University of New York Press.

Ogbu, J. U. (1991). Involuntary minorities. In M. A. Gibson & J. U. Ogbu (Eds.), *Minority status and schooling* (pp. 3–22). New York: Garland.

Ogbu, J., & Matute-Bianchi, M. E. (1986). Understanding sociocultural factors: Knowledge, identity and school adjustment. In D. D. Holt (Ed.), *Beyond language: Social and cultural factors in schooling language minority students* (pp. 73–142). Sacramento: California State Department of Education, Bilingual Education Office.

Orfield, G. (1998). Commentary. In M. Suárez-Orozco (Ed.), *Crossings: Mexican immigration in interdisciplinary perspectives* (pp. 248–249). Cambridge, MA: Harvard University Press.

Portes, A., & Rumbaut, R. G. (1996). *Immigrant America* (2nd ed.). Berkeley: University of California Press.

Sánchez-Jankowski, M. (1991). *Islands in the street: Gangs and American urban society.* Berkeley: University of California Press.

Stanton-Salazar, R. (1997). A social capital framework for understanding the socialization of racial minority children and youths. *Harvard Educational Review, 67,* 1–40.

Stanton-Salazar, R. (2001). *Manufacturing hope and despair: The school and kin support networks of U.S.-Mexican youth.* New York: Teachers College Press.

Stanton-Salazar, R., & Dornbusch, S. M. (1995). Social capital and the social reproduction of inequality: The formation of informational networks among Mexican-origin high school students. *Sociology of Education, 68,* 116–135.

Stern, D., Dayton, C., & Raby, M. (1992). *Career academies: Partnerships for reconstructing American high schools.* San Francisco: Jossey-Bass.

Stern, D., Dayton, C., & Raby, M. (1998). *Career academies and high school reform.* Berkeley, CA: University of California at Berkeley, Career Academy Support Network.

Suárez-Orozco, C., & Suárez-Orozco, M. (1995). *Transformations: Migration, family life, and achievement motivation among Latino adolescents.* Stanford, CA: Stanford University Press.

Trueba, H. (1998). The education of Mexican immigrant children. In M. Suárez-Orozco (Ed.), *Crossings: Mexican immigration in interdisciplinary perspectives* (pp. 253–275). Cambridge, MA: Harvard University Press.

U.S. Bureau of the Census. (1996). *Current population reports.* Washington, DC: Department of Commerce, Economics and Statistics Administration.

U.S. Bureau of the Census. (2001). *The Hispanic population: Census 2000 brief.* Washington, DC: U.S. Department of Commerce, Economics and Statistics Administration.

Vernez, G., & Abrahamse, A. (1996). *How immigrants fare in U.S. education.* Santa Monica, CA: RAND.

Vigil, D. J. (1988). *Barrio gangs: Street life and identity in southern California.* Austin: University of Texas Press.

Vigil, D. J. (1997). *Personas Mexicanas: Chicano high schoolers in a changing Los Angeles.* Fort Worth: Harcourt Brace College.

Weis, L. (1990). *Working class without work: High school students in a de-industrialized economy.* New York: Routledge.

Student Social Class and Teacher Expectations

The Self-Fulfilling Prophecy in Ghetto Education

Author's Introduction

The Enduring Dilemmas of Class and Color
in American Education

When asked by the editors of the *Harvard Educational Review* to prepare this short note as the introduction to the reprint of my 1970 article, my first reaction was that it cannot already be thirty years since the publication of "Student Social Class and Teacher Expectations." But it is, and thus I offer these brief observations on three areas germane to this piece: the state of urban education then and now; the qualitative research methods used then and now, especially the "insider-outsider" issue of myself as a White person doing research in the African American community; and, finally, several personal reflections.

The State of Urban Education

Raising this issue with a thirty-year retrospective is almost to enter a time warp. So much of what was the reality of the education of Black youth thirty years ago is no different today. Urban schools so often did not do well by their charges then, and in many ways, they still do not do so. Schools are still facing many of the same issues now as they did then. It would not be misleading, to paraphrase an old cliché, to say that the more time passes, the more things stay the same.

Intersecting with the highly visible and flammable issues in urban education of violence, drugs, academic failure, and collapsing infrastructures are the twin pivots of class and color. When I titled the original article, I emphasized the matter of student social class. I did so because the classrooms, the school, and

Harvard Educational Review Vol. 70 No. 3 Fall 2000, 257–265

its neighborhood community in St. Louis at that time were of one ethnic/racial group — African American. What I had observed was that as color was held constant, the realities of the social-class differences became not only apparent but pivotal in the construction of reality. Indeed, there was such a strong fit between the social class of the students and their academic tracking that it was striking how powerful this variable was for understanding their present and future treatment within that school setting. And when I expanded the analysis into a book, I again emphasized the class dimension by entitling the book, *The Urban School: A Factory for Failure* (1973).

Let me be clear. I was not then arguing that class superceded color, but that they together created a powerful interaction. I had colleagues at the time who were adamant in their arguments that one or the other was preeminent. Any number of them posited that color overrode any considerations of class. Stated differently, racism was so pervasive and so powerful in defining the situation in the United States that it had to be recognized as the dominant reality in any study of African Americans. Conversely, any number of my sociological colleagues at the time believed that the most appropriate analysis was through a framework of social class. In their opinion, Karl Marx was correct, and the best understanding of the situation of Black Americans was to view them as an exploited internal colony.

In contrast to this either-or approach, I found in the school a reality where class interacted with color. Of course, racism was powerful and ever present — otherwise why would the city schools of St. Louis be so entirely segregated that all-Black and all-White schools were the norm? And how could it be that I was the only White person to ever enter into that school building week after week after week? But social-class differentiation was equally a reality. Poor students in that school received neither the rewards nor the attention that was granted to the few middle-class students. Why is it that one might expect African Americans, including the teachers studied, not to respond to many of the same social-class forces that influence the behaviors and values of other groups in the society, whether majority or minority? In a school world of segregation, racism, and isolation, the power of social class was still evident. As an analyst, I could not avoid addressing the presence of both and how each played off against or in concert with the other.

The geographical compression of the broader social-class structure of the Black community into a restricted set of residential areas meant that the opportunities back in the 1960s to create geographically dispersed communities based on social class were few to nonexistent. (Indeed, the level of residential segregation in St. Louis was among the highest in the country.) Whereas White communities could differentiate among themselves on matters of social class with all the space they needed in the suburbs (where communities calibrated themselves at $10,000 intervals), the Black communities had no such opportunities. Thus, like an accordion squeezed shut, the Black community found its social classes compressed in on one another. And while I have no comparative data on urban White schools, my suspicion would be that the social-class diversity within each White school was less than in Black schools; that is, that poor

White students were going to school predominately or exclusively with other poor White students.

There is an ironic twist to one aspect of the improvement in race relations in the United States over these past three decades. As the Black middle class has grown and suburban housing has opened up, the Black children remaining in the urban schools are now overwhelmingly poor. Thus, a kind of perverse equality has emerged between poor urban Whites, poor urban Blacks, and poor urban Hispanics — they are now each in schools populated by other poor students.

Parenthetically, I see this reality as having played for years into the issue of school integration, as it also does now with vouchers. The bottom line is that non-poor folks do not like to see their children going to school with poor children. One of the realities that cut deep into the issue of school integration was that it meant poor Black children were being brought into schools of non-poor Whites. Color and class then collided. This I documented in another of my ethnographic studies, where I studied how thirty Black children came each day on a bus to integrate a school of more than seven hundred White children (Rist, 1978). The voucher issue also has the underlying issues of color and class front and center, regardless of the rhetoric of market tests, choice, and breaking up monopolies. Vouchers imply mobility for poor children, most of whom are minorities. Why this concept continues to stall on the American political scene is not just a matter of costs or teacher and school board opposition, but because of the intruding realities of color and class.

The issue thirty years after my article is that there is scant evidence that the urban schools are now any better prepared or positioned to address issues of color and class. Poor children in general have a hard time making it through school. Poor children who are also minority children have an even tougher time making it through. These children are just not likely to ever find a seat at the American Feast. At this time in American society when wealth absolutely abounds and money sloshes around in staggering amounts, between 18 and 20 percent of all children are living in poverty. (The numbers for Black children and Hispanic children are 36 percent and 34 percent, respectively.) Indeed, on several key statistics of the well-being of American children, for example, infant mortality and the percentage of children living in households below 50 percent of the national median, to name but two, American children now lag behind children in many developing countries (Federal Interagency Forum on Child and Family Statistics, 2000). The sobering reality is that when it comes to both color and class, U.S. schools tend to conform much more to the contours of American society than they transform it. And this appears to be a lesson that we are not wanting to learn.

The Methodology of Studying in a Public School

There was, in the 1960s, something of an upstart movement of social scientists who thought that if one wanted to know the realities of the social problems in the United States, they had to be experienced and observed first hand. This was in contrast, at the time, to the predominant emphasis on large survey research projects, on quantitative analysis, and on deductive theory building. The quantitative/qualitative debate in the social sciences was just coming on the scene. Thus, Elliot Liebow studied homeless men in Washington, DC, Joyce Ladner studied large public housing projects in St. Louis, Carol Stack studied women struggling to subsist on welfare in Boston, Gerald Suttles studied the social order of a Chicago slum, and James Spradley studied skid row alcoholics in Seattle, to name but five classical studies. In all of these and many more, researchers used field-based methods derived from anthropology and sociology. The conventional and mainline funding organizations seldom supported such work, be they the National Science Foundation, the National Institutes of Health, or the foundations. Three federal agencies that did nurture such studies were the National Institute of Mental Health (NIMH), the Office of Economic Opportunity (OEO), which was to coordinate the "War on Poverty" under both presidents Kennedy and Johnson, and the Department of Health, Education, and Welfare (HEW).

The study of U.S. education was not overlooked by those wanting in-depth, qualitative assessments of the conditions of American children. There were a number of studies that addressed the intersection of poverty and education (both urban and rural), early childhood learning (linked to the creation and early years of Head Start), the education of minority groups, and the treatment of children in schools. Popular books like *Death at an Early Age* and *Up the Down Staircase* fueled an interest in learning more about the dynamics of what was happening to students, particularly those in urban schools. School systems were being portrayed as killers of the spirits of students, as completely succumbing to bureaucratic rules and regimens, and using teachers as agents of social control over the poor.

There was in all this qualitative work a slant toward an "underdog" approach. There was clearly sympathy with those whom the American system treated as marginal. Indeed, there was a not too subtle political agenda in all this as well, for it was to the benefit of the OEO, HEW, and the NIMH, for example, to fund studies that would document and portray American citizens as being locked out of economic opportunity, denied a fair chance for a decent life, and crushed under a burden of poverty. If the necessary political will was to be mobilized to address these issues, American society needed to know just how desperate the straits were for so many of their fellow citizens. It was, of course, also in the best political survival instincts of these federal agencies to document the breadth and depth of the problems they were mandated to address.

The research project that generated "Student Social Class and Teacher Expectations" was supported for three years with a grant from the HEW to Washington University in St. Louis. Jules Henry, a cultural anthropologist, was the study director. Three graduate students (myself being one) received funding to spend up to three years documenting the socialization of Black youth into the St. Louis public schools. All three of us were to begin with a group of children from their first day of kindergarten and follow them through the second grade. Each of us was to be in a different public elementary school, and given the emphasis on the study of minority youth, it turned out that each school had only Black children enrolled. (Again, this was not surprising, given the residential segregation patterns in St. Louis.) The other two graduate students were both women, one White and one Black.

From the beginning, Jules Henry directed the study according to an intensive field-based and observational/ethnographic methodology. The expectation was that there would be up to fifteen hours per week of field work, either in the school and classrooms or in the students' homes. We were to prepare elaborate and detailed field notes on each site visit and then subsequently code according to an evolving coding scheme that the team developed. No testing, no psychometric assessments, no formal surveys, and no quantitative classroom observation instruments were ever used. The study was entirely based on the systematic gathering of qualitative data via the observation of behavior in natural settings — classrooms, playgrounds, living rooms, a city park, etc.

What strikes me about this approach thirty years later is that it is still entirely appropriate, though there may now be a greater preference for multimethod strategies for the study design and the subsequent data collection and analysis. The methodological approach embedded in qualitative research has lost none of its appeal — and indeed is now more prevalent and legitimated than in the 1960s. Field-based work in applied social science areas such as evaluation, monitoring, and action research all now use qualitative approaches as basic tools of the trade.

But there is a question to ask and for which there is no real clear answer — could this same study be done today as it was then? There are a number of factors that leave me thinking it could not be done as it was. First, the gatekeeping function (within the public school system and within the university) was much more rudimentary then than it is now. There were no human subjects committees in the university at the time and there were no review committees in the school system for either the research protocol itself or for community acceptance. It is my recollection that Jules Henry needed only the permission of one assistant superintendent and the study was up and running. There was also, so far as I remember, no permission ever garnered from the students, their parents, the teachers, or any of the administrators in the school. We simply showed up the first day of school and were shown to a kindergarten classroom where we could begin our observations. This is not to say that the design of this project was flawed or that it abused those studied, but only that without any oversight or serious review, we did our study.

Second, there was the matter of the race of the graduate students doing the data collection and that of the principal investigator himself. Two of the three graduate students and Jules Henry were White. I will say only for myself that I never felt unwelcome in the school, at the PTA meetings, or when I joined the faculty volleyball team. (Indeed, during my third year at the school, I was asked if I would join the board of the PTA. I think it was because I had had perfect attendance for the past two years!) These types of activities (plus bringing donuts on Friday mornings for the faculty lounge) were part of building trust and rapport with the faculty over the three years of the study. It is quite simply one of the strengths of qualitative research that comes with time and effort. I am not sure what a White graduate student might find today in an all-Black elementary school. To say it simply, race relations today in the United States are more subtle and the overlay of social-class distinctions have blurred the codes of interaction. The result has been a real tenuousness in figuring out how to behave. How the question of being a racial "outsider" might play itself out at present is not clear to me. And related to the point above, I am not sure how a university review panel or a school district review panel might respond to this kind of racial mix on the study — that is, only one of the four researchers was African American. And I am hard pressed now to identify in the past few years ethnographic studies undertaken by Whites in Black urban schools that would help answer this question. But maybe the absence of such studies is itself the answer.

Finally, there is the matter of the political rhetoric and ideology now linked to such work. Regardless of the methodological strategy, the issue is one of the political lens through which such an urban school would be described by the author. Is there a political correctness to how one approaches the study of minority urban education? Does an "underdog" bias still exist? Would those who argue that only an "insider's" perspective is valid in the study of minority communities and institutions ever accept analysis done by an "outsider"? The questions can go on and on, but the point of the political lens is the core issue. The study thirty years ago took a rather straightforward, if somewhat optimistic, approach that urban schools were shortchanging their minority students and needed to do better. The question now is what message would (or could be allowed to) come from an ethnographic study of an inner-city school in a blighted neighborhood with a 100 percent minority student enrollment.

Some Final Observations

To return to the theme at the beginning of this note, the issues of color and class inequality in American society are at the heart of the future of U.S. education. The basic challenge is that there is a profound disconnect between the rhetoric and the reality of American society for those on the bottom rung of the economic ladder. While the rhetoric is that of opportunity (be it through education, training, trickle-down economic growth, urban revitalization, etc.), the reality for those in the lowest 20 percent quintile of economic resources is quite different. Indeed, those in this bottom 20 percent have in the past thirty years actually lost ground to the rest of the society. The schism is real. The stratification of the American underclass is now more permanent and pervasive than thirty years ago. Add to this the isolation from the centers of economic growth of those who are both poor and minority and the picture is not a pretty one. That the present presidential campaign is silent on the matter is to be expected. But the fact remains, this condition is being ignored to the peril of the country.

The implications for urban schools are not upbeat. Into the foreseeable future, these schools now face the challenge of educating literally hundreds of thousands of children who are in both real and relative terms extremely poor.

These children come into the schools each morning from poor surroundings and go back to them each afternoon. The ability of these schools to generate social and economic opportunities for this massive group of children when the rest of the social structure works to block their way onto the mobility escalator is simply quite limited. And never mind the growing digital divide (and is not this divide along color and class lines?) separating those with the access to and knowledge of these new ways of accumulating and managing information from those without.

Another issue facing urban schools that was emphasized in the original article, but not yet mentioned here, is that of the teachers — their quality, their longevity, and their intentions toward the poor. The question is straightforward: Who now wants to teach in urban schools and why? If it is now difficult to fill the teaching vacancies in the strong and wealthy suburban schools, how greater are the difficulties for the urban schools? Thirty years ago, teaching jobs in city schools were a sure means of middle-class stability and mobility for thousands of Black people. Indeed, the teachers college in St. Louis, Harris Teachers College, supplied Black professionals for the school system for decades. But now, those in the African American community who desire to be teachers are no longer restricted to looking only for positions in the city schools. The urban schools therefore no longer have a guaranteed work force of minority professionals. Thus the question of who comes to teach in urban classrooms.

The policy implications for the country in general and for urban districts in particular are multiple. Presuming that the United States can treat the present situation in urban schools with a business-as-usual mentality only leads to a continual downward spiral. Our strategies for urban schools and the teachers within them seem caught in a cul de sac. We go round and round with the same remedies and the situation does not improve. Defining schooling to involve entire families and their learning needs, continual training of the teachers, breaking the barriers on certification of teachers, opening facilities on an 18-hour-a-day, year-round basis, school/private sector partnerships that mean more than the private sector donating used computers, and true performance standards with real accountability are but a few propositions to consider that might start to send urban education in a new direction. Even these might be insufficient to the task at hand.

Finally, two personal comments: First, thirty years after publishing this article based on a qualitative design and methodology, I find myself more than ever convinced that the information that comes from this approach is vital to understanding the inner workings of American society, be it in board rooms or in classrooms. But while those with power and resources have access to the media and can shape perceptions to their own benefit, the same is not available to the poor. Thus, giving voice to those who are not often heard or seen is a distinct contribution of qualitative research. Their voice comes through unmuted by the aggregation of survey results and the unexplained variance in regression equations. Having a window into the actual lives and views of others, especially those who are not like one's self, can be a powerful means of conveying information and creating new awareness.

Second, and to some degree the other side of the coin, is my view that policy-makers truly need this kind of information and analysis. I have spent more than fifteen years in the U.S. government (both executive and legislative branches), and now almost four years in an international development bank. I have been taken aback time and again about how those in positions of authority think they "know" what poor and marginalized peoples believe/want/need. In reality, these decisionmakers so often did not have a clue. Without a means of giving voice to the poor and marginalized, decisions will be made that reflect nothing more than the perceptions and values of those making the decisions. Bringing the views and beliefs of those on the outside to those on the inside is no small feat. But to not hear the voices of the poor, to not legitimate the stake they have in their own future, and to incorrectly assume commonly shared realities is to ensure their peripheral status in American society.

References

Federal Interagency Forum on Child and Family Statistics. (2000). *America's children: Key national indicators of well-being, 2000.* Washington, DC: Author.

Rist, R. C. (1973). *The urban school: A factory for failure.* Cambridge, MA: MIT Press.

Rist, R. C. (1978). *The invisible children: School integration in American society.* Cambridge, MA: Harvard University Press.

The views expressed here are those of the author and no endorsement by the World Bank Group is intended or should be inferred.

Student Social Class and Teacher Expectations

The Self-Fulfilling Prophecy in Ghetto Education

A dominant aspect of the American ethos is that education is both a necessary and a desirable experience for all children. To that end, compulsory attendance at some type of educational institution is required of all youth until somewhere in the middle teens. Thus on any weekday during the school year, one can expect slightly over 35,000,000 young persons to be distributed among nearly 1,100,000 classrooms throughout the nation (Jackson, 1968).

There is nothing either new or startling in the statement that there exist gross variations in the educational experience of the children involved. The scope of analysis one utilizes in examining these educational variations will reveal different variables of importance. There appear to be at least three levels at which analysis is warranted. The first is a macro-analysis of structural relationships where governmental regulations, federal, state, and local tax support, and the presence or absence of organized political and religious pressure all affect the classroom experience. At this level, study of the policies and politics of the Board of Education within the community is also relevant. The milieu of a particular school appears to be the second area of analysis in which one may examine facilities, pupil-teacher ratios, racial and cultural composition of the faculty and students, community and parental involvement, faculty relationships, the role of the principal, supportive services such as medical care, speech therapy, and library facilities — all of which may have a direct impact on the quality as well as the quantity of education a child receives.

Analysis of an individual classroom and the activities and interactions of a specific group of children with a single teacher is the third level at which there may be profitable analysis of the variations in the educational experience. Such micro-analysis could seek to examine the social organization of the class, the development of norms governing interpersonal behavior, and the variety of roles that both the teacher and students assume. It is on this third level — that of the individual classroom — that this study will focus. Teacher-student relationships and the dynamics of interaction between the teacher and students are far from uniform. For any child within the classroom, variations in the experience of success or failure, praise or ridicule, freedom or control, creativity or docility, comprehension or mystification may ultimately have significance far beyond the boundaries of the classroom situation (Henry, 1955, 1959, 1963).

Harvard Educational Review Vol. 40 No. 3 August 1970, 411–451

It is the purpose of this paper to explore what is generally regarded as a crucial aspect of the classroom experience for the children involved — the process whereby expectations and social interactions give rise to the social organization of the class. There occurs within the classroom a social process whereby, out of a large group of children and an adult unknown to one another prior to the beginning of the school year, there emerge patterns of behavior, expectations of performance, and a mutually accepted stratification system delineating those doing well from those doing poorly. Of particular concern will be the relation of the teacher's expectations of potential academic performance to the social status of the student. Emphasis will be placed on the initial presuppositions of the teacher regarding the intellectual ability of certain groups of children and their consequences for the children's socialization into the school system. A major goal of this analysis is to ascertain the importance of the initial expectations of the teacher in relation to the child's chances for success or failure within the public school system. (For previous studies of the significance of student social status to variations in educational experience, see also Becker, 1953; Hollingshead, 1949; Lynd, 1937; Warner, Havighurst, & Loeb, 1944).

Increasingly, with the concern over intellectual growth of children and the long and close association that children experience with a series of teachers, attention is centering on the role of the teacher within the classroom (Sigel, 1969). A long series of studies have been conducted to determine what effects on children a teacher's values, beliefs, attitudes, and, most crucial to this analysis, a teacher's expectations may have. Asbell (1963), Becker (1952), Clark (1963), Gibson (1965), Harlem Youth Opportunities Unlimited (1964), Katz (1964), Kvaraceus (1965), MacKinnon (1962), Riessman (1962, 1965), Rose (1956), Rosenthal and Jacobson (1968), and Wilson (1963) have all noted that the teacher's expectations of a pupil's academic performance may, in fact, have a strong influence on the actual performance of that pupil. These authors have sought to validate a type of educational self-fulfilling prophecy: if the teacher expects high performance, she receives it, and vice versa. A major criticism that can be directed at much of the research is that although the studies may establish that a teacher has differential expectations and that these influence performance for various pupils, they have not elucidated either the basis upon which such differential expectations are formed or how they are directly manifested within the classroom milieu. It is a goal of this paper to provide an analysis both of the factors that are critical in the teacher's development of expectations for various groups of her pupils and of the process by which such expectations influence the classroom experience for the teacher and the students.

The basic position to be presented in this paper is that the development of expectations by the kindergarten teacher as to the differential academic potential and capability of any student was significantly determined by a series of subjectively interpreted attributes and characteristics of that student. The argument may be succinctly stated in five propositions. First, the kindergarten teacher possessed a roughly constructed "ideal type" as to what characteristics were necessary for any given student to achieve "success" both in the public school and in the larger society. These characteristics appeared to be, in significant part, related to social class criteria. Second, upon first meeting her students at the beginning of the school year, subjective evaluations were made of the students as to possession or absence of the desired traits necessary for anticipated "success." On the basis of the evaluation, the class was divided into groups expected to succeed (termed by the teacher "fast learners") and those anticipated to fail (termed "slow learners"). Third, differential treatment was accorded to the two groups in the classroom, with the group designated as "fast learners" receiving the majority of the teaching time, reward-directed behavior, and attention from the teacher. Those designated as "slow learners" were taught infrequently, subjected to more frequent control-oriented behavior, and received little if any supportive behavior from the teacher. Fourth, the interactional patterns between the teacher and the various groups in her class became rigidified, taking on caste-like characteristics, during the course of the school year, with the gap in completion of academic material between the two groups widening as the school year progressed. Fifth, a similar process occurred in later years of schooling, but the teachers no longer relied on subjectively interpreted data as the basis for ascertaining differences in students. Rather, they were able to utilize a variety of informational sources related to past performance as the basis for classroom grouping.

Though the position to be argued in this paper is based on a longitudinal study spanning two and one-half years with a single group of Black children, additional studies suggest that the grouping of children both between and within classrooms is a rather prevalent situation within American elementary classrooms. In a report released in 1961 by the National Education Association related to data collected during the 1958–1959 school year, an estimated 77.6 percent of urban school districts (cities with a population above 2500) indicated that they practiced between-classroom ability grouping in the elementary grades. In a national survey of elementary schools, Austin and Morrison (1963) found that "more than 80% reported that they 'always' or 'often' use readiness tests for pre-reading evaluation [in first grade]." These findings would suggest that within-classroom grouping may be an even more prevalent condition than between-classroom grouping. In evaluating data related to grouping within American elementary classrooms, Smith (1971) concludes, "Thus group assignment on the basis of measured 'ability' or 'readiness' is an accepted and widespread practice."

Two grouping studies which bear particular mention are those by Borg (1964) and Goldberg, Passow, and Justman (1966). Lawrence (1969) summarizes the import of these two studies as "the two most carefully designed and controlled studies done concerning ability grouping during the elementary years." Two school districts in Utah, adjacent to one another and closely comparable in size, served as the setting for the study conducted by Borg. One of the two districts employed random grouping of students, providing all students with "enrichment," while the second school district adopted a group system with acceleration mechanisms present which sought to adapt curricular materials to ability level and also to enable varying rates of presentation of materials. In summarizing Borg's findings, Lawrence states:

> In general, Borg concluded that the grouping patterns had no consistent, general effects on achievement at any level. . . . Ability grouping may have motivated bright pupils to realize their achievement potential more fully, but it seemed to have little effect on the slow or average pupils. (p. 1)

The second study by Goldberg, Passow, and Justman was conducted in the New York City Public Schools and represents the most comprehensive study to date on elementary school grouping. The findings in general show results similar to those of Borg indicating that narrowing the ability range within a classroom on some basis of academic potential will in itself do little to produce positive academic change. The most significant finding of the study is that "variability in achievement from classroom to classroom was generally greater than the variability resulting from grouping pattern or pupil ability" (Lawrence, 1969). Thus one may tentatively conclude that teacher differences were at least as crucial to academic performance as were the effects of pupil ability or methods of classroom grouping. The study, however, fails to investigate within-in-class grouping.

Related to the issue of within-class variability are the findings of the Coleman Report (1966) which have shown achievement highly correlated with individual social class. The strong correlation present in the first grade does not decrease during the elementary years, demonstrating, in a sense, that the schools are not able effectively to close the achievement gap initially resulting from student social class (pp. 290–325). What variation the Coleman Report does find in achievement in the elementary years results largely from within- rather than between-school variations. Given that the report demonstrates that important differences in achievement do not arise from variations in facilities, curriculum, or staff, it concludes:

> One implication stands out above all: That schools bring little influence to bear on a child's achievement that is independent of his background and general social context; and that this very lack of independent effect means that the inequalities imposed on children by their home, neighborhood, and peer environment are carried along to become the inequalities with which they confront adult life at the end of school. For equality of educational opportunity through the schools must imply a strong effect of schools that is independent of the child's immediate social environment, and that strong independent effect is not present in American Schools. (p. 325)

It is the goal of this study to describe the manner in which such "inequalities imposed on children" become manifest within an urban ghetto school and the resultant differential educational experience for children from dissimilar social class backgrounds.

Methodology

Data for this study were collected by means of twice weekly one and one-half hour observations of a single group of Black children in an urban ghetto school who began kindergarten in September of 1967. Formal observations were conducted throughout the year while the children were in kindergarten and again in 1969 when these same children were in the first half of their second-grade year. The children were also visited informally four times in the classroom during their first-grade year.[1] The difference between the formal and informal observations consisted in the fact that during formal visits, a continuous handwritten account was taken of classroom interaction and activity as it occurred. Smith and Geoffrey (1968) have labeled this method of classroom observation "microethnography." The informal observations did not include the taking of notes during the classroom visit, but comments were written after the visit. Additionally, a series of interviews were conducted with both the kindergarten and the second-grade teachers. No mechanical devices were utilized to record classroom activities or interviews.

I believe it is methodologically necessary, at this point, to clarify what benefits can be derived from the detailed analysis of a single group of children. The single most apparent weakness of the vast majority of studies of urban education is that they lack any longitudinal perspective. The complexities of the interactional processes which evolve over time within classrooms cannot be discerned with a single two- or three-hour observational period. Second, education is a social process that cannot be reduced to variations in IQ scores over a period of time. At best, IQ scores merely give indications of potential, not of process. Third, I do not believe that this school and the classrooms within it are atypical from others in urban Black neighborhoods (see also both the popular literature [Kohl, 1967; Kozol, 1967] and the academic literature [Eddy, 1967; Fuchs, 1969; Leacock, 1969; Moore, 1967] on urban schools). The school in which this study occurred was selected by the District Superintendent as one of five available to the research team. All five schools were visited during the course of the study and detailed observations were conducted in four of them. The principal at the school reported upon in this study commented that I was very fortunate in coming to his school since his staff (and kindergarten teacher in particular) were equal to "any in the city." Finally, the utilization of longitudinal study as a research method in a ghetto school will enhance the possibilities of gaining further insight into mechanisms of adaptation utilized by Black youth to what appears to be a basically White, middle-class value-oriented institution.

The School

The particular school which the children attend was built in the early part of the 1960s. It has classes from kindergarten through the eighth grade and a single special educational class. The enrollment fluctuates near the 900 level while the teaching staff consists of twenty-six teachers, in addition to a librarian, two physical education instructors, the principal, and an assistant principal. There are also at the school, on a part-time basis, a speech therapist, social worker, nurse, and doctor, all employed by the Board of Education. All administrators, teachers, staff, and pupils are Black. (The author is Caucasian.) The school is located in a blighted urban area that has 98 percent Black population within its census district. Within the school itself, nearly 500 of the 900 pupils (55%) come from families supported by funds from Aid to Dependent Children, a form of public welfare.

The Kindergarten Class

Prior to the beginning of the school year, the teacher possessed several different kinds of information regarding the children that she would have in her class. The first was the pre-registration form completed by thirteen mothers of children who would be in the kindergarten class. On this form, the teacher was supplied with the name of the child, his age, the name of his parents, his home address, his phone number, and whether he had had any pre-school experience. The second source of information for the teacher was supplied two days before the beginning of school by the school social worker who provided a tentative list of all children enrolled in the kindergarten class who lived in homes that received public welfare funds.

The third source of information on the child was gained as a result of the initial interview with the mother and child during the registration period, either in the few days prior to the beginning of school or else during the first days of school. In this interview, a major concern was the gathering of medical information about the child as well as the ascertaining of any specific parental concern related to the child. This latter information was noted on the "Behavioral Questionnaire" where the mother was to indicate her concern, if any, on twenty-eight different items. Such items as thumb-sucking, bed-wetting, loss of bowel control, lying, stealing, fighting, and laziness were included on this questionnaire.

The fourth source of information available to the teacher concerning the children in her class was both her own experiences with older siblings, and those of other teachers in the building related to behavior and academic performance of children in the same family. A rather strong informal norm had developed among teachers in the school such that pertinent information, especially that related to discipline matters, was to be passed on to the next teacher of the student. The teachers' lounge became the location in which they would discuss the performance of individual children as well as make comments concerning the parents and their interests in the student and the school. Frequently, during the first days of the school year, there were admonitions to a specific teacher to "watch out" for a child believed by a teacher to be a "trouble-maker." Teachers would also relate techniques of controlling the behavior of a student who had been disruptive in the class. Thus, a variety of information concerning students in the school was shared, whether that information regarded academic performance, behavior in class, or the relation of the home to the school.

It should be noted that not one of these four sources of information to the teacher was related directly to the academic potential of the incoming kindergarten child. Rather, they concerned various types of social information revealing such facts as the financial status of certain families, medical care of the child, presence or absence of a telephone in the home, as well as the structure of the family in which the child lived, that is, number of siblings, whether the child lived with both, one, or neither of his natural parents.

The Teacher's Stimulus

When the kindergarten teacher made the permanent seating assignments on the eighth day of school, not only had she the above four sources of information concerning the children, but she had also had time to observe them within the classroom setting. Thus the behavior, degree and type of verbalization, dress, mannerisms, physical appearance, and performance on the early tasks assigned during class were available to her as she began to form opinions concerning the capabilities and potential of the various children. That such evaluation of the children by the teacher was beginning, I believe, there is little doubt. Within a few days, only a certain group of children were continually being called on to lead the class in the Pledge of Allegiance, read the weather calendar each day, come to the front for "show and tell" periods, take messages to the office, count the number of children present in the class, pass out materials for class projects, be in charge of equipment on playground, and lead the class to the bathroom, library, or on a school tour. This one group of children, that continually were physically close to the teacher and had a high degree of verbal interaction with her, she placed at Table 1.

As one progressed from Table 1 to Table 2 and Table 3, there was an increasing dissimilarity between each group of children at the different tables on at least four major criteria. The first criterion appeared to be the physical appearance of the child. While the children at Table 1 were all dressed in clean clothes that were relatively new and pressed, most of the children at Table 2, and with only one exception at Table 3, were all quite poorly dressed. The clothes were old and often quite dirty. The children at Tables 2 and 3 also had a noticeably different quality and quantity of clothes to wear, especially during the winter months. Whereas the children at Table 1 would come on cold days with heavy coats and sweaters, the children at the other two tables often wore very thin spring coats and summer clothes. The single child at Table 3 who came to school quite nicely dressed came from a home in which the mother was receiving welfare funds, but was supplied with clothing for the children by the families of her brother and sister.

An additional aspect of the physical appearance of the children related to their body odor. While none of the children at Table 1 came to class with an odor of urine on them, there were two children at Table 2 and five children at Table 3 who frequently had such an odor. There was not a clear distinction among the children at the various tables as to the degree of "Blackness" of their skin, but there were more children at the third table with very dark skin (five in all) than there were at the first table (three). There was also a noticeable distinction among the various groups of children as to the condition of their hair. While the three boys at Table 1 all had short hair cuts and the six girls at the same table had their hair "processed" and combed, the number of

201

TABLE I   *Distribution of Socio-Economic Status Factors by Seating Arrangement at the Three Tables in the Kindergarten Classroom*

| Factors | Seating Arrangement* | | |
	Table 1	Table 2	Table 3
Income			
1) Families on welfare	0	2	4
2) Families with father employed	6	3	2
3) Families with mother employed	5	5	5
4) Families with both parents employed	5	3	2
5) Total family income below $3,000/yr**	0	4	7
6) Total family income above $12,000/yr**	4	0	0
Education			
1) Father ever grade school	6	3	2
2) Father ever high school	5	2	1
3) Father ever college	1	0	0
4) Mother ever grade school	9	10	8
5) Mother ever high school	7	6	5
6) Mother ever college	4	0	0
7) Children with pre-school experience	1	1	0
Family Size			
1) Families with one child	3	1	0
2) Families with six or more children	2	6	7
3) Average number of siblings in family	3–4	5–6	6–7
4) Families with both parents present	6	3	2

* There are nine children at Table 1, eleven at Table 2, and ten at Table 3.

** Estimated from stated occupation.

children with either matted or unprocessed hair increased at Table 2 (two boys and three girls) and eight of the children at Table 3 (four boys and four girls). None of the children in the kindergarten class wore their hair in the style of a "natural."

A second major criteria which appeared to differentiate the children at the various tables was their interactional behavior, both among themselves and with the teacher. The several children who began to develop as leaders within the class by giving directions to other members, initiating the division of the class into teams on the playground, and seeking to speak for the class to the teacher ("We want to color now"), all were placed by the teacher at Table 1. This same group of children displayed considerable ease in their interaction with her. Whereas the children at Tables 2 and 3 would often linger on the periphery of groups surrounding the teacher, the children at Table 1 most often crowded close to her.

TABLE 2 *Distribution of Socio-Economic Status Factors by Seating Arrangement in the Three Reading Groups in the Second-Grade Classroom*

	Seating Arrangement*		
Factors	Tigers	Cardinals	Clowns
Income			
1) Families on welfare	2	4	7
2) Families with father employed	8	5	1
3) Families with mother employed	7	11	6
4) Families with both parents employed	7	5	1
5) Total family income below $3,000/yr**	1	5	8
6) Total family income above $12,000/yr**	4	0	0
Education			
1) Father ever grade school	8	6	1
2) Father ever high school	7	4	0
3) Father ever college	0	0	0
4) Mother ever grade school	12	13	9
5) Mother ever high school	9	7	4
6) Mother ever college	3	0	0
7) Children with pre-school experience	1	0	0
Family Size			
1) Families with one child	2	0	1
2) Families with six or more children	3	8	5
3) Average number of siblings in family	3–4	6–7	7–8
4) Families with both parents present	8	6	1

* There are twelve children in the Tiger group, fourteen in the Cardinal group, and nine in the Clown group.

** Estimated from stated occupation.

The use of language within the classroom appeared to be the third major differentiation among the children. While the children placed at the first table were quite verbal with the teacher, the children placed at the remaining two tables spoke much less frequently with her. The children placed at the first table also displayed a greater use of Standard American English within the classroom. Whereas the children placed at the last two tables most often responded to the teacher in Black dialect, the children at the first table did so very infrequently. In other words, the children at the first table were much more adept at the use of "school language" than were those at the other tables. The teacher utilized Standard American English in the classroom and one group of children were able to respond in a like manner. The frequency of a "no response" to a question from the teacher was recorded at a ratio of nearly three to one for the children at the last two tables as opposed to Table 1. When questions were asked, the children who were placed at the first table most often gave a response.

TABLE 3   *Variations in Teacher-Directed Behavior for Three Second-Grade Reading Groups During Three Observational Periods Within a Single Classroom*

| Item | *Variations in Teacher-Directed Behavior* | | |
	Control	*Supportive*	*Neutral*
Observational Period #1			
Tigers	5% (6)**	7% (8)	87% (95)
Cardinals	10% (7)	8% (5)	82% (58)
Clowns	27% (27)	6% (6)	67% (67)
Observational Period #2			
Tigers	7% (14)	8% (16)	85% (170)
Cardinals	7% (13)	8% (16)	85% (170)
Clowns	14% (44)	6% (15)	80% (180)
Observational Period #3			
Tigers	7% (15)	6% (13)	86% (171)
Cardinals	14% (20)	10% (14)	75% (108)
Clowns	15% (36)	7% (16)	78% (188)

* Forty-eight (48) minutes of unequal teacher access (due to one group's being out of the room) was eliminated from the analysis.

** Value within the parentheses indicates total number of units of behavior within that category.

The final apparent criterion by which the children at the first table were quite noticeably different from those at the other tables consisted of a series of social factors which were known to the teacher prior to her seating the children. Though it is not known to what degree she utilized this particular criterion when she assigned seats, it does contribute to developing a clear profile of the children at the various tables. Table 1 gives a summary of the distribution of the children at the three tables on a series of variables related to social and family conditions. Such variables may be considered to give indication of the relative status of the children within the room, based on the income, education, and size of the family. (For a discussion of why these three variables of income, education, and family size may be considered as significant indicators of social status, see also Frazier, 1962; Freeman et al., 1959; Gebhard et al., 1958; Kahl, 1957; Notestein, 1953; Reissman, 1959; Rose, 1956; Simpson & Yinger, 1958.)

Believing, as I do, that the teacher did not randomly assign the children to the various tables, it is then necessary to indicate the basis for the seating arrangement. I would contend that the teacher developed, utilizing some combination of the four criteria outlined above, a series of expectations about the potential performance of each child and then grouped the children according to perceived similarities in expected performance. The teacher herself informed me that the first table consisted of her "fast learners" while those at the last two tables "had no idea of what was going on in the classroom." What becomes crucial in this discussion is to ascertain the basis upon which the teacher developed her criteria of "fast learner" since there had been no formal testing of the children as to their academic potential or capacity for cognitive development. She made evaluative judgments of the expected capacities of the children to perform academic tasks after eight days of school.

Certain criteria became indicative of expected success and others became indicative of expected failure. Those children who closely fit the teacher's "ideal type" of the successful child were chosen for seats at Table 1. Those children that had the least "goodness of fit" with her ideal type were placed at the third table. The criteria upon which a teacher would construct her ideal type of the successful student would rest in her perception of certain attributes in the child that she believed would make for success. To understand what the teacher considered as "success," one would have to examine her perception of the larger society and whom in that larger society she perceived as successful. Thus, in the terms of Merton (1957), one may ask which was the "normative reference group" for Mrs. Caplow that she perceived as being successful.[2] I believe that the reference group utilized by Mrs. Caplow to determine what constituted success was a mixed Black-White, well-educated middle class. Those attributes most desired by educated members of the middle class became the basis for her evaluation of the children. Those who possessed these particular characteristics were expected to succeed while those who did not could be expected not to succeed. Highly prized middle-class status for the child in the classroom was attained by demonstrating ease of interaction among adults; high degree of verbalization in Standard American English; the ability to become a leader; a neat and clean appearance; coming from a family that is educated, employed, living together, and interested in the child; and the ability to participate well as a member of a group.

The kindergarten teacher appeared to have been raised in a home where the above values were emphasized as important. Her mother was a college graduate, as were her brother and sisters. The family lived in the same neighborhood for many years, and the father held a responsible position with a public utility company in the city. The family was devoutly religious and those of the family still in the city attend the same church. She and other members of her family were active in a number of civil rights organizations in the city. Thus, it appears that the kindergarten teacher's "normative reference group" coincided quite closely with those groups in which she did participate and belong. There was little discrepancy between the normative values of the mixed Black-White educated middle class and the values of the groups in which she held membership. The attributes indicative of "success" among those of the educated middle class had been attained by the teacher. She was a college graduate, held positions of respect and responsibility in the Black community, lived in a comfortable middle-class section of the city in a well-furnished and spacious home, together with her husband earned over $20,000 per year, was active in a number of community organizations, and had parents, brother, and sisters similar in education, income, and occupational positions.

The teacher ascribed high status to a certain group of children within the class who fit her perception of the criteria necessary to be among the "fast learners" at Table 1. With her reference group orientation as to what constitute the qualities essential for "success," she responded favorably to those children who possessed such necessary attributes. Her resultant preferential treatment of a select group of children appeared to be derived from her belief that certain behavioral and cultural characteristics are more crucial to learning in school than are others. In a similar manner, those children who appeared not to possess the criteria essential for success were ascribed low status and described as "failures" by the teacher. They were relegated to positions at Table 2 and 3. The placement of the children then appeared to result from their possessing or lacking the certain desired cultural characteristics perceived as important by the teacher.

The organization of the kindergarten classroom according to the expectation of success or failure after the eighth day of school became the basis for the differential treatment of the children for the remainder of the school year. From the day that the class was assigned permanent seats, the activities in the classroom were perceivably different from previously. The fundamental division of the class into those expected to learn and those expected not to permeated the teacher's orientation to the class.

The teacher's rationalization for narrowing her attention to selected students was that the majority of the remainder of the class (in her words) "just had no idea of what was going on in the classroom." Her reliance on the few students of ascribed high social status reached such proportions that on occasion, the teacher would use one of these students as an exemplar that the remainder of the class would do well to emulate:

> (It is Fire Prevention Week and the teacher is trying to have the children say so. The children make a number of incorrect responses, a few of which follow:) Jim, who had raised his hand, in answer to the question, "Do you know what week it is?" says, "October." The teacher says "No, that's the name of the month. Jane, do you know what special week this is?" and Jane responds, "It cold outside." Teacher says, "No, that is not it either. I guess I will have to call on Pamela. Pamela, come here and stand by me and tell the rest of the boys and girls what special week this is." Pamela leaves her chair, comes and stands by the teacher, turns and faces the rest of the class. The teacher puts her arm around Pamela, and Pamela says, "It fire week." The teacher responds, "Well Pamela, that is close. Actually it is Fire Prevention Week."

On another occasion, the Friday after Halloween, the teacher informed the class that she would allow time for all the students to come to the front of the class and tell of their experiences. She, in reality, called on six students, five of whom sat at Table 1 and the sixth at Table 2. Not only on this occasion, but on others, the teacher focused her attention on the experiences of the higher status students:[3]

> (The students are involved in acting out a skit arranged by the teacher on how a family should come together to eat the evening meal.) The students acting the roles of mother, father, and daughter are all from Table 1. The boy playing the

son is from Table 2. At the small dinner table set up in the center of the class-room, the four children are supposed to be sharing with each other what they had done during the day — the father at work, the mother at home, and the two chil-dren at school. The Table 2 boy makes few comments. (In real life he has no fa-ther and his mother is supported by ADC funds.) The teacher comments, "I think that we are going to have to let Milt (Table 1) be the new son. Sam, why don't you go and sit down. Milt, you seem to be one who would know what a son is supposed to do at the dinner table. You come and take Sam's place."

In this instance, the lower-status student was penalized, not only for failing to have verbalized middle-class table talk, but more fundamentally, for lacking middle-class experiences. He had no actual father to whom he could speak at the dinner table, yet he was expected to speak fluently with an imaginary one.

Though the blackboard was long enough to extend parallel to all three ta-bles, the teacher wrote such assignments as arithmetic problems and drew all illustrations on the board in front of the students at Table 1. A rather poignant example of the penalty the children at Table 3 had to pay was that they often could not see the board material:

> Lilly stands up out of her seat. Mrs. Caplow asks Lilly what she wants. Lilly makes no verbal response to the question. Mrs. Caplow then says rather firmly to Lilly, "Sit down." Lilly does. However, Lilly sits down sideways in the chair (so she is still facing the teacher). Mrs. Caplow instructs Lilly to put her feet under the table. This Lilly does. Now she is facing directly away from the teacher and the black-board where the teacher is demonstrating to the students how to print the letter, "O."

The realization of the self-fulfilling prophecy within the classroom was in its final stages by late May of the kindergarten year. Lack of communication with the teacher, lack of involvement in the class activities and infrequent instruc-tion all characterized the situation of the children at Tables 2 and 3. During one observational period of an hour in May, not a single act of communication was directed towards any child at either Table 2 or 3 by the teacher except for twice commanding "sit down." The teacher devoted her attention to teaching those children at Table 1. Attempts by the children at Table 2 and 3 to elicit the attention of the teacher were much fewer than earlier in the school year.

In June, after school had ended for the year, the teacher was asked to com-ment on the children in her class. Of the children at the first table, she noted,

> I guess the best way to describe it is that very few children in my class are excep-tional. I guess you could notice this just from the way the children were seated this year. Those at Table 1 gave consistently the most responses throughout the year and seemed most interested and aware of what was going on in the classroom.

Of those children at the remaining two tables, the teacher commented,

> It seems to me that some of the children at Table 2 and most all the children at Table 3 at times seem to have no idea of what is going on in the classroom and were off in another world all by themselves. It just appears that some can do it and some cannot. I don't think that it is the teaching that affects those that cannot do it, but some are just basically low achievers.

The Students' Response

The students in the kindergarten classroom did not sit passively, internalizing the behavior the teacher directed towards them. Rather, they responded to the stimuli of the teacher, both in internal differentiations within the class itself and also in their response to the teacher. The type of response a student made was highly dependent upon whether he sat at Table 1 or at one of the two other tables. The single classroom of Black students did not respond as a homogenous unit to the teacher-inspired social organization of the room.

For the high-status students at Table 1, the response to the track system of the teacher appeared to be at least three-fold. One such response was the directing of ridicule and belittlement towards those children at Tables 2 and 3. At no point during the entire school year was a child from Table 2 or 3 ever observed directing such remarks at the children at Table 1:

> Mrs. Caplow says, "Raise your hand if you want me to call on you. I won't call on anyone who calls out." She then says, "All right, now who knows that numeral? What is it, Tony?" Tony makes no verbal response but rather walks to the front of the classroom and stands by Mrs. Caplow. Gregory calls out, "He don't know. He scared." Then Ann calls out, "It sixteen, stupid." (Tony sits at Table 3, Gregory and Ann sit at Table 1.)
>
> Jim starts to say out loud that he is smarter than Tom. He repeats it over and over again, "I smarter than you. I smarter than you." (Jim sits at Table 1, Tom at Table 3.)
>
> Milt came over to the observer and told him to look at Lilly's shoes. I asked him why I should and he replied, "Because they so ragged and dirty." (Milt is at Table 1, Lilly at Table 3.)
>
> When I asked Lilly what it was that she was drawing, she replied, "A parachute." Gregory interrupted and said, "She can't draw nothin'."

The problems of those children who were of lower status were compounded, for not only had the teacher indicated her low esteem of them, but their peers had also turned against them. The implications for the future schooling of a child who lacks the desired status credentials in a classroom where the teacher places high value on middle-class "success" values and mannerisms are tragic.

It must not be assumed, however, that though the children at Tables 2 and 3 did not participate in classroom activities and were systematically ignored by the teacher, they did not learn. I contend that in fact they did learn, but in a fundamentally different way from the way in which the high-status children at Table 1 learned. The children at Table 2 and 3 who were unable to interact with the teacher began to develop patterns of interaction among themselves whereby they would discuss the material that the teacher was presenting to the children at Table 1. Thus I have termed their method of grasping the material "secondary learning" to imply that knowledge was not gained in direct interaction with the teacher, but through the mediation of peers and also through listening to the teacher though she was not speaking to them. That the children were grasping, in part, the material presented in the classroom, was indicated to me in home visits when the children who sat at Table 3 would relate material specifically taught by the teacher to the children at Table 1. It is not as though the children at Table 2 and 3 were ignorant of what was being taught in the class, but rather that the patterns of classroom interaction established by the teacher inhibited the low-status children from verbalizing what knowledge they had accumulated. Thus, from the teacher's terms of reference, those who could not discuss must not know. Her expectations continued to be fulfilled, for though the low-status children had accumulated knowledge, they did not have the opportunity to verbalize it and, consequently, the teacher could not know what they had learned. Children at Table 2 and 3 had learned material presented in the kindergarten class, but would continue to be defined by the teacher as children who could not or would not learn.

A second response of the higher status students to the differential behavior of the teacher towards them was to seek solidarity and closeness with the teacher and urge Table 2 and 3 children to comply with her wishes:

> The teacher is out of the room. Pamela says to the class, "We all should clean up before the teacher comes." Shortly thereafter the teacher has still not returned and Pamela begins to supervise other children in the class. She says to one girl from Table 3, "Girl, leave that piano alone." The child plays only a short time longer and then leaves.
>
> The teacher has instructed the students to go and take off their coats since they have come in from the playground. Milt says, "Ok y'al, let's go take off our clothes."
>
> At this time Jim says to the teacher, "Mrs. Caplow, they pretty flowers on your desk." Mrs. Caplow responded, "Yes, Jim, those flowers are roses, but we will not have roses much longer. The roses will die and rest until spring because it is getting so cold outside."
>
> When the teacher tells the students to come from their desks and form a semicircle around her, Gregory scoots up very close to Mrs. Caplow and is practically sitting in her lap.
>
> Gregory has come into the room late. He takes off his coat and goes to the coat room to hang it up. He comes back and sits down in the very front of the group and is now closest to the teacher.

The higher-status students in the class perceived the lower status and esteem the teacher ascribed to those children at Tables 2 and 3. Not only would the Table 1 students attempt to control and ridicule the Table 2 and 3 students, but they also perceived and verbalized that they, the Table 1 students, were better students and were receiving differential treatment from the teacher:

> The children are rehearsing a play, Little Red Riding Hood. Pamela tells the observer, "The teacher gave me the best part." The teacher overheard this comment, smiled, and made no verbal response.
>
> The children are preparing to go on a field trip to a local dairy. The teacher has designated Gregory as the "sheriff" for the trip. Mrs. Caplow stated that for the field trip today Gregory would be the sheriff. Mrs. Caplow simply watched as Gregory would walk up to a student and push him back into line saying, "Boy, stand where you suppose to." Several times he went up to students from Table 3 and showed them the badge that the teacher had given to him and said, "Teacher made me sheriff."

The children seated at the first table were internalizing the attitudes and behavior of the teacher towards those at the remaining two tables. That is, as the teacher responded from her reference group orientation as to which type of children were most likely to succeed and which type most likely to fail, she behaved towards the two groups of children in a significantly different manner. The children from Table 1 were also learning through emulating the teacher how to behave towards other Black children who came from low-income and poorly educated homes. The teacher, who came from a well-educated and middle-income family, and the children from Table 1 who came from a background similar to the teacher's, came to respond to the children from poor and uneducated homes in a strikingly similar manner.

The lower-status students in the classroom from Tables 2 and 3 responded in significantly different ways to the stimuli of the teacher. The two major responses of the Table 2 and 3 students were withdrawal and verbal and physical in-group hostility.

The withdrawal of some of the lower-status students as a response to the ridicule of their peers and the isolation from the teacher occasionally took the form of physical withdrawal, but most often it was psychological:

Betty, a very poorly dressed child, had gone outside and hidden behind the door. . . . Mrs. Caplow sees Betty leave and goes outside to bring her back, says in an authoritative and irritated voice, "Betty, come here right now." When the child returns, Mrs. Caplow seizes her by the right arm, brings her over to the group, and pushes her down to the floor. Betty begins to cry. . . . The teacher now shows the group a large posterboard with a picture of a White child going to school.

The teacher is demonstrating how to mount leaves between two pieces of wax paper. Betty leaves the group and goes back to her seat and begins to color.

The teacher is instructing the children in how they can make a "spooky thing" for Halloween. James turns away from the teacher and puts his head on his desk. Mrs. Caplow looks at James and says, "James sit up and look here."

The children are supposed to make United Nations flags. They have been told that they do not have to make exact replicas of the teacher's flag. They have before them the materials to make the flags. Lilly and James are the only children who have not yet started to work on their flags. Presently, James has his head under his desk and Lilly simply sits and watches the other children. Now they are both staring into space. . . . (5 minutes later) Lilly and James have not yet started, while several other children have already finished. . . . A minute later, with the teacher telling the children to begin to clean up their scraps, Lilly is still staring into space.

The teacher has the children seated on the floor in front of her asking them questions about a story that she had read to them. The teacher says, "June, your back is turned. I want to see your face." (The child had turned completely around and was facing away from the group.)

The teacher told the students to come from their seats and form a semi-circle on the floor in front of her. The girls all sit very close to the piano where the teacher is seated. The boys sit a good distance back away from the girls and away from the teacher. Lilly finishes her work at her desk and comes and sits at the rear of the group of girls, but she is actually in the middle of the open space separating the boys and the girls. She speaks to no one and simply sits staring off.

The verbal and physical hostility that the children at Tables 2 and 3 began to act out among themselves in many ways mirrored what the Table 1 students and the teacher were also saying about them. There are numerous instances in the observations of the children at Tables 2 and 3 calling one another "stupid," "dummy," or "dumb dumb." Racial overtones were noted on two occasions when one boy called another a "nigger," and on another occasion when a girl called a boy an "almond head." Threats of beatings, "whoppins," and even spitting on a child were also recorded among those at Tables 2 and 3. Also at Table 2, two instances were observed in which a single child hoarded all the supplies for the whole table. Similar manifestations of hostility were not observed among those children at the first table. The single incident of strong anger or hostility by one child at Table 1 against another child at the same table occurred when one accused the other of copying from his paper. The second denied it and an argument ensued.

In the organization of hostility within the classroom, there may be at least the tentative basis for the rejection of a popular "folk myth" of American society, which is that children are inherently cruel to one another and that this tendency towards cruelty must be socialized into socially acceptable channels. The evidence from this classroom would indicate that much of the cruelty displayed was a result of the social organization of the class. Those children at Tables 2 and 3 who displayed cruelty appeared to have learned from the teacher that it was acceptable to act in an aggressive manner towards those from low-income and poorly educated backgrounds. Their cruelty was not diffuse, but rather focused on a specific group — the other poor children. Likewise, the incidence of such behavior increased over time. The children at Tables 2 and 3 did not begin the school year ridiculing and belittling each other. This social process began to emerge with the outline of the social organization the teacher imposed upon the class. The children from the first table were also apparently socialized into a pattern of behavior in which they perceived that they could direct hostility and aggression towards those at Table 2 and 3, but not towards one another. The children in the class learned who was vulnerable to hostility and who was not through the actions of the teacher. She established the patterns of differential behavior which the class adopted.

First Grade

Though Mrs. Caplow had anticipated that only twelve of the children from the kindergarten class would attend the first grade in the same school, eighteen of the children were assigned during the summer to the first-grade classroom in the main building. The remaining children either were assigned to a new school a few blocks north, or were assigned to a branch school designed to handle the overflow from the main building, or had moved away. Mrs. Logan, the first-grade teacher, had had more than twenty years of teaching experience in the city public school system, and every school in which she had taught was more than 90 percent Black. During the 1968–1969 school year, four informal visits were made to the classroom of Mrs. Logan. No visits were made to either the branch school or the new school to visit children from the kindergarten class who had left their original school. During my visits to the first-grade room, I kept only brief notes of the short conversations that I had with Mrs. Logan; I did not conduct formal observations of the activities of the children in the class.

During the first-grade school year, there were thirty-three children in the classroom. In addition to the eighteen from the kindergarten class, there were nine children repeating the first grade and also six children new to the school. Of the eighteen children who came from the kindergarten class to the first grade in the main building, seven were from the previous year's Table 1, six from Table 2, and five from Table 3.

In the first-grade classroom, Mrs. Logan also divided the children into three groups. Those children whom she placed at "Table A" had all been Table 1 students in kindergarten. No student who had sat at Table 2 or 3 in kindergarten was placed at Table A in the first grade. Instead, all the students from Table 2 and 3 — with one exception — were placed together at "Table B." At the third table which Mrs. Logan called "Table C," she placed the nine children repeating the grade plus Betty who had sat at Table 3 in the kindergarten class. Of the six new students, two were placed at Table A and four at Table C. Thus the totals for the three tables were nine students at Table A, ten at Table B, and fourteen at Table C.

The seating arrangement that began in the kindergarten as a result of the teacher's definition of which children possessed or lacked the perceived necessary characteristics for success in the public school system emerged in the first grade as a caste phenomenon in which there was absolutely no mobility upward. That is, of those children whom Mrs. Caplow had perceived as potential "failures" and thus seated at either Table 2 or 3 in the kindergarten, not one was assigned to the table of the "fast learners" in the first grade.

The initial label given to the children by the kindergarten teacher had been reinforced in her interaction with those students throughout the school year. When the children were ready to pass into the first grade, their ascribed labels from the teacher as either successes or failures assumed objective dimensions. The first-grade teacher no longer had to rely on merely the presence or absence of certain behavioral and attitudinal characteristics to ascertain who would do well and who would do poorly in the class. Objective records of the "readiness" material completed by the children during the kindergarten year were available to her. Thus, upon the basis of what material the various tables in kindergarten had completed, Mrs. Logan could form her first-grade tables for reading and arithmetic.

The kindergarten teacher's disproportionate allocation of her teaching time resulted in the Table 1 students' having completed more material at the end of the school year than the remainder of the class. As a result, the Table 1 group from kindergarten remained intact in the first grade, as they were the only students prepared for the first-grade reading material. Those children from Tables 2 and 3 had not yet completed all the material from kindergarten and had to spend the first weeks of the first-grade school year finishing kindergarten level lessons. The criteria established by the school system as to what constituted the completion of the necessary readiness material to begin first-grade lessons insured that the Table 2 and 3 students could not be placed at Table A. The only children who had completed the material were those from Table 1, defined by the kindergarten teacher as successful students and whom she then taught most often because the remainder of the class "had no idea what was going on."

It would be somewhat misleading, however, to indicate that there was absolutely no mobility for any of the students between the seating assignments in kindergarten and those in the first grade. All of the students save one who had been seated at Table 3 during the kindergarten year were moved "up" to Table B in the first grade. The majority of Table C students were those having to repeat the grade level. As a tentative explanation of Mrs. Logan's rationale for the development of the Table C seating assignments, she may have assumed that within her class there existed one group of students who possessed so very little of the perceived behavioral patterns and attitudes necessary for success that they had to be kept separate from the remainder of the class. (Table C was placed by itself on the opposite side of the room from Tables A and B.) The Table C students were spoken of by the first-grade teacher in a manner reminiscent of the way in which Mrs. Caplow spoke of the Table 3 students the previous year.

Students who were placed at Table A appeared to be perceived by Mrs. Logan as students who not only possessed the criteria necessary for future success, both in the public school system and in the larger society, but who also had proven themselves capable in academic work. These students appeared to possess the characteristics considered most essential for "middle-class" success by the teacher. Though students at Table B lacked many of the "qualities" and characteristics of the Table A students, they were not perceived as lacking them to the same extent as those placed at Table C.

A basic tenet in explaining Mrs. Logan's seating arrangement is, of course, that she shared a similar reference group and set of values as to what constituted "success" with Mrs. Caplow in the kindergarten class. Both women were well educated, were employed in a professional occupation, lived in middle-income neighborhoods, were active in a number of charitable and civil rights organizations, and expressed strong religious convictions and moral standards. Both were educated in the city teacher's college and had also attained graduate degrees. Their backgrounds as well as the manner in which they described the various groups of students in their classes would indicate that they shared a similar reference group and set of expectations as to what constituted the indices of the "successful" student.

Second Grade

Of the original thirty students in kindergarten and eighteen in first grade, ten students were assigned to the only second-grade class in the main building. Of the eight original kindergarten students who did not come to the second grade from the first, three were repeating first grade while the remainder had moved. The teacher in the second grade also divided the class into three groups, though she did not give them number or letter designations. Rather, she called the first group the "Tigers." The middle group she labeled the "Cardinals," while the second-grade repeaters plus several new children assigned to the third table were designated by the teacher as "Clowns."[4]

In the second-grade seating scheme, no student from the first grade who had not sat at Table A was moved "up" to the Tigers at the beginning of second grade. All those students who in first grade had been at Table B or Table C and returned to the second grade were placed in the Cardinal group. The Clowns consisted of six second-grade repeaters plus three students who were new to the class. Of the ten original kindergarten students who came from the first grade, six were Tigers and four were Cardinals. Table 2 illustrates that the distribution of social economic factors from the kindergarten year remained essentially unchanged in the second grade.

By the time the children came to the second grade, their seating arrangement appeared to be based not on the teacher's expectations of how the child might perform, but rather on the basis of past performance of the child. Available to the teacher when she formulated the seating groups were grade sheets from both kindergarten and first grade, IQ scores from kindergarten, listing of parental occupations for approximately half of the class, reading scores from a test given to all students at the end of the first grade, evaluations from the speech teacher and also the informal evaluations from both the kindergarten and first-grade teachers.

The single most important data utilized by the teacher in devising seating groups were the reading scores indicating the performance of the students at the end of the first grade. The second-grade teacher indicated that she attempted to divide the groups primarily on the basis of these scores. The Tigers were designated as the highest reading group and the Cardinals the middle. The Clowns were assigned a first-grade reading level, though they were, for the most part, repeaters from the previous year in second grade. The caste character of the reading groups became clear as the year progressed, in that all three groups were reading in different books and it was school policy that no child could go on to a new book until the previous one had been completed. Thus there was no way for the child, should he have demonstrated competence at a higher reading level, to advance, since he had to continue at the pace of the rest of his reading group. The teacher never allowed individual reading in order that a child might finish a book on his own and move ahead. *No matter how well a child in the lower reading groups might have read, he was destined to remain in the same reading group. This is, in a sense, another manifestation of the self-fulfilling prophecy in that a "slow learner" had no option but to continue to be a slow learner, regardless of performance or potential.* Initial expectations of the kindergarten teacher two years earlier as to the ability of the child resulted in placement in a reading group, whether high or low, from which there appeared to be no escape. The child's journey through the early grades of school at one reading level and in one social grouping appeared to be pre-ordained from the eighth day of kindergarten.

The expectations of the kindergarten teacher appeared to be fulfilled by late spring. Her description of the academic performance of the children in June had a strong "goodness of fit" with her stated expectations from the previous September. For the first- and second-grade teachers alike, there was no need to rely on intuitive expectations as to what the performance of the child would be. They were in the position of being able to base future expectations upon past performance. At this point, the relevance of the self-fulfilling prophecy again is evident, for the very criteria by which the first- and second-grade teachers established their three reading groups were those manifestations of performance most affected by the previous experience of the child. That is, which reading books were completed, the amount of arithmetic and reading readiness material that had been completed, and the mastery of basic printing skills all became the significant criteria established by the Board of Education to determine the level at which the child would begin the first grade. A similar process of standard evaluation by past performance on criteria established by the board appears to have been the basis for the arrangement of reading groups within the second grade. Thus, again, the initial patterns of expectations and her acting upon them appeared to place the kindergarten teacher in the position of establishing the parameters of the educational experience for the various children in her class. The parameters, most clearly defined by the seating arrangement at the various tables, remained intact through both the first and second grades.

The phenomenon of teacher expectation based upon a variety of social status criteria did not appear to be limited to the kindergarten teacher alone. When the second-grade teacher was asked to evaluate the children in her class by reading group, she responded in terms reminiscent of the kindergarten teacher. Though such a proposition would be tenuous at best, the high degree of similarity in the responses of both the kindergarten and second-grade teachers suggests that there may be among the teachers in the school a common set of criteria as to what constitutes the successful and promising student. If such is the case, then the particular individual who happens to occupy the role of kindergarten teacher is less crucial. For if the expectations of all staff within the school are highly similar, then with little difficulty there could be an interchange of teachers among the grades with little or no noticeable effect upon the performance of the various groups of students. If all teachers have similar expectations as to which types of students perform well and which types perform poorly, the categories established by the kindergarten teacher could be expected to reflect rather closely the manner in which other teachers would also have grouped the class.

As the indication of the high degree of similarity between the manner in which the kindergarten teacher described the three tables and the manner in which the second-grade teacher described the "Tigers, Cardinals, and Clowns," excerpts of an interview with the second-grade teacher are presented, where she stated her opinions of the three groups.

Concerning the Tigers:

Q: Mrs. Benson, how would you describe the Tigers in terms of their learning ability and academic performance?

R: Well, they are my fastest group. They are very smart.

Q: Mrs. Benson, how would you describe the Tigers in terms of discipline matters?

R: Well, the Tigers are very talkative. Susan, Pamela, and Ruth, they are always running their mouths constantly, but they get their work done first. I don't have much trouble with them.

Q: Mrs. Benson, what value do you think the Tigers hold for an education?

R: They all feel an education is important and most of them have goals in life as to what they want to be. They mostly want to go to college.

The same questions were asked of the teacher concerning the Cardinals.

Q: Mrs. Benson, how would you describe the Cardinals in terms of learning ability and academic performance?

R: They are slow to finish their work . . . but they get finished. You know, a lot of them, though, don't care to come to school too much. Rema, Gary, and Toby are absent quite a bit. The Tigers are never absent.

Q: Mrs. Benson, how would you describe the Cardinals in terms of discipline matters?

R: Not too bad. Since they work so slow they don't have time to talk. They are not like the Tigers who finish in a hurry and then just sit and talk with each other.

Q: Mrs. Benson, what value do you think the Cardinals hold for an education?

R: Well, I don't think they have as much interest in education as do the Tigers, but you know it is hard to say. Most will like to come to school, but the parents will keep them from coming. They either have to baby sit, or the clothes are dirty. These are the excuses the parents often give. But I guess most of the Cardinals want to go on and finish and go on to college. A lot of them have ambitions when they grow up. It's mostly the parents' fault that they are not at the school more often.

In the kindergarten class, the teacher appeared to perceive the major ability gap to lie between the students at Table 1 and those at Table 2. That is, those at Tables 2 and 3 were perceived as more similar in potential than were those at Tables 1 and 2. This was not the case in the second-grade classroom. The teacher appeared to perceive the major distinction in ability as lying between the Cardinals and the Clowns. Thus she saw the Tigers and the Cardinals as much closer in performance and potential than the Cardinals and the Clowns. The teacher's responses to the questions concerning the Clowns lends credence to this interpretation:

Q: Mrs. Benson, how would you describe the Clowns in terms of learning ability and academic performance?

R: Well, they are really slow. You know most of them are still doing first-grade work.

Q: Mrs. Benson, how would you describe the Clowns in terms of discipline matters?

R: They are very playful. They like to play a lot. They are not very neat. They like to talk a lot and play a lot. When I read to them, boy, do they have a good time. You know, the Tigers and the Cardinals will sit quietly and listen when I read to them, but the Clowns, they are always so restless. They always want to stand up. When we read, it is really something else. You know — Diane and Pat especially like to stand up. All these children, too, are very aggressive.

Q: Mrs. Benson, what value do you think the Clowns hold for an education?

R: I don't think very much. I don't think education means much to them at this stage. I know it doesn't mean anything to Randy and George. To most of the kids, I don't think it really matters at this stage.

Further Notes on the Second Grade: Reward and Punishment

Throughout the length of the study in the school, it was evident that both the kindergarten and second-grade teachers were teaching the groups within their classes in a dissimilar manner. Variations were evident, for example, in the amount of time the teachers spent teaching the different groups, in the manner in which certain groups were granted privileges which were denied to others, and in the teacher's proximity to the different groups. Two additional considerations related to the teacher's use of reward and punishment.

Though variations were evident from naturalistic observations in the kindergarten, a systematic evaluation was not attempted of the degree to which such differential behavior was a significant aspect of the classroom interactional patterns. When observations were being conducted in the second grade, it appeared that there was on the part of Mrs. Benson a differentiation of reward and punishment similar to that displayed by Mrs. Caplow. In order to examine more closely the degree to which variations were present over time, three observational periods were totally devoted to the tabulation of each of the individual behavioral units directed by the teacher towards the children. Each observational period was three and one-half hours in length, lasting from 8:35 a.m. to 12:00 noon. The dates of the observations were the Fridays at the end of eight, twelve, and sixteen weeks of school — October 24, November 21, and December 19, 1969, respectively.

A mechanism for evaluating the varieties of teacher behavior was developed. Behavior on the part of the teacher was tabulated as a "behavioral unit" when there was clearly directed towards an individual child some manner of communication, whether it be verbal, nonverbal or physical contact. When, within the interaction of the teacher and the student, there occurred more than one type of behavior, that is, the teacher spoke to the child and touched him, a count was made of both variations. The following is a list of the nine variations in teacher behavior that were tabulated within the second-grade classroom. Several examples are also included with each of the alternatives displayed by the teacher within the class.

1. Verbal Supportive — "That's a very good job." "You are such a lovely girl." "My, but your work is so neat."
2. Verbal Neutral — "Laura and Tom, let's open our books to page 34." "May, your pencil is on the floor." "Hal, do you have milk money today?"
3. Verbal Control — "Lou, sit on that chair and shut up." "Curt, get up off that floor." "Mary and Laura, quit your talking."
4. Nonverbal Supportive — Teacher nods her head at Rose. Teacher smiles at Liza. Teacher claps when Laura completes her problem at the board.
5. Nonverbal Neutral — Teacher indicates with her arms that she wants Lilly and Shirley to move farther apart in the circle. Teacher motions to Joe and Tom that they should try to snap their fingers to stay in beat with the music.
6. Nonverbal Control — Teacher frowns at Lena. Teacher shakes finger at Amy to quit tapping her pencil. Teacher motions with hand for Rose not to come to her desk.
7. Physical Contact Supportive — Teacher hugs Laura. Teacher places her arm around Mary as she talks to her. Teacher holds Trish's hand as she takes out a splinter.
8. Physical Contact Neutral — Teacher touches head of Nick as she walks past. Teacher leads Rema to new place on the circle.
9. Physical Contact Control — Teacher strikes Lou with stick. Teacher pushes Curt down in his chair. Teacher pushes Hal and Doug to the floor.

Table 3 which follows is presented with all forms of control, supportive, and neutral behavior grouped together within each of the three observational periods. As a methodological precaution, since the categorization of the various types of behavior was decided as the interaction occurred and there was no cross-validation check by another observer, all behavior was placed in the appropriate neutral category which could not be clearly distinguished as belonging to one of the established supportive or control categories. This may explain the large percentage of neutral behavior tabulated in each of the three observational periods.

The picture of the second-grade teacher, Mrs. Benson, that emerges from analysis of these data is of one who distributes rewards quite sparingly and equally, but who utilizes somewhere between two and five times as much control-oriented behavior with the Clowns as with the Tigers. Alternatively, whereas with the Tigers the combination of neutral and supportive behavior never dropped below 93 percent of the total behavior directed towards them by the teacher in the three periods, the lowest figure for the Cardinals was 86 percent and for the Clowns was 73 percent. It may be assumed that neutral and supportive behavior would be conducive to learning while punishment or control-oriented behavior would not. Thus for the Tigers, the learning situation was one with only infrequent units of control, while for the Clowns, control behavior constituted one-fourth of all behavior directed towards them on at least one occasion.

Research related to leadership structure and task performance in voluntary organizations has given strong indications that within an authoritarian setting there occurs a significant decrease in performance on assigned tasks that does not occur with those in a non-authoritative setting (Kelly & Thibaut, 1954; Lewin, Lippitt, & White, 1939). Further investigations have generally confirmed these findings.

Of particular interest within the classroom are the findings of Adams (1945), Anderson (1946), Anderson et al. (1946), Preston and Heintz (1949), and Robbins (1952). Their findings may be generalized to state that children within an authoritarian classroom display a decrease in both learning retention and performance, while those within the democratic classroom do not. In extrapolating these findings to the second-grade classroom of Mrs. Benson, one cannot say that she was continually "authoritarian" as opposed to "democratic" with her students, but that with one group of students there occurred more control-oriented behavior than with other groups. The group which was the recipient of this control-oriented behavior was that group which she had defined as "slow and disinterested." On at least one occasion Mrs. Benson utilized nearly five times the amount of control-oriented behavior with the Clowns as with her perceived high-interest and high-ability group, the Tigers. For the Clowns, who were most isolated from the teacher and received the least amount of her teaching time, the results noted above would indicate that the substantial control-oriented behavior directed towards them would compound their difficulty in experiencing significant learning and cognitive growth.

Here discussion of the self-fulfilling prophecy is relevant: given the extent to which the teacher utilized control-oriented behavior with the Clowns, data from the leadership and performance studies would indicate that it would be more difficult for that group to experience a positive learning situation. The question remains unanswered, though, as to whether the behavior of uninterested students necessitated the teacher's resorting to extensive use of control-oriented behavior, or whether that to the extent to which the teacher utilized control-oriented behavior, the students responded with uninterest. If the prior experience of the Clowns was in any way similar to that of the students in kindergarten at Table 3 and Table C in the first grade, I am inclined to opt for the latter proposition.

A very serious and, I believe, justifiable consequence of this assumption of student uninterest related to the frequency of the teacher's control-oriented behavior is that the teachers themselves contribute significantly to the creation of the "slow learners" within their classrooms. Over time, this may help to account for the phenomenon noted in the Coleman Report (1966) that the gap between the academic performance of the disadvantaged students and the national norms increased the longer the students remained in the school system. During one of the three and one-half hour observational periods in the second grade, the percentage of control-oriented behavior oriented toward the entire class was about 8 percent. Of the behavior directed toward the Clowns, however, 27 percent was control-oriented behavior — more than three times the amount of control-oriented behavior directed to the class as a whole. Deutsch (1968), in a random sampling of New York City public school classrooms of the fifth through eighth grades, noted that the teachers utilized between 50 and 80 percent of class time in discipline and organization. Unfortunately, he fails to specify the two individual percentages and thus it is unknown whether the classrooms were dominated by either discipline or organization as opposed to their combination. If it is the case, and Deutsch's findings appear to lend indirect support, that the higher the grade level, the greater the discipline and control-oriented behavior by the teacher, some of the unexplained aspects of the "regress phenomenon" may be unlocked.

On another level of analysis, the teacher's use of control-oriented behavior is directly related to the expectations of the ability and willingness of "slow learners" to learn the material she teaches. That is, if the student is uninterested in what goes on in the classroom, he is more apt to engage in activities that the teacher perceives as disruptive. Activities such as talking out loud, coloring when the teacher has not said it to be permissible, attempting to leave the room, calling other students' attention to activities occurring on the street, making comments to the teacher not pertinent to the lesson, dropping books, falling out of the chair, and commenting on how the student cannot wait for recess, all prompt the teacher to employ control-oriented behavior toward that student. The interactional pattern between the uninterested student and the teacher literally becomes a "vicious circle" in which control-oriented behavior is followed by further manifestations of uninterest, followed by further control behavior and so on. The stronger the reciprocity of this pattern of interaction, the greater one may anticipate the strengthening of the teacher's expectation of the "slow learner" as being either unable or unwilling to learn.

The Caste System Falters

A major objective of this study has been to document the manner in which there emerges within the early grades a stratification system, based both on teacher expectations related to behavioral and attitudinal characteristics of the child and also on a variety of socioeconomic status factors related to the background of the child. As noted, when the child begins to move through the grades, the variable of past performance becomes a crucial index of the position of the child within the different classes. The formulation of the system of stratification of the children into various reading groups appears to gain a caste-like character over time in that there was no observed movement into the highest reading group once it had been initially established at the beginning of the kindergarten school year. Likewise, there was no movement out of the highest reading group. There was movement between the second and third reading groups, in that those at the lowest reading table one year are combined with the middle group for a following year, due to the presence of a group of students repeating the grade.

Though formal observations in the second-grade class of Mrs. Benson ended in December of 1969, periodic informal visits to the class continued throughout the remainder of the school year. The organization of the class remained stable save for one notable exception. For the first time during observations in either kindergarten, first or second grade, there had been a reassignment of two students from the highest reading group to the middle reading group. Two students from the Tiger group were moved during the third week of January, 1970 from the Tiger group to the Cardinal group. Two Cardinal group students were assigned to replace those in the Tiger group. Mrs. Benson was asked the reason for the move and she explained that neither of the two former Tiger group students "could keep a clean desk." She noted that both of the students constantly had paper and crayons on the floor beside their desks. She stated that the Tigers "are a very clean group" and the two could no longer remain with the highest reading group because they were "not neat." The two Cardinals who were moved into the Tiger reading group were both described as "extremely neat with their desk and floor."

Poor Kids and Public Schools

It has been a major goal of this paper to demonstrate the impact of teacher expectations, based upon a series of subjectively interpreted social criteria, on both the anticipated academic potential and subsequent differential treatment accorded to those students perceived as having dissimilar social status. For the kindergarten teacher, expectations as to what type of child may be anticipated as a "fast learner" appear to be grounded in her reference group of a mixed White-Black educated middle class. That is, students within her classroom who displayed those attributes which a number of studies have indicated are highly desired in children by middle-class educated adults as being necessary for future success were selected by her as possessing the potential to be a "fast learner." On the other hand, those children who did not possess the desired qualities were defined by the teacher as "slow learners." None of the criteria upon which the teacher appeared to base her evaluation of the children were directly related to measurable aspects of academic potential. Given that the IQ test was administered to the children in the last week of their kindergarten year, the results could not have been of any benefit to the teacher as she established patterns of organization within the class.[5] The IQ scores may have been significant factors for the first- and second-grade teachers, but I assume that consideration of past performance was the major determinant for the seating arrangements which they established.[6]

For the first-grade teacher, Mrs. Logan, and the second-grade teacher, Mrs. Benson, the process of dividing the class into various reading groups, apparently on the basis of past performance, maintained the original patterns of differential treatment and expectations established in the kindergarten class. Those initially defined as "fast learners" by the kindergarten teacher in subsequent years continued to have that position in the first group, regardless of the label or name given to it.

It was evident throughout the length of the study that the teachers made clear the distinctions they perceived between the children who were defined as fast learners and those defined as slow learners. It would not appear incorrect to state that within the classroom there was established by the various teachers a clear system of segregation between the two established groups of children. In the one group were all the children who appeared clean and interested, sought interactions with adults, displayed leadership within the class, and came from homes which displayed various status criteria valued in the middle class. In the other were children who were dirty, smelled of urine, did not actively participate in class, spoke a linguistic dialect other than that spoken by the teacher and students at Table 1, did not display leadership behavior, and came from poor homes often supported by public welfare. I would contend that within the system of segregation established by the teachers, the group perceived as slow learners were ascribed a caste position that sought to keep them apart from the other students.

The placement of the children within the various classrooms into different reading groups was ostensibly done on the promise of future performance in the kindergarten and on differentials of past performance in later grades. However, the placement may rather have been done from purely irrational reasons that had nothing to do with academic performance. The utilization of academic criteria may have served as the rationalization for a more fundamental process occurring with the class whereby the teacher served as the agent of the larger society to ensure that proper "social distance" was maintained between the various strata of the society as represented by the children.

Within the context of this analysis there appear to be at least two interactional processes that may be identified as having occurred simultaneously within the kindergarten classroom. The first was the relation of the teacher to the students placed at Table 1. The process appeared to occur in at least four stages. The initial stage involved the kindergarten teacher's developing expectations regarding certain students as possessing a series of characteristics that she considered essential for future academic "success." Second, the teacher reinforced through her mechanisms of "positive" differential behavior those characteristics of the children that she considered important and desirable.

Third, the children responded with more of the behavior that initially gained them the attention and support of the teacher. Perceiving that verbalization, for example, was a quality that the teacher appeared to admire, the Table 1 children increased their level of verbalization throughout the school year. Fourth, the cycle was complete as the teacher focused even more specifically on the children at Table 1 who continued to manifest the behavior she desired. A positive interactional scheme arose whereby initial behavioral patterns of the student were reinforced into apparent permanent behavioral patterns, once he had received support and differential treatment from the teacher.

Within this framework, the actual academic potential of the students was not objectively measured prior to the kindergarten teacher's evaluation of expected performance. The students may be assumed to have had mixed potential. However, the common positive treatment accorded to all within the group by the teacher may have served as the necessary catalyst for the self-fulfilling prophecy whereby those expected to do well did so.

A concurrent behavioral process appeared to occur between the teacher and those students placed at Tables 2 and 3. The student came into the class possessing a series of behavioral and attitudinal characteristics that within the frame of reference of the teacher were perceived as indicative of "failure." Second, through mechanisms of reinforcement of her initial expectations as to the future performance of the student, it was made evident that he was not perceived as similar or equal to those at the table of fast learners. In the third stage, the student responded to both the definition and actual treatment given to him by the teacher which emphasized his characteristics of being an educational "failure." Given the high degree of control-oriented behavior directed toward the "slower" learner, the lack of verbal interaction and encouragement, the disproportionally small amount of teaching time given to him, and the ridicule and hostility, the child withdrew from class participation. The fourth stage was the cyclical repetition of behavioral and attitudinal characteristics that led to the initial labeling as an educational failure.

As with those perceived as having high probability of future success, the academic potential of the failure group was not objectively determined prior to evaluation by the kindergarten teacher. This group also may be assumed to have come into the class with mixed potential. Some within the group may have had the capacity to perform academic tasks quite well, while others perhaps did not. Yet the reinforcement by the teacher of the characteristics in the children that she had perceived as leading to academic failure may, in fact, have created the very conditions of student failure. With the "negative" treatment accorded to the perceived failure group, the teacher's definition of the situation may have ensured its emergence. What the teacher perceived in the children may have served as the catalyst for a series of interactions, with the result that the child came to act out within the class the very expectations defined for him by the teacher.

As an alternative explanation, however, the teacher may have developed the system of caste segregation within the classroom, not because the groups of children were so similar they had to be handled in an entirely different manner, but because they were, in fact, so very close to one another. The teacher may have believed quite strongly that the ghetto community inhibited the development of middle-class success models. Thus, it was her duty to "save" at least one group of children from the "streets." Those children had to be kept separate who could have had a "bad" influence on the children who appeared to have a chance to "make it" in the middle class of the larger society. Within this framework, the teacher's actions may be understood not only as an attempt to keep the slow learners away from those fast learners, but to ensure that the fast learners would not so be influenced that they themselves become enticed with the "streets" and lose their apparent opportunity for future middle-class status.

In addition to the formal separation of the groups within the classroom, there was also the persistence of mechanisms utilized by the teacher to socialize the children in the high reading group with feelings of aversion, revulsion, and rejection towards those of the lower reading groups. Through ridicule, belittlement, physical punishment, and merely ignoring them, the teacher was continually giving clues to those in the high reading group as to how one with high status and a high probability of future success treats those of low status and low probability of future success. To maintain within the larger society the caste aspects of the position of the poor vis à vis the remainder of the society, there has to occur the transmission from one generation to another the attitudes and values necessary to legitimate and continue such a form of social organization.

Given the extreme intercomplexity of the organizational structure of this society, the institutions that both create and sustain social organization can neither be held singularly responsible for perpetuating the inequalities nor for eradicating them (see also Leacock, 1969). The public school system, I believe, is justifiably responsible for contributing to the present structure of the society, but the responsibility is not its alone. The picture that emerges from this study is that the school strongly shares in the complicity of maintaining the organizational perpetuation of poverty and unequal opportunity. This, of course, is in contrast to the formal doctrine of education in this country to ameliorate rather than aggravate the conditions of the poor.

The teachers' reliance on a mixed Black-White educated middle class for their normative reference group appeared to contain assumptions of superiority over those of lower-class and status positions. For they and those members of their reference group, comfortable affluence, education, community participation, and possession of professional status may have afforded a rather stable view of the social order. The treatment of those from lower socioeconomic backgrounds within the classrooms by the teachers may have indicated that the values highly esteemed by them were not open to members of the lower groups. Thus the lower groups were in numerous ways informed of their lower status and were socialized for a role of lower self expectations and also for respect and deference towards those of higher status. The social distance between the groups within the classrooms were manifested in its extreme form by the maintenance of patterns of caste segregation whereby those of lower positions were not allowed to become a part of the peer group at the highest level. The value system of the teachers appeared to necessitate that a certain group be ostracized due to "unworthiness" or inherent inferiority. The very beliefs which legitimated exclusion were maintained among those of the higher social group which then contributed to the continuation of the pattern of social organization itself.

It has not been a contention of this study that the teachers observed could not or would not teach their students. They did, I believe, teach quite well. But the high quality teaching was not made equally accessible to all students in the class. For the students of high socioeconomic background who were perceived by the teachers as possessing desirable behavioral and attitudinal characteristics, the classroom experience was one where the teachers displayed interest in them, spent a large proportion of teaching time with them, directed little control-oriented behavior toward them, held them as models for the remainder of the class and continually reinforced statements that they were "special" students. Hypothetically, if the classrooms observed had contained only those students perceived by the teachers as having a desirable social status and a high probability of future success outside the confines of the ghetto community, the teachers could be assumed to have continued to teach well, and under these circumstances, to the entire class.

Though the analysis has focused on the early years of schooling for a single group of Black children attending a ghetto school, the implications are far-reaching for those situations where there are children from different status backgrounds within the same classroom. When a teacher bases her expectations of performance on the social status of the student and assumes that the higher the social status, the higher the potential of the child, those children of low social status suffer a stigmatization outside of their own choice or will. Yet there is a greater tragedy than being labeled as a slow learner, and that is being treated as one. The differential amounts of control-oriented behavior, the lack of interaction with the teacher, the ridicule from one's peers, and the caste aspects of being placed in lower reading groups all have implications for the future life style and value of education for the child.

Though it may be argued from the above that the solution to the existence of differential treatment for students is the establishment of schools catering to only a single segment of the population, I regard this as being antithetical to the goals of education — if one views the ultimate value of an education as providing insights and experience with thoughts and persons different from oneself. The thrust of the educational experience should be towards diversity, not homogeneity. It may be utopian to suggest that education should seek to encompass as wide a variety of individuals as possible within the same setting, but it is no mean goal to pursue.

The success of an educational institution and any individual teacher should not be measured by the treatment of the high-achieving students, but rather by the treatment of those not achieving. As is the case with a chain, ultimate value is based on the weakest member. So long as the lower-status students are treated differently in both quality and quantity of education, there will exist an imperative for change.

It should be apparent, of course, that if one desires this society to retain its present social class configuration and the disproportional access to wealth, power, social and economic mobility, medical care, and choice of life styles, one should not disturb the methods of education as presented in this study. This contention is made because what develops a "caste" within the classrooms appears to emerge in the larger society as "class." The low-income children segregated as a caste of "unclean and intellectually inferior" persons may very well be those who in their adult years become the car washers, dishwashers, welfare recipients, and participants in numerous other un- or underemployed roles within this society. The question may quite honestly be asked, "Given the treatment of low-income children from the beginning of their kindergarten experience, for what class strata are they being prepared other than that of the lower class?" It appears that the public school system not only mirrors the configurations of the larger society, but also significantly contributes to maintaining them. Thus the system of public education in reality perpetuates what it is ideologically committed to eradicate — class barriers which result in inequality in the social and economic life of the citizenry.

Notes

1. The author, due to a teaching appointment out of the city, was unable to conduct formal observations of the children during their first-grade year.
2. The names of all staff and students are pseudonyms. Names are provided to indicate that the discussion relates to living persons, and not to fictional characters by the author.
3. Through the remainder of the paper, reference to "high" or "low" status students refers to status ascribed to the student by the teacher. Her ascription appeared to be based on perceptions of valued behavioral and cultural characteristics present or absent in any individual student.
4. The names were not given to the groups until the third week of school, though the seating arrangement was established on the third day.
5. The results of the IQ Test for the kindergarten class indicated that, though there were no statistically significant differences among the children at the three tables, the scores were skewed slightly higher for the children at Table 1. There were, however, children at Tables 2 and 3 who did score higher than several students at Table 1. The highest score came from a student at Table 1 (124) while the lowest came from a student at Table 3 (78). There appear to be at least three alternative explanations for the slightly higher scores by students at Table 1. First, the scores may represent the result of differential treatment in the classroom by Mrs. Caplow, thus contributing to the validation of the self-fulfilling prophecy. That is, the teacher by the predominance of teaching time spent with the Table 1 students, better prepared the students to do well on the examination than was the case for those students who received less teaching time. Second, the tests themselves may have reflected strong biases towards the knowledge and experience of middle-class children. Thus, students from higher-status families at Table 1 could be expected to perform better than did the low-status students from Table 3. The test resulted not in a "value free" measure of cognitive capacity, but in an index of family background. Third, of course, would be the fact that the children at the first table did possess a higher degree of academic potential than those at the other tables, and the teacher was intuitively able to discern these differences. This third alternative, however, is least susceptible to empirical verification.
6. When the second-grade teacher was questioned as to what significance she placed in the results of IQ tests, she replied, "They merely confirm what I already know about the student."

References

Adams, R. G. (1945). *The behavior of pupils in democratic and autocratic social climates.* Abstracts of dissertations, Stanford University.

Anderson, H. (1946). *Studies in teachers' classroom personalities.* Stanford, CA: Stanford University Press.

Anderson, H., Brewer, J., & Reed, M. (1946). *Studies of teachers' classroom personalities, III: Follow-up studies of the effects of dominative and integrative contacts on children's behavior* (Applied Psychology Monograph). Stanford, CA: Stanford University Press.

Asbell, B. (1963, October). Not like other children. *Redbook*, pp. 114–118.

Austin, M. C., & Morrison, C. (1963). *The first r: The Harvard report on reading in elementary schools*. New York: Macmillan.

Becker, H. S. (1952). Social class variation in teacher-pupil relationship. *Journal of Educational Sociology, 25,* 451–465.

Borg, W. (1964). *Ability grouping in the public schools* (Cooperative Research Project No. 557). Salt Lake City: Utah State University.

Clark, K. B. (1963). Educational stimulation of racially disadvantaged children. In A. H. Passow (Ed.), *Education in depressed areas*. New York: Columbia University Press.

Coleman, J. S., et al. (1966). *Equality of educational opportunity*. Washington, DC: U.S. Government Printing Office.

Deutsch, M. (1967). Minority groups and class status as related to social and personality factors in scholastic achievement. In M. Deutsch et al. (Eds.), *The disadvantaged child*. New York: Basic Books.

Eddy, E. (1967). *Walk the white line*. Garden City, NY: Doubleday.

Frazier, E. F. (1957). *Black bourgeoisie*. New York: Free Press.

Freeman, R., Whelpton, P., & Campbell, A. (1959). *Family planning, sterility and population growth*. New York: McGraw-Hill

Fuchs, E. (1967). *Teachers talk*. Garden City, NY: Doubleday.

Gebhard, P., Pomeroy, W., Martin, C., & Christenson, C. (1958). *Pregnancy, birth and abortion*. New York: Harper & Row.

Gibson, G. (1965). Aptitude tests. *Science, 149,* 583.

Goldberg, M., Passow, A., & Justman, J. (1966). *The effects of ability grouping*. New York: Teachers College Press, Columbia University.

Harlem Youth Opportunities Unlimited. (1964). *Youth in the ghetto*. New York: HARYOU.

Henry, J. (1955). Docility, or giving the teacher what she wants. *Journal of Social Issues, 11,* 2.

Henry, J. (1959). The problem of spontaneity, initiative and creativity in suburban classrooms. *American Journal of Orthopsychiatry, 29,* 1.

Henry, J. (1963). Golden rule days: American schoolrooms. In *Culture against man*. New York: Random House.

Hollingshead, A. (1949). *Elmtown's youth*. New York: John Wiley & Sons.

Jackson, P. (1968). *Life in classrooms*. New York: Holt, Rinehart & Winston.

Kahl, J. A. (1957). *The American class structure*. New York: Holt, Rinehart & Winston.

Katz, I. (1964). Review of evidence relating to effects of desegregation on intellectual performance of Negroes. *American Psychologist, 19,* 381–399.

Kelly, H., & Thibaut, J. (1954). Experimental studies of group problem solving and process. In G. Lindzey (Ed.), *Handbook of social psychology, vol. 2*. Reading, MA: Addison-Wesley.

Kohn, H. (1967). *36 children*. New York: New American Library.

Kozol, J. (1967). *Death at an early age*. Boston: Houghton Mifflin.

Kvaraceus, W. C. (1965). *Disadvantaged children and youth: Programs of promise or pretense?* (Mimeograph). Burlingame: California Teachers Association.

Lawrence, S. (1969). *Ability grouping*. Unpublished manuscript, Harvard Graduate School of Education, Center for Educational Policy Research, Cambridge, MA.

Leacock, E. (1969). *Teaching and learning in city schools*. New York: Basic Books.

Lewin, K., Lippitt, R., & White, R. (1939). Patterns of aggressive behavior in experimentally created social climates. *Journal of Social Psychology, 10,* 271–299.

Lynd, H., & Lynd, R. (1937). *Middletown in transition*. New York: Harcourt, Brace & World.

MacKinnon, D. W. (1962). The nature and nurture of creative talent. *American Psychologist, 17,* 484–495.

Merton, R. K. (1957). *Social theory and social structure* (rev. ed.). New York: Free Press.

Moore, A. (1967). *Realities of the urban classroom*. Garden City, NY: Doubleday.

Notestein, F. (1953). Class differences in fertility. In R. Bendix & S. Lipset (Eds.), *Class, status and power*. New York: Free Press.

Preston, M., & Heintz, R. (1949). Effects of participatory versus supervisory leadership on group judgment. *Journal of Abnormal Social Psychology, 44,* 345–355.

Reissman, L. (1959). *Class in American society*. New York: Free Press.

Riessman, F. (1962). *The culturally deprived child*. New York: Harper and Row.

Riessman, F. (1965). *Teachers of the poor: A five point program* (Mimeographed). Burlingame: California Teachers Association.

Robbins, F. (1952). The impact of social climate upon a college class. *School Review, 60,* 275–284.

Rose, A. (1956). *The Negro in America.* Boston: Beacon Press.

Rosenthal, R., & Jacobson, L. (1968). *Pygmalion in the classroom.* New York: Holt, Rinehart & Winston.

Sigel, I. (1969). The Piagetian system and the world of education. In D. Elkind & J. Flavell (Eds.), *Studies in cognitive development.* New York: Oxford University Press.

Simpson, G., & Yinger, J. M. (1958). *Racial and cultural minorities.* New York: Harper and Row.

Smith, L., & Geoffrey, W. (1968). *The complexities of an urban classroom.* New York: Holt, Rinehart & Winston.

Smith, M. (1971). Equality of educational opportunity: The basic findings reconsidered. In F. Mosteller & D. P. Moynihan (Eds.), *On equality of educational opportunity.* New York: Random House.

Warner, W. L., Havighurst, R., & Loeb, M. (1944). *Who shall be educated?* New York: Harper and Row.

Wilson, A. B. (1963). Social stratification and academic achievement. In A. H. Passow (Ed.), *Education in depressed areas.* New York: Teachers College Press, Columbia University.

Part Three

Expanding Opportunities,
Fostering Achievement

Part Three

Introduction

n a 1986 article in the *Harvard Educational Review,* noted scholar Jim Cummins advocated for personal and institutional redefinitions to reverse the pattern of minority student failure.[1] He outlined three kinds of interactions or structures that needed to be transformed for this purpose: classroom interactions between teachers and students; the relationships between schools and minority communities; and intergroup power relations within society as a whole. The achievement differences that exist between different groups of students in the United States thus reflect not only structures in societies and broader policy, but also reflect the extent to which individual educators respond to the structures and policies that benefit some students and disadvantage others. Twenty years later we are still looking for ways to change these patterns of minority student failure. But who is failing? Is it the students? Or is it us as educators, as policymakers, as community members who are failing to provide adequate opportunities for our students? In what ways have we been able to redefine the problem of inequity as Jim Cummins was urging us to?

The authors in Part Three direct us to initiatives in practice and research where these redefinitions have been attempted at the various levels that Cummins advocates for, in the hope of bridging the opportunity gap for minority students and moving towards the lofty goal of achieving educational opportunity for all. These initiatives though exemplary, are by no means meant to be an exhaustive list of best practices to resolve the achievement and opportunity gaps. Rather, they represent some significant, albeit humble, efforts to guide us as we begin to reenvision the realm of educational opportunity. Each of the chapters included in this section remind us that the challenge of providing equal educational opportunity calls for a collective response — the coordinated efforts and action of multiple players in the field of education.

In *The Algebra Project: Organizing in the Spirit of Ella,* Robert Moses, Mieko Kamii, Susan Swap, and Jeff Howard discuss the intersection of civil rights organizing with educational efforts in the realm of middle school mathematics education. The authors examine in depth The Algebra Project, an ongoing multiyear project created to establish a pedagogy of mathematics that encourages every student to study algebra at the middle school level. Moses, in his role as civil rights activist, math educator, and parent, provides an elaborate narrative that brings together these three different perspectives in the service of providing all children to access to a rigorous mathematics curriculum designed to prepare them not just for college, but to participate fully in an economy driven by rapid technological change and innovation. The authors inform us of the centrality of mathematics as a medium that can empower students to transcend their disadvantages and become leaders in their communities. Yet, as the authors point out, the subjects of mathematics and algebra are often mystified, perceived as inaccessible, and frustrating to students. The authors seek to reverse this injustice by questioning policies (such as ability grouping or tracking) and providing a vision of high expectations for all students to engage in algebra at the middle school level. They reinforce the need to coordinate efforts of teachers, parents, community organizers, policymakers, and philanthropists to develop fresh and innovative curricula that are culturally responsive, linked to students' everyday lives, and that empower them to succeed in school and in their lives.

Christopher Kliewer, Linda May Fitzgerald, Jodi Meyer-Mork, Patresa Hartman, Pat English-Sand, and Donna Raschke, in *Citizenship for All in Literate Community: An Ethnography of Young Children with Significant Disabilities in Inclusive Early Childhood Settings*, take us to another cornerstone of academic success — literacy. The authors draw on their varying roles — as special educator, professors specializing in special education and disabilities, and school psychologist — to highlight an intervention aimed at developing literacy in children with significant disabilities. The study, which spanned two years and was set in nine preschool and kindergarten classrooms where children with and without disabilities were learning in the same space. Kliewer, et al. emphasize the importance of linking instruction with the experiences and narratives of students, and in viewing them as competent and capable of achievement. Though the article is about teaching students with significant disabilities, the lessons shared by the authors can be used in multiple contexts and educational settings. The use of ethnography by authors who occupy different places in the realm of education, demonstrates that any intervention to correct the inequality in educational opportunity needs long and hard reflection, research, and a coordinated and persistent effort from researchers and practitioners. The authors assert that we must necessarily start with *imagination* — with a belief in the abilities of all students and a recognition of all students as full citizens who are each able to make meaning, albeit in their own way.

Sonia Nieto, who closes Part Three with *Lessons from Students on Creating a Chance to Dream*, reaffirms Moses's and Kliewer's respect for the inherent abilities and meaning-making skills of students. Nieto, a researcher, educator, and activist, urges us to turn to students — that is, to those who are the most affected by educational reform — and include them in the dialogue about expanding educational opportunities. Instead of focusing on their vulnerabilities, Nieto focuses on their resilience and the wealth of personal experience that they bring to the educational settings they inhabit.

She uses interviews to develop case studies of high school students from a wide variety of ethnic, racial, linguistic, and social-class backgrounds, asking them their thoughts about school policies and practices and how they impact their experience of inequities in educational opportunity. In giving voice to the experiences and opinions of students, Nieto teaches us that listening to students is crucial if we are to develop antiracist, critical pedagogy that is rooted in social justice and geared toward providing equal opportunity for all. This argument takes on special relevance when we consider that a huge percentage of students in U.S. schools today are first-generation school-goers and that their populations are not adequately represented in the school faculty or administration.

In Nieto's research, as with the work of the other authors included in this section, there is an implication that expanding educational opportunities implies a transformation not only of schools but also "of our hearts and minds." Nieto reminds us that there is a need to transform our attitude of looking at deficits or achievement gaps into an attitude of tapping into the great strengths that each student brings to the classroom and providing them with opportunities to maximize these strengths and experience success and fulfillment.

Notes

1. Jim Cummins, "Empowering Minority Students: A Framework for Intervention," *Harvard Educational Review* 56, no. 1 (1986): 18-36.

The Algebra Project

Organizing in the Spirit of Ella

ROBERT PARRIS MOSES
MIEKO KAMII
SUSAN MCALLISTER SWAP
JEFF HOWARD

The United States is beginning to address, in a fundamental way, the teaching of mathematics in its middle schools. The National Science Foundation (1989), for instance, has issued a request for proposals to develop materials for middle school mathematics instruction that sets out the technical elements of the problem in great detail. At the heart of math-science education issues, however, is a basic political question: If the current technological revolution demands new standards of mathematics and science literacy, will all citizens be given equal access to the new skills, or will some be left behind, denied participation in the unfolding economic and political era? Those who are concerned about the life chances for historically oppressed people in the United States must not allow math-science education to be addressed as if it were purely a matter of technical instruction.

The Algebra Project, a math-science program in Cambridge, Massachusetts, has organized local communities to help make algebra available to all seventh- and eighth-grade students, regardless of their prior level of skill development or academic achievement. The project's philosophy is that access to algebra will enable students to participate in advanced high school math and science courses, which in turn are a gateway for college entrance. The project offers a new curriculum and a five-step curricular process for sixth-graders that provides the following: a smooth transition from the concepts of arithmetic to those of algebra, increasing the likelihood of mastery of seventh- and eighth-grade algebra; a home, community, and school culture involving teachers, parents, community volunteers, and school administrators in activities that support students' academic achievement; and a model of intellectual development that is based on motivation rather than ability.

The belief that ability is the essential ingredient driving intellectual development and is necessary for mastering advanced school mathematics is the ba-

Harvard Educational Review Vol. 59 No. 4 November 1989, 423–443

sis for the differentiation in mathematics curricula at the eighth-grade level as well as the widespread practice of offering eighth-grade algebra only to students who are "mathematically inclined" or "gifted." The developers of the Algebra Project have called upon the traditions of the civil rights movement to assist communities in organizing a challenge to the ability model and its institutional expressions.

Traditions of the Civil Rights Movement in Mississippi

Through the Public Broadcasting System's (PBS) Eyes on the Prize series, the American public has been given an opportunity to revisit the civil rights movement's community mobilization tradition. Masses of people were mobilized to participate in large-scale events such as the Birmingham campaign, the March on Washington, and the Selma-to-Montgomery March, which were aimed at achieving equal access for Southern Blacks to public facilities and institutions. The tradition is epitomized by Dr. Martin Luther King, Jr., who lifted the movement by inspiring immense crowds in vast public spaces.

Within the civil rights movement was an older, yet less well known, community organizing tradition. This tradition laid the foundation for Mississippi Freedom Summer (1964), which revolutionized race relations in Mississippi, and for the Voting Rights Act of 1965, which altered politics throughout the South during the last quarter of this century. Its leader was Ella Baker, a community organizer and fundi whose wisdom and counsel guided the Black veterans of the first wave of student sit-ins through the founding and establishment of the Student Nonviolent Coordinating Committee (SNCC).[1] She inspired in SNCC field secretaries a spiritual belief in human dignity, a faith in the capacity of Blacks to produce leaders from the ranks of their people, and a perseverance when confronting overwhelming obstacles. Baker symbolizes the tradition in the civil rights movement of quiet places and the organizers who liked to work in them.[2] Just as her spirit, consciousness, and teaching infused the Mississippi Movement, they permeated the Algebra Project from its inception.

Three aspects of the Mississippi organizing tradition underlie the Algebra Project: the centrality of families to the work of organizing; the empowerment of grassroots people and their recruitment for leadership; and the principle of "casting down your bucket where you are," or organizing in the context in which one lives and works, and working the issues found in that context.[3]

Families and Organizing

Of central importance to the Mississippi Movement was the capacity of Black families to adopt, nurture, love, and protect civil rights organizers as if they were family members. This practice, known in the literature as "informal absorption," allowed SNCC and CORE (Congress of Racial Equality) field secretaries and organizers to move from place to place in Mississippi with scarcely a dollar in their pockets, knowing full well that a family welcome awaited them at the end of their journeys. The absorption of civil rights organizers into Black families was spiritual gold for the Mississippi Movement, and it empowered movement organizers with the one credential that they could never earn: being one of the community's children. This credential contradicted the label of "outside agitator" used in Mississippi by the White power structure to negate the impact of the movement. By the same token, movement organizers empowered their adoptive families by reinforcing and enlarging the connections between them and the larger movement family, with its extensive networks across the land.

Grassroots People and Grassroots Leadership

The Mississippi Movement's message of empowerment for grassroots people was delivered to the entire country on national television at the 1964 Democratic National Convention by the Black sharecroppers, domestic workers, and farmers who formed the rank and file of the Mississippi Freedom Democratic Party (MFDP). Thereafter, the message of empowerment was carried by Black and White community organizers into many areas of community activity, including education, health, welfare, religion, and politics. However, neither the MFDP nor other grassroots organizations took root and flourished into a strong national movement for empowering Black people. The echoes heard — from the Democratic party to the federal government and from the religious sector to public school systems — were the same: institutionalizing empowerment in the hands of Black "folk" is too risky a notion to attract lasting political support.

The issue of community empowerment in the public schools, first raised by Black community organizers in Harlem in 1965, also found expression in White, liberal America. For example, in 1969 the Open Program of the Martin Luther King, Jr., School was established as a magnet program in the Cambridge public schools, in part because of the clamoring of Cambridge parents for more open education programs for their children, and in part because of the response to desegregation of the Cambridge schools.[4]

"Cast down your bucket where you are"

To master the art of organizing that strives to empower grassroots people, one needs to learn to "cast down your bucket where you are." In 1976, Bob and Janet Moses, both former organizers for SNCC in Mississippi, cast down their bucket in Cambridge and looked to the Open Program of the King School as a place to educate their children.[5] What would later become the Algebra Project began in 1982 when their eldest daughter, Maisha, entered the Open Program's eighth grade.

The Algebra Project

Before 1982, Moses, whose background included teaching secondary school mathematics in New York City and in Tanzania, had been teaching math to his children at home. Maisha, now a junior at Harvard University, recalls these lessons, conducted weekly during the school year and daily during the summer and vacations:

> Doing math at home was always a lot harder than math at school. It was somewhat like a chore. In our family, extra reading with my mom when we were much younger and math with my dad was part of our responsibility in the family, like taking out the garbage or doing the laundry.

Moses faced a familiar challenge: the resistance of adolescent children to performing what they regarded as a "household chore." Maisha explains:

> As we were getting older, it was a lot harder to get us to do math at home. We battled a lot more and complained. "Why do we have to do this? No one else has to do this." Dad would say, "It's important. I want you to do it. You need to do it." But we wouldn't be satisfied. I didn't really want to do it. Dad would have to sit there and force answers out of me. Finally he decided that the only way to get me to do algebra was to go into school.

In the fall of 1982, Mary Lou Mehrling, Maisha's eighth-grade teacher, invited Moses into her seventh/eighth-grade classroom to work with Maisha and three other eighth graders on algebra. That spring, Maisha and two others took the Cambridge citywide algebra test that was offered to students who wished to bypass Algebra I and go directly into honors algebra or honors geometry in the ninth grade. All three passed, becoming the first students in the history of the King School to be eligible to pursue the honors math and science curriculum at Cambridge's only high school, Cambridge Rindge and Latin.[6]

With one eye on his eldest son, who was about to enter the Open Program's seventh grade, Moses decided to continue working the next year (1983–1984) with Mehrling and another seventh/eighth-grade teacher. The number of eighth-graders studying algebra with Moses increased to nine. Partway through the year, the teachers selected seven seventh-graders they thought were likely to begin algebra the following year, creating the first group of "high-ability" seventh-graders for Moses to direct. That spring, all nine of Moses's eighth-graders took the citywide algebra test, and six passed.

In the following year the program expanded again, but it was no longer quite the same. As early as 1983–1984, it was evident that in spite of the commitment to meeting the educational needs of all its pupils, mathematics instruction in the Open Program was unwittingly skewed along racial lines.[7] Children in the two seventh/eighth-grade classrooms were clustered into separate ability groups: above-grade-level tracks primarily composed of middle-class Whites; below-grade-level tracks made up almost exclusively of Blacks and other children of color; and grade-level tracks that were racially mixed. The Open Program's system of ability groups effectively shunted most students of color onto the no-algebra track, imbuing too many youngsters with the self-fulfilling notion that little was expected of them.

Additionally, Moses and Mehrling became aware that some high-achieving Black males felt uncomfortable joining the algebra group, for it meant being separated from their friends who were on other math tracks. On the whole, young people feel the need to be as similar to their peers as possible. Separating academically talented adolescents from their peers for the sake of participation in the academic "fast track" potentially aggravates the anxiety that accompanies adolescents' identity development.[8] Moreover, enduring attitudes toward math are shaped by math instruction at the seventh- and eighth-grade levels. Traditionally, very few new math principles are introduced in these two grades, when attention focuses instead on review (Usiskin, 1987). Moses and Mehrling hypothesized that using the seventh and eighth grades to lay a groundwork of competence in algebra might enhance students' general self-confidence and provide them with the mathematical background necessary for advanced high school courses.

The Mississippi Movement's organizing tradition utilized everyday issues of ordinary people and framed them for the maximum benefit of the community. In Mississippi the issue was the right to vote; technically: "What are the legal, judicial, political, and constitutional obstacles to the right to vote? How can we initiate court cases, introduce legislation, and mobilize political support to remove these obstacles?" SNCC and CORE workers pursued this goal by establishing beachheads, through Black families, in the most resistant counties throughout the state. But the Mississippi organizers did something of even greater importance, and that was to conceive of the issue of voting in its broadest political sense. Midway through voter registration efforts, they began to ask themselves and the Black community: "What is the vote for? Why do we want it in the first place? What must we do right now to ensure that when we have the vote, it will work for us to benefit our communities?" After the organizers and key community groups had worked and reworked these and other questions, they shifted the organizing strategy from increasing voter registration to laying the basis for a community-based political party, which eventually became the Mississippi Freedom Democratic Party. Creating a new political party became the Mississippi Movement's focus, because of its greater potential for involving community people in a substantive long-term effort. Participants would come to own the political questions and their responses to them.[9]

In the Open Program the everyday issue was teaching algebra in the seventh and eighth grades. Moses, the parent-as-organizer in the program, instinctively used the lesson he had learned in Mississippi, transforming the everyday issue into a broader political question for the Open Program community to consider: What is algebra for? Why do we want children to study it? What do we need to include in the mathematics education of every middle school student, to provide each and every one of them with access to the college preparatory mathematics curriculum in high school? Why is it important to gain such access?

By linking the content of math education to the future prospects of inner-city children, Moses transformed what had previously been a purely curricular issue into a broader political question. Drawing on his experience as an organizer, educator, and parent, Moses transformed the dialogue among parents, teachers, and school administrators in the Open Program into one that centered on questions that would get at the heart of educational practice: How can a culture be created in the Open Program in which every child is expected to be as good as possible in his or her mathematical development? What should the content of middle school mathematics be? What curricular processes make that content available to all students?

A cornerstone of the evolving Algebra Project thus became the expectation that every child in the Open Program could achieve math literacy, an ethos powerful enough to suffuse both the peer and adult culture. The components of this effort included changing the content and methods of teaching math, involving parents in activities that would enable them to better support their children's learning, teaching students to set goals and motivating them to achieve, and reaching out to Black college graduates in the Boston area who would serve as tutors and role models of academic success.

Teachers as Learners

From the beginning, Mehrling and Moses modeled the notion that there is no shame in confessing ignorance — if it is the first step in learning. Mehrling, an ex-music teacher, took courses in mathematics, beginning with algebra, and eventually achieved state certification in math. But she did something more profound: she turned her inexperience with math content into a component of learning by adopting a position of mutual inquiry with her students and by presenting herself to them as a learner. As she states, she "developed methods of responding to students' questions that helped both the students and me to think through the problems." When she had questions, she would ask Moses for help, on the spot:

> Presenting myself as a learner, in front of my students, helped me to understand what they were experiencing, and helped them to feel comfortable asking for help. Students no longer felt threatened if they did not understand a problem or a concept, for they saw that we all were learners and we all learn in different ways.

Because Mehrling presented herself openly and honestly as a student of the subject she was teaching, she was able to help build her students' confidence. She overtly transmitted the message, "if I [your teacher] can risk embarrassment to learn this subject, surely you can, too." But she also conveyed to them a powerful latent message:

> I am confident that people who don't know this subject can learn it; to learn it they have, at all times, to be ready not to pretend to understand what they do not truly understand; to learn it they must be comfortable asking for help and willing to risk embarrassment.

Mehrling's message recapitulated a memorable message that Fannie Lou Hamer and others conveyed at the height of the MFDP challenge to the Democratic National Convention of 1964 — confidence that people who did not know the business of politics could learn it by asking direct questions and risking embarrassment. Each confronted their inexperience with honesty and integrity, turning potential liabilities into strengths.

Involving Parents

From its inception, the Open Program had evolved a set of policies and practices that encouraged parents' active involvement in staff hiring, curriculum development, observation and evaluation of teachers, and governance and administration of the school. Parental involvement in the Algebra Project grew naturally in this context.

Parents who served on the program's seventh/eighth-grade committee in 1984–1985 concluded that decisions about studying algebra in the seventh and eighth grades could not be left up to individual sixth-graders. These children were too young to fully understand the long-range implications of their decisions for college entrance. Nor should such decisions rest solely with the teachers, curriculum coordinators, or school or district-wide administrators, each of whom had their own ideas about who should study algebra and in which grade. Rather, parents needed to be involved in making educational choices for their children at both individual and policymaking levels. They also had to be better informed about details of the middle school math curriculum so that they would be able to make informed decisions and protect the best interests of their children.

During the spring of 1985, a parent from the Open Program's seventh/eighth-grade committee collaborated with Moses to distribute a letter to the parents of all the sixth-graders, asking whether they thought that every seventh-grader should study algebra, and whether they thought their own child should study algebra in the seventh grade. In reply, a few parents said they thought that some seventh- graders probably weren't ready, but no parent thought his or her own child should be denied access to algebra in the seventh grade. Exposing the contradictions between parental assessments of their children's capabilities and curricular assumptions at the community level provided a means for building consensus around educational outcomes for all children.

This was the catalyst for inviting all Open Program children entering the seventh grade in the fall of 1985 to study algebra three times a week. With the exception of a few eighth-graders who in their teacher's judgment were not ready, the invitation to study algebra was extended to the entire eighth grade as well. The consensus statement from parents launched a change in school policy and culture. Currently, every Open Program student is expected to study algebra in the seventh and eighth grades.

As the project evolved, parental participation increased as parents volunteered in classrooms and participated in workshops on student self-esteem and achievement. Parents from throughout the King School were invited to attend "Honors Bound" parent groups, which prepared students of color to accept the challenge of taking honors courses in high school and created a home-school culture that would nurture and support serious intellectual effort. A Saturday morning algebra course for parents was offered, teaching algebra in the same way that it was being taught to their children.

Parents who took algebra during the Saturday classes committed themselves to making the project "theirs" in a fundamental sense. A grateful parent captured the multiple dimensions of this experience in a 1987 letter to the Cambridge School Committee:

> . . . this program exemplifies to me all that I hope most for in the education of my daughter and other young people in our community: a positive orientation to

learning; a rich understanding of advanced mathematics; recognition of the relationship between what is learned in the classroom and what goes on in life; and a sense of personal empowerment.

As a sixth grader in her first year in the program, my daughter began to overcome her fear of math and distorted perceptions of what she is capable of doing and why it is important. I believe this was due to several factors, including the climate of learning in the classroom (in part, a sense that students, teachers and aides alike were learning together); the demystification of the subject by relating it to life experiences; and by the fact that her mother, along with other parents and community members, was simultaneously overcoming latent math panic by taking the course on Saturdays.

This experience not only helped me understand the program (and learn math); it also greatly enhanced my comprehension of the life of the school and neighborhood community and of problems that as a citizen I can help to resolve.
. . .

Parents were barraged with letters and opportunities to talk, to ask questions, and to join in planning, all as an acknowledgment of the centrality of parents in the construction of a home-school culture of high achievement.

Creating a New Teaching and Learning Environment for Math

As an adjunct to opening up algebra to all seventh and eighth graders in 1985, ability grouping was replaced with individual and small-group instruction. Students were taught skills for learning hard material "on their own." In conferences with teachers, students were asked to set their own short-term objectives (for example, deciding how many lesson sets they wished to complete each week), and longer-range goals (for example, deciding to prepare for the citywide test). Parents were informed about the goals and were asked to sign their child's goal statement each semester. The pace and scope of students' mathematical studies therefore came under student control. Mehrling tells a story that reflects the individual and group motivation that such goal-setting can foster:

> Andrea spoke up at one of our first meetings and said, "I'm going to do four lessons a week because I want to finish such-and-such by the end of seventh grade, so I can finish the book by the end of the eighth grade, so I can be in honors geometry in the ninth grade." This was a twelve-year-old. The others looked at her — this hadn't come from a teacher — and said, "Are you crazy?" She said, "That's what I'm going to do." Bob [Moses] was there, and he started to frame for them why what Andrea had just done was a very mature and farsighted act, and how maybe they weren't ready to do that yet. But it gave Andrea a lot of support and affirmation for having said that in the group. And it changed what the others were going to say next. Everything from then on was in terms of Andrea: "Well, I'm not going to do quite what Andrea is, but . . . ."

Students also learned to work harder than they had before. They were encouraged to develop habits of concentration, patience, and perseverance in approaching their daily math work. Students decided which of several resources to consult — the textbook, the instructor, or a peer — when they had a question or ran into difficulties in solving a problem. Teachers met with small groups for brief lessons on specific concepts and regularly held small-group review sessions. Reflecting on this decision, Mehrling recently explained:

> Adolescent learners can sometimes interrelate with materials, and it's not nearly as threatening as interacting with an adult. If they can go to an adult to ask a question about the materials when they're ready to go to an adult, it's wholly different from being in a group, being pinpointed and put on the spot, and feeling vulnerable about the pieces they don't have in place yet. Once they start to interact with materials, they get not only very possessive of them, but very reluctant to go back to any kind of teacher-directed lessons. They're empowered, in a curious way, around materials — something I would never have even thought about. The Open Program generally is a very teacher-intensive kind of program. We motivate, we bring in materials from everywhere, and our teaching is interpersonal. We discovered at the seventh- and eighth-grade level that that was one of the problems with students who felt vulnerable: It put them on the spot.

As part of the new curricular, pedagogical, and social environment for studying math, the seventh- and eighth-grade teachers assumed the role of "coach" as opposed to "lecturer" in their relationship with students.

The project produced its first full graduating class in the spring of 1986. When they entered high school the following autumn, 39 percent of the graduates were placed in Honors Geometry or Honors Algebra. Not a single student in that cohort ended up at Cambridge Rindge and Latin School in lower-level math courses, such as Algebra I.

Curricular Expansion

By 1986, attention turned to the preparation of students for seventh-grade algebra. With all students in the seventh and eighth grades taking the subject, lower grade teachers began to question the adequacy of their own math curricula as preparation for algebra. To address this question systematically, the entire staff of the Open Program participated in a year-long institute centered on the issue of math literacy.

After the institute, teachers at all levels (K–8) implemented new curricula in mathematics appropriate for the age and grade levels they taught. Some teachers found it unsettling to devise their own curricular practices around the needs of children and their own teaching styles. The results of the Algebra Project suggest that flexibility leads to better pedagogy. For example, when fifth/sixth-grade teachers tried a materials-centered approach with sixth-graders that had worked very well at the seventh/eighth-grade level, they found that younger children, accustomed to more teacher-centered instruction, needed more teacher-child and small-group interaction in the sixth-grade transition curriculum. The teachers modified their classroom technique, but retained the principle of encouraging greater self-reliance in finding answers to problems. Improved adaptation of curriculum was itself beneficial. But equally important, this process gave teachers the same sense of empowerment experienced by students. Teachers who participated in the innovation and trained themselves in how to present the curriculum were more likely to understand, appreciate, and foster the skill of self-education that was central to the Algebra Project. One teacher explained:

> Bob was affirming what we were doing while he was helping us change. He didn't come in and say, "We're throwing this out, it's junk." He came in and said, "You guys are great. Wanna try something different?" When we asked, "How will it work?" he turned it around and asked, "Well, how do you think it should work? What do you want to have happen?" He didn't really give us a way, which admittedly was frustrating, but it also gave us ownership around it. Bob didn't have all of the answers. At first I was really annoyed that he was making me go through this process. I kept saying, "Bob has an agenda. Why doesn't he tell us? We're wasting so much time!" But he knew that it had to come from us. He knew he couldn't impose, because he didn't know what would work. He wasn't a classroom teacher. He just had the vision. If he could help us catch the vision, we would make it work.

A second outcome was that Moses agreed to develop a curriculum for the sixth grade that would provide a conceptual transition from arithmetic to algebra. The main features of what has come to be called the Algebra Project, and the philosophy that guided its construction, are discussed below.

What to Teach and How to Teach It

The opening of algebra to everyone in 1985–1986 gave Moses the opportunity to work closely with several students who had great difficulty with the initial chapters of the algebra textbook. In particular, one Black male student took many months to complete the first few lessons. Moses wondered precisely where the student's conceptual knot lay. Was it possible to lead the student from arithmetic to algebra by mapping a conceptual trail, beginning with concepts that were obvious and proceeding by equally obvious steps?

After working with a number of students who were having difficulty, Moses came to the conclusion that the heart of the problem lay in their concept of number. In arithmetic, the distinctive feature of a number is magnitude or quantity. In algebra, a number has two distinctive features: one is quantitative; the other is qualitative and must be explicitly taught. Students of arithmetic have in their minds one question that they associate with counting numbers: "How many?" Students of algebra need to have two: "How many?" and another questions, such as "Which way?" as points of reference for the intuitive concept of opposites. Children understand the question, "Which way?" from their early years, but it is not a question that they associate with numbers. The number concept used in arithmetic must be generalized in algebra, and failure to make this generalization blocks students' understanding. Once students have generalized their concept of number, they must also generalize their knowledge of basic operations such as subtraction.

Moses gradually arrived at a five-step teaching and learning process that takes students from physical events to a symbolic representation of those events, thereby accelerating sixth graders' grasp of key concepts needed in the study of algebra.[10] The five steps are:

1. Physical event
2. Picture of model of this event

3. Intuitive (idiomatic) language description of this event
4. A description of this event in "regimented" English
5. Symbolic representation of the event

The purpose of the five steps is to avert student frustration in "the game of signs," or the misapprehension that mathematics is the manipulation of a collection of mysterious symbols and signs. Chad, a young Black seventh-grader, recently looked up from reading a page in the first chapter of a traditional algebra text and said to his mother, "It's all just words." For too many youngsters, mathematics is a game of signs they cannot play. They must be helped to understand what those signs really mean and to construct for themselves a basis of evidence for mathematics. When middle-school students use the five-step process to construct symbolic representations of physical events (representations that they themselves make up), they forge, through direct experience, their own platform of mathematical truths. Their personally constructed symbolic representations enter into a system of mathematical truths that has content and meaning.

At the Open Program, students initiate this process with a trip on the Red Line of Boston's subway system (the physical event). This experience provides the context in which a number of obvious questions may be asked: At what station do we start? Where are we going? How many stops will it take to get there? In what direction do we go? These questions have obvious answers, forming the basis for the mathematics of trips. When they return, students are asked to write about their trip, draw a mural or construct a three-dimensional model, make graphs for trips that they create, and collect statistical data about them. The purpose is to fuse in their minds the two questions "How many?" and "which way?" and to anchor these questions to physical events.

Students then use this process to explore the concept of equivalence in the broad cultural context of everyday events, such as cooking, coaching, teaching, painting, and repairing. They explore any concept in which object A is substituted for object B to achieve a certain goal. They conclude the discussion of equivalence in subway travel with open-ended constructions of equivalent trips, leading to an introduction of displacements as "trips that have the same number of stops and go in the same direction."

Once displacements are introduced, they investigate the concept of "comparing" as a prelude to generalizing their concept of subtraction. Most algebra texts introduce subtraction as a transformed addition problem. Students are asked to think of subtraction $(3 - (-2) = +5)$ as "adding the opposite" or "finding the missing addend" $(3 - ? = 5)$, which provides one group of signs as a reference for another. But students look for concrete experiences, pictures, or at least a concept, to link directly to algebraic subtraction. The problem is compounded because students have over-learned "take-away" as the concept underlying subtraction. In algebra, "take-away" no longer has a straightforward application to subtraction. Within a couple of months of beginning algebra, students confront subtraction statements that have no discernable content, have only indirect meaning in relation to an associated addition problem, and are not at all obvious.

To give additional content, meaning, and clarity to subtraction in beginning algebra, students begin with the physical event of comparing the heights of two students, Coastocoast, who is six feet tall, and Watchme, who is four feet tall. The class works with a picture of this event, generating questions that can be used to compare heights:

1. Which one is taller?
2. What is the difference in their heights?
3. How much shorter is Watchme than Coastocoast?
4. Who is shorter?
5. How much taller is Coastocoast than Watchme?

In arithmetic there are two subtraction concepts, the concept of "take-away" and the concept of "the difference between." The latter provides the appropriate entry into subtraction in algebra, as illustrated in the above set of questions. Students will readily identify an answer to the second question by subtracting to find the difference in the heights. This prepares them to accept subtraction as the best approach to answering comparative questions — questions that belong to algebra and not arithmetic.

The answers to these questions are carefully processed in three stages: intuitive language, regimented English, and symbolic representations. "How much taller is Coastocoast than Watchme?" is explored in the following way:

- *Intuitive language:* "Coastocoast is two feet taller than Watchme."
- *Regimented English:* "The height of Coastocoast compared to the height of Watchme is two feet taller."
- *Symbolic representations:*
    - (5a) H(C) compared to H(W) is 2'
    - (5b   H(C) – H(W) = 2' ↑
    - (5c) 6' ↑ – 4' ↑ = 2' ↑
    - (that is, 6' is 2' taller than 4')

"How much shorter is Watchme than Coastocoast?" proceeds along a similar track.

- *Intuitive language:* "Watchme is two feet shorter than Coastocoast."
- *Regimented English:* "The height of Watchme compared to the height of Coastocoast is two feet shorter."
- *Symbolic representations:*
    - (3a) H(W) compared to H(C) is 2' ⁻
    - (3b) H(W) – H(C) = 2' ↓
    - (3c) 4' ↑ – 6' ↑ = 2' ↓
    - (that is, a height of 4' is 2' shorter than a height of 6')

This way of comparing physical quantities is easily reinforced with work stations at which students compare weights, lengths, temperatures, and speeds. They may return to their experience on the subway to compare positions of stations on the Red Line, using the following model:

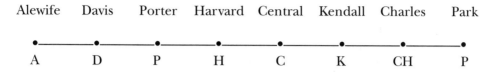

Alewife	Davis	Porter	Harvard	Central	Kendall	Charles	Park
A	D	P	H	C	K	CH	P

When asked, "What is the position of Harvard compared to Kendall?" students work through the following steps:

- *Intuitive language:* "Harvard is two stops outbound from Kendall."
- *Regimented English:* "The position of Harvard compared to the position of Kendall is two stops outbound."
- *Symbolic representations:*
    - (a) P(H) compared to P(K) is 2
    - (b) P(H) – P(K) = 2

In a similar way the question, "What is the position of Kendall relative to Harvard?" yields

$$P(K) - P(H) = 2$$

As soon as integers are introduced as a system of coordinates, students are ready to generate their own subtraction problems. The notion of an arbitrary point of reference having been introduced earlier, systems of coordinates are assigned to the stations, with the zero point alternately assigned to various stations. Each assignment generates a different subtraction problem for the question, "What is the position of Harvard relative to Kendall?"

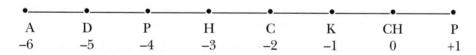

A	D	P	H	C	K	CH	P
–6	–5	–4	–3	–2	–1	0	+1

- (a) P(H) compared to P(K) is 2
- (b) P(H) – P(K) = 2
- (c) –3 – (–1) = –2

By similar reasoning, the question, "what is the position of Kendall relative to Harvard?" yields

$$P(K) - P(H) = 2$$
$$-1 - (-3) = +2$$

The opposite comparisons [P(H) compared to P(K), and P(K) compared to P(H)] lead to opposite expressions [(–3) – (–1), and (–1) – (–3)] as well as opposite integers [(–2) and (+2)], in a way that gives direct, intuitive meaning to subtraction of integers and provides students and teachers alike with control over the generation of simple subtraction problems and equations. The curriculum and curricular process used in the sixth grade have made algebra accessible for all middle school students. The project has demonstrated that all seventh- and eighth-grade students in the King School's Open Program can study algebra, and that the entire school community expects them to do so.

Community Participation in Creating a Culture of Achievement

For youngsters who have felt excluded from the culture of academic achievement in school, the expectation that they, too, can learn is crucial. During the 1987–88 school year, the project's response to children who did not think they were likely to succeed in math was to institute a series of measures designed to create a culture of mathematical and scientific literacy, not only in the Open Program, but in other programs within the King School as well. The Seymour Institute for Advanced Christian Studies, a service organization conceived by Black Harvard graduates to support community-based development in urban areas, provided Black role models to go into classes to tutor students and to run before-school algebra study halls four mornings a week. The study halls were open to seventh and eighth graders from all of the King School's four programs. The tutors, who came from Harvard, MIT, Wentworth Institute, and Boston University, established relationships with individual children and became role models of academically successful young adults for seventh and eighth graders to emulate. A Harvard Law School student and tutor wrote:

> I have been impressed by the fact that these seventh and eighth graders are able to read and understand their math textbooks, already have some understanding of algebraic concepts, and are willing to come out at 7:30 a.m. in order to work on their mathematical skills. . . . The students in the Algebra Project are able to help themselves, and each other, by using their books. Helping each other has another important role in the Project. I believe that it is their friendships that keep them coming to early morning study halls; relationships that support educational achievement are being established outside the classroom.

As the Algebra Project developed, the message that each child could learn was more systematically articulated by the Efficacy Institute.[11] Emphasizing confidence and effective effort as key ingredients in the process of intellectual development, the Efficacy model provides educators, parents, and students with an explicit alternative to the ability model of learning. Efficacy assumes that children, who are well enough endowed to master the fundamentals of language at an early age, are fully capable of learning mathematics. In order to learn, children are required to marshal effective effort. They must learn to work with commitment, focused attention, and reliable strategies. When learning is perceived as a function of effective effort, one seeks factors inhibiting children when they are having difficulties learning or understanding a concept, rather than looking for "disabilities" that prevent learning.

Many children of color learn from an early age that there are doubts concerning their capacity to develop intellectually. Messages communicated from school (low- ability placements in the primary grades), from peers (pervasive anti-intellectualism within the peer group), and the media (expectations of inferiority) all serve to impress upon them that they may not be up to the task of advanced studies. The lack of confidence engendered by the internalization of these messages shapes the meaning of any failure ("I guess this proves I'm not smart") and undermines the capacity to work ("Why bang my head against the wall if I'm unable to learn the stuff anyway?").

To redress these circumstances, Efficacy works to plant an alternative idea in the child's mind: "If I work hard enough, I can get smart."

Confidence	$\rightarrow$	Effective Effort	$\rightarrow$	Development
(Think you can)		*(Work hard)*		*(Get smart)*

Emphasis is placed on the process of development and some measure of control is returned to the child.

Teachers are the carriers of Efficacy ideas, and it is to them that responsibility falls for building confidence and shaping strong effort in children. Teachers attend an intensive, five-day seminar to learn the Efficacy model of development and study its implications for their own teaching. They are then provided with a formal curriculum to use with their students over the course of an academic year. The curriculum gives teachers and students a shared language and a conceptual framework for reworking questions, such as why a particular child has been unable to "do math" in the past. The teacher is able to impress upon the child that learning is a function of effort, not of innate ability. The curriculum helps the students to raise their consciousness so they can affirm for themselves their own need for self-development. Such affirmation on their part is a critical prerequisite to confronting obstacles to their own development and acquiring attitudes and habits that will ensure success in many endeavors, including the algebra program.

In 1988, a sixth-grade teacher in the Open Program began teaching the Efficacy curriculum to all the sixth graders twice a week. She explains:

> We all consider ourselves to be good teachers, and yet we know that we are failing some students. Bob talked to us about a way that could help us to help those children achieve. We realized what that will mean not only to those students but to all of the children in our classrooms, and from there, what that will mean to the community at large.

The Project Continues

The Algebra Project continues at the Open Program. The Efficacy and algebra curricula are taught to sixth-graders, and algebra is studied by all seventh- and eighth-graders. The project is now challenging other schools to make the political decision to alter their own math curricula. For example, discussions are proceeding with administrators and teachers in Boston, where three schools have volunteered to experiment with both the Efficacy and Algebra Project curricula and receive training in their implementation. Moses has also begun to train selected middle school teachers in Atlanta. Currently, the project is exploring relationships with school systems in other cities.

Conclusion

Community Organizing and Educational Innovation

The community organizing approach to educational innovation differs from traditional educational interventions in several important ways. The principle of "casting down your bucket where you are" stands in marked contrast to research programs originating in universities, where scholars design interventions they hypothesize will result in outcomes that they articulate in advance and that are replicable. Researchers in universities and consulting firms must have well-designed, highly articulated interventions in order to convince funding agencies that their projects have promise. Depending upon the focus of the investigation, the researcher generally targets selected neighborhoods, schools, or organizations for participation based on their demographic or similarly quantifiable characteristics. Additionally, researchers have intellectual roots in their own disciplines and view problems through lenses that are consonant with their disciplines, rather than through the eyes of a community.

In contrast to the university-based researcher, the organizer working in the tradition of Ella gradually becomes recognized by community members as having a commitment to their overall well-being. The organizer immerses himself or herself in the life of the community, learning its strengths, resources, concerns, and ways of conducting business. The organizer does not have a comprehensive, detailed plan for remedying a perceived problem but takes an "evolutionary" view of his or her own role in the construction of the solution. He or she understands that the community's everyday concerns can be transformed into broader political questions of general import. The form they will take is not always known in advance.

Once political questions are identified, the organizer's agenda must remain simultaneously focused and fluid — sharply focused on the long-range goal, but fluid with respect to how the goal will be attained. The organizer seeks out views of community participants who have strong interests in the issue and informally educates community members who are uninvolved but whose interests are at stake. It is the organizer's task to help community members air their opinions, question one another, and then build consensus, a process that usually takes a good deal of time to complete.

Improving the mathematics curriculum and curricular process in a middle school has gradually become the focus of the Algebra Project. At the outset, Moses did not know that the project would become a vehicle for raising questions about ability grouping, effective teaching for children of color, or the community's roles in educational decisionmaking. He did not imagine that it would trigger an interest in teaching algebra to inner-city middle school students beyond his daughter's classroom.

As we have seen, the program's innovations relied on the involvement of the entire community: teachers, parents, school administrators, students, tutors, and consultants from the Greater Boston community. In her review of programs that have been helpful in breaking the cycle of disadvantage, Lisbeth

Schorr (1988) highlights the importance of comprehensive, flexible, and intensive approaches to reform:[12]

> Many interventions have turned out to be ineffective not because seriously disadvantaged families are beyond help, but because we have tried to attack complex, deeply rooted tangles of troubles with isolated fragments of help, with help rendered grudgingly in one-shot forays, with help designed less to meet the needs of beneficiaries than to conform to professional or bureaucratic convenience, with help that may be useful to middle-class families but is often irrelevant to families struggling to survive. (pp. 263–264)

The work of discovering new solutions, building a broad base of support, and overcoming barriers takes time. Moses's effort to work with teachers, parents, and administrators to transform the middle school mathematics curriculum and curricular process in the Open Program began seven years ago. We note that it took fifteen years for James Comer's efforts at comprehensive reform in two New Haven schools to yield striking improvements in test scores (Comer, 1980, 1988).[13] Durable reforms are possible, but there are no shortcuts in bottom-up implementation.

In the Open Program, faculty volunteered to participate, committing themselves to working together to discover better ways to teach math and struggling to reach consensus. Parents were deeply involved as learners, supporters, contributors, and decisionmakers. Students voluntarily set goals for themselves and came to 7:30 a.m. study halls four mornings a week. School administrators supported teachers as they tried out new strategies, worked to secure funding, and acted as spokespersons for the project. The strengths of various contributors were recognized, and they were empowered to adapt, create, and evaluate their progress in attaining a shared vision.

Others have learned that it is through struggling with a problem and shaping the solutions that commitment to change really occurs. Schorr (1988) reports:

> Dr. Comer wanted to make sure I understood that the essence of his intervention is a process, not a package of materials, instructional methods, or techniques. "It is the creation of a sense of community and direction for parents, school staff, and students alike." (p. 234)

Comer is pointing to the fact that significant innovations must transform the culture, and transformation requires a broad base of voluntary support. It is crucial that participants have time to understand an idea, explore their commitment, and adapt the innovation to their needs.

Henry Levin (1988) also emphasizes the importance of process.[14] He states:

> Underlying the organizational approach are two major assumptions: First, the strategy must "empower" all of the major participants rather than decrying their weaknesses. (p. 5)

Many will find it useful to follow the precept "cast down your bucket where you are," as Jaime Escalante did in Los Angeles when he began offering calculus to disadvantaged youth. The starting point for reform is less important than whether the issue is powerful and inspiring enough to generate enthusiasm, reveal broader political questions, compel devoted leadership, and serve as a vehicle for community commitment.

Funding to Support Innovation

The Algebra Project would not have developed as it did had it not been for the MacArthur "no strings attached" Fellowship that allowed Moses to work in the Open Program for five years without having to account for the way he spent his time. Subsequent funding has been difficult. For eighteen months, Wheelock College in Boston supported Moses as he looked for resources to provide release time for teachers, cover materials and reproduction costs, and secure consultation from the broader academic community. Moses is still spending an enormous amount of time trying to secure long-term funding to support the continuation and dissemination of the Algebra Project.

Finding support can be a depleting struggle for many innovative efforts. National funding sources are hesitant to fund projects with grassroots leadership, a community focus, a long timeframe, and a philosophy that casts educational issues in political as well as technical terms. Declining state and local budgets also threaten commitment to comprehensive, long-term reforms. But only when major political questions are addressed (for instance, that all children can benefit from and should have access to algebra in their middle school years) can we discover the most appropriate ways to organize knowledge, develop curriculum, and encourage home, school, and community participation.

Transforming School Culture

Teachers and parents in the Open Program came to believe that ability grouping in mathematics seriously impaired the capacity of middle school females and students of color to learn as well as they might. Questioning the policy was the first step toward comprehensive change. Others concur that differentiating students harms those who are disadvantaged or placed in lower tracks.[15] After articulating a vision of high expectations in algebra for all students, participants worked to transform the culture of the school, so that policies, teaching strategies, and the Efficacy curriculum could together help students.

The project speaks to the importance of family as a link to school success. Henderson (1987) concludes her review of research concerning parental involvement in student achievement by categorically stating that "the evidence is beyond dispute: parent involvement improves student achievement" (p. 1). This finding holds for middle- as well as low-income families, at different grade levels, and within a broad spectrum of interventions. As the U.S. population becomes more diverse, it is absolutely fundamental that schools join with families to define and support school success. Continuity between home and school must be forged for all children, and we must draw on the strengths and resources that families can provide.

Curriculum and Curricular Process

Among the strengths of the faculty and volunteers in the Open Program was their curiosity about why some children were not succeeding in mathematics and their willingness to explore the possibility that their own teaching strategies might be a factor. Moses and the teachers became classroom researchers — analyzing student errors, locating conceptual knots, and experimenting with materials and teaching processes that might improve students' mathematical development. A sixth-grade transition curriculum that allows students to relate everyday experiences to mathematical concepts represented symbolically should be disseminated widely.

In 1964, national attention was focused on the disenfranchised citizens of the South. In 1989, another kind of disenfranchisement exists, as many poor, indigenous, and immigrant children of color are denied access to programs and teaching that support their success in school. The success of the Algebra Project stands as a challenge to public school teachers, administrators, scholars, and, most important, those individuals who have traditionally advocated for the democratization of the society and schools: Will you wage a campaign for mathematical literacy, which acknowledges that every middle school student can and should learn algebra while simultaneously empowering the child's community and family? Will you organize in the spirit of Ella?

Notes

1. Fundi is a Swahili term for a person who has an expertise valued by society, and who passes on his or her art to the young by example and instruction. Ella Baker was a fundi to the SNCC workers learning the art of community organizing.
2. One such quiet place was Amite County, in a remote corner of southwest Mississippi, where E. W. Steptoe's family welcomed Bob Moses, SNCC's first field secretary, into the community in the summer of 1961. Mr. Steptoe was president of Amite County's NAACP chapter in the late 1950s when the county sheriff raided a chapter meeting and confiscated the group's books, thus exposing the members to economic reprisals and physical danger. By the time the first wave of SNCC organizers spread out across the rural South, activities at places like the Steptoe farmhouse had ground to a halt.
3. "Cast down your bucket where you are" was used by Booker T. Washington in an address at the Atlanta Exposition, September 18, 1895.
4. The King School is a large, modern facility built on the site of a school that had served Cambridge's Black community for many years. By the late 1970s, the King School housed four programs for grades K–8: a regular program composed of personnel from the former school; a magnet Open Program; and smaller bilingual and special needs programs.
5. Because some but not all authors of this article are also the subjects of discussion, we have chosen to use third-person references throughout to avoid confusion.
6. The fourth student opted to go to a private high school, and did not take the test.
7. See Delpit (1986) for a discussion of the differences between the instructional needs of mainstream and minority children.
8. See Fordham (1988) for a discussion of the tensions high-achieving Black students feel when they strive for academic success.
9. It was only in Mississippi, where the entire state was structured along a community organizing tradition, that the issue of the right to vote was perceived as a broad political question.

10. This model is a synthesis of ideas derived from three sources. The first was the Open Program itself. Moses observed teaching practices in the Open Program and attended workshops with teachers in which Virginia Chalmers and others explained the teaching and learning ideas that they had developed for primary grades. The second was Quine's (1981) notion of "mathematization in situ." "A progressive sharpening and regimenting of ordinary idioms: this is what led to arithmetic, symbolic logic, and set theory, and this is mathematization" (p. 150). Quine insisted that "set theory, arithmetic, and symbolic logic are all of them products of the straightforward mathematization of ordinary interpreted discourse . . . " (p. 151). The third source was Dubinsky (1987), who shared his insight that in the future, mathematics education would center on a "fixed curricular process" rather than a "fixed curriculum."

11. The Efficacy model of intellectual development is based on motivation. The role of motivation in self-development was studied by Jeffrey Howard, Director of the Efficacy Institute, who, in collaboration with educators, developed the model summarized here.

12. As a participant of the Harvard University Working Group on Early Life and Adolescence, Lisbeth Schorr believed that with the knowledge currently available, society could prevent the damaging outcomes for adolescents associated with disadvantage, such as teenage pregnancy, juvenile crime, school failure, and unemployment. She visited an array of health and education programs that were successful in interrupting the cycle of disadvantage and discovered that what the programs had in common was a comprehensive, flexible, and intensive approach to reform.

13. In 1968, James Comer, a psychiatrist at the Yale Child Study Center, began a program of reform in the two New Haven schools that had the lowest achievement scores and the worst attendance and behavior records in the system. Today, although the community is still impoverished, these demonstration schools now boast top achievement scores in the New Haven system (ranking third and fourth), no serious behavior problems, and superior attendance records. The critical components of the reform, now disseminated to fourteen other sites, include a school planning and management team (composed of the principal, parents, and teachers), a mental health team that provides coordinated services to children in conflict, and extensive parent involvement.

14. Henry Levin is the director of the very successful Accelerated Schools Project in the San Francisco Bay Area, whose mission is "bringing children into the educational mainstream so that they can fully benefit from future schooling and their adult opportunities" (1988, p. 3).

15. Levin (1988) argued that the major reason for the failure of many disadvantaged children is low teacher expectation, which in turn leads to pull-out programs based on tedious drill-and-practice curricula. Peterson (1989) conducted a study in Utah, concluding that ability grouping is harmful to remedial students, and that participation in accelerated programs is a more effective route to higher achievement.

References

Comer, J. (1988). Maggie's American dream. New York: New American Library.

Comer, J. (1980). School power. New York: Free Press.

Delpit, L. (1986). Skills and other dilemmas of a progressive Black educator. Harvard Educational Review, 56, 379–385.

Dubinsky, E. (1987). How Piaget's and related work should influence K–12 curriculum design. Unpublished manuscript.

Fordham, S. (1988). Racelessness as a factor in Black students' school success: Pragmatic strategy or Pyrrhic victory? Harvard Educational Review, 58, 54–84.

Henderson, A. (1987). The evidence continues to grow: Parent involvement improves student achievement. Columbia, MD: National Committee for Citizens in Education.

Levin, H. (1988). Don't remediate: Accelerate. In Proceedings of the Stanford University Centennial Conference, Accelerating the Education of At-Risk Students. Stanford, CA: Stanford University, Center for Educational Research.

National Science Foundation. (1989). Materials for middle school mathematics instruction. Catalog of Federal Domestic Assistance no. 47.067, Materials Development, Research, and Informal Science Education.

Peterson, J. (1989). Remediation is no remedy. Educational Leadership, 46(6), 24–25.

Quine, W. V. (1981). Theories and things. Cambridge, MA: Harvard University Press.

Saxon, J. H., Jr. (1982). Algebra I: An incremental development. Norman, OK: Saxon Publishers.

Schorr, L. (1988). Within our reach: Breaking the cycle of disadvantage. New York: Anchor Press/Doubleday.

Usiskin, Z. (1987). Why elementary algebra can, should, and must be an eighth-grade course for average students. Mathematics Teacher, 80, 428–437.

The authors wish to thank the following people for their contributions to this article: Theresa Perry, Daniel Cheever, Barney Brawer, Ceasar McDowell, and, finally, the teachers and administrators of the Open Program of the Martin Luther King, Jr., School.

Citizenship for All
in the Literate Community

An Ethnography of Young Children
with Significant Disabilities in Inclusive
Early Childhood Settings[1]

CHRISTOPHER KLIEWER
LINDA MAY FITZGERALD
JODI MEYER-MORK
PATRESA HARTMAN
PAT ENGLISH-SAND
DONNA RASCHKE

You can have no fun at school! There is to be no fun at school!" were the playfully stated phrases that greeted us as we opened the door to the Corner Nook, the given name of a dynamic combined preschool/kindergarten classroom within the Shoshone School, an early childhood education center located in an urban industrial community we refer to as Empire City.[2] While the building that housed Shoshone was old and crumbling, a reflection of the surrounding neighborhood, its interior was colorful and filled with life.

This vibrancy was one of several factors that led us to include the Corner Nook as the first of what would become nine school settings that served as research sites in our ethnography of literacy development in young children with significant disabilities — children often entirely excluded from school-based literacy opportunities. Other factors common among our classroom settings included (a) a focus on preschool- to kindergarten-aged children; (b) educational environments where children with significant disabilities and those without disabilities were taught together;[3] (c) educational environments in which faculty generally viewed literacy development as integral to all aspects of the early childhood curriculum; (d) an established research relationship between the ethnographers and the school; and (e) educational environments with widespread reputations of excellence among their respective communities.

Harvard Educational Review   Vol. 74   No. 4   Winter 2004, 373–403

The Literate Community of an Inclusive Early Childhood Classroom

Shayne Robbins, lead teacher to seventeen preschool- and kindergarten-aged children in the Corner Nook classroom, repeated, "I said, 'There's to be no fun at school!'" Shayne was on her knees, forehead-to-forehead with Steven, a four-year-old who stood his ground. With finger jabbing toward Shayne, he made a series of enunciations that ran together like the sounds of a spoken sentence, but without discernible words. Shayne, however, appeared to understand perfectly. "You say you're going to have fun?" she asked. "I say, 'No way!'" Steven threw his head back and shook with laughter. Labeled with autism spectrum disorder, Steven had only two recognizable spoken words and thus was considered to have significant communication disabilities. In the class, he was one of five children labeled with disabilities.

Steven had arrived at school that morning in an extremely angry mood. He had scowled at peers, and during the first few minutes of the initial period of play, a time he generally enjoyed, Steven sat in a corner with his back to the classroom. Steven's closest friend, a nondisabled child named Soo-Nei, approached him with a toy car in hand, but Steven had swatted at his pal, and Soo-Nei retreated. Shayne Robbins, keeping one eye on the situation, approached Steven and said, "We have a new rule, and that new rule is that there will be no fun at school!"

While Steven argued with Shayne, Soo-Nei shouted, "Yes, fun at school!" Shayne said, "No fun at school! I am going to write the new rule on this strip [of paper] and I will hang it on the wall with the class rules, and then it will be our new official rule." The class rules were hung at the front of the room. Certain rules changed on an almost weekly basis, as children and adults gathered to discuss emerging issues and concerns. Implicit in these interactions were both the power and dynamic nature of the written word. Rules were not static but evolving, and authority could be captured and conveyed through graphic (i.e., recorded and observable) symbols. During this particular observation, a number of children now gathered near Shayne and watched intently as she wrote in large letters: "No fun at school." Two giggling students attempted to grab the strip away from Shayne.

A classroom teaching assistant, Aaron, approached Steven, Soo-Nei, and the rest of the children. He said to them, "If you're going to protest a rule you have to do it right. You need to have an official protest with signs saying what you're against." Steven watched with intensity as Aaron got out a piece of poster board and asked, "What should our protest sign say?" Soo-Nei shouted, "Yes, fun at school!" Another child called out in response to Aaron, "No Shayne at school!" Children were gathering, laughing, and chattering with excitement. Aaron wrote out the words, "Yes fun at school." Soo-Nei got his own piece of paper and followed Aaron's lead, writing out, "Yes fun at scool." With his own crayon in hand, Steven sat next to Soo-Nei and made several line marks on the same poster board.

By this point other students had gotten their own posterboard, and with the support of various adults in the class had created a variety of protest signs. One read, "No Shayne at school." Another read, "Yes fun at school." One child drew a quick picture of the school building then added a circle with a slash through it, apparently meaning something akin to "No school" at all. Lori, a four-year-old child with severe physical disabilities, was sitting with an associate teacher, Margaret, watching the excitement grow. Margaret said to her, "Do you want to make a sign?" Lori had a DynaVox positioned beside her. The DynaVox is a computerized communication device with voice output that Lori used to communicate. However, in this interaction, Lori chose the more efficient communication mode of smiling and bending forward — her sign for "yes."

Margaret carried Lori to a table where other children were making their signs. She asked Lori, "What do you want your sign to say?" Lori reached out to the DynaVox and touched an icon. The device stated in an automated fashion, "Yes" — the same word she had just indicated through body movement and facial signs. Lori was more apt to use the DynaVox when her language was directing another to write, draw, or otherwise symbolize her thoughts, combining expressive modalities. She followed up the "yes," however, with an uttered, "Muh-huh," her manner for orally articulating Margaret's name. Margaret said in a voice loud enough for Shayne to hear, "You want your sign to say 'Yes Margaret'? Does that mean 'No Shayne'?" Lori doubled forward, laughing with mouth wide open. Shayne called out, "Hey, why am I always the bad guy?" With Margaret's hand guiding Lori's, the two wrote in big letters across the poster board, "Yes Margaret." Any indication that surrounding adults did not believe Lori was capable of this level of sophisticated humor was entirely absent from the interaction.

Aaron announced to all the participating children, "Okay, if this is going to be a real protest, we need to march with our signs and chant. Where should we march to?" One child yelled out, "The office." "To the office it is!" Aaron cried, "Let's chant, 'Yes fun at school.'" Thirteen children filed out the door, led by Aaron, with Soo-Nei close behind and Steven holding onto a corner of Soo-Nei's sign. Margaret carried Lori and Lori's sign. Several children joined the chant, "Yes fun at school. Yes fun at school." When the protest ended, Shayne called all the children to a carpeted area of the room where class meetings were held. She said, "Okay, so this is a democracy, and we'll vote on whether 'No fun at school' becomes a rule." The vote against the rule was unanimous. Shayne said to a beaming Steven, "I guess you win this one."

In this hectic scene of preschool/kindergarten "hallway-level" democracy, a vibrant, literate community is clearly discernible. Shared graphic (i.e., observable, recorded) symbols (including alphabetic text) are used by children and adults of the Corner Nook as social tools for formulating, conveying, interpreting, debating, and reformulating ideas into personal and collective narratives. An intriguing aspect of this literate community, and the ethnographic focus of our research, was the seemingly natural and full citizenship of children with significant disabilities, children often excluded by tradition and convention from oral literacy-learning opportunities (Erickson & Koppenhaver, 1995; Koppenhaver & Erickson, 2003; Mirenda, 2003).

Three of the five students labeled with disabilities in the Corner Nook classroom (including Steven and Lori) were considered to have moderate to severe disabilities. Testing on developmental assessments for all three had only months earlier generated cognitive scores more usually associated with infant and toddler levels of development. Shayne Robbins and her classroom colleagues, however, perceived capacity and possibility for these children where prevalent professional disability discourses focused primarily on presumed defect and limitation (see also Mirenda, 2003). This fundamental presumption of human competence, including literate potential, translated into the described classroom-based actions such that the children with significant disabilities were seamlessly understood and supported as full citizens of the literate community. These actions included (a) Shayne converting her argument with Steven into a written phrase to be hung on the wall with other written rules, (b) Steven participating on his own initiative with Soo-Nei to construct a protest sign, and (c) Lori making use of icons on a screen to communicate direction and ideas.

With our ethnographic gaze affixed on the literate citizenship of children whose disability label commonly precludes community participation due to cultural assumptions, we sought to both continue and build on our previous interpretive studies of early childhood literacy with a particular interest in young children with significant developmental disabilities (Kliewer, 1998a, 1998b; Kliewer & Biklen, 2001; Kliewer & Landis, 1999). We were guided in our research by two questions: In the nine inclusive classrooms involved in this study, how are preschool and kindergarten students labeled with moderate to significant disabilities supported as full, competent citizens of the dynamic literate community? What obstacles hinder this full acceptance?

In exploring how each classroom approached the substance of our guiding questions, we developed an increasingly holistic sense of the nature of the literate community itself. Our effort here is designed to be both directly pragmatic and paradigmatic: We believe the rich descriptions of children with significant disabilities participating in the literate dynamics of general preschool and kindergarten classrooms can serve as a model for establishing particular forms of literate communities and supporting the active participation of other children who, based on cultural assumptions, are often and without question excluded. We also believe that our findings ultimately raise serious concerns about the current direction of research and policy in early literacy in general.

Cultural Constructions of Literacy and Significant Developmental Disability

Perceptions of literacy development in early childhood schooling have historically been influenced by shifting discourses about what literacy is and how acts of literacy occur (see Crawford, 1995, for an excellent discussion). In the mid-twentieth century, educators primarily viewed young children as passive recipients of texts read to them. This prepared them for a later stage when they might begin to learn the skills and subskills of decoding and then encoding printed language (Crawford, 1995). Over the past three decades, the discourse of passive preparation has been slowly subverted, first by an active developmental model described as emergent literacy, and more recently by one of systematic, direct phonics instruction along linear trajectories of phonemic, alphabetic, oral language, and orthographic skill development (Barratt-Pugh, 2000; Crawford, 1995).[4] Previously, direct drill was most prominent beginning in the primary years of elementary school, but it is now being used with ever-younger children (Richgels, 2001).

Clearly, no single, absolute, all-encompassing, or timeless sense of literacy development exists. Indeed, while the lead or predominant discourse of the moment always takes on the appearance of objective or scientific truth (Kliewer & Drake, 1998), in actuality the meaning of the term *literacy* and the inferences cast by the term *literate citizen* shift across time and place. For instance, into the nineteenth century, a distinction of literate citizenship was made between those who could and could not sign their own names — a skill that fewer than half the adult populations of even the most industrialized Western European countries possessed (Fernandez, 2001; Resnick & Resnick, 1977).

Within the first author's own family, old documents demonstrate that into the twentieth century in the United States many of his Mennonite ancestors had to place an "X" where a name was required.[5] How could these skilled farmers, parents, builders, craftspeople, and artisans (most often rolled into one) have been unable to perform this seemingly basic literate act expected today of five-year-old children? The answer, of course, lies in the social nature of literacy. What seemed so objectively real just a century ago now seems objectionably bizarre and unreal. The seemingly natural reality of whole classes of people necessarily living in an illiterate state was, in fact, an entirely unnecessary, unnatural — and at times vicious — social creation that was then reified through a myriad of collective informal and formal social means.[6]

Though the shifting nature of literacy is evident, the current predominant discourse on the development of literacy in young children has largely taken on an essential, objective, and fixed mechanistic aura. Within this paradigmatic view, literacy is considered a point reached along a trajectory of sequenced, mechanized skills adhering solely to abilities with alphabetic texts (Whitehurst & Lonigan, 2001). The literate citizen, according to this framework, is ultimately one who has — through formal instruction and drill — mastered and combined sets of phonemic subskills in linear fashion at a normative pace associated with efficient movement through the educational grades (see Adams, 2001; Adams, Foorman, Lunberg, & Beeler, 1997).

The Ladder to Literacy as Predominant Discourse

Elsewhere we have associated this linear, subskill model with a metaphoric ladder to literacy (Kliewer & Biklen, 2001). Each rung of the ladder constitutes increasingly complex, normative subskills, with the first or earliest rungs primarily associated with letter and phonemic abilities, as identified in school-based reading programs. Only later are the rungs associated with understanding and meaning of text. Adams (2001), for example, likens learning to read to an individual child's bodily kinesthetic maturation. "In any complex endeavor," she writes, "children must learn to walk [i.e., decipher phonemes] before they run [i.e., understand text]. Learning [to read] must start somewhere: if not with letters and phonemes, then where?" (p. 68).

It follows that instructional systems currently laying claim to the coveted title of scientifically based reading programs are entirely focused on detached, decontextualized phonics instruction.[7] These published reading methods craft a generic blueprint of literacy development for all children with no consideration given to the backgrounds (natured or nurtured) with which they arrive at school (Shannon, 1995). All children, according to these phonics-based plans, must first be made phonemic decoders in the exact manner of all other children. Only after achieving phonic mastery is there any systematic consideration given to a child's understanding of a text's message or meaning. In effect, the literate construction of meaning is reserved only for those children who have survived the early skill-and-drill efforts around phoneme awareness.

Lacking Literacy: Young Children with Significant Disabilities

Nearly absent from discussions of early literacy development and instruction is an interest in young children with what we refer to as *significant* developmental disabilities, including presumed moderate to severe intellectual disabilities (Kliewer & Biklen, 2001). For these children, eventual citizenship in the literate community following the ladder-to-literacy model is considered to be, at best, an intellectual improbability. Mirenda (2003) explained that "despite the fact that many individuals [with developmental disabilities] are able to demonstrate skills directly related to literacy, they are often seen as 'too cognitively impaired' or 'not ready for instruction' in this area" (p. 271). As Erickson and Koppenhaver (1995) write:

> It's not easy trying to learn to read and write if you're a child with severe disabilities in U.S. public schools today. . . . Your preschool teachers are unlikely to be aware of emergent literacy research or to include written language activities in your early intervention program. Many of the teachers you encounter across your public school career do not view you as capable of learning to read and write and consequently provide you with few opportunities to learn written language. (p. 676)

Erickson and Koppenhaver concluded that, for the few children with significant disabilities who do find themselves in settings that provide some literacy opportunities, instruction tends to reflect the ladder model, with these children decidedly stuck at the lower rungs. "You [the student] are likely," the researchers write, "to engage largely in word-level skill-and-drill activities, seldom reading or listening to text and even more rarely composing text" (p. 676).

As was the case with particular social classes from previous centuries, children with construed significant developmental disabilities are today primarily considered to be naturally illiterate — cerebrally unable to master the sequenced subskills thought to precede literate citizenship. While the assumed natural literacy limitations ascribed in previous eras to slaves or agrarian workers have come to be understood as the cultural imposition of subliteracy on one class by another more powerful group, the severely limited literacy skills associated today with children labeled developmentally disabled are considered to be organic and innate. So-called manifestations of global cortical defects are thought to be beyond sociohistorical creation, construction, or ideology; they are, in effect, thought to be objectively real (Kliewer & Fitzgerald, 2001).

In contrast to disability doctrine, however, there is a relatively small but accumulating body of work that documents the development of literacy skills on the part of individuals generally considered to be hopelessly illiterate due to presumed intellectual deficits.[8] In several of our own ethnographies of literacy (Kliewer, 1998a; Kliewer & Landis, 1999; Kliewer & Biklen, 2001), it became apparent that this awareness of human possibility arose in environments where the adults, both parents and teachers, had challenged the paradigm of historic segregation of children with disabilities and the model of a singular ladder to citizenship in the literate community. By emphasizing a holistic vision of the literate community over rigid adherence to sequenced phonemic subskill mastery, teachers appeared to open up citizenship to young children who were traditionally excluded.

On Methods

In this study we have used ethnographic research methods to study literacy and young children with significant disabilities. Several important principles of ethnography guided our efforts. First, we studied real-world settings. We were interested in the literate citizenship of young children with significant disabilities, so we purposefully (Bogdan & Biklen, 2003) entered inclusive settings where preschool and kindergarten students with significant disabilities were actively participating in literacy opportunities. The study originated in the Corner Nook classroom at the Shoshone School, where Shayne Robbins was lead teacher. As coding schemes developed out of themes from our Shoshone data, we turned to other inclusive early childhood settings to confirm, deepen, and refine our tentative findings. Ultimately, this study is based on data gathered in nine classrooms across five separate schools and education programs.

Second, our data were primarily narrative and were collected using multiple methods historically associated with ethnography and phenomenology. We conducted participant observations in the classrooms, as well as interviews with participating adults. We also systematically collected documents associated with the contexts under study. Our team composed field notes following observations that resulted in interpretive memos. We have more than twenty hours of transcribed/described video footage from the classrooms, in addition to interview transcriptions.

Third, our analysis was interpretive and grounded in the narrative data (Strauss & Corbin, 1994). The research team met biweekly and shared field notes, observational anecdotes, emergent themes, and coding categories. Our analysis was primarily inductive. For instance, we initially focused on observing children's use of alphabetic text and how children with significant disabilities struggled in this regard (thus acknowledging certain of our preconceived notions and biases). As the findings of this study will illustrate, our perceptions of literacy changed through the process of this research. Discussions with the teachers and participant observation taught us to look for a broadened under-standing of the meaning of literacy in young children's experiences.

Finally, we are concerned that the theory presented herein accurately re-flects the social settings and observations from which it is derived. To this end, this research effort included:

- field observations conducted in nine classrooms across five programs over two years
- observation of 213 children, sixty-two of whom had disabilities, and forty-five of whom were labeled with moderate to severe (i.e., significant) disabilities[9]
- 226 observations and interviews, detailed in field notes conducted by five researchers
- biweekly research meetings attended by four of the five researchers to dis-cuss ongoing data analysis
- participating teachers' intimate involvement in data analysis through mem-ber checks, and their participation in presentations of the data at interna-tional, regional, and local conferences, as well as in graduate classes

The thoroughness of the study combined with the open-door policy that was provided the participating teachers suggests that the data analysis is reflective of the classrooms under study.

Findings: Literacy as Making Sense and Children with Significant Disabilities as Sense-Makers

In the introduction to this article, we described the children in Shayne Rob-bins' Corner Nook classroom at the Shoshone School as they protested their lead teacher's initiation of the new rule, "There will be no fun at school." Our interest in the literacy development of young children, including those with significant disabilities, clearly focused our attention on the various printed language aspects that were such a natural part of the scene. In a number of research interviews, however, Shayne Robbins emphasized that, in order to understand early literacy, our attention should be equally directed toward chil-dren's play, imagination, interests, stories, experiences, interactions, and ac-tions that underlie and ultimately may be expressed through the social tools of printed language and symbols.

In one interview, Shayne said, "I think the most important literacy we do in here is . . . the way they pretend. [It] is their way into [literacy]." In another in-terview she expressed a similar sentiment: "It's really all about literacy. There's very little we do that's not literacy related, even when it doesn't look like read-ing the way you and I look when we sit down and read a book." Shayne later clarified her view of literacy, saying, "It's about making sense. It's about mean-ing. . . . It's kids being able to have something to tell, and to be able to tell it and hear it in a lot of ways so that it's understood."

Children's sense-making and meaning take shape in multiple symbolic forms of what we refer to as narrative: ideas, thoughts, concerns, interests, desires, and stories that may be told, made sense of, understood, retold, or altered in such a way that a symbolic connectedness — in essence, a literate community — is crafted in the classroom.[10] For Shayne, narrative is the story to be told, whether that is arguing against a new rule such as "No fun at school!" or drafting a protest sign. Narrative is the organizing principle, the central core of the literate community.

Shirley Kehoe, co-teacher at the inclusive St. John Nursery School located in the basement of a Lutheran church on the far west side of Empire City, echoed Shayne Robbins' assertion of early literacy as children's narrative:

> Literacy is taking the kids seriously at every level — their experiences they come with, their emotions, their interests. You put them in a setting where all those things are acknowledged and built on, and they all realize they have something to say, and they say it in so many ways. Sometimes with their voice, but just as often in a lot of other ways. And their expressiveness just grows and they start to read — each other, books, art.

Like Shayne Robbins, when considering literacy development, Kehoe focused her attention less on traditional text and more on the multiple modalities children used to express and understand stories emerging from their experiences.

The Teacher's Imagination and the Participation of Children with Significant Disabilities

Fostering the idea of a literate community crafted on children's narrative does not automatically support the citizenship of young children with significant disabilities who are conventionally excluded from literate opportunities. Our observations and interviews suggested that teachers must also shed conventional disability orthodoxy if they are to see in all children the capacity to generate and interpret narrative. Dianna Lowell, lead teacher of a preschool classroom of seventeen students that included two children with severe developmental disabilities, insisted, "It's very difficult to predict what a child — any child — is ever going to be capable of. Especially regarding [disability] labels. You assume the child is able and you start from there."

Lowell's sense that a teacher needs to assume the competence of children with disabilities and open narrative opportunities based on that assumption was echoed by other teachers in this study. At the Shoshone School, Shayne Robbins took a sip of coffee during an interview and said, "You know, after all these years, I really, really see it as about my imagination for a kid. Like Elijah, his only limitations were how I imagined he could do things." Elijah was a former student of Robbins' who had Down's syndrome.

When Elijah entered Shayne's classroom, his speech was extremely limited and highly irregular for a three-year-old. His only consistently understandable word was "No!" Elijah was also labeled cognitively impaired. Developmental assessments suggested that he was functioning cognitively in the ninth- to eleventh-month age range. Yet, Shayne Robbins suggested that Elijah's possibilities were as expansive as her own imagination allowed. This is a radical reconfiguration of convention, influenced by the medical model that places limitations and impairments within the body of the person labeled and not in the minds of others.

Demonstrating Belief in the Narrative Lives of Children with Significant Disabilities

The presumption that children's limitations are limitations in the imaginations of surrounding adults resulted in the participating teachers opening narrative forms to all children in their classrooms. Active opportunities to pretend, imagine, dramatize, role play, and tell and interpret stories are considered fundamental to contemporary conceptualizations of healthy early childhood development — unless the discussion is focused on young children with significant developmental disabilities.

Classrooms segregated for children with moderate to severe disabilities commonly have no child-oriented books or pretend-play opportunities, based on the assumption that such opportunities lack function in the lives of children so labeled (Kliewer, Fitzgerald, & Raschke, 2001; Kliewer & Landis, 1999; Mirenda, 2003). In a previous ethnography, Kliewer and Biklen (2001) identified one stark theme: that for many children with significant disabilities, any participation in a literate community was commonly limited to extremely brief, adult-designed expressions of physical demands. A child with limited spoken language might, for example, have a communication board with "Bathroom" and "Eat" symbolized, and little else. The expectation was that a child with significant disabilities had nothing to say beyond what might be termed *immediate need* narratives. Consequently, when that did in fact become the only narrative form engaged in by the child, professional assumptions about the child's impaired capacity appeared to be confirmed.

In the classrooms involved in this study, however, teachers actively sought to support students with significant disabilities alongside their nondisabled peers in the full range of narrative forms comprising the early childhood literate community. Thus, the participating teachers demonstrated a fundamental belief in the capacity of children with significant developmental disabilities to engage in narratives of transcendence, in which the imaginations and interests of young children prodded their focus from the here and now, and shifted it to the abstractions of play and stories.

An example of supporting a child with significant disabilities as a part of the imaginative life of a classroom occurred during an observation conducted at Corner Nook. On this particular day, a pretend-play restaurant scene unfolded. In the center of the room, teachers had arranged a few tables with salt shakers, plastic utensils, and various menus borrowed from local establishments. Several children sat at the tables, poring over the menus, shouting out orders to a "waiter," who scribbled on a pad and exhibited tremendous control over his customers. "I want the hamburger," one student yelled. "You get the pizza," the waiter explained, scribbling furiously on his pad. "How much is my supper?" a student asked the waiter, grabbing a stack of fake money. "Eight hundred dollars," the waiter responded. "I don't have eight hundred dollars," the patron retorted. "Then you're out of the restaurant!" the waiter yelled. "I don't have eight hundred dollars either," another customer said. "Then you're kicked out too," the waiter responded.

As the drama unfolded, we watched Jamie sit on the periphery of the play, piecing together a jigsaw puzzle but taking numerous quick glances toward the children involved in the restaurant scene. Jamie, who was labeled with autism, was considered moderately to severely developmentally disabled. He had only recently begun to use any spoken language. Children with such a high degree of autistic behavior are commonly considered to reside at a pre-symbolic stage. As such, pretend play is thought to be an impossibility (Maurice, 1993). In obvious contradiction to this characterization, Jamie appeared extremely intrigued by the restaurant play.

Eventually one of the patrons kicked out of the restaurant by the dictatorial waiter stumbled over Jamie, and the two rolled on the floor, giggling, until a teacher cut short the roughhousing. The boy continued on, and Jamie stood and walked to one of the restaurant tables. In discussing this vignette, Margaret, one of Shayne Robbins' associate teachers, explained that Jamie often appeared "stuck" until the touch of another seemed to allow him to initiate actions of participation. "It's not that he can't do the things," Margaret explained. "It's more like he's stuck until someone can give him that little nudge." Rather than cloaking this apparent need for physical facilitation in clinical descriptions of impairment, Margaret chose to instead normalize Jamie's behavior: "We all need different kinds of nudges," she said.

On entering the restaurant scene, Jamie sat and picked up a menu, holding it upside down. A passing teacher noticed and paused to further support Jamie's participation. The teacher turned the menu over in Jamie's hand and said, "What are you going to order? What're the choices?" With the teacher's hand over his, Jamie pointed to the word hamburger (which had a picture of a hamburger next to it). He quietly voiced, "Hamburger." They repeated this with several choices.

After reviewing the menu, the teacher said, "Okay, what're you going to order?" Then she cried out, "Oh waiter, we're ready to make an order." The waiter appeared, pad and pen poised, and waited while the teacher quietly voiced in Jamie's ear, "I want to order the —." Jamie paused, then finished the sentence, "hamburger." "Hamburger," the waiter said, scribbling into his pad, "That'll be eight hundred dollars please." The matter-of-fact manner in which the waiter stood by while Jamie hesitated in his order, and the way the waiter responded to Jamie and not to the teacher, demonstrated the general acceptance of Jamie in this classroom, despite certain unusual behaviors. In short order, Jamie, like every other patron, had been kicked out of the restaurant for lack of money.

From the above scene, elements that appeared helpful to Jamie's increasingly sophisticated social participation included other children serving as models and understanding Jamie's behavioral uniqueness, an intervening teacher who understood how to foster Jamie's independent participation, and various props, including the photo- and text-based menu. Underlying each of these, however, and making Jamie's competent participation possible, was the fundamental belief in his capacity to engage in narrative as a rightful member of the classroom's literate community.

In Tammy Wolcott's class at the Lincoln Early Childhood Center, located in a midwestern city, we noticed through systematic observation that, in contrast to Shayne Robbins' Corner Nook class, her six students with significant disabilities rarely engaged in dramatic or pretend play. This seemed to be the result of the degree of disability segregation built into the instructional model of this classroom. Tammy Wolcott's six students, all labeled with significant disabilities, joined ten children without disabilities from a day-care center for a part of each day. Otherwise the two groups were separated, with Wolcott's students in a segregated special education classroom and the children without disabilities returning to their day-care classroom.

Tammy Wolcott expressed a desire to increase the children's interaction in pretend-play situations, but had also found other paths to narrative engagement for her students with developmental disabilities. Importantly, she used storytelling narratives to bring the children, disabled and nondisabled, together. This required Tammy's fundamental belief in the capacity of her students with significant disabilities to understand and make meaning of story narratives. It appeared that this belief held tremendous developmental opportunities for Tammy's students. For instance, during one particular observation, three-year-old Paulie approached a researcher copying down a poem from an easel. The poem had been the centerpiece of the morning meeting, with children reciting and acting out the rhyme under adult guidance. Paulie was one of Tammy's six students with significant disabilities. He was considered to have global developmental delays, including cognitive and communication disabilities.

Paulie faced the researcher and patted his stomach with both hands. In a telling misinterpretation of his communication, the researcher asked, "Are you hungry, Paulie?" In actuality, Paulie was attempting to join her in discussing the poem, but the researcher's immediate reaction was to assume Paulie was conveying an immediate physical need, hunger. Paulie, recognizing the misinterpretation, attempted to correct the researcher by pointing to the easel. The eight-line poem she had been copying was a fictional account of the meeting between a snowman and rabbit. A picture icon appeared after each line representing the key idea contained in that line. The first icon was of the snowman. Paulie pointed to it. Patting the stomach was the sign used in the class to represent the word "snowman."

On Paulie's clarification, the researcher said, "Oh, the snowman. Do you want to read the poem?" Paulie affirmed this by moving closer to the easel. The researcher read out loud, "A pudgy little snowman." Paulie repeated his sign for snowman. The researcher read, "Had a carrot nose." Paulie gestured with his right hand, signing a representation of a growing nose. As the researcher continued reading, Paulie — with clear delight — continued adding symbolic gestures representing the picture icons. It was a very interactive recitation that demonstrated Paulie's ability to focus on the poem during the morning meeting, his adeptness at translating his thoughts into sign systems, and a general sophistication with literacy that confounded assessment descriptions of Paulie that suggested a severe cognitive impairment.

After the poem was completed, Paulie immediately went to a shelf filled with children's storybooks. He looked across the shelf and, with definite intent, pulled down a particular book. He carried it to the researcher and the two adjusted themselves, with Paulie sitting on the researcher's lap. Paulie continued signing key words, this time related to the saga of a lost mitten, in spite of the fact that there were no picture icons as cues.

Storybooks as well as poetry are narrative opportunities of the imagination, allowing children to get lost in the fables and imagery presented. At the time of this observation, the students with disabilities in Tammy Wolcott's classroom struggled to join the play of their nondisabled counterparts. However, while concerned about expanding pretend-play skills, Tammy also worked to consistently bring literature into her students' lives. As such, she was demonstrating a fundamental belief in their capacity to understand and engage in narratives. It was here, in story texts, that Paulie clearly demonstrated sophisticated emergent skills and interest in symbolically making sense of the larger world.

Multiple Literacies in the Inclusive Early Childhood Classroom

In the data vignettes of Jamie at the Shoshone School and Paulie at the Lincoln Early Childhood Center, both boys were described as using a variety of representational social tools for participation. Despite his limited spoken language, Jamie made use of recognizable (albeit teacher-supported), interactive pretend-play behaviors, meaningful gestures toward a text- and photo-based menu, and some use of pretend money. Paulie effectively used picture icons, systematically gestured using the classroom version of signed English, and interpreted printed language in the form of a written poem and storybooks.

In an interview, Shirley Kehoe, a research participant and coteacher at the St. John Nursery School, rattled off a list of symbolic social tools used by children in her classroom to both organize and convey meaning and understanding across the literate community. "It's all the signing we do," she explained, "the art, music, pictures, the symbols, all the symbols and tools we use in play, and of course the stories we write and read and perform, like the skits we put on, books we act out. It's everywhere."

Our data ultimately contained descriptions of multiple sign, movement, pictorial, numerical, graphic, and printed-language systems that citizens of the early childhood literate community made use of as social tools to interpret, understand, and express narratives. Narrative gives shape to the literate community, and these multiple semiotic systems are the social tools that give shape to the various narrative forms.

Our borrowing the term *semiotic systems* (Barton & Hamilton, 1998, p. 9) suggests a range of coherent bodies of meaningful and at least semiformalized symbols, signs, sounds, and gestures conceived as a means of communicating or interpreting thought, emotion, or experience, and the systems or rules for their common usage. Spoken language is an example. However, our use of the term *literacies* reflects observable, tactile, or otherwise graphically knowable semiotic systems used as social tools to bring forth and give literate shape to narrative. Certainly, the graphic nature of the final "text" ranged dramatically from highly fleeting (e.g., observing one another's body language during pretend play) to relatively permanent written products (e.g., a painted protest sign or a story book). Ultimately, literacy is the development of increasing sophistication and competence in children's use of graphic semiotic systems to meaningfully participate in, generate, and sustain narrative.

Providing a Range of Literate Opportunities

A teacher's sense of students as capable sense-makers in the construction and interpretation of narrative forms appeared to be fundamental to literate citizenship for children with significant disabilities. Our data suggest that this presumption of competence was fostered by giving the children with disabilities thoughtful opportunities across a range of literacies (i.e., multiple semiotic systems contextualized in, and lending shape to, a variety of narrative forms). This finding contradicts a deeply ensconced professional belief that children with disabilities require more restrictive programs and activities than do their nondisabled counterparts, and that as the so-called severity of the disability increases, the degree of options and opportunities must be narrowed (for a critique of this historic truthism, see Kluth, Straut, & Biklen, 2003).

The importance of giving young children with significant disabilities opportunities with multiple literacies was exemplified in an observation of Damian, a nearly five-year-old child in Diana Lowell's inclusive preschool classroom. Damian was defined as having intellectual and communication disabilities.

This particular observation of Damian occurred over a regularly scheduled 45-minute period of the day called Centers Time, during which children could choose to spend time in a variety of teacher-created activities generally independent of direct teacher supervision. As the vignette suggests, had Damian not been provided with a range of opportunities, a sense of his literate presence might have been severely restricted.

Damian began Centers Time in the classroom's cooking area. He and a nondisabled friend, Paula, followed a large, laminated set of directions that led to making blueberry muffins in paper cups. Damian stood next to Paula and ran his finger, left to right, across one line of the directions. His words approximated the sentence, "Gots to four spoons." The actual line of the directions read, "Add four teaspoons of muffin mix." The sentence was followed by the outline of four teaspoons and a line drawing of the muffin mix box.

Diana Lowell, the lead teacher, had set up this particular center with a number of objectives in mind. With little direct teacher support but in cooperation with one another, she wanted children to decipher alphabetic, numeric, and picture-symbol text in order to come away with a completed product. In so doing, students were experiencing a number of semiotic systems within the familiar narrative forms of baking/cooking and cooperating with peers toward a shared goal. The center was also linked to a previous field trip the students had taken to a bakery, so there was a wider community orientation as well. Damian's relatively sophisticated ability to interpret and make sense of the text appeared to be fostered by the drawn icons, the active involvement of peers, and the meaningful context, both in the immediate sense that Damian understood he was to create a muffin and in the sense of the familiarity he had with cooking as a daily, relatively independent activity in the class.

Paula, Damian's friend, also counted the teaspoon outlines, "One, two, three, four, five, six." Two of the outlines she counted twice, pounding with her index finger. "Nuh-huh," Damian responded with some distress. Shoving her hand away, he re-counted, touching each spoon outline only once. The two pushed and shoved against one another, and their focus seemed to stray from the recipe to a larger struggle over the chair. Eventually an adult noticed the altercation and intervened. The two returned to the recipe, with each scooping far more mix into their cups than four or six full spoons.

Several more lines of the laminated directions eventually led to the command, "Place in microwave for forty-five seconds." Again there was a line drawing, this one depicting a muffin cup in a microwave oven. Paula and Damian raced to the microwave, with Paula arriving first. She positioned her body to block Damian, put her cup in the oven, slammed the door, and — demonstrating an expert's familiarity — typed in the desired number of seconds, which for her was ninety-three. Damian watched with growing agitation. He ran back to the directions and pounded on the indicated "forty-five seconds." "Four-five," he said several times. Paula smiled at him, confirmed that none of the teachers was paying attention, then pushed the "Start" button, thus establishing a new narrative of rule-breaking around microwave muffin experimentation.

Damian moved to a small "computer area" of the classroom that was secluded by shelves. Damian sat at one of the two old Apple computers and gestured for an observing researcher to sit beside him. A nondisabled student quickly followed and sat down at the open computer. Damian played a matching game, narrating as he proceeded for the observer, "One, two, three, . . . eight" (as he counted, his finger touched the screen). "Find eight," he said, clicking on various animated pictures to see if the numeral eight appeared. When he matched the correct numeral to the number of dots, the picture on the computer screen exploded with sound and lights. Damian stood each time this happened, with hands over head, awaiting applause from the researcher.

Next to him, the other student opened a game in which a picture of an object appeared with space to label it. The required letters were scrambled below the space. The object was to click on the letters in correct sequence to spell the name of the object. If a child chose letters out of sequence, the computer simply "waited" until the correct one was chosen. The child appeared to click on letters randomly until the correct word was spelled.

This appeared to annoy Damian, who began to monitor both his own game and the game next to him. A picture of a bed appeared on the second computer screen. The child clicked on the letter that appeared first in the mixed-up sequence, letter "E." Damian cried out, "Bed, bed, bed. B! B, b, b!" His hand shot over to maneuver the mouse, and the other student slammed her fist down on his fingers. Damian, with one eye on his own screen, formed a fist and whacked his neighbor's shoulder with an overhand punch. With surprising immediacy, each then refocused on his or her own computer screen.

Damian next moved to an area labeled "Dramatic Play." Much noise and activity had been emanating from here throughout Centers Time, as one of the students, Alyssa, had used dress-up clothing and other props to organize her own wedding. Damian rarely entered the pretend play of other children, and during this observation he stood quietly on the periphery. He watched as children created ever-shifting scenes and dialogue with one another, but he did not join in. While he had been actively engaged in the multiple literacies involved in the various narratives at the other two stops, in Dramatic Play he took on the role of observer. Eventually Damian left the Dramatic Play area and drifted back to the muffin-making area.

Evident in the observation of Damian was the importance of not reducing all of early literacy to a set of teacher-directed drills. Although nothing in our data suggested that drill-and-skill opportunities should not be provided, it was precisely in the vast, active, engaging range of choices that we were able to see literate abilities emerge. For instance, with both the muffin recipe and the computer games, Damian demonstrated the capacity to recognize and make use of numerals, alphabetic text, and pictorial representations. He demonstrated spelling skills, letter recognition, and left-to-right orientations within meaningful narrative forms. All of these were aspects of the formal, constructivist classroom curricula, but here Damian was demonstrating his abilities without teacher direction. He did so in an active, self-directed manner, and at his own thoughtful pace. Diana Lowell explained: "Damian shines when he's allowed to be independent. That's when you really see some of his skills that you really didn't see at the beginning of the year. Of course he had never really been a part of an inclusion situation before."

In contrast to his active cooking and computer use, however, Damian's participation in the narratives of dramatic play appeared to be limited to the role of observer. "Pretending is not really his strong suit," Diana Lowell mentioned in a brief discussion with a researcher. "It's something we need to work on." Again, had this preschool classroom been primarily organized around dramatic play, Damian's literate abilities may not have been fully realized. His skills were found in the active use of text across other narrative forms.

Providing Teacher-Guided Literate Opportunities

Damian's experience at Centers Time demonstrated that a teacher's presumption of potential literate citizenship in children, including those with significant disabilities, allowed literate opportunities to be presented across a range of play and activities performed independent of direct adult oversight. However, some children with significant disabilities struggled to keep pace with these seemingly natural, often spontaneous, highly fluid literacy opportunities.

Lori, the four-year-old mentioned earlier as she communicated with a Dyna-Vox, experienced this struggle with the hectic pace of her preschool/kindergarten class. Lori's serious physical disabilities meant that her movement around the classroom required adult support or supervision. Her speech was limited to a few easily articulated sounds and was primarily discernible only to adults. Thus, the DynaVox, an alternative to speech, was theoretically liberating but had its limitations. For instance, stretching to touch the screen icons required patience from both Lori and those around her, who awaited the voice-output message. Certain adapted switches had been tested, but the required physical manipulation remained difficult and awkward.

Supporting Lori's participation in spontaneous literate exchanges appeared to require extensive adult intervention. Such intervention, of course, altered the spontaneity of the event, and it often took on a much more work-like (as opposed to play-like) appearance. Because of this struggle, Lori's teachers commonly made use of other more structured, teacher-guided opportunities to foster and support Lori's full communicative and literate classroom participation. For instance, several classrooms in this research, including Corner Nook, had a *Child of the Week* activity, a show-and-tell opportunity where a particular child was selected to bring in photographs, mementos, and other objects to share with peers.

When Lori was named child of the week, she brought in a bulletin board with several photographs showing her on vacations or at home with her family. The pictures were all neatly labeled with sentences describing the scene (one read, "Lori goes horseback riding"). Lori sat with Shayne at the front of the class, the photographs facing her peers. Shayne said, "Which picture do you want to show first?" With a wide smile, Lori slowly stretched toward a preprogrammed icon on her DynaVox. The device responded with a female child's voice, "I am go-ing horseback riding in Ver-mont."

The other students, many on their knees trying to get a better look, scanned Lori's photographs. Some began shouting about their own horseback riding experiences. Shayne interrupted, saying, "Stop and remember. Who has a . . ." She paused, pointing to a board that read, "Wh Questions: Who? What? When? Where? Why?" Several students shouted "W-h question!" and hands shot up with students calling, "I have a question!"

The teacher-guided *Child of the Week* period provided a format and pace that allowed Lori to skillfully use the DynaVox, one of her most effective symbolic modes of participation. The logo- and text-based icons of the DynaVox, the photos with text explanations, the "W-h" question board, and teacher support all played a role in Lori's literate ability to provide her peers with a deeper sense of her experiences, tastes, likes, and dislikes. The children appeared completely at ease with the technology when it fit so seamlessly into the structured meeting.

Pertinent to Lori's moments of success with the DynaVox, however, was the role her mother played in programming the device. For *Child of the Week*, Lori's mother had entered and recorded a separate icon for each photograph, as well as some related messages. In one research interview, Shayne expressed a sentiment she often repeated in conversations about Lori. "I don't know what we would do without her mom," Shayne said. "We just don't have all the time we need to program the DynaVox and we really rely on her. It's like a full-time job for her." Shayne's acknowledgment of the essential role Lori's mother played in supporting her daughter's classroom participation, even in a setting like the Shoshone School, filled with professional educators and language therapists, illustrated the complexity of active citizenship for young children with significant disabilities.

Alternative Goals within Multiple Literacies

Our participating teachers' presumption of the literate citizenship of all their children did not translate into a general belief that each child would participate in the literate community in exactly the same fashion. Our teachers appeared instead to direct their attention to creating communal opportunities for all children to engage in a variety of semiotic systems across narrative forms, but would often emphasize literate goals considered specific to a particular child's determined ability, need, or interest.[11] An example of this curricular individualization occurred during a lesson on graphing data in lead teacher Sheila Oswald's preschool class, which included sixteen three- and four-year-old children, three of whom had disability labels.

During one observation, Sheila Oswald had her children graph the frequency of classroom birthdays across the twelve months. This provided the children with a new representational and symbolic manner for organizing information about their class. The semiotic systems at play included alphabetic text, numbers, three-dimensional bodies in movement, and two-dimensional graphs. Jordan, a child labeled with communication and intellectual disabilities, sat among his peers holding a printed number line. Sheila called out, "Everyone with birthdays in January, stand up."

Sheila scanned the children standing and compared the result to a birthday chart. She pointed to a written name on the chart and said, "One more of you should be up. Who's not up?" Several students, reading the name, called out, "Joey." Joey was startled out of his apparent day-dream and leapt to his feet. Shelia Oswald then called to Jordan, "How many January birthdays, Jordan?" An associate teacher seated behind Jordan peeked over his head as he started jabbing at the number line with his index finger. She reached around and put her hand over his, slowing down what appeared to be impulsive pointing. He pointed to the four. The associate said, "No, count again. How many kids?" With her hand over his, they arrived at the three on the number line. "Three," she called out. Sheila said, "Good. Come up here, Jordan, and we'll put three down for January." Jordan was immediately on his feet, moving to Sheila, who helped him stick three circles above the word "January" on what would become a birthday bar graph. The lesson continued like this for each of the twelve months.

Sheila Oswald's motivation for Jordan's participation in this activity did not necessarily stem from a firm belief in his ability to grasp the abstract nature of graphing information. Oswald later explained in a research interview, "Is [Jordan] getting everything? Probably not. We're not sure what he grasps and what he doesn't, but he's working on things like responding on cue, being part of conversations, being aware." He also had goals of developing one-to-one correspondence and numeral recognition. Sheila Oswald believed these objectives neatly fit into an activity where it was thought most of the other students were engaged in a more abstract manner. Still, though Sheila expressed skepticism about Jordan's ability to understand, she acknowledged the possibility that he was cognizant, and she did not deny him the opportunity to engage in and perhaps develop graphing skills.

Turning Children's Strengths into Literate Opportunities

Jamie, a child introduced earlier who took part in the pretend-play restaurant scenario in Shayne Robbins's classroom, was fascinated with the maps and globes Shayne made available and often used in the classroom. Conventional interpretations of severe autism, Jamie's label, might dismiss his keen interest as nothing more than a bizarre mode of self-stimulation or compulsive, perseverative behavior that lacked intellectual meaning (see Mirenda, 2003, for a critique of this still-common approach to explaining the performance of people labeled autistic). In the classrooms involved in this study, children with significant disabilities were considered to be sense-makers in the flow of narrative forms. A child's intense focus or interest was never dismissed in such patronizing fashion. Thus, Jamie's curiosity with maps was considered just that — a healthy interest that could further support his citizenship in the literate community.

In one observation, we watched Mushi, Shayne Robbins's graduate-level student teacher, lead a class circle time discussing how she missed and remained in contact with her family in South Korea. She had the classroom globe beside her. Mushi called Jamie to the front of the room. Shayne and Mushi had decided earlier that Jamie should be Mushi's helper for the circle time because he was the child most adept at using and understanding maps. Mushi later explained in an informal interview on the activity: "Jamie can do things with maps like no one else in here, and it's nice for his friends to see. He's still not talking so much at all so sometimes I think the other ones think he's younger [and] forget how smart he is."

Once called forward, Jamie received a gentle nudge from a nearby adult and he stood and tentatively approached Mushi. He clapped quickly several times and let out a "Yee-ah" sound he often made when excited. She pointed to the globe and said, "Show the kids where we are located — where we are now. Show them [our state]." Jamie excitedly dropped to his knees. He spun the globe. Other children moved in. Shayne called out, "Everyone needs to stay on their spot so that everyone can see." Jamie pointed to the correct state, but only Mushi could see. She said, "Show all the kids." He moved awkwardly in an effort to stop blocking the view of the globe. She then said, "Okay, now show my home, Korea." Again, Jamie spun the globe and seemed to become transfixed. Finally, Mushi and Shayne asked, "Can you find Korea?" He quickly landed his finger on Korea. Mushi emphasized how Jamie's finger had to "cross the ocean," just as she had done, in order to find Korea.

Mushi continued with the lesson, weaving multiple literacies throughout. She discussed maintaining contact with her parents through letters, email, and phone calls. She showed the students postcards she received from Korea, written, of course, in Korean. Jamie, still beside her, studied the postcards with tremendous intensity. In discussing the lesson later, Mushi said, "Jamie and I have looked at the globe together a lot. I have shown him Korea, Seoul, many times. I talk about home a lot. I think of all the kids, he really understands."

Shayne and Mushi were uncertain how much Jamie understood the abstract nature of crossing oceans, missing family far away, and sending postcards. However, the same uncertainty exists for any young child, and exposure to constructs of worlds separated by time and distance is considered healthy and important in developing a sense of self, others, and community. Shayne Robbins believed the same importance applied to Jamie's experience as it did to the experiences of nondisabled students. In turning that belief into a literate experience for Jamie, she enabled him to demonstrate and further his literate capacities.

Turning Experience into Text

The emergence of phonemic awareness as the beginning of literate citizenship in early childhood has had the unfortunate effect of skill-and-drill phonics activities largely displacing activities in which young children represent stories through text, symbol, and drawing as a route to reading (Adams, 1990; McGuinness, 1997). In our participating classrooms, however, where multiple literacies appeared to be valued, writing was considered an integral part of full citizenship, and children were supported in turning their experiences into written or otherwise graphically represented texts. For instance, one classroom had a daily "journaling" period during which children "wrote" to their parents, describing events they had participated in over the course of a school day.

Jessica, a child with Down's syndrome and significant motor and communication disabilities, worked daily with an adult, using multiple options to complete her journal. For instance, one line of a mimeographed sheet read, "I played in the ____ area." Jessica usually filled in the blank by pointing to a symbol reflecting an area of the room in which she had spent time. With the adult's assistance, the symbol was then glued over the blank in the sentence. However, Jessica was always given a choice of how she wanted to journal, and some days she chose to manipulate a marker or pencil, scribbling lines in the blank. A teacher then wrote next to Jessica's form of writing where Jessica had spent time.

Jessica's teacher, Cheryl Bigelow, noted the development of a number of skills related to Jessica's expressive communication. In a research interview, Cheryl told us:

> [Jessica] has really developed a sense of her own place in this classroom. Just lately it seems . . . she's pointing to symbols and some written words to really say things, and she's making demands and letting her voice be heard. If you don't make sure she has options, there's hell to pay! She really is into making decisions.

Previous developmental assessments measured Jessica's cognitive level as topping out at approximately what was expected of a child aged one year, six months — far below her chronological age of four years, five months. Cheryl, however, pointed out that Jessica's symbol and text use, apparently just beginning to flower, was influencing perceptions of her competence and abilities.

A notebook children maintained at the St. John nursery school was similar to Jessica's experience, but related to the early childhood narrative in the domain of science. Teacher Janet Vaughn had ordered a package of live butterfly eggs that, if properly cared for, could be hatched in order to study the metamorphosis process. Janet had the children observe and record the transformation of the butterflies from eggs, through larva, pupa, and finally into butterflies. One student in the class, Marty, was nonverbal, with a label of pervasive developmental disorder (PPD). He participated in the activity daily by choosing from a series the picture he felt most closely resembled the current lifecycle. The picture he pointed to was then pasted in his butterfly notebook.

Turning Text into Experience

Studying butterflies at St. John also served to illustrate the importance that the participating teachers placed on turning text and symbols into visible, active experience when promoting the literate citizenship of all children. Teachers at St. John, as in each classroom under study, regularly made use of both formal and informal role-play opportunities to bring storybooks and tales into three dimensions.

In addition to traditional role play, the St. John faculty had incorporated the physical therapy the children with disabilities received into its general community. The visiting therapist led the children both with and without disabilities through an early childhood version of yoga. For instance, during the unit on butterflies, the therapist organized a twenty-minute yoga session following the life-cycle theme. She used a chart made by a teacher depicting the four stages of a butterfly's life, complete with drawings and written labels. In silence, the therapist pointed to the chart's depiction of a larva emerging from its egg. The classroom staff and the children, including those with disabilities, followed the therapist's lead in silently and symbolically moving through the four stages.

Including Basic Phonemic Skills

As described earlier, the current predominant discourse on literacy skills development is focused on fluencies surrounding phonemic awareness and certain other skills (e.g., Good & Kaminski, 2002). Participating faculty in this study were generally resistant to the rigidity of this narrow focus in defining and fostering literate citizenship, but did view instruction in and exposure to the idea of basic literacy skills as one useful dimension of a multidimensional approach to literacy.

In the Corner Nook classroom at Shoshone School, Shayne Robbins had begun a "weird word book" when one child had noticed the nonphonetic nature of many spelled words. "Why is *phone* spelled like that?" he had asked. Soon after, another child asked, "Why is there an 'R' in Feb-*U*-ary?" Initially with Shayne's involvement, strangely spelled and nonphonetic words were added to the book daily, but within a matter of just a few weeks, a number of students became the primary instigators of using the weird word book. This, of course, required their understanding of and involvement in analyzing the graphemes of written language — a discourse many had been unaware of before the weird word book creation.

In one class meeting that involved the weird word book, Shayne announced, "Sean, tell us where you're just back from. Where did you go to see your grandma?" Sean was a child with physical disabilities and very limited speech. The teaching team had prepared for this meeting by making up a word board with relevant words that he could point to in response to questions. Sean leaned forward and pointed to "Ottawa." An adult seated next to him called out, "Ottawa." A friend without disabilities immediately burst out, "Sean oughta went to Ottawa!" What ensued then, making use of a white board and marker, was a lengthy discussion of the spelling and pronunciation of the words "Ottawa," "Ought [with emphasis on the 'gh']," "Ought to," and the slangy "Oughta," all of which were dutifully entered into the weird word book. While Sean's attention appeared riveted, his participation in the weird word discussion was limited because the spontaneous conversation had, of course, been unplanned. However, his ability to use written words for communication purposes demonstrated an emergent reading capacity beyond that of many of his nondisabled peers.

Historically, the semiotic system of most value in terms of citizenship in the literate community has been alphabetic text. The focus in the participating classrooms on multiple symbolic modes of narrative participation (i.e., citizenship), not just alphabetic text, may be construed by some as a devaluation of the skills and subskills currently thought to underlie literacy development. In fact, there was no devaluation of printed alphabetic language abilities. We determined from our data that valuing multiple symbolic modes of narrative participation both indirectly and directly affected children's development of printed-language skills. First, such a values framework opened opportunities for children with significant disabilities to participate in classrooms with a rich, literate curriculum. A rigid requirement that only nondisabled children with conventional, normative participation skills belong in regular preschool and kindergarten programs obviously cuts out students with moderate to severe disabilities and sends them into segregated programs that quite commonly offer very little in the way of literacy experiences of any kind (Kliewer & Landis, 1999; Kliewer & Raschke, 2002; Mirenda, 2003).

Second, fostering a degree of participation in the literate community for children who are commonly segregated from such participation opened opportunities to weave further and more sophisticated symbolic modes into the children's experiences. For instance, some children with significant communication disabilities pointed to picture symbols to communicate immediate needs and desires. In some classrooms, as the children's facility with pictures appeared to increase, teachers added written labels. In time, some of these children were actually constructing their own words and sentences out of letter options.

Third, as children's competencies were recognized with multiple semiotic systems, teachers appeared to grow increasingly comfortable shifting their instructional support between children's general skills with sense-making to specific skills associated with the narrative form of basic literacy skill instruction. Our participating teachers generally agreed that creative instruction associated with phonemes, graphemes, or orthography might benefit the printed-language skills of any child, including those with significant disabilities. Teacher Cheryl Bigelow noted, "I am very interested in our children understanding that words can be taken apart, put back together, read from left-to-right, sounded out, turned upside down, whatever. It's a part of the whole picture."

Literacy and the Subterranean Culture of Children

Supporting students with significant disabilities as sense-makers and as full participants in the classroom's literate community created certain ambiguities related to child behavior for participating teachers in this study. For instance, the question emerged, "How do you support a child to misbehave?" In early childhood, subterranean youth cultures already emerge with profound implications for what might be termed normal socialization (Paley, 1988, 1992). Indeed, children's "misbehavior" may in fact be part of normal socialization. Those concerned with children's full participation recognized the importance of a child fitting into social patterns separate from adult oversight and control.

In early childhood, subterranean cultures stereotypically involve such things as "potty talk," inane riddles, cliquish ganging up, or teasing. Graphic semiotic systems giving shape to youth culture are most commonly associated with adolescence, from note passing in class to symbols used to associate with a particular teenage clique. However, using multiple literacies as a way to connect certain children while excluding adults and other students who do not fit in clearly begins in the preschool and kindergarten classrooms.

By its very definition, the subterranean culture, with its many narrative forms, is child-initiated and quite separate from adult influence — factors that appear to make participation difficult for children with significant disabilities who often rely on high levels of adult support. Once adults actively begin to assist a child, any ongoing narratives are no longer subterranean. Still, in our observations we noted children with disabilities at times finding their way into subterranean discourses, with multiple literacies playing a role. For instance, in the Corner Nook classroom, we observed several girls take over a corner of the room where both boys and girls tended to play. Led by Kassie, a nondisabled child, the girls engaged in the literate act of producing two signs with markers and crayons. One read, "No boys," and the other had a bright red circle with a slash mark over the word "Boys," meaning, again, "No boys allowed." Lori, the girl with severe disabilities, was included in the group. While she was not directly involved in the fast-paced action of creating the signs, she was a part of the giggling conspiracy.

Some of the classroom boys began to take notice of the signs being posted and attempted to enter the area — only to be greeted by girls who would not allow them in. "No boys allowed," was the mantra. The boys' primary focus was to wrench down the signs. This central effort demonstrated the power of the written form. It was as if the signs were the key to the girls' authority; remove them and order would be restored.

Jamie, the child with autism introduced earlier, moved about skittishly at the edge of the group trying to break into the area. He was largely ignored by both the boys and girls, suggesting perhaps that in this struggle his presence was considered nonthreatening. At times he found himself in the middle of a shoving match, and he would giggle and clap his hands and go running. Suddenly, in a flash, Jamie reached out and grabbed one sign. He ran from the scene shrieking with laughter, several girls after him and several boys shouting support. The commotion brought the classroom adults to the scene to end the play, but not until after Jamie had taken on the rare role of hero.

While teachers primarily remained outside the subterranean narratives, other than to shut them down, there was ambivalent recognition that such participation was healthy for the children with significant disabilities. Shayne Robbins, later discussing Jamie's role in the narrative just described, said, "It's so much what inclusion is about. . . . [Jamie] came in this year, he was so clueless in the beginning about all the social stuff — reaching out to other kids, asserting himself, standing up to others and for his rights." Shayne said she had noticed dramatic growth in terms of Jamie's ability to fit in with groups of children: "It's amazing to watch him now. Sometimes I'll just stand back and watch, and he's a leader. He gets kids doing things. He's just so important in this class." Shayne continued, "That's the important stuff. Sometimes you kind of have to look the other direction, let him break a rule or two, because he's learning how to fit in, how to just be a normal part."

Conclusions: Constructing Contexts of Support for Literacy

Inclusive education appeared to be fundamental to the literate citizenship of children with significant disabilities. In its rejection of the status quo of segregated schooling, inclusion immersed students in the wonderfully chaotic patterns, semiotic systems, and narrative forms of the early childhood literate community. Beyond mere presence, however, was the teachers' active belief that literacy was many things and that all students, including those with the most complex disabilities, were capable sense-makers. Through a teacher's educational imagination, children were supported in the literate engagement of a variety of narrative forms made available in their hectic classrooms.

We are not the first researchers to have explored young children's narratives as fundamental to literacy. Most notably, Kieran Egan and colleagues have systematically examined the varied stories of children and their relationship to a literate culture (Egan, 1999; McEwan & Egan, 1995; see endnote 11). Narrative, in McEwan and Egan's (1995) definition, is the language-based story that grows around, gives shape to, and symbolically extends the experience. They note, "What distinguishes narrative is that it takes shape, in however attenuated a form, as a rhythm that ultimately springs from patterns implicit in human life and interaction" (McEwan & Egan, 1995, p. vii). In relation to our own research, "human life and interaction" corresponds to the meaning, understanding, and sense-making that emerged as a motivating force in the lives of all young children.

The rhythm of which McEwan and Egan (1995) write is also described as a "pattern" out of which "more developed [e.g., less attenuated, increasingly sophisticated] patterns may emerge" (p. vii). In an insightful essay exploring the origins of literacy in preschool narratives, Egan (1999) cautiously noted certain links between the community young children create in early childhood classrooms and the sophisticated oral cultures out of which literacy itself once emerged thousands of years ago. He noted that, as with oral cultures, young children and surrounding adults build messages of importance into "developing narratives" or spoken stories. These stories provide the first "firm structures" for the abstractions of childhood ideas and understanding; they, in effect, "catch and fix meaning" (p. 16).

According to Egan (1999), as preschoolers grow in sophistication, so too do their stories and the manner in which those stories are caught and fixed. Young children's oral narratives engage the tools of rhyme, rhythm, meter, repetition of formulae, redundancy, and visual imagery (i.e., figures of speech) to expand and deepen messages of importance. These same tools, Egan asserted, are important in written texts aimed at a preschool audience (e.g., nursery rhymes and Dr. Seuss books), and in the early textual-representational efforts on the part of young children themselves.

Kieran Egan's descriptions of children's oral-based communities eventually merging with the literate, text-sated realities of the formal school agenda added depth to our own observations of narratives. However, his descriptive efforts, focused as they are on oral culture, could not capture the complexities of literate citizenship in inclusive early childhood classrooms where many of the children labeled with significant disabilities exhibited extreme problems with spoken language and were, in fact, at the margins of oral language participation.

Yet, teachers in the classrooms where our participant observations played out were firmly committed to the notion that all children, including those with the most complex disabilities, could be citizens of the literate community. Hence, while Egan and colleagues may argue that oral narrative is the origin of literacy, the efforts of our participating teachers and students suggested that narrative expressed through any of a variety of semiotic systems served as the basis for and developing sophistication in literacy for all children.

Notes

1. The contents of this research were developed under a grant from the U.S. Department of Education (No. H324D010031). However, the contents do not necessarily represent the policy of the DOE, and no endorsement by the federal government should be assumed.

2. All proper names, including those of classrooms, schools, cities, adults, and children, have been altered, and identifying information has been obscured in order to maintain confidentiality.

3. Referred to in the disability education literature as inclusive education (see Biklen, 1992; Kliewer, 1998b).

4. Currently, the most visible proponents of direct subskill instruction for literacy development in early childhood (e.g., Adams, 1990, 2001; Adams, Foorman, Lundberg, & Beeler, 1997; McGuiness, 1997) conclude that teaching must directly focus, through drill, on three components. The first, considered most important to literacy, is referred to as phonemic awareness and is composed of a myriad of subcomponents. It is the conscious awareness on the part of young children that words are made up of phonemes. The second is commonly referred to as the alphabetic principle, and is a general description of knowledge about the alphabet, including awareness that phonemes can be graphically represented by letters and letter combinations. The third, oral language, is associated with vocabulary development and correct English usage. A fourth component that may be included in descriptions of the need for direct instruction is orthography, or direct instruction in spelling and the rules associated with spelling.

5. Based on records maintained in the archives of the Mennonite Heritage Museum, Mountain Lake, Minnesota.

6. One type of source among many vividly documenting the viciousness of imposed illiteracy is the autobiographical genre described as slave narrative, which emerged from the stories of freed and escaped American slaves prior to the Civil War (see Gates, 1987).

7. *Scientific-based* and *evidence-based* are current, synonymous educational catch-phrases related to particular forms of what is termed in psychology to be experimental research and the practices that are formulated therein. In reading research, it appears that only phonics-based instruction and assessment is currently branded as scientifically based. An example of qualifying research and derivative practice is the reading assessment referred to by its trade-marked title, *Dynamic Indicators of Basic Early Literacy Skills* (DIBELS; Good & Kaminski, 2002). DIBELS materials state that the *big ideas* of early literacy include phonological awareness, the alphabetic principle, and accuracy and fluency with connected text. In preschool, DIBELS' focus is placed on assessing initial sound fluency and word- use fluency (which refers to using apparently random words correctly in random sentences). In kindergarten, letter-naming fluency, phoneme-segmentation fluency, and nonsense-word fluency are added to the assessed literacy skills. Not until first grade do we see an expectation around understanding and meaning (referred to in DIBELS lexicon as retell fluency).

8. An extremely narrow selection of this body of work includes, for example, biographical, autobiographical, clinical, and ethnographic accounts of the development of highly sophisticated literacies on the part of people with Down's syndrome (Andrews, 1995; Buck, 1955; Buckley, 1995; Burke & McDaniel, 1991; Goode, 1992; Hunt, 1966; Seagoe, 1964), autism (Biklen, 1992; Grandin & Scariano, 1986), and severe physical disabilities (Brown, 1989; Crossley & McDonald, 1984).

9. Different states, and even different Local Education Agencies (e.g., school districts) within a single state, vary in how children are labeled. All children defined here as having a significant disability are students who qualify for special education services under the Individuals with Disabilities Education Act (IDEA). In addition, they are children who qualify for a significant level of resources because of the presumed degree of disability. Many but not all of the children had specific disability labels or diagnoses (e.g., autism, Down's syndrome, cerebral palsy, etc.). Preschool children (and now older students), however, may receive services with a generic label (e.g., developmental disability [D.D.], entitled individual [E.I.], etc.).

10. Narrative is, of course, a broad construct. Our use of the term reflects McEwan and Egan's (1995) sense that "narrative is basically extended language configured in such a way that its earlier embodiment in life becomes revealed" (p. vii). The earlier embodiment may be a thought, idea, emotion, or experience, and its revelation may take on the configuration of, among other expressive or receptive communication forms, literacy.

11. Emphasizing a specific child's unique or idiosyncratic needs within a general curriculum is traditionally associated with inclusive education and is commonly considered a process of making curricular adaptations or modifications. Initially it was termed the Principle of Partial Participation (Baumgart et al., 1982), and has more recently been referred to as multilevel learning (Falvey, Givner, & Kimm, 1996) and differentiated instruction (Tomlinson, 1999).

References

Adams, M. J. (1990). *Beginning to read: Thinking and learning about print.* Cambridge, MA: MIT Press.

Adams, M. J. (2001). Alphabetic anxiety and explicit, systematic phonics instruction: A cognitive science perspective. In S. B. Neuman & D. K. Dickinson (Eds.), *Handbook of early literacy research* (pp. 66–80). New York: Guilford Press.

Adams, M. J., Foorman, B. R., Lundberg, I., & Beeler, T. (1997). *Phonemic awareness in young children: A classroom curriculum.* Baltimore: Brookes.

Andrews, S. S. (1995). Life in Mendocino: A young man with Down syndrome in a Northern California town. In S. J. Taylor, R. Bogdan, & Z. M. Lutfiyya (Eds.), *The variety of community experience: Qualitative studies of family and community life* (pp. 101–116). Baltimore: Brookes.

Barratt-Pugh, C. (2000). The socio-cultural context of literacy learning. In C. Barratt-Pugh & M. Rohl (Eds.), *Literacy learning in the early years* (pp. 1–26). Buckingham, Eng.: Open University Press.

Barton, D., & Hamilton, M. (1998). *Local literacies: Reading and writing in one community.* New York: Routledge.

Baumgart, D., Brown, L., Pumpian, I., Nisbet, J., Ford, A., Sweet, M., Messina, R., & Schroeder, J. (1982). Principle of partial participation and individualized adaptations in educational programs for severely handicapped students. *Journal of the Association for the Severely Handicapped, 7,* 17–27.

Biklen, D. (1992). *Schooling without labels: Parents, educators, and inclusive education.* Philadelphia: Temple University Press.

Bogdan, R., & Biklen, S. K. (2003). *Qualitative research for education: An introduction to theory and methods* (4th ed.). Boston: Allyn & Bacon.

Brown, C. (1989). *My left foot.* New York: Simon & Schuster.

Buck, J. N. (1955). The sage: An unusual mongoloid. In A. Burton & R. Harris (Eds.), *Clinical studies of personality* (vol. 3, pp. 455–481). New York: Harper & Row.

Buckley, S. (1995). Teaching children with Down syndrome to read and write. In L. Nadel & D. Rosenthal (Eds.), *Down syndrome: Living and learning in the community* (pp. 158–169). New York: Wiley-Liss.

Burke, C., & McDaniel, J. B. (1991). *A special kind of hero.* New York: Dell.

Crawford, P. A. (1995). Early literacy: Emerging perspectives. *Journal of Research in Childhood Education, 10,* 71–86.

Crossley, R., & McDonald, A. (1984). *Annie's coming out.* New York: Penguin.

Egan, K. (1999). *Children's minds, talking rabbits, and clockwork oranges.* New York: Teachers College Press.

Erickson, K. A., & Koppenhaver, D. A. (1995). Developing a literacy program for children with severe disabilities. *Reading Teacher, 48,* 676–684.

Falvey, M., Givner, C. C., & Kimm, C. (1996). What do I do Monday morning? In S. Stainback & W. Stainback (Eds.), *Inclusion: A guide for educators* (pp. 117–140). Baltimore: Paul Brookes.

Fernandez, R. (2001). *Imagining literacy: Rhizomes of knowledge in American culture and literature.* Austin: University of Texas Press.

Gates, H. L., Jr. (1987). *The classic slave narratives.* New York: Mentor.

Good, R. H., & Kaminski, R. A. (2002). *Dynamic indicators of basic early literacy skills* (6th ed.). Eugene, OR: Institute for the Development of Educational Achievement.

Goode, D. A. (1992). Who is Bobby? Ideology and method in the discovery of a Down syndrome person's competence. In P. M. Ferguson, D. L. Ferguson, & S. J. Taylor (Eds.), *Interpreting disability: A qualitative reader* (pp. 197–212). New York: Teachers College Press.

Grandin, T., & Scariano, M. M. (1986). *Emergence: Labeled autistic.* Novato, CA: Arena Press.

Hunt, N. (1966). *The world of Nigel Hunt: The diary of a mongoloid youth.* New York: Garrett.

Kliewer, C. (1998a). Citizenship in the literate community: An ethnography of children with Down syndrome and the written word. *Exceptional Children, 64,* 167–180.

Kliewer, C. (1998b). *Schooling children with Down syndrome: Toward an understanding of possibility.* New York: Teachers College Press.

Kliewer, C. & Biklen, D. (2001). "School's not really a place for reading": A research analysis of the literate lives of people with severe disabilities. *Journal of the Association for Persons with Severe Disabilities, 26,* 1–12.

Kliewer, C., & Drake, S. (1998). Disability, eugenics, and the current ideology of segregation: A modern moral tale. *Disability and Society, 13,* 95–111.

Kliewer, C., & Fitzgerald, L. M. (2001). Disability, schooling, and the artifacts of colonialism. *Teachers College Record, 103,* 450–470.

Kliewer, C., Fitzgerald, L. M., & Raschke, D. (2001). Young children's citizenship in the literate community: Significant disability and the power of early childhood inclusion. *TASH Connections, 27*(11/12), 8–11.

Kliewer, C., & Landis, D. (1999). Individualizing literacy instruction for young children with moderate to severe disabilities. *Exceptional Children, 66,* 85–100.

Kliewer, C., & Raschke, D. (2002). Beyond the metaphor of merger: Confronting the moral quagmire of segregation in early childhood special education. *Disability, Culture, and Education, 1,* 41–62.

Kluth, P., Straut, D. M., & Biklen, D. P. (Eds.). (2003). *Access to academics for all students: Critical approaches to inclusive curriculum, instruction, and policy.* Mahwah, NJ: Lawrence Erlbaum Associates.

Koppenhaver, D. A., & Erickson, K. A. (2003). Natural emergent literacy supports for preschoolers with autism and severe communication impairments. *Topics in Language Disorders, 23,* 283–292.

Maurice, C. (1993). *Let me hear your voice: A family's triumph over autism.* New York: Knopf.

McEwan, H., & Egan, K. (Eds.). (1995). *Narrative in teaching, learning, and research.* New York: Teachers College Press.

McGuiness, D. (1997). *Why our children can't read.* New York: Free Press.

Mirenda, P. (2003). "He's not really a reader": Perspectives on supporting literacy development in individuals with autism. *Topics in Language Disorders, 23,* 271–282.

Paley, V. G. (1988). *Bad guys don't have birthdays: Fantasy play at four.* Chicago: University of Chicago Press.

Paley, V. G. (1992). *You can't say you can't play.* Cambridge, MA: Harvard University Press.

Resnick, D. P., & Resnick, L. B. (1977). The nature of literacy: An historical exploration. *Harvard Educational Review, 47,* 370–385.

Richgels, D. J. (2001). Invented spelling, phonemic awareness, and reading and writing instruction. In S. B. Neuman & D. K. Dickinson (Eds.), *Handbook of early literacy research* (pp. 142–155). New York: Guilford Press.

Seagoe, M. V. (1964). *Yesterday was Tuesday, all day and all night: The story of a unique education.* Boston: Little, Brown.

Shannon, P. (1995). *Text, lies, and videotape: Stories about life, literacy, and learning.* Portsmouth, NH: Heinemann.

Strauss, A., & Corbin, J. (1994). Grounded theory methodology: An overview. In N. K. Denzin & Y. S. Lincoln (Eds.), *Handbook of qualitative research* (pp. 273–285). Thousand Oaks, CA: Sage.

Tomlinson, C. (1999). *The differentiated classroom: Responding to the needs of all learners.* Alexandria, VA: Association for Supervision and Curriculum Development.

Whitehurst, G. J., & Lonigan, C. J. (2001). Emergent literacy: Development from prereaders to readers. In S. B. Neuman & D. K. Dickinson (Eds.), *Handbook of early literacy research* (pp. 11–29). New York: Guilford Press.

Lessons from Students on Creating a Chance to Dream

SONIA NIETO

> How does it come about that the one institution that is said to be the
> gateway to opportunity, the school, is the very one that is most effec-
> tive in perpetuating an oppressed and impoverished status in society?
> (Stein, 1971, p. 178)

The poignant question above was posed in this very journal almost a quarter of a century ago by Annie Stein, a consistent critic of the schools and a
relentless advocate for social justice. This question shall serve as the central motif of this article because, in many ways, it remains to be answered
and continues to be a fundamental dilemma standing in the way of our society's stated ideals of equity and equal educational opportunity. Annie Stein's
observations about the New York City public schools ring true today in too
many school systems throughout the country and can be used to examine some
of the same policies and practices she decried in her 1971 article.

It is my purpose in this article to suggest that successfully educating all students in U.S. schools must begin by challenging school policies and practices
that place roadblocks in the way of academic achievement for too many young
people. Educating students today is, of course, a far different and more complex proposition than it has been in the past. Young people face innumerable
personal, social, and political challenges, not to mention massive economic
structural changes not even dreamed about by other generations of youth in
the twentieth century. In spite of the tensions that such challenges may pose,
U.S. society has nevertheless historically had a social contract to educate *all*
youngsters, not simply those who happen to be European American, English
speaking, economically privileged, and, in the current educational reform jar-
gon, "ready to learn."[1] Yet, our schools have traditionally failed some youngsters, especially those from racially and culturally dominated and economically
oppressed backgrounds. Research over the past half century has documented

Harvard Educational Review   Vol. 64   No. 4   Winter 1994, 392–426

285

a disheartening legacy of failure for many students of all backgrounds, but especially children of Latino, African American, and Native American families, as well as poor European American families and, more recently, Asian and Pacific American immigrant students. Responding to the wholesale failure of so many youngsters within our public schools, educational theorists, sociologists, and psychologists devised elaborate theories of genetic inferiority, cultural deprivation, and the limits of "throwing money" at educational problems. Such theories held sway in particular during the 1960s and 1970s, but their influence is still apparent in educational policies and practices today.[2]

The fact that many youngsters live in difficult, sometimes oppressive conditions is not at issue here. Some may live in ruthless poverty and face the challenges of dilapidated housing, inadequate health care, and even abuse and neglect. They and their families may be subject to racism and other oppressive institutional barriers. They may have difficult personal, psychological, medical, or other kinds of problems. These are real concerns that should not be discounted. But, despite what may seem to be insurmountable obstacles to learning and teaching, some schools are nevertheless successful with young people who live in these situations. In addition, many children who live in otherwise onerous situations also have loving families willing to sacrifice what it takes to give their children the chance they never had during their own childhoods. Thus, poverty, single-parent households, and even homelessness, while they may be tremendous hardships, do not in and of themselves doom children to academic failure (see, among others, Clark, 1983; Lucas, Henze, & Donato, 1990; Mehan & Villanueva, 1993; Moll, 1992; Taylor & Dorsey-Gaines, 1988). These and similar studies point out that schools that have made up their minds that their students deserve the chance to learn do find the ways to educate them successfully in spite of what may seem to be overwhelming odds.

Educators may consider students difficult to teach simply because they come from families that do not fit neatly into what has been defined as "the mainstream." Some of them speak no English; many come from cultures that seem to be at odds with the dominant culture of U.S. society that is inevitably reflected in the school; others begin their schooling without the benefit of early experiences that could help prepare them for the cognitive demands they will face. Assumptions are often made about how such situations may negatively affect student achievement and, as a consequence, some children are condemned to failure before they begin. In a study by Nitza Hidalgo, a teacher's description of the students at an urban high school speaks to this condemnation: "Students are generally poor, uneducated and come from broken families who do not value school. Those conditions that produce achievers are somewhere else, not here. We get street people" (Hidalgo, 1991, p. 58). When such viewpoints guide teachers' and schools' behaviors and expectations, little progress can be expected in student achievement.

On the other hand, a growing number of studies suggest that teachers and schools need to build on rather than tear down what students bring to school. That is, they need to understand and incorporate cultural, linguistic, and experiential differences, as well as differences in social class, into the learning process (Abi-Nader, 1993; Hollins, King, & Hayman, 1994; Lucas et al., 1990; Moll & Díaz, 1993). The results of such efforts often provide inspiring examples of success because they begin with a belief that all students deserve a chance to learn. In this article, I will highlight these efforts by exploring the stories of some academically successful young people in order to suggest how the policies and practices of schools can be transformed to create environments in which all children are capable of learning.

It is too convenient to fall back on deficit theories and continue the practice of blaming students, their families, and their communities for educational failure. Instead, schools need to focus on where they *can* make a difference, namely, their own instructional policies and practices. A number of recent studies, for example, have concluded that a combination of factors, including characteristics of schools as opposed to only student background and actions, can explain differences between high- and low-achieving students. School characteristics that have been found to make a positive difference in these studies include an enriched and more demanding curriculum, respect for students' languages and cultures, high expectations for all students, and encouragement for parental involvement in their children's education (Lee, Winfield, & Wilson, 1991; Lucas et al., 1990; Moll, 1992). This would suggest that we need to shift from a single-minded focus on low- or high-achieving students to the conditions that create low- or high-achieving schools. If we understand school policies and practices as being enmeshed in societal values, we can better understand the manifestations of these values in schools as well. Thus, for example, "tracked" schools, rather than reflecting a school practice that exists in isolation from society, reflect a society that is itself tracked along racial, gender, and social-class lines. In the same way, "teacher expectations" do not come from thin air, but reflect and support expectations of students that are deeply ingrained in societal and ideological values.

Reforming school structures alone will not lead to substantive differences in student achievement, however, if such changes are not also accompanied by profound changes in how we as educators think about our students; that is, in what we believe they deserve and are capable of achieving. Put another way, changing policies and practices is a necessary but insufficient condition for total school transformation. For example, in a study of six high schools in which Latino students have been successful, Tamara Lucas, Rosemary Henze, and Rubén Donato (1990) found that the most crucial element is a shared belief among teachers, counselors, and administrators that all students are capable of learning. This means that concomitant changes are needed in policies and practices *and* in our individual and collective will to educate all students. Fred Newmann (1993), in an important analysis of educational restructuring, underlines this point by emphasizing that reform efforts will fail unless they are accompanied by a set of particular commitments and competencies to guide them, including a commitment to the success of all students, the creation of new roles for teachers, and the development of schools as caring communities.

Another crucial consideration in undertaking educational change is a focus on what Jim Cummins (1994) has called the "relations of power" in schools. In proposing a shift from coercive to collaborative relations of power, Cummins argues that traditional teacher-centered transmission models can limit the potential for critical thinking on the part of both teachers and students, but especially for students from dominated communities whose cultures and languages have been devalued by the dominant canon.[3] By encouraging collaborative relations of power, schools and teachers can begin to recognize other sources of legitimate knowledge that have been overlooked, negated, or minimized because they are not part of the dominant discourse in schools.

Focusing on concerns such as the limits of school reform without concomitant changes in educators' attitudes towards students and their families, and the crucial role of power relationships in schools may help rescue current reform efforts from simplistic technical responses to what are essentially moral and political dilemmas. That is, such technical changes as tinkering with the length of the school day, substituting one textbook for another, or adding curricular requirements may do little to change student outcomes unless these changes are part and parcel of a more comprehensive conceptualization of school reform. When such issues are considered fundamental to the changes that must be made in schools, we might more precisely speak about *transformation* rather than simply about reform. But educational transformation cannot take place without the inclusion of the voices of students, among others, in the dialogue.

Why Listen to Students?

One way to begin the process of changing school policies and practices is to listen to students' views about them; however, research that focuses on student voices is relatively recent and scarce. For example, student perspectives are for the most part missing in discussions concerning strategies for confronting educational problems. In addition, the voices of students are rarely heard in the debates about school failure and success, and the perspectives of students from disempowered and dominated communities are even more invisible. In this article, I will draw primarily on the words of students interviewed for a previous research study (Nieto, 1992). I used the interviews to develop case studies of young people from a wide variety of ethnic, racial, linguistic, and social-class backgrounds who were at the time students in junior or senior high school. These ten young people lived in communities as diverse as large urban areas and small rural hamlets, and belonged to families ranging from single-parent households to large, extended families. The one common element in all of their experiences turned out to be something we as researchers had neither planned nor expected: they were all successful students.[4]

The students were selected in a number of ways, but primarily through community contacts. Most were interviewed at home or in another setting of their choice outside of school. The only requirement that my colleagues and I determined for selecting students was that they reflect a variety of ethnic and racial backgrounds, in order to give us the diversity for which we were looking. The students selected self-identified as Black, African American, Mexican, Native American, Black and White American (biracial), Vietnamese, Jewish, Lebanese, Puerto Rican, and Cape Verdean. The one European American was the only student who had a hard time defining herself, other than as "American" (for a further analysis of this issue, see Nieto, 1992). That these particular students were academically successful was quite serendipitous. We defined them as such for the following reasons: they were all either still in school or just graduating; they all planned to complete at least high school, and most hoped to go to college; they had good grades, although they were not all at the top of their class; they had thought about their future and had made some plans for it; they generally enjoyed school and felt engaged in it (but they were also critical of their own school experiences and that of their peers, as we shall see); and most described themselves as successful. Although it had not been our initial intention to focus exclusively on academically successful students, on closer reflection it seemed logical that such students would be more likely to want to talk about their experiences than those who were not successful. It was at that point that I decided to explore what it was about these students' specific experiences that helped them succeed in school.

Therefore, the fact that these students saw themselves as successful helped further define the study, whose original purpose was to determine the benefits of multicultural education for students of diverse backgrounds. I was particularly interested in developing a way of looking at multicultural education that went beyond the typical "Holidays and Heroes" approach, which is too superficial to have any lasting impact in schools (Banks, 1991; Sleeter, 1991).[5] By exploring such issues as racism and low expectations of student achievement, as well as school policies and practices such as curriculum, pedagogy, testing, and tracking, I set about developing an understanding of multicultural education as anti-racist, comprehensive, pervasive, and rooted in social justice. Students were interviewed to find out what it meant to be from a particular background, how this influenced their school experience, and what about that experience they would change if they could. Although they were not asked specifically about the policies and practices in their schools, they nevertheless reflected on them in their answers to questions ranging from identifying their favorite subjects to describing the importance of getting an education. In this article, I will revisit the interviews to focus on students' thoughts about a number of school policies and practices and on the effects of racism and other forms of discrimination on their education.

The insights provided by the students were far richer than we had first thought. Although we expected numerous criticisms of schools and some concrete suggestions, we were surprised at the depth of awareness and analysis the students shared with us. They had a lot to say about the teachers they liked, as well as those they disliked, and they were able to explain the differences between them; they talked about grades and how these had become overly important in determining curriculum and pedagogy; they discussed their parents' lack of involvement, in most cases, in traditional school activities such as P.T.O. membership and bake sales, but otherwise passionate support for their children's academic success; they mused about what schools could do to encourage more students to learn; they spoke with feeling about their cultures, languages, and communities, and what schools could do to capitalize on these factors; and they gave us concrete suggestions for improving schools for young people of all backgrounds. This experience confirmed my belief that educators can benefit from hearing students' critical perspectives, which might cause them to modify how they approach curriculum, pedagogy, and other school practices. Since doing this research, I have come across other studies that also focus on young people's perspectives and provide additional powerful examples of the lessons we can learn from them. This article thus begins with "lessons from students," an approach that takes the perspective proposed by Paulo Freire, that teachers need to become students just as students need to become teachers in order for education to become reciprocal and empowering for both (Freire, 1970).

This focus on students is not meant to suggest that their ideas should be the final and conclusive word in how schools need to change. Nobody has all the answers, and suggesting that students' views should be adopted wholesale is to accept a romantic view of students that is just as partial and condescending as excluding them completely from the discussion. I am instead suggesting that if we believe schools must provide an equal and quality education for all, students need to be included in the dialogue, and that their views, just as those of others, should be problematized and used to reflect critically on school reform.

Selected Policies and Practices and Students' Views about Them

School policies and practices need to be understood within the sociopolitical context of our society in general, rather than simply within individual schools' or teachers' attitudes and practices. This is important to remember for a number of reasons. First, although "teacher bashing" provides an easy target for complex problems, it fails to take into account the fact that teachers function within particular societal and institutional structures. In addition, it results in placing an inordinate amount of blame on some of those who care most deeply about students and who struggle every day to help them learn. That some teachers are racist, classist, and mean-spirited and that others have lost all creativity and caring is not in question here, and I begin with the assumption that the majority of teachers are not consciously so. I do suggest, however, that although many teachers are hardworking, supportive of their students, and talented educators, many of these same teachers are also burned out, frustrated, and negatively influenced by societal views about the students they teach. Teachers could benefit from knowing more about their students' families and experiences, as well as about students' views on school and how it could be improved.

How do students feel about the curriculum they must learn? What do they think about the pedagogical strategies their teachers use? Is student involvement a meaningful issue for them? Are their own identities important considerations in how they view school? What about tracking and testing and disciplinary policies? These are crucial questions to consider when reflecting on what teachers and schools can learn from students, but we know very little about students' responses. When asked, students seem surprised and excited about being included in the conversation, and what they have to say is often compelling and eloquent. In fact, Patricia Phelan, Ann Locke Davidson, and Hanh Thanh Cao (1992), in a two-year research project designed to identify students' thoughts about school, discovered that students' views on teaching and learning were remarkably consistent with those of current theorists concerned with learning theory, cognitive science, and the sociology of work. This should come as no surprise when we consider that students spend more time in schools than anybody else except teachers (who are also omitted in most discussions of school reform, but that is a topic for another article). In the following sections, I will focus on students' perceptions concerning the curriculum, pedagogy, tracking, and grades in their schools. I will also discuss their attitudes about racism and other biases, how these are manifested in their schools and classrooms, and what effect they may have on students' learning and participation in school.

Curriculum

The curriculum in schools is at odds with the experiences, backgrounds, hopes, and wishes of many students. This is true of both the tangible curriculum as expressed through books, other materials, and the actual written curriculum guides, as well as in the less tangible and "hidden" curriculum as seen in the bulletin boards, extracurricular activities, and messages given to students about their abilities and talents. For instance, Christine Sleeter and Carl Grant (1991) found that a third of the students in a desegregated junior high school they studied said that *none* of the class content related to their lives outside class. Those who indicated some relevancy cited only current events, oral history, money and banking, and multicultural content (because it dealt with prejudice) as being relevant. The same was true in a study by Mary Poplin and Joseph Weeres (1992), who found that students frequently reported being bored in school and seeing little relevance in what was taught for their lives or their futures. The authors concluded that students became more disengaged as the curriculum, texts, and assignments became more standardized. Thus, in contrast to Ira Shor's (1992) suggestion that "What students bring to class is where learning begins. It starts there and goes places" (p. 44), there is often a tremendous mismatch between students' cultures and the culture of the school. In many schools, learning starts not with what students bring to class, but with what is considered high-status knowledge; that is, the "canon," with its overemphasis on European and European American history, arts, and values. This seldom includes the backgrounds, experiences, and talents of the majority of students in U.S. schools. Rather than "going elsewhere," their learning therefore often goes nowhere.

That students' backgrounds and experiences are missing in many schools is particularly evident where the native language of most of the students is not English. In such settings, it is not unusual to see little or no representation of those students' language in the curriculum. In fact, there is often an insistence that students "speak only English" in these schools, which sends a powerful message to young people struggling to maintain an identity in the face of overpowering messages that they must assimilate. This was certainly the case for Marisol, a Puerto Rican girl of sixteen participating in my research, who said:

> I used to have a lot of problems with one of my teachers 'cause she didn't want us to talk Spanish in class and I thought that was like an insult to us, you know? Just telling us not to talk Spanish, 'cause they were Puerto Ricans and, you know, we're free to talk whatever we want, . . . I could never stay quiet and talk only English, 'cause sometimes . . . words slip in Spanish. You know, I think they should understand that.

Practices such as not allowing students to speak their native tongue are certain to influence negatively students' identities and their views of what constitutes important knowledge. For example, when asked if she would be interested in taking a course on Puerto Rican history, Marisol was quick to answer: "I don't think [it's] important. . . . I'm proud of myself and my culture, but I think I know what I should know about the culture already, so I wouldn't take the course." Ironically, it was evident to me after speaking with her on several occasions that Marisol knew virtually nothing about Puerto Rican history. However, she had already learned another lesson well: given what she said about the courses she needed to take, she made it clear that "important" history is U.S. history, which rarely includes anything about Puerto Rico.

Messages about culture and language and how they are valued or devalued in society are communicated not only or even primarily by schools, but by the media and community as a whole. The sociopolitical context of the particular city where Marisol lived, and of its school system, is important to understand: there had been an attempt to pass an ordinance restricting the number of Puerto Ricans coming into town based on the argument that they placed an undue burden on the welfare rolls and other social services. In addition, the "English Only" debate had become an issue when the mayor had ordered all municipal workers to speak only English on the job. Furthermore, although the school system had a student body that was 65 percent Puerto Rican, there was only a one-semester course on Puerto Rican history that had just recently been approved for the bilingual program. In contrast, there were two courses, which although rarely taught were on the books, that focused on apartheid and the Holocaust, despite the fact that both the African American and Jewish communities in the town were quite small. That such courses should be part of a comprehensive multicultural program is not being questioned; however, it is ironic that the largest population in the school was ignored in the general curriculum.

In a similar vein, Nancy Commins's (1989) research with four first-generation Mexican American fifth-grade students focused on how these students made decisions about their education, both consciously and unconsciously, based on their determination of what counted as important knowledge. Her research suggests that the classroom setting and curriculum can support or hinder students' perceptions of themselves as learners based on the languages they speak and their cultural backgrounds. She found that although the homes of these four students provided rich environments for a variety of language uses and literacy, the school did little to capitalize on these strengths. In their classroom, for instance, these children rarely used Spanish, commenting that it was the language of the "dumb kids." As a result, Commins states: "Their reluctance to use Spanish in an academic context also limited their opportunities to practice talking about abstract ideas and to use higher level cognitive skills in Spanish" (p. 35). She also found that the content of the curriculum was almost completely divorced from the experiences of these youngsters, since the problems of poverty, racism, and discrimination, which were prominent in their lives, were not addressed in the curriculum.

In spite of teachers' reluctance to address such concerns, they are often compelling to students, particularly those who are otherwise invisible in the curriculum. Vinh, an 18-year-old Vietnamese student attending a high school in a culturally heterogeneous town, lived with his uncle and younger brothers and sisters. Although grateful for the education he was receiving, Vinh expressed concern about what he saw as insensitivity on the part of some of his teachers to the difficulties of adjusting to a new culture and learning English:

> [Teachers] have to know about our culture. . . . From the second language, it is very difficult for me and for other people.

Vinh's concern was echoed by Manuel, a nineteen-year-old Cape Verdean senior who, at the time of the interviews, was just getting ready to graduate, the first in his family of eleven children to do so:

> I was kind of afraid of school, you know, 'cause it's different when you're learning the language. . . . It's kind of scary at first, especially if you don't know the language and like if you don't have friends here.

In Manuel's case, the Cape Verdean Crioulo bilingual program served as a linguistic and cultural mediator, negotiating difficult experiences that he faced in school so that, by the time he reached high school, he had learned enough English to "speak up." Another positive curricular experience was the theater workshop he took as a sophomore. There, students created and acted in skits focusing on their lived experiences. He recalled with great enthusiasm, for example, a monologue he did about a student going to a new school, because it was based on his personal experience.

Sometimes a school's curriculum is unconsciously disrespectful of students' cultures and experiences. James, a student who proudly identified himself as Lebanese American, found that he was invisible in the curriculum, even in supposedly multicultural curricular and extracurricular activities. He mentioned a language fair, a multicultural festival, and a school cookbook, all of which omitted references to the Arabic language and to Lebanese people. About the cookbook, he said:

> They made this cookbook of all these different recipes from all over the world. And I would've brought in some Lebanese recipes if somebody'd let me know.

> And I didn't hear about it until the week before they started selling them. . . . I asked one of the teachers to look at it and there was nothing Lebanese in there.

James made an effort to dismiss this oversight, and although he said that it didn't matter, he seemed to be struggling with the growing realization that it mattered very much indeed:

> I don't know, I guess there's not that many Lebanese people in . . . I don't know; you don't hear really that much . . . Well, you hear it in the news a lot, but I mean, I don't know, there's not a lot of Lebanese kids in our school. . . . I don't mind, 'cause I mean, I don't know, just I don't mind it. . . . It's not really important. It *is* important for me. It would be important for me to see a Lebanese flag.

Lebanese people were mentioned in the media, although usually in negative ways, and these were the only images of James's ethnic group that made their way into the school. He spoke, for example, about how the Lebanese were characterized by his peers:

> Some people call me, you know, 'cause I'm Lebanese, so people say, "Look out for the terrorist! Don't mess with him or he'll blow up your house!" or some stuff like that. . . . But they're just joking around, though. . . . I don't think anybody's serious 'cause I wouldn't blow up anybody's house — and they know that. . . . I don't care. It doesn't matter what people say. . . . I just want everybody to know that, you know, it's not true.

Cultural ambivalence, both pride and shame, were evident in the responses of many of the students. Although almost all of them were quite clear that their culture was important to them, they were also confronted with debilitating messages about it from society in general. How to make sense of these contradictions was a dilemma for many of these young people.

Fern, who identified herself as Native American, was, at thirteen, one of the youngest students interviewed. She reflected on the constant challenges she faced in the history curriculum in her junior high school. Her father was active in their school and community and he gave her a great deal of support for defending her position, but she was the only Native American student in her entire school in this mid-size city in Iowa. She said:

> If there's something in the history book that's wrong, my dad always taught me that if it's wrong, I should tell them that it is wrong. And the only time I ever do is if I know it's *exactly* wrong. Like we were reading about Native Americans and scalping. Well, the French are really the ones that made them do it so they could get money. And my teacher would not believe me. I finally just shut up because he just would not believe me.

Fern also mentioned that her sister had come home angry one day because somebody in school had said "Geronimo was a stupid chief riding that stupid horse." The connection between an unresponsive curriculum and dropping out of school was not lost on Fern, and she talked about this incident as she wondered aloud why other Native Americans had dropped out of the town's schools. Similar sentiments were reported by students in Virginia Vogel Zanger's (1994) study of twenty Latinos from a Boston high school who took part in a panel discussion in which they reflected on their experiences in school. Some of the students who decided to stay in school claimed that dropping out among their peers was a direct consequence of the school's attempts to "monoculture" them.

Fern was self-confident and strong in expressing her views, despite her young age. Yet she too was silenced by the way the curriculum was presented in class. This is because schools often avoid bringing up difficult, contentious, or conflicting issues in the curriculum, especially when these contradict the sanctioned views of the standard curriculum, resulting in what Michelle Fine has called "silencing." According to Fine: "Silencing is about who can speak, what can and cannot be spoken, and whose discourse must be controlled" (1991, p. 33). Two topics in particular that appear to have great saliency for many students, regardless of their backgrounds, are bias and discrimination, yet these are among the issues most avoided in classrooms. Perhaps this is because the majority of teachers are European Americans who are unaccustomed, afraid, or uncomfortable in discussing these issues (Sleeter, 1994); perhaps it is due to the pressure teachers feel to "cover the material"; maybe it has to do with the tradition of presenting information in schools as if it were free of conflict and controversy (Kohl, 1993); or, most likely, it is a combination of all these things. In any event, both students and teachers soon pick up the message that racism, discrimination, and other dangerous topics are not supposed to be discussed in school. We also need to keep in mind that these issues have disparate meanings for people of different backgrounds, and are often perceived as particularly threatening to those from dominant cultural and racial groups. Deidre, one of the young African American women in Fine's 1991 study of an urban high school, explained it this way: "White people might feel like everything's over and OK, but we remember" (p. 33).

Another reason that teachers may avoid bringing up potentially contentious issues in the curriculum is their feeling that doing so may create or exacerbate animosity and hostility among students. They may even believe, as did the reading teacher in Jonathan Kozol's 1967 classic book on the Boston Public Schools, *Death at an Early Age,* that discussing slavery in the context of U.S. history was just too complicated for children to understand, not to mention uncomfortable for teachers to explain. Kozol writes of the reading teacher:

> She said, with the very opposite of malice but only with an expression of the most intense and honest affection for the children in the class: "I don't want these children to have to think back on this year later on and to have to remember that we were the ones who told them they were Negro. (p. 68)

More than a quarter of a century later, the same kinds of disclaimers are being made for the failure to include in the curriculum the very issues that would engage students in learning. Fine (1991) found that although over half of the students in the urban high school she interviewed described experiences with racism, teachers were reluctant to discuss it in class, explaining, in the words of one teacher, "It would demoralize the students, they need to feel positive and optimistic — like they have a chance. Racism is just an excuse they use to not try harder" (p. 37). Some of these concerns may be sincere expressions of protectiveness towards students, but others are merely self-serving and manifest teachers' discomfort with discussing racism.

The few relevant studies I have found concerning the inclusion of issues of racism and discrimination in the curriculum suggest that discussions about these topics can be immensely constructive if they are approached with sensitivity and understanding. This was the case in Melinda Fine's description of the "Facing History and Ourselves" (FHAO) curriculum, a project that started in the Brookline (Massachusetts) Public Schools almost two decades ago (Fine, 1993). FHAO provides a model for teaching history that encourages students to reflect critically on a variety of contemporary social, moral, and political issues. Using the Holocaust as a case study, students learn to think critically about such issues as scapegoating, racism, and personal and collective responsibility. Fine suggests that moral dilemmas do not disappear simply because teachers refuse to bring them into the schools. On the contrary, when these realities are separated from the curriculum, young people learn that school knowledge is unrelated to their lives, and once again, they are poorly prepared to face the challenges that society has in store for them.

A good case in point is Vanessa, a young European American woman in my study who was intrigued by "difference" yet was uncomfortable and reluctant to discuss it; although she was active in a peer education group that focused on such concerns as peer pressure, discrimination, and exclusion, these were rarely discussed in the formal curriculum. Vanessa, therefore, had no language with which to talk about these issues. In thinking about U.S. history, she mused about some of the contradictions that were rarely addressed in school:

> It seems weird . . . because people came from Europe and they wanted to get away from all the stuff that was over there. And then they came here and set up all the stuff like slavery, and I don't know, it seems the opposite of what they would have done.

The curriculum, then, can act to either enable or handicap students in their learning. Given the kind of curriculum that draws on their experiences and energizes them because it focuses precisely on those things that are most important in their lives, students can either soar or sink in our schools. Curriculum can provide what María Torres-Guzmán (1992) refers to as "cognitive empowerment," encouraging students to become confident, active critical thinkers who learn that their background experiences are important tools for further learning. The connection of the curriculum to real life and their future was mentioned by several of the students interviewed in my study. Avi, a Jewish boy of sixteen who often felt a schism between his school and home lives, for instance, spoke about the importance of school: "If you don't go to school, then you can't learn about life, or you can't learn about things that you need to progress [in] your life." And Vanessa, who seemed to yearn for a more socially conscious curriculum in her school, summed up why education was important to her: "A good education is like when you personally learn something . . . like growing, expanding your mind and your views."

Pedagogy

If curriculum is primarily the *what* of education, then pedagogy concerns the *why* and *how*. No matter how interesting and relevant the curriculum may be, the way in which it is presented is what will make it engaging or dull to students. Students' views echo those of educational researchers who have found that teaching methods in most classrooms, and particularly those in secondary schools, vary little from traditional "chalk and talk" methods; that textbooks are the dominant teaching materials used; that routine and rote learning are generally favored over creativity and critical thinking; and that teacher-centered transmission models prevail (Cummins, 1994; Goodlad, 1984; McNeil, 1986). Martin Haberman is especially critical of what he calls "the pedagogy of poverty," that is, a basic urban pedagogy used with children who live in poverty and which consists primarily of giving instructions, asking questions, giving directions, making assignments, and monitoring seat work. Such pedagogy is based on the assumption that before students can be engaged in creative or critical work, they must first master "the basics." Nevertheless, Haberman asserts that this pedagogy does not work and, furthermore, that it actually gets in the way of real teaching and learning. He suggests instead that we look at exemplary pedagogy in urban schools that actively involves students in real-life situations, which allows them to reflect on their own lives. He finds that good teaching is taking place when teachers welcome difficult issues and events and use human difference as the basis for the curriculum; design collaborative activities for heterogeneous groups; and help students apply ideals of fairness, equity, and justice to their world (Haberman, 1991).

Students in my study had more to say about pedagogy than about anything else, and they were especially critical of the lack of imagination that led to boring classes. Linda, who was just graduating as the valedictorian of her class in an urban high school, is a case in point. Her academic experiences had not always been smooth sailing. For example, she had failed both seventh and eighth grade twice, for a combination of reasons, including academic and medical problems. Consequently, she had experienced both exhilarating and devastating educational experiences. Linda had this to say about pedagogy:

> I think you have to be creative to be a teacher; you have to make it interesting. You can't just go in and say, "Yeah, I'm going to teach the kids just that; I'm gonna teach them right out of the book and that's the way it is, and don't ask questions." Because I know there were plenty of classes where I lost complete interest. But those were all because the teachers just, "Open the books to this page." They never made up problems out of their head. Everything came out of the book. You didn't ask questions. If you asked them questions, then the answer was "in the book." And if you asked the question and the answer *wasn't* in the book, then you shouldn't have asked that question!

Rich, a young Black man, planned to attend pharmacy school after graduation, primarily because of the interest he had developed in chemistry. He too talked about the importance of making classes "interesting":

> I believe a teacher, by the way he introduces different things to you, can make a class interesting. Not like a normal teacher that gets up, gives you a lecture,

or there's teachers that just pass out the work, you do the work, pass it in, get a grade, good-bye!

Students were especially critical of teachers' reliance on textbooks and blackboards, a sad indictment of much of the teaching that encourages student passivity. Avi, for instance, felt that some teachers get along better when they teach from the point of view of the students: "They don't just come out and say, `All right, do this, blah, blah, blah.' . . . They're not so *one-tone voice*." Yolanda said that her English teacher didn't get along with the students. In her words, "She just does the things and sits down." James mentioned that some teachers just don't seem to care: "They just teach the stuff. `Here,' write a couple of things on the board, `see, that's how you do it. Go ahead, page 25.' " And Vinh added his voice to those of the students who clearly saw the connection between pedagogy and caring: "Some teachers, they just go inside and go to the blackboard. . . . They don't care."

Students did more than criticize teachers' pedagogy, however; they also praised teachers who were interesting, creative, and caring. Linda, in a particularly moving testimony to her first-grade teacher, whom she called her mentor, mentioned that she would be "following in her footsteps" and studying elementary education. She added:

> She's always been there for me. After the first or second grade, if I had a problem, I could always go back to her. Through the whole rest of my life, I've been able to go back and talk to her. . . . She's a Golden Apple Award winner, which is a very high award for elementary school teachers. . . . She keeps me on my toes. . . . When I start getting down . . . she peps me back up and I get on my feet.

Vinh talked with feeling about teachers who allowed him to speak Vietnamese with other students in class. Vinh loved working in groups. He particularly remembered a teacher who always asked students to discuss important issues, rather than focusing only on learning what he called "the word's meaning" by writing and memorizing lists of words. The important issues concerned U.S. history, the students' histories and cultures, and other engaging topics that were central to their lives. Students' preference for group work has been mentioned by other educators as well. Phelan et al. (1992), in their research on students' perspectives concerning school, found that both high- and low-achieving students of all backgrounds expressed a strong preference for working in groups because it helped them generate ideas and participate actively in class.

James also appreciated teachers who explained things and let everybody ask questions because, as he said, "There could be someone sitting in the back of the class that has the same question you have. Might as well bring it out." Fern contrasted classes where she felt like falling asleep because they're just "blah," to chorus, where the teacher used a "rap song" to teach history and involve all the students. And Avi, who liked most of his teachers, singled out a particular math teacher he had had in ninth grade for praise:

> 'Cause I never really did good in math until I had him. And he showed me that it wasn't so bad, and after that I've been doing pretty good in math and I enjoy it.

Yolanda had been particularly fortunate to have many teachers she felt understood and supported her, whether they commented on her bilingual ability, or referred to her membership in a folkloric Mexican dance group, or simply talked with her and the other students about their lives. She added:

> I really got along with the teachers a lot. . . . Actually, 'cause I had some teachers, and they were always calling my mom, like I did a great job. Or they would start talking to me, or they kinda like pulled me up some grades, or moved me to other classes, or took me somewhere. And they were always congratulating me.

Such support, however, rarely represented only individual effort on the part of some teachers, but rather was often manifested by the school as a whole; that is, it was integral to the school's practices and policies. For instance, Yolanda had recently been selected "Student of the Month" and her picture had been prominently displayed in her school's main hall. In addition, she received a certificate and was taken out to dinner by the principal. Although Linda's first-grade teacher was her special favorite, she had others who also created an educational context in which all students felt welcomed and connected. The entire Tremont Elementary School had been special for Linda, and thus the context of the school, including its leadership and commitment, were the major ingredients that made it successful:

> All of my teachers were wonderful. I don't think there's a teacher at the whole Tremont School that I didn't like. . . . It's just a feeling you have. You know that they really care for you. You just know it; you can tell. Teachers who don't have you in any of their classes or haven't ever had you, they still know who you are. . . . The Tremont School in itself is a community. . . . I love that school! I want to teach there.

Vanessa talked about how teachers used their students' lives and experiences in their teaching. For her, this made them especially good teachers:

> [Most teachers] are really caring and supportive and are willing to share their lives and are willing to listen to mine. They don't just want to talk about what they're teaching you; they also want to know you.

Aside from criticism and praise, students in this study also offered their teachers many thoughtful suggestions for making their classrooms more engaging places. Rich, for instance, said that he would "put more activities into the day that can make it interesting." Fern recommended that teachers involve students more actively in learning: "More like making the whole class be involved, not making only the two smartest people up here do the whole work for the whole class." Vanessa added, "You could have games that could teach anything that they're trying to teach through notes or lectures." She suggested that in learning Spanish, for instance, students could act out the words, making them easier to remember. She also thought that other books should be required "just to show some points of view," a response no doubt to the bland quality of so many of the textbooks and other teaching materials available in schools. Avi thought that teachers who make themselves available to students ("You know, I'm here after school. Come and get help.") were most helpful.

Vinh was very specific in his suggestions, and he touched on important cultural issues. Because he came from Vietnam when he was fifteen, learning English was a difficult challenge for Vinh, and he tended to be very hard on himself, saying such things as "I'm not really good, but I'm trying" when asked to describe himself as a student. Although he had considered himself smart in Vietnam, he felt that because his English was not perfect, he wasn't smart anymore. His teachers often showered him with praise for his efforts, but Vinh criticized this approach:

> Sometimes, the English teachers, they don't understand about us. Because something we not do good, like my English is not good. And she say, "Oh, your English is great!" But that's the way the American culture is. But my culture is not like that. . . . If my English is not good, she has to say, "Your English is not good. So you have to go home and study." And she tell me what to study and how to study and get better. But some Americans, you know, they don't understand about myself. So they just say, "Oh! You're doing a good job! You're doing great! Everything is great!" Teachers talk like that, but my culture is different. . . . They say, "You have to do better."

This is an important lesson not only because it challenges the overuse of praise, a practice among those that María de la Luz Reyes (1992) has called "venerable assumptions," but also because it cautions teachers to take into account both cultural and individual differences. In this case, the practice of praising was perceived by Vinh as hollow, and therefore insincere. Linda referred to the lesson she learned when she failed seventh and eighth grade and "blew two years":

> I learned a lot from it. As a matter of fact, one of my college essays was on the fact that from that experience, I learned that I don't need to hear other people's praise to get by. . . . All I need to know is in here [pointing to her heart] whether I tried or not.

Students have important messages for teachers about what works and what doesn't. It is important, however, not to fall back on what Lilia Bartolomé (1994) has aptly termed the "methods fetish," that is, a simplistic belief that particular methods will automatically resolve complex problems of underachievement. According to Bartolomé, such a myopic approach results in teachers avoiding the central issue of why some students succeed and others fail in school and how political inequality is at the heart of this dilemma. Rather than using this or that method, Bartolomé suggests that teachers develop what she calls a "humanizing pedagogy" in which students' languages and cultures are central. There is also the problem that Reyes (1992) has called a "one-size-fits all" approach, where students' cultural and other differences may be denied even if teachers' methods are based on well-meaning and progressive pedagogy. The point here is that no method can become a sacred cow uncritically accepted and used simply because it is the latest fad. It is probably fair to say that teachers who use more traditional methods but care about their students and believe they deserve the chance to dream may have more of a positive effect than those who know the latest methods but do not share these beliefs. Students need more than such innovations as heterogeneous grouping, peer tutoring, or cooperative groups. Although these may in fact be excellent and effective teaching methods, they will do little by themselves unless accompanied by changes in teachers' attitudes and behaviors.

The students quoted above are not looking for one magic solution or method. In fact, they have many, sometimes contradictory, suggestions to make about pedagogy. While rarely speaking with one voice, they nevertheless have similar overriding concerns: too many classrooms are boring, alienating, and disempowering. There is a complex interplay of policies, practices, and attitudes that cause such pedagogy to continue. Tracking and testing are two powerful forces implicated in this interplay.

Tracking/Ability Grouping/Grades and Expectations of Student Achievement

> It is not low income that matters but low status. And status is always created and imposed by the ones on top. (Stein, 1971, p. 158)

In her 1971 article, Annie Stein cited a New York City study in which kindergarten teachers were asked to list in order of importance the things a child should learn in order to prepare for first grade. Their responses were coded according to whether they were primarily socialization or educational goals. In the schools with large Puerto Rican and African American student populations, the socialization goals were always predominant; in the mixed schools, the educational goals were first. Concluded Stein, "In fact, in a list of six or seven goals, several teachers in the minority-group kindergartens forgot to mention any educational goals at all" (p. 167). A kind of tracking, in which students' educational goals were being sacrificed for social aims, was taking place in these schools, and its effects were already evident in kindergarten.

Most recent research on tracking has found it to be problematic, especially among middle- and low-achieving students, and suggestions for detracking schools have gained growing support (Oakes, 1992; Wheelock, 1992). Nevertheless, although many tracking decisions are made on the most tenuous grounds, they are supported by ideological norms in our society about the nature of intelligence and the distribution of ability. The long-term effects of ability grouping can be devastating for the life chances of young people. John Goodlad (1984) found that first- or second-grade children tracked by teachers' judgments of their reading and math ability or by testing are likely to remain in their assigned track *for the rest of their schooling*. In addition, he found that poor children and children of color are more likely to face the negative effects of tracking than are other youngsters. For example, a recent research project by Hugh Mehan and Irene Villanueva (1993) found that when low-achieving high school students are detracked, they tend to benefit academically. The study focused on low-achieving students in the San Diego City Schools. When these students, mostly Latinos and African Americans, were removed from a low track and placed in college-bound courses with high-achieving students, they benefitted in a number of ways, including significantly higher college enrollment. The researchers concluded that a rigorous academic program serves the educational and social interests of such students more effectively than remedial and compensatory programs.

Most of the young people in my study did not mention tracking or ability grouping by name, but almost all referred to it circuitously, and usually in negative ways. Although by and large academically successful themselves, they were quick to point out that teachers' expectations often doomed their peers to failure. Yolanda, for instance, when asked what suggestions she would give teachers, said, "I'd say to teachers, 'Get along more with the kids that are not really into themselves. . . . Have more communication with them.' " When asked what she would like teachers to know about other Mexican American students, she quickly said, "They try real hard, that's one thing I know." She also criticized teachers for having low expectations of students, claiming that materials used in the classes were "too low." She added, "We are supposed to be doing higher things. And like they take us too slow, see, step by step. And that's why everybody takes it as a joke." Fern, although she enjoyed being at the "top of my class," did not like to be treated differently. She spoke about a school she attended previously where "you were all the same and you all got pushed the same and you were all helped the same. And one thing I've noticed in Springdale is they kind of teach 25 percent and they kinda leave 75 percent out." She added that, if students were receiving bad grades, teachers did not help them as much: "In Springdale, I've noticed if you're getting D's and F's, they don't look up to you; they look down. And you're always the last on the list for special activities, you know?"

These young people also referred to expectations teachers had of students based on cultural or class differences. Vanessa said that some teachers based their expectations of students on bad reputations, and found least helpful those teachers who "kind of just move really fast, just trying to get across to you what they're trying to teach you. Not willing to slow down because they need to get in what they want to get in." Rich, who attended a predominately Black school, felt that some teachers there did not expect as much as they should from the Black students: "Many of the White teachers there don't push. . . . Their expectations don't seem to be as high as they should be. . . . I know that some Black teachers, their expectations are higher than White teachers. . . . They just do it, because they know how it was for them. . . . Actually, I'd say, you have to be in Black shoes to know how it is." Little did Rich know that he was reaching the same conclusion as a major research study on fostering high achievement for African American students. In this study, Janine Bempechat determined that "across all schools, it seems that achievement is fostered by high expectations and standards" (Bempechat, 1992, p. 43).

Virginia Vogel Zanger's research with Latino and Latina students in a Boston high school focused on what can be called "social tracking." Although the students she interviewed were high-achieving and tracked in a college-bound course, they too felt the sting of alienation. In a linguistic analysis of their comments, she found that students conveyed a strong sense of marginalization, using terms such as "left out," "below," "under," and "not joined in" to reflect their feelings about school (Zanger, 1994). Although these were clearly academically successful students, they perceived tracking in the subordinate status they were assigned based on their cultural backgrounds and on the racist climate established in the school. Similarly, in a study on dropping out among Puerto Rican students, my colleague Manuel Frau-Ramos and I found some of the same kind of language. José, who had dropped out in eleventh grade, explained, "I was alone. . . . I was an outsider" (Frau-Ramos & Nieto, 1993, p. 156). Pedro, a young man who had actually graduated, nevertheless felt the same kind of alienation. When asked what the school could do to help Puerto Ricans stay in school, he said, *"Hacer algo para que los boricuas no se sientan aparte"* (Do something so that the Puerto Ricans wouldn't feel so separate) (p. 157).

Grading policies have also been mentioned in relation to tracking and expectations of achievement. One study, for example, found that when teachers de-emphasized grades and standardized testing, the status of their African American and White students became more equal, and White students made more cross-race friendship choices (Hallinan & Teixeira, 1987). In my own research, I found a somewhat surprising revelation: although the students were achieving successfully in school, most did not feel that grades were very helpful. Of course, for the most part they enjoyed receiving good grades, but it was not always for the expected reason. Fern, for instance, wanted good grades because they were one guarantee that teachers would pay attention to her. Marisol talked about the "nice report cards" that she and her siblings in this family of eight children received, and said, "and, usually, we do this for my mother. We like to see her the way she wants to be, you know, to see her happy."

But they were also quick to downplay the importance of grades. Linda, for instance, gave as an example her computer teacher, who she felt had been the least helpful in her high school:

> I have no idea about computer literacy. I got A's in that course. Just because he saw that I had A's, and that my name was all around the school for all the "wonderful things" I do, he just automatically assumed. He didn't really pay attention to who I was. The grade I think I deserved in that class was at least a C, but I got A just because everybody else gave me A's. . . . He didn't help me at all because he didn't challenge me.

She added,

> To me, they're just something on a piece of paper. . . . [My parents] feel just about the same way. If they ask me, "Honestly, did you try your best?" and I tell them yes, then they'll look at the grades and say okay.

Rich stated that, although grades were important to his mother, "I'm comfortable setting my own standards." James said, without arrogance, that he was "probably the smartest kid in my class." Learning was important to him and, unlike other students who also did the assignments, he liked to "really get into the work and stuff." He added,

> If you don't get involved with it, even if you do get, if you get perfect scores and stuff . . . it's not like really gonna sink in. . . . You can memorize the words, you know, on a test . . . but you know, if you memorize them, it's not going to do you any good. You have to *learn* them, you know?

Most of the students made similar comments, and their perceptions challenge schools to think more deeply about the real meaning of education. Linda was not alone when she said that the reason for going to school was to "make yourself a better person." She loved learning, and commented that "I just want to keep continuously learning, because when you stop learning, then you start dying." Yolanda used the metaphor of nutrition to talk about learning: "[Education] is good for you. . . . It's like when you eat. It's like if you don't eat in a whole day, you feel weird. That's the same thing for me." Vanessa, also an enthusiastic student, spoke pensively about success and happiness: "I'm happy. Success is being happy to me, it's not like having a job that gives you a zillion dollars. It's just having self-happiness."

Finally, Vinh spoke extensively about the meaning of education, contrasting the difference between what he felt it meant in the United States and what it meant in his home culture:

> In Vietnam, we go to school because we want to become educated people. But in the United States, most people, they say, "Oh, we go to school because we want to get a good job." But my idea, I don't think so. I say, if we go to school, we want a good job *also*, but we want to become a good person.
>
> [Grades] are not important to me. Important to me is education. . . . I not so concerned about [test scores] very much. . . . I just know I do my exam very good. But I don't need to know I got A or B. I have to learn more and more.
>
> Some people, they got a good education. They go to school, they got master's, they got doctorate, but they're just helping *themselves*. So that's not good. I don't care much about money. So, I just want to have a normal job that I can take care of myself and my family. So that's enough. I don't want to climb up compared to other people.

Racism and Discrimination

The facts are clear to behold, but the BIG LIE of racism blinds all but its victims. (Stein, 1971, p. 179)

An increasing number of formal research studies, as well as informal accounts and anecdotes, attest to the lasting legacy of various forms of institutional discrimination in the schools based on race, ethnicity, religion, gender, social class, language, and sexual orientation. Yet, as Annie Stein wrote in 1971, these are rarely addressed directly. The major reason for this may be that institutional discrimination flies in the face of our stated ideals of justice and fair play and of the philosophy that individual hard work is the road to success. Beverly Daniel Tatum, in discussing the myth of meritocracy, explains why racism is so often denied, downplayed, or dismissed: "An understanding of racism as a system of advantage presents a serious challenge to the notion of the United States as a just society where rewards are based solely on one's merits" (Tatum, 1992, p. 6).

Recent studies point out numerous ways in which racism and other forms of discrimination affect students and their learning. For instance, Angela Taylor found that, to the extent that teachers harbor negative racial stereotypes, the African American child's race *alone* is probably sufficient to place him or her at risk for negative school outcomes (Taylor, 1991). Many teachers, of course, see it differently, preferring to think instead that students' lack of academic achievement is due solely to conditions inside their homes or communities. But the occurrence of discriminatory actions in schools, both by other students and by teachers and other staff, has been widely documented. A 1990 study of Boston high school students found that while 57 percent had witnessed a racial attack and 47 percent would either join in or feel that the group being attacked deserved it, only a quarter of those interviewed said they would report a racial incident to school officials (Ribadeneira, 1990). It should not be surprising, then, that in a report about immigrant students in California, most believed that Americans felt negatively and unwelcoming toward them. In fact, almost every immigrant student interviewed reported that they had at one time or another been spat upon, and tricked, teased, and laughed at because of their race, accent, or the way they dressed. More than half also indicated that they had been the victims of teachers' prejudice, citing instances where they were punished, publicly embarrassed, or made fun of because of improper use of English. They also reported that teachers had made derogatory comments about immigrant groups in front of the class, or had avoided particular students because of the language difficulty (Olsen, 1988). Most of the middle and high school students interviewed by Mary Poplin and Joseph Weeres (1992) had also witnessed incidents of racism in school. In Karen Donaldson's study in an urban high school where students used the racism they experienced as the content of a peer education program, over 80 percent of students surveyed said that they had perceived racism to exist in school (Donaldson, 1994).

Marietta Saravia-Shore and Herminio Martínez found similar results in their ethnographic study of Puerto Rican young people who had dropped out of school and were currently participating in an alternative high school program. These adolescents felt that their former teachers were, in their words, "against Puerto Ricans and Blacks" and had openly discriminated against them. One reported that a teacher had said, "Do you want to be like the other Puerto Rican women who never got an education? Do you want to be like the rest of your family and never go to school?" (Saravia-Shore & Martínez, 1992, p. 242). In Virginia Vogel Zanger's study of high-achieving Latino and Latina Boston high school students, one young man described his shock when his teacher called him "spic" right in class; although the teacher was later suspended, this incident had left its mark on him (Zanger, 1994). Unfortunately, incidents such as these are more frequent than schools care to admit or acknowledge. Students, however, seem eager to address these issues, but are rarely given a forum in which such discussions can take place.

How do students feel about the racism and other aspects of discrimination that they see around them and experience? What effect does it have on them? In interviews with students, Karen Donaldson found three major ways in which they said they were affected: White students experienced guilt and embarrassment when they became aware of the racism to which their peers were subjected; students of color sometimes felt they needed to overcompensate and overachieve to prove they were equal to their White classmates; and students of color also mentioned that discrimination had a negative impact on their self-esteem (Donaldson, 1994). The issue of self-esteem is a complicated one and may include many variables. Children's self-esteem does not come fully formed out of the blue, but is *created* within particular contexts and responds to conditions that vary from situation to situation, and teachers' and schools' complicity in creating negative self-esteem certainly cannot be discounted. This was understood by Lillian, one of the young women in Nitza Hidalgo's study of an urban high school, who commented, "That's another problem I have, teachers, they are always talking about how we have no type of self-esteem or anything like that. . . . But they're the people that's putting us down. That's why our self-esteem is so low" (Hidalgo, 1991, p. 95).

The students in my research also mentioned examples of discrimination based on their race, ethnicity, culture, religion, and language. Some, like Manuel, felt it from fellow students. As an immigrant from Cape Verde who came to the United States at the age of eleven, he found the adjustment difficult:

> When American students see you, it's kinda hard [to] get along with them when you have a different culture, a different way of dressing and stuff like that. So kids really look at you and laugh, you know, at the beginning.

Avi spoke of anti-Semitism in his school. The majority of residents in his town were European American and Christian. The Jewish community had dwindled significantly over the years, and there were now very few Jewish students in his school. On one occasion, a student had walked by him saying, "Are you ready for the second Holocaust?" He described another incident in some detail:

> I was in a woods class, and there was another boy in there, my age, and he was in my grade. He's also Jewish and he used to come to the temple sometimes and went to Hebrew school. But then, of course, he started hanging around with the wrong people and some of these people were in my class, and I guess they were . . . making fun of him. And a few of them starting making swastikas out of wood. . . . So I saw one and I said to some kid, "What are you doing?" and the kid said to me, "Don't worry. It's not for you, it's for him." And I said to him, "What?!"

Other students talked about discrimination on the part of teachers. Both Marisol and Vinh specifically mentioned language discrimination as a problem. For Marisol, it had happened when a particular teacher did not allow Spanish to be spoken in her room. For Vinh, it concerned teachers' attitudes about his language: "Some teachers don't understand about the language. So sometimes, my language, they say it sounds funny." Rich spoke of the differences between the expectations of White and Black teachers, and concluded that all teachers should teach the curriculum *as if they were in an all-White school*, meaning that then expectations would be high for everybody. Other students were the object of teasing, but some, including James, even welcomed it, perhaps because it at least made his culture visible. He spoke of Mr. Miller, an elementary teacher he had been particularly fond of, who had called him "Gonzo" because he had a big nose and "Klinger" after the *M.A.S.H.* character who was Lebanese. James said, "And then everybody called me Klinger from then on. . . . I liked it, kind of . . . everybody laughing at me."

It was Linda who had the most to say about racism. As a young woman who identified herself as mixed because her mother was White and her father Black, Linda had faced discrimination or confusion on the part of both students and teachers. For example, she resented the fact that when teachers had to indicate her race, they came to their own conclusions without bothering to ask her. She explained what it was like:

> [Teachers should not] try to make us one or the other. And God forbid you should make us something we're totally not. . . . Don't write down that I'm Hispanic when I'm not. Some people actually think I'm Chinese when I smile. . . . Find out. Don't just make your judgments. . . . If you're filling out someone's report card and you need to know, then ask.

She went on to say:

> I've had people tell me, "Well, you're Black." I'm not Black; I'm Black and White. I'm Black and White American. "Well, you're Black!" No, I'm not! I'm both. . . . I mean, I'm not ashamed of being Black, but I'm not ashamed of being White either, and if I'm both, I want to be part of both. And I think teachers need to be sensitive to that.

Linda did not restrict her criticisms to White teachers, but also spoke of a Black teacher in her high school. Besides Mr. Benson, her favorite teacher of all, there was another Black teacher in the school:

> The other Black teacher, he was a racist, and I didn't like him. I belonged to the Black Students Association, and he was the advisor. And he just made it so obvious: he was all for Black supremacy. . . . A lot of times, whether they deserved it or not, his Black students passed, and his White students, if they deserved an A, they got a B. . . . He was insistent that only Hispanics and Blacks be allowed in the club. He had a very hard time letting me in because I'm not all Black. . . . I just really wasn't that welcome there. . . . He never found out what I was about. He just made his judgments from afar.

It was clear that racism was a particularly compelling issue for Linda, and she thought and talked about it a great deal. The weight of racism on her mind was evident when she said, "It's hard. I look at history and I feel really bad for what some of my ancestors did to some of my other ancestors. Unless you're mixed, you don't know what it's like to be mixed." She even wrote a poem about it, which ended like this:

> But all that I wonder is who ever gave
> them the right to tell me
> What I can and can't do
> Who I can and can't be
> God made each one of us
> Just like the other
> the only difference is,
> I'm darker in color.

Implications of Students' Views for
Transformation of Schools

Numerous lessons are contained within the narratives above. But what are the implications of these lessons for the school's curriculum, pedagogy, and tracking? How can we use what students have taught us about racism and discrimination? How can schools' policies and practices be informed through dialogue with students about what works and doesn't work? Although the students in my study never mentioned multicultural education by name, they were deeply concerned with whether and in what ways they and their families and communities were respected and represented in their schools. Two implications that are inherently multicultural come to mind, and I would suggest that both can have a major impact on school policies and practices. It is important that I first make explicit my own view of multicultural education: It is my understanding that multicultural education should be *basic for all students, pervasive in the curriculum and pedagogy, grounded in social justice, and based on critical pedagogy* (Nieto, 1992). Given this interpretation of multicultural education, we can see that it goes beyond the "tolerance" called for in numerous proclamations about diversity. It is also a far cry from the "cultural sensitivity" that is the focus of many professional development workshops (Nieto, 1994). In fact, "cultural sensitivity" can become little more than a condescending "bandaid" response to diversity, because it often does little to solve deep-seated problems of inequity. Thus, a focus on cultural sensitivity in and of itself can be superficial if it fails to take into account the structural and institutional barriers that reflect and reproduce power differentials in society. Rather than promoting cultural sensitivity, I would suggest that multicultural education needs to be understood as "arrogance reduction"; that is, as encompassing *both* individual *and* structural changes that squarely confront the individual biases, attitudes, and behaviors of educators, as well as the policies and practices in schools that emanate from them.

Affirming Students' Languages, Cultures, and Experiences

Over twenty years ago, Annie Stein reported asking a kindergarten teacher to explain why she had ranked four of her students at the bottom of her list, noting that they were "mute." "'Yes,' she said, 'they have not said one word for six months and they don't appear to hear anything I say.' 'Do they ever talk to the other children?' we asked. 'Sure,' was her reply. 'They cackle to each other in Spanish all day.'" (Stein, 1971, p. 161). These young children, although quite vocal in their own language, were not heard by their teacher because the language they spoke was bereft of all significance in the school. The children were not, however, blank slates; on the contrary, they came to school with a language, culture, and experiences that could have been important in their learning. Thus, we need to look not only at the individual weaknesses or strengths of particular students, but also at the way in which schools assign status to entire groups of students based on the sociopolitical and linguistic context in which they live. Jim Cummins addressed this concern in relation to the kinds of superficial antidotes frequently proposed to solve the problem of functional illiteracy among students from culturally and economically dominated groups: "A remedial focus only on technical aspects of functional illiteracy is inadequate because the causes of educational underachievement and 'illiteracy' among subordinated groups are rooted in the systematic devaluation of culture and denial of access to power and resources by the dominant group" (1994, pp. 307–308). As we have seen in many of the examples cited throughout this article, when culture and language are acknowledged by the school, students are able to reclaim the voice they need to continue their education successfully.

Nevertheless, the situation is complicated by the competing messages that students pick up from their schools and society at large. The research that I have reviewed makes it clear that, although students' cultures are important to them personally and in their families, they are also problematic because they are rarely valued or acknowledged by schools. The decisions young people make about their identities are frequently contradictory and mired in the tensions and struggles concerning diversity that are reflected in our society. Schools are not immune to such debates. There are numerous ways in which students' languages and cultures are excluded in schools: they are invisible, as with James, denigrated, as in Marisol's case, or simply not known, as happened with Vinh. It is no wonder then that these young people had conflicted feelings about their backgrounds. In spite of this, all of them spoke about the strength they derived from family and culture, and the steps they took to maintain it. James and Marisol mentioned that they continued to speak their native languages at home; Fern discussed her father's many efforts to maintain their Native American heritage; Manuel made it clear that he would always consider himself first and foremost Cape Verdean. Vinh spoke movingly about what his culture meant to him, and said that only Vietnamese was allowed in the home and that his sisters and brothers wrote to their parents in Vietnamese weekly. Most of these young people also maintained solid ties with their religion and places of worship as an important link to their heritage.

Much of the recent literature on educating culturally diverse students is helping to provide a radically different paradigm that contests the equation *education = assimilation* (Trueba, 1989). This research challenges the old assumptions about the role of the school as primarily an assimilationist agent, and provides a foundation for policy recommendations that focus on using students' cultural background values to promote academic achievement. In the case of Asian Pacific American youth, Peter Kiang and Vivian Wai-Fun Lee state the following:

> It is ironic that strengths and cultural values of family support which are so often praised as explanations for the academic achievement of Asian Pacific American students are severely undercut by the lack of programmatic and policy support for broad-based bilingual instruction and native language development, particularly in early childhood education. (Kiang & Lee, 1993, p. 39)

A study by Jeannette Abi-Nader of a program for Hispanic youth provides an example of how this can work. In the large urban high school she studied, stu-

309

dents' cultural values, especially those concerned with *familia,* were the basis of everyday classroom interactions. Unlike the dismal dropout statistics prevalent in so many other Hispanic communities, up to 65 percent of the high school graduates in this program went on to college. Furthermore, the youth attributed their academic success to the program, and made enthusiastic statements about it, including this one written on a survey: "The best thing I like about this class is that we all work together and we all participate and try to help each other. We're family!" (Abi-Nader, 1993, p. 213).

The students in my research also provided impassioned examples of the effect that affirming their languages and cultures had on them and, conversely, on how negating their languages and cultures negated a part of them as well. The attitudes and behaviors of the teachers in Yolanda's school, for example, were reflected in policies that seemed to be based on an appreciation for student diversity. Given the support of her teachers and their affirmation of her language and her culture, Yolanda concluded, "Actually, it's fun around here if you really get into learning. . . . I like learning. I like really getting my mind working." Manuel also commented on how crucial it was for teachers to become aware of students' cultural values and backgrounds. This was especially important for Manuel, since his parents were immigrants unfamiliar with U.S. schools and society, and although they gave him important moral support, they could do little to help him in school. He said of his teachers:

> If you don't know a student there's no way to influence him. If you don't know his background, there's no way you are going to get in touch with him. There's no way you're going to influence him if you don't know where he's been.

Fern, on the other hand, as the only Native American student in her school, spoke about how difficult it was to discuss values that were different from those of the majority. She specifically mentioned a discussion about abortion in which she was trying to express that for Native Americans, the fetus is alive: "And, so, when I try to tell them, they just, 'Oh, well, we're out of time.' They cut me off, and we've still got half an hour!" And Avi, although he felt that teachers tried to be understanding of his religion, also longed for more cultural affirmation. He would have welcomed, for example, the support of the one Jewish teacher at school who Avi felt was trying to hide his Jewishness.

On the contrary, in Linda's case, Mr. Benson, her English teacher, who was also her favorite teacher, provided just that kind of affirmation. Because he was racially mixed like Linda, she felt that he could relate to the kinds of problems she confronted. He became, in the words of Esteban Díaz and his colleagues, a "sociocultural mediator" for Linda by assigning her identity, language, and culture important roles in the learning environment (Díaz, Flores, Cousin, & Soo Hoo, 1992). Although Linda spoke English as her native language, she gave a wonderful example of how Mr. Benson encouraged her to be "bilingual," using what she referred to as her "street talk." Below is her description of Mr. Benson and the role he played in her education:

> I've enjoyed all my English teachers at Jefferson. But Mr. Benson, my English Honors teacher, he just threw me for a whirl! I wasn't going to college until I met

this man. . . . He was one of the few teachers I could talk to . . . 'cause Mr. Benson, he says, I can go into Harvard and converse with those people, and I can go out in the street and "rap with y'all." It's that type of thing. I love it. I try and be like that myself. I have my street talk. I get out in the street and I say "ain't" this and "ain't" that and "your momma" or "wha's up?" But I get somewhere where I know the people aren't familiar with that language or aren't accepting that language, and I will talk properly. . . . I walk into a place and I listen to how people are talking and it just automatically comes to me.

Providing time in the curriculum for students and teachers to engage in discussions about how the language use of students from dominated groups is discriminated against would go a long way in affirming the legitimacy of the discourse of *all* students (Delpit, 1992). According to Margaret Gibson (1991), much recent research has confirmed that schooling may unintentionally contribute to the educational problems of students from culturally dominated groups by pressuring them to assimilate against their wishes. The conventional wisdom that assimilation is the answer to academic underachievement is thus severely challenged. One intriguing implication is that the more students are involved in resisting assimilation while maintaining their culture and language, the more successful they will be in school. That is, maintaining culture and language, although a conflicted decision, seems to have a positive impact on academic success. In any case, it seems to be a far healthier response than adopting an oppositional identity that effectively limits the possibility of academic success (Fordham & Ogbu, 1986; Skutnabb- Kangas, 1988). Although it is important not to overstate this conclusion, it is indeed a real possibility, one that tests the "melting pot" ideology that continues to dominate U.S. schools and society.

We know, of course, that cultural maintenance is not true in all cases of academic success, and everybody can come up with examples of students who felt they needed to assimilate to be successful in school. But the question remains whether this kind of assimilation is healthy or necessary. For instance, in one large-scale study, immigrant students clearly expressed a strong desire to maintain their native languages and cultures and to pass them on to their children (Olsen, 1988). Other research has found that bilingual students specifically appreciate hearing their native language in school, and want the opportunity to learn in that language (Poplin & Weeres, 1992). In addition, an intriguing study of Cambodian refugee children by the Metropolitan Indochinese Children and Adolescent Service found that the more successful they became at modeling their behavior to be like U.S. children, the more their emotional adjustment worsened (National Coalition, 1988). Furthermore, a study of Southeast Asian students found a significant connection between grades and culture: in this research, higher grade point averages correlated with the *maintenance* of traditional values, ethnic pride, and close social and cultural ties with members of the same ethnic group (Rumbaut & Ima, 1987).

All of the above suggests that it is time to look critically at policies and practices that encourage students to leave their cultures and languages at the schoolhouse door. It also suggests that schools and teachers need to affirm, maintain, and value the differences that students bring to school as a foundation for their learning. It is still too common to hear teachers urging parents to "speak only English," as my parents were encouraged to do with my sister and me (luckily, our parents never paid attention). The ample literature cited throughout this article concerning diverse student populations is calling such practices into question. What we are learning is that teachers instead need to encourage parents to speak their *native* language, not English, at home with their children. We are also learning that they should emphasize the importance of family values, not in the rigid and limiting way that this term has been used in the past to create a sense of superiority for those who are culturally dominant, but rather by accepting the strong ethical values that all cultural groups and all kinds of families cherish. As an initial step, however, teachers and schools must first learn more about their students. Vinh expressed powerfully what he wanted teachers to know about him by reflecting on how superficial their knowledge was:

> They understand something, just not all Vietnamese culture. Like they just understand something *outside*. . . . But they cannot understand something inside our hearts.

Listen to Students

Although school is a place where a lot of talk goes on, it is not often student talk. Student voices sometimes reveal the great challenges and even the deep pain young people feel when schools are unresponsive, cold places. One of the students participating in a project focusing on those "inside the school," namely students, teachers, staff, and parents, said, "This place hurts my spirit" (Poplin & Weeres, 1992, p. 11). Ironically, those who spend the most time in schools and classrooms are often given the least opportunity to talk. Yet, as we saw in the many examples above, students have important lessons to teach educators and we need to begin to listen to them more carefully. Suzanne Soo Hoo captured the fact that educators are losing a compelling opportunity to learn from students while working on a project where students became coresearchers and worked on the question, "What are the obstacles to learning?" a question that, according to Soo Hoo, "electrified the group" (1993, p. 386). Including students in addressing such important issues places the focus where it rightfully belongs, said Soo Hoo: "Somehow educators have forgotten the important connection between teachers and students. We listen to outside experts to inform us, and consequently, we overlook the treasure in our very own backyards: our students" (p. 390). As Mike, one of the coresearchers in her project, stated, "They think just because we're kids, we don't know anything" (p. 391).

When they are treated as if they do know something, students can become energized and motivated. For the ten young people in my study, the very act of speaking about their schooling experiences seemed to act as a catalyst for more critical thinking about them. For example, I was surprised when I met Marisol's mother and she told me that Marisol had done nothing but speak about our interviews. Most of the students in the study felt this enthusiasm and these feelings are typical of other young people in similar studies. As Laurie Olsen

(1988) concluded in an extensive research project in California in which hundreds of immigrant students were interviewed, most of the students were gratified simply to have the opportunity to speak about their experiences. These findings have several implications for practice, including using oral histories, peer interviews, interactive journals, and other such strategies. Simply providing students with time to talk with one another, including group work, seems particularly helpful.

The feeling that adults do not listen to them has been echoed by many young people over the years. But listening alone is not sufficient if it is not accompanied by profound changes in what we expect our students to accomplish in school. Even more important than simply *listening* is *assisting* students to become agents of their own learning and to use what they learn in productive and critical ways. This is where social action comes in, and there have been a number of eloquent accounts of critical pedagogy in action (Peterson, 1991; Torres-Guzmán, 1992). I will quote at length from two such examples that provide inspiring stories of how listening to students can help us move beyond the written curriculum.

Iris Santos Rivera wrote a moving account of how a Freirian "problem-posing" approach was used with K–6 Chicano students in a summer educational program of the San Diego Public Schools in 1975 (Santos Rivera, 1983–1984). The program started by having the students play what she called the "Complain, Moan, and Groan Game." Using this exercise, in which students dialogued about and identified problems in the school and community, the young people were asked to identify problems to study. One group selected the school lunch program. This did not seem like a "real" problem to the teacher, who tried to steer the children toward another problem. Santos Rivera writes: "The teacher found it hard to believe in the problem's validity as an issue, as the basis for an action project, or as an integrating theme for education" (p. 5). She let the children talk about it for awhile, convinced that they would come to realize that this was not a serious issue. However, when she returned, they said to her, "Who is responsible for the lunches we get?" (p. 6). Thus began a summer-long odyssey in which the students wrote letters, made phone calls, traced their lunches from the catering truck through the school contracts office, figured out taxpayers' cost per lunch, made records of actual services received from the subcontractors, counted sandwiches and tested milk temperatures, and, finally, compared their findings with contract specifications, and found that there was a significant discrepancy. "We want to bring in the media," they told the teacher (p. 6). Both the local television station and the major networks responded to the press releases sent out by the students, who held a press conference to present the facts and answer reporters' questions. When a reporter asked who had told them all this, one nine-year old girl answered, "We found this stuff out. Nobody had to tell us anything. You know, you adults give yourselves too much credit" (p. 7). The postscript to this story is that state and federal laws had to be amended to change the kinds of lunches that students in California are served, and tapes from the students in this program were used in the state and federal hearings.

In a more recent example, Mary Ginley, a student in the doctoral program at the School of Education at the University of Massachusetts and a gifted teacher in the Longmeadow (Massachusetts) Public Schools, tries to help her second-graders develop critical skills by posing questions to them daily. Their responses are later discussed during class meeting time. Some of these questions are fairly straightforward ("Did you have a good weekend?"), while others encourage deeper thinking; the question posed on Columbus Day, "Was Columbus a hero?" was the culmination of much reading and dialogue that had previously taken place. Another activity she did with her students this year was to keep a daily record of sunrise and sunset. The students discovered to their surprise that December 21 was *not* the shortest day of the year. Using the daily almanac in the local newspaper, the students verified their finding and wrote letters to the editor. One, signed by Kaolin, read (spelling in original):

> Dear Editor,
>
> Acorting to our chart December 21 was not the shotest day of the year. But acorting to your paper it is. Are teacher says it happens evry year! What's going on?

As a result of this letter, the newspaper called in experts from the National Weather Service and a local planetarium. One of them said, "It's a fascinating question that [the pupils] have posed. . . . It's frustrating we don't have an adequate answer."(Kelly, 1994, p. 12). Katie, one of the students in Mary's class, compared her classmates to Galileo, who shook the scientific community by saying that the earth revolved around the sun rather than the other way around. Another, Ben, said, "You shouldn't always believe what you hear," and Lucy asserted, "Even if you're a grown-up, you can still learn from a second grader!"

In the first part of this article, I posed the question, "Why listen to students?" I have attempted to answer this question using numerous comments that perceptive young people, both those from my study and others, have made concerning their education. In the final analysis, the question itself suggests that it is only by first listening *to* students that we will be able to learn to talk *with* them. If we believe that an important basis of education is dialogue and reflection about experience, then this is clearly the first step. Yolanda probably said it best when she commented, "'Cause you learn a lot from the students. That's what a lot of teachers tell me. They learn more from their students than from where they go study."

Conclusion

I have often been struck by how little young people believe they deserve, especially those who do not come from economically privileged backgrounds. Although they may work hard at learning, they somehow believe that they do not deserve a chance to dream. This article is based on the notion that all of our students deserve to dream and that teachers and schools are in the best position for "creating a chance" to do so, as referred to in the title. This means developing conditions in schools that let students know that they have a right to envision other possibilities beyond those imposed by traditional barriers of race, gender, or social class. It means, even more importantly, that those traditional barriers can no longer be viewed as impediments to learning.

The students in my study also showed how crucial extracurricular activities were in providing needed outlets for their energy and for teaching them important leadership skills. For some, it was their place of worship (this was especially true for Avi, Manuel, and Rich); for others, it was hobbies (Linda loved to sing); and for others, sports were a primary support (Fern mentioned how she confronted new problems by comparing them to the sports in which she excelled: "I compare it to stuff, like, when I can't get science, or like in sewing, I'll look at that machine and I'll say, 'This is a basketball; I can overcome it'"). The schools' responsibility to provide some of these activities becomes paramount for students such as Marisol, whose involvement in the Teen Clinic acted almost like a buffer against negative peer pressure.

These students can all be characterized by an indomitable resilience and a steely determination to succeed. However, expecting all students, particularly those from subordinated communities, to be resilient in this way is an unfair burden, because privileged students do not need this quality, as the schools generally reflect their backgrounds, experiences, language, and culture. Privileged students learn that they are the "norm," and although they may believe this is inherently unfair (as is the case with Vanessa), they still benefit from it.

Nevertheless, the students in this research provide another important lesson about the strength of human nature in the face of adversity. Although they represented all kinds of families and economic and social situations, the students were almost uniformly upbeat about their future and their lives, sometimes in spite of what might seem overwhelming odds. The positive features that have contributed to their academic success, namely, caring teachers, affirming school climates, and loving families, have helped them face such odds. "I don't think there's anything stopping me," said Marisol, whose large family lived on public assistance because both parents were disabled. She added, "If I know I can do it, I should just keep on trying." The determination to keep trying was evident also in Fern, whose two teenage sisters were undergoing treatment for alcohol and drug abuse, but who nevertheless asserted, "I succeed in everything I do. If I don't get it right the first time, I always go back and try to do it again," adding, "I've always wanted to be president of the United States!" And it was evident as well in the case of Manuel, whose father cleaned downtown offices in Boston while his mother raised the remaining children at home, and who was the first of the eleven children to graduate from high school: "I can do whatever I want to do in life. Whatever I want to do, I know I could make it. I believe that strongly." And, finally, it was also clear in the case of Rich, whose mother, a single parent, was putting all three of her children through college at the same time. Rich had clearly learned a valuable lesson about self-reliance from her, as we can see in this striking image: "But let's not look at life as a piece of cake, because eventually it'll dry up, it'll deteriorate, it'll fall, it'll crumble, or somebody will come gnawing at it." Later he added, "As they say, self-respect is one gift that you give yourself."

Our students have a lot to teach us about how pedagogy, curriculum, ability grouping, and expectations of ability need to change so that greater numbers of young people can be reached. In 1971, Annie Stein expressed the wishes and hopes of students she talked with, and they differ little from those we have heard through the voices of students today: "The demands of high school youth are painfully reasonable. They want a better education, a more 'relevant' curriculum, some voice in the subject matter to be taught and in the running of the school, and some respect for their constitutional and human rights" (1971, p. 177). Although the stories and voices I have used in this article are primarily those of individual students, they can help us to imagine what it might take to transform entire schools. The responsibility to do so cannot be placed only on the shoulders of individual teachers who, in spite of the profound impact they can have on the lives of particular students, are part of a system that continues to be unresponsive to too many young people. In the final analysis, students are asking us to look critically not only at structural conditions, but also at individual attitudes and behaviors. This implies that we need to undertake a total transformation not only of our schools, but also of our hearts and minds.

Notes

1. I recognize that overarching terms, such as "European American," "African American," "Latino," etc., are problematic. Nevertheless, "European American" is more explicit than "White" with regard to culture and ethnicity, and thus challenges Whites also to think of themselves in ethnic terms, something they usually reserve for those from more clearly identifiable groups (generally, people of color). I have a more in-depth discussion of this issue in chapter two of my book, Affirming Diversity (1992).
2. The early arguments for cultural deprivation are well expressed by Carl Bereiter and Siegfried Englemann (1966) and by Frank Reissman (1962). A thorough review of a range of deficit theories can be found in Herbert Ginsburg (1986).
3. "Critical thinking," as used here, is not meant in the sense that it has come to be used conventionally to imply, for example, higher order thinking skills in math and science as disconnected from a political awareness. Rather, it means developing, in the Freirian (1970) sense, a consciousness of oneself as a critical agent in learning and transforming one's reality.
4. I was assisted in doing the interviews by a wonderful group of colleagues, most of whom contacted the students, interviewed them, and gave me much of the background information that helped me craft the case studies. I am grateful for the insights and help the following colleagues provided: Carlie Collins Tartakov, Paula Elliott, Haydée Font, Maya Gillingham, Mac Lee Morante, Diane Sweet, and Carol Shea.
5. "Holidays and Heroes" refers to an approach in which multicultural education is understood as consisting primarily of ethnic celebrations and the acknowledgment of "great men" in the history of particular cultures. Deeper structures of cultures, including values and lifestyle differences, and an explicit emphasis on power differentials as they affect particular cultural groups, are not addressed in this approach. Thus, this approach is correctly perceived as one that tends to romanticize culture and treat it in an artificial way. In contrast, multicultural education as empowering and liberating pedagogy confronts such structural issues and power differentials quite directly.

References

Abi-Nader, J. (1993). Meeting the needs of multicultural classrooms: Family values and the motivation of minority students. In M. J. O'Hair & S. Odell (Eds), *Diversity and teaching: Teacher education yearbook 1* (pp. 212–236). Fort Worth, TX: Harcourt Brace Jovanovich.

Banks, J. A. (1991). *Teaching strategies for ethnic studies* (6th ed.). Boston: Allyn & Bacon.

Bartolomé, L. (1994). Beyond the methods fetish: Toward a humanizing pedagogy. *Harvard Educational Review, 64,* 173–194.

Bempechat, J. (1992). *Fostering high achievement in African American children: Home, school, and public policy influences.* New York: ERIC Clearinghouse on Urban Education, Teachers College, Columbia University.

Bereiter, C., & Englemann, S. (1966). *Teaching disadvantaged children in the preschool.* Englewood Cliffs, NJ: Prentice Hall.

Clark, R. M. (1983). *Family life and school achievement: Why poor Black children succeed or fail.* Chicago: University of Chicago Press.

Commins, N. L. (1989). Language and affect: Bilingual students at home and at school. *Language Arts, 66,* 29–43.

Cummins, J. (1994). From coercive to collaborative relations of power in the teaching of literacy. In B. M. Ferdman, R-M. Weber, & A. G. Ramírez (Eds.), *Literacy across languages and cultures* (pp. 295–331). Albany: State University of New York Press.

Delpit, L. (1992). The politics of teaching literate discourse. *Theory into Practice, 31,* 285–295.

Díaz, E., Flores, B., Cousin, P. T., & Soo Hoo, S. (1992, April). *Teacher as sociocultural mediator.* Paper presented at the Annual Meeting of the AERA, San Francisco.

Donaldson, K. (1994). Through students' eyes. *Multicultural Education, 2*(2), 26–28.

Fine, M. (1991). *Framing dropouts: Notes on the politics of an urban public high school.* Albany: State University of New York Press.

Fine, M. (1993). "You can't just say that the only ones who can speak are those who agree with your position": Political discourse in the classroom. *Harvard Educational Review, 63,* 412–433.

Fordham, S., & Ogbu, J. (1986) Black students' school success: Coping with the "burden of acting White". *Urban Review, 18,* 176–206.

Frau-Ramos, M., & Nieto, S. (1993). "I was an outsider": Dropping out among Puerto Rican youths in Holyoke, Massachusetts. In R. Rivera & S. Nieto (Eds.), *The education of Latino students in Massachusetts: Research and policy considerations* (pp. 143–166). Boston: Gastón Institute.

Freire, P. (1970). *Pedagogy of the oppressed.* New York: Seabury Press.

Gibson, M. (1991). Minorities and schooling: Some implications. In M. A. Gibson & J. U. Ogbu (Eds.), *Minority status and schooling: A comparative study of immigrant and involuntary minorities* (pp. 357–381). New York: Garland.

Ginsburg, H. (1986). The myth of the deprived child: New thoughts on poor children. In U. Neisser (Ed.), *The school achievement of minority children: New perspectives.* Hillsdale, NJ: Lawrence Erlbaum.

Goodlad, J. I. (1984). *A place called school.* New York: McGraw-Hill.

Haberman, M. (1991). The pedagogy of poverty versus good teaching. *Phi Delta Kappan, 73,* 290–294.

Hallinan, M., & Teixeira, R. (1987). Opportunities and constraints: Black-White differences in the formation of interracial friendships. *Child Development, 58,* 1358–1371.

Hidalgo, N. M. (1991). *"Free time, school is like a free time": Social relations in City High School classes.* Unpublished doctoral dissertation, Harvard University.

Hollins, E. R., King, J. E., & Hayman, W. C. (Eds.). (1994). *Teaching diverse populations: Formulating a knowledge base.* Albany: State University of New York Press.

Kelly, R. (1994, January 11). Class searches for solstice. *Union News,* p. 12.

Kiang, P. N., & Lee, V. W-F. (1993). Exclusion or contribution? Education K–12 policy. In *The State of Asian Pacific America: Policy Issues to the Year 2020* (pp. 25–48). Los Angeles: LEAP Asian Pacific American Public Policy Institute and UCLA Asian American Studies Center.

Kohl, H. (1993). The myth of "Rosa Parks, the tired." *Multicultural Education, 1*(2), 6–10.

Kozol, J. (1967). *Death at an early age: The destruction of the hearts and minds of Negro children in the Boston Public Schools.* New York: Houghton Mifflin.

Lee, V. E., Winfield, L. F., & Wilson, T. C. (1991). Academic behaviors among high-achieving African-American students. *Education and Urban Society, 24*(1), 65–86.

Lucas, T., Henze, R., & Donato, R. (1990). Promoting the success of Latino language-minority students: An exploratory study of six high schools. *Harvard Educational Review, 60,* 315–340.

McNeil, L. M. (1986). *Contradictions of control: School structure and school knowledge.* New York: Routledge & Kegan Paul.

Mehan, H., & Villanueva, I. (1993). Untracking low achieving students: Academic and social consequences. In *Focus on Diversity* (Newsletter available from the National Center for Research on Cultural Diversity and Second Language Learning, 399 Kerr Hall, University of California, Santa Cruz, CA 95064).

Moll, L. (1992). Bilingual classroom studies and community analysis: Some recent trends. *Educational Researcher, 21*(2), 20–24.

Moll, L., & Díaz, S. (1993). Change as the goal of educational research. In E. Jacob & C. Jordan (Eds.), *Minority education: Anthropological perspectives* (pp. 67–79). Norwood, NJ: Ablex.

National Coalition of Advocates for Students. (1988). *New voices: Immigrant students in U.S. public schools.* Boston: Author.

Newmann, F. M. (1993). Beyond common sense in educational restructuring: The issues of content and linkage. *Educational Researcher, 22*(2), 4–13, 22.

Nieto, S. (1992). *Affirming diversity: The sociopolitical context of multicultural education.* White Plains, NY: Longman.

Nieto, S. (1994). Affirmation, solidarity, and critique: Moving beyond tolerance in multicultural education. *Multicultural Education, 1*(4), 9–12, 35–38.

Oakes, J. (1992). Can tracking research inform practice? *Educational Researcher, 21*(4), 12–21.

Olsen, L. (1988). *Crossing the schoolhouse border: Immigrant students and the California public schools.* San Francisco: California Tomorrow.

Peterson, R. E. (1991). Teaching how to read the world and change it: Critical pedagogy in the intermediate grades. In C. E. Walsh (Ed.), *Literacy as praxis: Culture, language, and pedagogy* (pp. 156–182). New Jersey: Ablex.

Phelan, P., Davidson, A. L., & Cao, H. T. (1992). Speaking up: Students' perspectives on school. *Phi Delta Kappan, 73,* 695–704.

Poplin, M., & Weeres, J. (1992). *Voices from the inside: A report on schooling from inside the classroom.* Claremont, CA: Claremont Graduate School, Institute for Education in Transformation.

Reissman, F. (1962). *The culturally deprived child.* New York: Harper & Row.

Reyes, M. de la Luz (1992). Challenging venerable assumptions: Literacy instruction for linguistically different students. *Harvard Educational Review, 62,* 427–446.

Ribadeneira, D. (1990, October 18). Study says teen-agers' racism rampant. *Boston Globe,* p. 31.

Rumbaut, R. G., & Ima, K. (1987). *The adaptation of Southeast Asian refugee youth: A comparative study.* San Diego: Office of Refugee Resettlement.

Santos Rivera, I. (1983–1984, October-January). Liberating education for little children. In *Alternativas* (Freirian newsletter from Río Piedras, Puerto Rico, no longer published).

Saravia-Shore, M., & Martínez, H. (1992). An ethnographic study of home/school role conflicts of second generation Puerto Rican adolescents. In M. Saravia-Shore & S. F. Arvizu (Eds.), *Cross-cultural literacy: Ethnographies of communication in multiethnic classrooms* (pp. 227–251). New York: Garland.

Shor, I. (1992). *Empowering education: Critical teaching for social change.* Chicago: University of Chicago Press.

Skutnabb-Kangas, T. (1988). Resource power and autonomy through discourse in conflict: A Finnish migrant school strike in Sweden. In T. Skutnabb-Kangas & J. Cummins (Eds.),

Minority education: From shame to struggle (pp. 251–277). Clevedon, England: Multilingual Matters.

Sleeter, C. E. (1991). *Empowerment through multicultural education.* Albany: State University of New York Press.

Sleeter, C. E. (1994). White racism. *Multicultural Education, 1*(4), 5–8, 39.

Sleeter, C. E., & Grant, C. A. (1991). Mapping terrains of power: Student cultural knowledge vs. classroom knowledge. In C. E. Sleeter (Ed.), *Empowerment through multicultural education* (pp. 49–67). Albany: State University of New York Press.

Soo Hoo, S. (1993). Students as partners in research and restructuring schools. *Educational Forum, 57,* 386–393.

Stein, A. (1971). Strategies for failure. *Harvard Educational Review, 41,* 133–179.

Tatum, B. D. (1992). Talking about race, learning about racism: The application of racial identity development theory in the classroom. *Harvard Educational Review, 62,* 1–24.

Taylor, A. R. (1991). Social competence and the early school transition: Risk and protective factors for African-American children. *Education and Urban Society, 24*(1), 15–26.

Taylor, D., & Dorsey-Gaines, C. (1988). *Growing up literate: Learning from inner-city families.* Portsmouth, NH: Heinemann.

Torres-Guzmán, M. (1992). Stories of hope in the midst of despair: Culturally responsive education for Latino students in an alternative high school in New York City. In M. Saravia-Shore & S. F. Arvizu (Eds.), *Cross-cultural literacy: Ethnographies of communication in multiethnic classrooms* (pp. 477–490). New York: Garland.

Trueba, H. T. (1989). *Raising silent voices: Educating the linguistic minorities for the twenty-first century.* Cambridge, MA: Newbury House.

Wheelock, A. (1992). *Crossing the tracks: How "untracking" can save America's schools.* New York: New Press.

Zanger, V. V. (1994). Academic costs of social marginalization: An analysis of Latino students' perceptions at a Boston high school. In R. Rivera & S. Nieto (Eds.), *The education of Latino students in Massachusetts: Research and policy considerations* (pp. 167–187). Boston: Gastón Institute.

Afterword

Opportunity Now: Raising Achievement in Spite of Structural Impediments

RONALD F. FERGUSON

This volume assembles an impressive anthology of papers published in the *Harvard Education Review* (*HER*) over the past few decades. The aim is to address what the *HER* editors perceive as an imbalance in contemporary policy and discourse on closing achievement gaps among the nation's children from different racial, ethnic, and social-class backgrounds. The editors caution that if we fail to address the *opportunity* gaps that these papers highlight, No Child Left Behind (NCLB), like many previous reform efforts, will fail to substantially reduce the achievement gaps that the legislation is supposed to help close. This timely volume joins what promises to be an extensive and often turbulent national debate preceding the NCLB reauthorization. I agree with various commentators who argue that the specific accountability mechanisms in NCLB are not sustainable and need to be fixed. I am cautiously optimistic that an alternative and wiser law will result from the coming national debate.

What will be the role of racial achievement gaps in that debate? There is growing recognition among political analysts that the way issues are framed affects both how social and political forces mobilize to address them and what interests are ultimately served. NCLB frames the goal as raising achievement and closing gaps, with explicit attention to racial subgroups. Some suggest that such racially specific goals represent a calculated move by political conservatives to produce a conspicuous national failure when the goals are not met.[1] Such failure, some believe, will help support arguments for abandoning racial equality as a national goal. As if in response, more socially liberal writers assert that racial gaps are fundamentally socioeconomic in nature and they seek to remove race from such explicit consideration in the NCLB legislation.[2] Some argue, at least in private, that the nation is more likely to embrace socioeconomic than racial goals and that socioeconomic goals are, in any case, more fair. Others, however, believe that only through ongoing efforts to highlight the racial dimensions of the challenge — dimensions that may defy standard socioeconomic classification schemes — will we earnestly and relentlessly come to terms with all the social, political, and cultural forces that impede progress toward raising achievement for all groups, while also narrowing racial gaps.[3]

While this volume is in no way a plea to deemphasize race *per se*, its emphasis on addressing opportunity gaps could inadvertently contribute to an imbalance in public understanding and action, especially in non-White communities. This emphasis may play a role in muting a self-critical but nonetheless constructive discourse inside these non-White (including middle class) communities on the full range of issues that contribute to the perpetuation of racial achievement gaps. My point concerns the need to nurture several lines of work simultaneously, some related to opportunity gaps and some concerning strategic options for progress that are already within reach of many Black, Hispanic, and other non-White households.

The stakes are high for the entire society. The United States is moving rapidly toward a time when non-Whites collectively will be the majority of the population. A child born today will be between forty and fifty years old — still in his or her prime working years — when this happens.[4] How internationally competitive and socially stable will the nation be by the time Whites are a numeric minority? Will Whites still predominate in positions of influence and authority? Societies dominated by racial minorities, even if only by virtue of their superior academic preparation, are likely to be socially turbulent.[5] Even as we strive to help all children excel, the entire nation will benefit if we resolve that Black and Brown children, in particular, will rise as rapidly as possible to nationally and internationally competitive levels of achievement.

Certainly there is nothing in our collective experience to show that this goal is achievable, but there are still reasons for cautious optimism. First, there was dramatic progress in narrowing racial gaps between 1970 and 1990 in the National Assessment of Educational Progress (NAEP) Long Term Trend Assessment; almost two-thirds of the reading score gap in the NAEP between Black and White seventeen-year-olds disappeared between 1971 and 1988.[6] Second, the Black-White IQ gap is estimated to have narrowed by more than 25 percent between 1972 and 2002, indicating that not even IQ gaps are fixed in nature.[7] And third, the national Early Childhood Longitudinal Study finds virtually no group-level mental ability gaps among infants approaching their first birthday.[8]

Getting entirely serious about closing racial gaps in achievement will be a huge social and political undertaking that needs to be sustained over several decades, often on the basis of hope, faith, and stubborn determination. This volume and other research and commentaries make the point repeatedly that a variety of forces, both past and ongoing, have conspired to produce and sustain the disparities that concern us. As the editors emphasize, there is an opportunity gap in America that helps to sustain the achievement gap. The challenge to overcome that gap is daunting.

One way to understand how daunting and pervasive the challenge remains is to recognize that the Black-White achievement gaps among twelfth graders on the NAEP over the past decade have tended to be largest among students who report their parents as college educated.[9] Hence, the racial achievement gap is not simply a problem among the poor and disadvantaged. Even more troubling is that NAEP scores among twelfth grade Blacks who report that their parents have sixteen or more years of schooling, are lower than for Whites who report that their parents attended school for twelve years or less.[10] This does not offset the fact, as I indicated above, that there was impressive progress in the NAEP Long Term Trend Assessment between 1970 and 1990. That period of gap-narrowing showed that progress is possible. Still, there is a long way to go and many impediments to overcome.

One nontrivial impediment is that we must often conduct our fast-paced public discourse in slogans that cast issues of balance inappropriately as either/or propositions. We communicate about complex policy issues using metaphors selected for their capacity to conjure up particular feelings and propensities to support or resist particular policy options, and this makes it difficult to get the right mix as we seek to combine problem solving (or opportunity-exploiting) approaches into effective strategies.[11]

For example, this volume aims to refocus public discourse and policy choices on closing the "opportunity gap," thereby deemphasizing the "achievement gap" as a way of framing the problem. By highlighting opportunity gaps, the editors may aim to mobilize fellow subscribers to the lofty principal that children from all walks of life should have equal opportunity to achieve academically. Once mobilized, our allies in the struggle may target structural forces in the society that serve to perpetuate the gaps in opportunity. These same allies may share an impulse to deemphasize the achievement gap because it may implicitly demean the groups on the bottom side of the gap and place the burden of improvement too much on their shoulders.

Similarly, the language used by the editors implies a focus on children's assets instead of their deficits, where, again, to focus on deficits may seem too degrading. The same desire to subdue demeaning stereotypes and stigmas and to avoid "blaming the victim" leads many to focus mostly on structural forces instead of on cultural patterns in communities of color where achievement levels are lowest.

My view is that these apparently competing frames and emphases present us with false dichotomies, each calculated to set right what the *HER* editors and the authors in this volume perceive as an imbalance in public perceptions. I am quite sympathetic to their concerns. However, by focusing too much on either side of a dichotomy, we forfeit the benefits that might accrue from careful and sustained attention to the other. We need a balance.

First, it seems obvious to me that opportunity gaps, both past and present, are primarily to blame for achievement gaps. However, must every opportunity gap be overcome in order to narrow achievement gaps? Can some simply be circumvented? If not, why not? If yes, then which ones? We are unlikely to answer these questions effectively if we focus too much on opportunity gaps and divert our active attention from the purpose — that is, closing achievement gaps. Opportunity and achievement gaps need to be elements of (but not the totality of) an integrated understanding of our shared sense of mission and collective endeavor.

Second, children arrive at schools with assets, but they may also have deficits in their skills and knowledge in relationship to particular standards. If we aim to help them reach or exceed the standards, how can we address and fill the deficits if we refuse to acknowledge their existence? I once asked a group of math educators what methods they use to identify gaps in children's math knowledge in order to help them catch up with classmates. They refused to accept the wording of my question, insisting on rephrasing it as, "How do we identify the assets a child brings in order to build effectively upon them." I then wrote a poem, suggesting to them that their refusal to acknowledge and talk about weaknesses may be as limiting as the low expectations that "asset" language is meant to counteract. Children do bring assets, but they may also have deficits in their knowledge.

Third, a one-sided focus on removing structural forces that constrain choices, to the exclusion of addressing routines and lifestyles that have momentum of their own, is limiting as well. Even among the college-educated, there are racial differences in parenting practices and youth culture that may contribute to enduring gaps.[12] Admittedly, the research base in this domain is still developing and not entirely definitive. Still, there is enough to warrant an active discourse about *lifestyle* in communities of color and to launch new efforts aimed at positive, collective change. Especially among households where material hardship is limited (for example, among the college educated), I believe that parents of color are willing and able to make use of ideas on how changes in reading habits, television viewing, nutrition, sleep, and patterns of warmth and discipline in the family can make a positive difference in academic and other life outcomes.

Structural inequities and opportunity gaps that help to sustain racial disparities in achievement outcomes are real. Judicial decisions, political mobilization, and various policy measures will be needed to overcome them. This seems certain to be true long past the time when non-Whites become the nation's majority. Still, some forces that appear to be constraints — social, political, and cultural forces — are not absolute impediments. We should strive to remove them, but we should not use them, even inadvertently, as excuses for not doing what we can while they exist.

Writing as an African American parent who is focused both privately and professionally on the issues that this book addresses, I believe that there is much within our reach. My continuing research and intervention work to address racial gaps is based on the belief that achievement gaps among racial groups are not facts of nature. The future stability and vitality of the nation may well depend upon our collective capacity to demonstrate that this belief is accurate. I believe we can, if we face the challenge squarely and strike the right balances in our rhetoric and strategies. This collection of papers from the *Harvard Education Review* is a worthy contribution to what we all hope will be a lively, extended period of searching together for ways to propel our children toward life-long success and our twenty-first century society toward moral fairness, economic prosperity, and social stability.

Notes

1. Glenn C. Loury, speech given at the 2nd Annual Conference of the Achievement Gap Initiative at Harvard University, June 2006. See a video of the speech, available at http://agi.harvard.edu/events/Videos.php. Also see, George Lakoff, *Don't Think of an Elephant: Know your Values and Frame the Debate* (White River Junction, VT: Chelsea Green Publishing, 2004). Lakoff discusses how political conservatives use liberal imagery of nurturant values to manipulate voter loyalties. He briefly cites NCLB as an example.

2. For example, Richard Rothstein, *Class and Schools: Using Social, Educational, and Economic Reforms to Close the Black-White Achievement Gap* (New York: Teachers College Press, 2004)

3. This is essentially the position that I am taking here. See also Ronald F. Ferguson, *Toward Skillful Parenting and Transformed Schools inside a National Movement for Excellence with Equity* (The First Educational Equity Symposium of the Campaign for Educational Equity, Teachers College, Columbia University, October 24 and 25, 2005; accessed December 19, 2006, from http://agi.harvard.edu/events/Papers.php).

4. The United States is projected to be majority non-White by the year 2050. For further information see http://www.census.gov/ipc/www/usinterimproj/.

5. I am no expert on such matters, but the issue is complex and the examples are many. Simply conduct an internet search on the phrase "ethnic minority dominance" or "racial minority dominance," to see the great number and variety of books and papers that surface on problems of societies where minority groups are economically or politically dominant. Turmoil is not inevitable in such circumstances, but it is quite common.

6. U.S. Department of Education, *The Nation's Report Card. NAEP 2004 Trends in Academic Progress: Three Decades of Student Performance in Reading and Mathematics* (Washington, DC: U.S. Department of Education, 2005).

7. William T. Dickens and James R. Flynn, *Black Americans Reduce the Racial IQ Gap: Evidence from Standardization Samples* (Washington, DC: Brookings Institution Press, 2005). See http://agi.harvard.edu/events/Papers.php.

8. U.S. Department of Education, National Center for Education Statistics, Early Childhood Longitudinal Study, Birth Cohort (ECLS–B), Restricted-Use File (NCES 2004–093), previously unpublished tabulation (January 2005). The table can be viewed at http://agi.harvard.edu/Topics/coe_table_35_3.xls?tableID=303. Also see Roland G. Fryer Jr. and Steven D. Levitt, *Testing for Racial Differences in the Mental Ability of Young Children*, available at http://agi.harvard.edu/events/Papers.php.

9. U.S. Department of Education, *National Assessment of Educational Progress Reading Report Card for the Nation* (Washington, DC: U.S. Department of Education, 2002, 2004).

10. U.S. Department of Education, *National Assessment of Educational Progress Reading Report Card for the Nation* (Washington, DC: U.S. Department of Education, 2002, 2004).

11. See Lakoff, *Don't Think of an Elephant.*

12. See, for example, Ronald F. Ferguson, "Why America's Black-White School Achievement Gap Persists," in *Ethnicity, Social Mobility and Public Policy: Comparing the U.S. and Great Britain*, ed. Glenn Loury, Tariq Modood, and Steve Teles (New York: Cambridge University Press, 2005). Other papers on parenting among the college educated are forthcoming from this author and others, as part of an effort of the Achievement Gap Initiative at Harvard University to inform and mobilize parents for improvement.

About the Authors

Gilberto Q. Conchas is an associate professor of education, Chicano/Latino studies, and sociology at the University of California, Irvine. He is the author of *The Color of Success: Race and High-Achieving Urban Youth* (2006) and coauthor of *Small Schools and Urban Youth: Size, Culture, and Personalization* (forthcoming).

Raewyn Connell (formerly R. W. Connell), a professor at the University of Sydney, is interested in social justice in education and in other settings. Her current research concerns gender dynamics, intellectual labor, neoliberalism, and social theory in the global South. She is the author of *Schools and Social Justice* (1993), *Gender* (2002), *Masculinities* (2nd ed., 2005), and coauthor of *Making the Difference* (with D. J. Ashenden et al., 1982) and *Education, Change, and Society* (with C. Campbell et al., 2006).

Pat English-Sand has been a public school inclusion coordinator and a teacher of students with significant disabilities for the past eighteen years. She is currently an assistant professor at Fordham University.

Ronald F. Ferguson is an economist and senior research associate with the Malcolm Wiener Center for Social Policy at the Harvard University John F. Kennedy School of Government. His teaching and publications cover a variety of issues related to education and economic development, and much of his research since the mid-1990s has focused on racial achievement gaps. He is the creator and director of the Tripod Project for School Improvement, and is also the faculty cochair and director of the Achievement Gap Initiative at Harvard University.

Linda May Fitzgerald is an associate professor of curriculum and instruction and a research fellow in the Regents' Center for Early Developmental Education, University of Northern Iowa. Her current research involves dispositions for inclusion and social justice in teacher education. Fitzgerald is the coauthor of "Disability, Schooling, and the Artifacts of Colonialism" in *Teachers College Record* (with C. Kliewer, 2001), and coeditor of *Self-Study and Diversity* (with D. Tidwell, 2006).

Patresa Hartman is a school psychologist with the Heartland Area Education Agency, in Johnston, Iowa, and an adjunct instructor with Des Moines Area Community College. Her professional interests include teaching students with disabilities to be strong self-advocates.

Jeff Howard, president of the Efficacy Institute in Waltham, Massachusetts, is interested in building Campaigns for Proficiency, a program based on school-community partnerships. He is author of "You Can't Get There from Here: The Need for a New Logic in Education Reform" in *Daedalus* (1995) and "Still at Risk: The Causes and Costs of Failure to Educate Poor and Minority Children for the Twenty-First Century" in *A Nation Reformed? American Education 20 Years After a Nation at Risk* (edited by D. Gordon, 2003).

Mieko Kamii is an associate professor of psychology and education at Wheelock College in Boston. Her current research centers on equity and diversity in preK-16 educational practices and in standards and performance assessments in teacher preparation, and on race, ethnicity, and culture in workplace behavior and decisionmaking. Her recent publications include "Project QUEST: A Journey of Discovery With Beginning Teachers in Urban Schools" in *Equity and Excellence in Education* (2006) and "My History Lesson" in *In Praise of Our Teachers* (edited by G. Wade Gayles, 2003).

Rafa M. Kasim is an assistant professor in the Department of Educational Foundations and Special Services, College and Graduate School of Education, Health, and Human Services, at Kent State University. His major area of professional interest is measurement and quantitative methods. His current work focuses on exploring efficient ways of estimating effect sizes for single subject design studies through multilevel models. He is coauthor of "Understanding Prevention Effectiveness in Real World Settings: The National Cross-Site Evaluation of High-Risk Youth Programs" in *The American Journal of Drug and Alcohol Abuse* (with S. Sambrano et al., 2005) and "Effectiveness of Culturally Specific Approaches to Substance Abuse Prevention" in the *Journal of Ethnic and Cultural Diversity in Social Work* (with J. F. Springer et al., 2004).

Christopher Kliewer is a professor of special education at the University of Northern Iowa. He teaches coursework on inclusive education and conducts inquiry into the literacy development of young children with significant disabilities. He is the author of *Schooling Children with Down Syndrome: Toward an Understanding of Possibility* (1998), and his numerous articles include "Literacy as Cultural Practice" in *Reading and Writing Quarterly* (2003).

Robert A. LeVine is the Roy E. Larsen Professor of Education and Human Development, Emeritus, at Harvard University. A specialist in the comparative study of human development, his books include *Childcare and Culture: Lessons from Africa* (1994) and *Human Conditions: The Cultural Basis of Educational Development* (with M. I. White, 1986).

Sarah E. LeVine is an associate in the Department of Sanskrit and Indian Studies at Harvard University. Her areas of research are the effects of maternal literacy in developing countries, including Mexico, Zambia, and Nepal, and modern Buddhism in South Asia and the United States. She is author of *Mothers and Wives: Gusii Women of East Africa* (1979) and *Dolor y Alegría: Women and Social Change in Urban Mexico* (1993), and coauthor of *Rebuilding Buddhism: The Theravada Revival Movement in Nepal* (with D. Gellner, 2005).

Jodi Meyer-Mork is a visiting professor at Clarke College in Dubuque, Iowa. Her research interests are in inclusive practices, early childhood education, and the self-study of teacher education. Her publications include "Walking the Labyrinth: Journey to Awareness" in *Journeys of Hope: Risking Self-Study in a Diverse World* (edited by D. Tidwell et al., 2004).

Robert Parris Moses is president of the Algebra Project, which he founded. A mathematics educator, curriculum developer, and teacher trainer, his goal with the project is to establish a pedagogy of mathematics that expects and encourages every student to succeed at algebra in middle school, and supports their efforts to do so. He is currently an Eminent Scholar at the Florida International University Center for Urban Education and Innovation.

Sonia Nieto is the Professor Emerita of Education, University of Massachusetts, Amherst. Her research focuses on multicultural education, teacher education, and on the education of Latinos, immigrants, and other students of culturally and linguistically diverse backgrounds. Her books include *The Light in Their Eyes: Creating Multicultural Learning Communities* (1999) and *What Keeps Teachers Going?* (2003). Her articles include "Public Education in the Twentieth Century and Beyond: High Hopes, Broken Promises, and an Uncertain Future" which appeared in the *Harvard Educational Review 75th Anniversary Issue* (2005).

Donna Raschke is a professor of early childhood special education at the University of Northern Iowa. She coordinates the graduate education of many early childhood teachers focused on inclusive schooling. Raschke's numerous publications include "A Unified-Birth Through

Grade Three Early Childhood Endorsement: Challenges to the IHE Faculty across Iowa" in *Teacher Education and Special Education* (with S. Maude et al., 2001).

Stephen W. Raudenbush is the Lewis-Sebring Distinguished Service Professor and chair of the Committee on Education at the University of Chicago. His primary research interests are statistical methods for longitudinal and multilevel data, and the process and consequences of schooling. His research involves the development, testing, refinement, and application of statistical methods for individual change, as well as the effects of social settings on change. Raudenbush has coauthored a series of articles in *Psychological Methods* on the design of multilevel and longitudinal experiments, and has authored recent articles in *Science, Sociological Methodology,* and *The American Journal of Sociology.* He is also the coauthor of *Hierarchical Linear Models: 2nd Edition* (with A. S. Bryk, 2002).

Ray C. Rist is a senior evaluation officer in the World Bank. His long career has included fifteen years in the U.S. Government, with appointments at the Department of Health, Education, and Welfare and the U.S. General Accounting Office, as well as academic appointments at Cornell University, Johns Hopkins University, and George Washington University. He serves on the editorial boards of nine professional journals and on the governing board of the School of Business at Durham University in the United Kingdom. Rist has authored, edited, or coedited 25 books and has written more than 135 articles. He is the editor of the *Comparative Policy Evaluation* book series for Transaction Books.

Beatrice Schnell-Anzola (formerly Schnell) is a literacy consultant and research associate of the Maternal Schooling Project at the Harvard Graduate School of Education. Her major professional interests are early child language and literacy development and the effects of maternal input from a cross-cultural perspective. She is coauthor of "Literacy as a Pathway between Schooling and Maternal Health Skills: A Venezuelan Study" in the *International Journal of Educational Development* (with M. Rowe and R. LeVine, 2005).

Irene Serna is a research associate at the Graduate School of Education and Information Studies at the University of California, Los Angeles. Her primary areas of professional interest are detracking reform, demographic change and school reform, and minorities in the educational system.

Susan McAllister Swap (deceased) was chair of the Department of Professional Studies and professor of education and psychology at Wheelock College in Boston. Her published works include *Enhancing Parent Involvement in Schools* (1987), *Managing an Effective Staff Development Program* (1987), and *Building Home-School Partnerships with America's Changing Families* (with L. Braun, 1987).

Amy Stuart Wells is a professor of sociology and education and the deputy director for research of the Campaign for Educational Equity at Teachers College, Columbia University. Her research and writing have focused broadly on issues of race and education and, more specifically, on educational policies such as school desegregation, school choice, charter schools, and tracking, and how they shape and constrain opportunities for students of color. Wells is the coeditor of *Bringing Equity Back: Research for a New Era in Educational Policy Making* (with J. Petrovich, 2005), editor of *Where Charter School Policy Fails: The Problems of Accountability and Equity* (2002), and author of "The 'Consequences' of School Desegregation Take Two: The Mismatch Between the Research and the Rationale" in *Hastings Constitutional Law Quarterly* (2001).

About the Editors

Carol DeShano da Silva is a doctoral student in Administration, Planning, and Social Policy, with a focus on International Education, at the Harvard Graduate School of Education. Her research interests include early reading instruction, teacher education, the impact of policy on practice and student achievement, and equity in education for poor and marginalized communities. Her current research is on social entrepreneurs in the field of literacy instruction in Latin America. She is the coauthor of "Where Is the 'Education' in Conditional Cash Transfers in Education?", a paper published by the UNESCO Institute of Statistics. Da Silva was previously an English-as-a-Second-Language instructor and international student advisor in Boston.

James Philip Huguley is a doctoral student in Human Development and Psychology at the Harvard Graduate School of Education, with a focus on adolescent development in urban education. Huguley's professional experience is in nonprofit management, curriculum design, teacher training, academic advising, classroom instruction, fundraising and development, and family support services. He was formerly the codirector of Providence Summerbridge, an academic enrichment program for low-income inner-city middle school students in Rhode Island, and a teacher at the Wheeler School, an independent preK-12 school in Providence.

Zenub Kakli is a doctoral student in Administration, Planning, and Social Policy at the Harvard Graduate School of Education. Her research interests include public engagement in education, family-community-school partnerships, and community organizing for school reform. Her current research is on how school districts engage families and communities in decisionmaking. Kakli is a coauthor of *Focus on Families! How to Build and Support Family-Centered Practices in After School* (with T. Buck et al., 2006). She is a former elementary school teacher.

Radhika Rao is a doctoral student in Learning and Teaching at the Harvard Graduate School of Education, with a focus on the arts in education. Her research interests include drama/theater in education, moral education, peace and citizenship education, and the links between these realms. Her current work focuses on programs that use theater in educational settings to generate civic dialogue for social justice and peace and citizenship education. Rao previously worked with a professional theater group in New Delhi, India, and taught drama and life skills to secondary school students.